Praise for *Choosing the Future*

"*Choosing the Future* by Erik Stavrand is a compelling exploration of the transformative power of category management and AI in procurement. Through realistic scenarios and engaging storytelling, the book provides valuable insights into strategic leadership, organizational change, and the integration of innovative technologies to drive business success. A must-read for professionals seeking to navigate the evolving landscape of procurement and corporate strategy."

—Chris Sawchuk | Principal and Global Procurement Applied Intelligence Practice Leader

"*Choosing the Future* tells a story of implementing and sustaining transformational change in an organization; it is also a companion piece to *The Global Category Manager's Handbook*. Based on decades of collaborations with Procurement Executives and Leaders across multiple global industries, Erik has created a reality based fictional organization and people who clearly demonstrate the leadership commitment, directed corporate culture evolution, and sustained measurable effort required to drive change that produces competitive advantage. *Choosing the Future* is a relevant read for anyone in any industry undergoing change."

—Scot Buessow, Retired at Canis Major Consulting

"A breakthrough in how to understand the vast potential of category management that so many miss. In this groundbreaking work Stavrand tells a compelling story and brings to life the typical challenges whilst enlightening the reader towards what is actually required for good practical application in an AI driven world."

—Jonathan O'Brien, Author, Host of The Procurement Show Podcast and Founder and CEO Positive Purchasing

"Very well written and deeply engaging—I haven't been this drawn into an educational book since reading *The Goal*. The author does an excellent job setting the stage with Frontier's challenges, bringing Margot's role to life while highlighting the all-too-common gap between procurement activity and true value creation. If you've ever questioned what "good" really looks like in procurement or want a realistic, insightful look at transformation, this book is absolutely worth reading."

—John Boullie, VP, Integrated Supply Chain, Apollo Neuroscience

"Erik Stavrand's *Choosing the Future*: Leading at the Intersection of Category Management and AI is a masterful exploration of the transformative power of strategic procurement and artificial intelligence in reshaping organizational culture and driving business success. As a senior HR leader and consultant, I found the book to be an invaluable resource for understanding how procurement can evolve from a tactical function to a strategic powerhouse, fostering collaboration, innovation, and alignment across all levels of an organization. Stavrand's insights into leadership, change management, and the integration of AI are both timely and essential for any leader looking to navigate the complexities of modern business."

—Gene Carroll, Retired HR executive and consultant

"Erik Stavrand brings over 30 years of hard-earned, hands-on expertise in category management and change management. In *Choosing the Future*, he masterfully bridges strategic vision with practical reality, offering clear insights that help leaders navigate complex transformations with confidence. This book is an invaluable guide for anyone responsible for driving meaningful change while preserving operational excellence in an increasingly uncertain world."

—Chris Shanahan, Board member, senior advisor and CPO

"The world of purchasing is full of stories, about approaches and initiatives that worked and people that didn't, of suppliers' successes and of changes. It's rare to see all of that pulled together into a coherent narrative, and even more rare for it to illustrate the way in which changes in procurement approach need insight, leadership and ambition.

Erik, with his comprehensive knowledge of how large businesses work in practice, has woven together an entirely believable world and set of characters, infused with a very believable description of how category management can be brought to life. We're all aware of those big change levers that happen infrequently but drive considerable upheaval, and to explore AI as a change agent brings relevance and insight into the storyline.

The pace of storytelling means individual strands are brought in and explored swiftly, but it is also true to say that each of those strands is a deep insight which could easily be expanded on. The challenge for the reader is to hang on to the richness of the story and to gather the insights as they pass by, to reflect on later for our own interpretation.

For those wanting to explore an end-to-end view of procurement change, this is a great way to get a sense of what is involved, and in a way that takes you on a journey, wanting to turn the next page."

—Mark Hubbard, Partner, Future Purchasing

"*Choosing the Future* brings procurement to life through engaging storytelling, guiding readers from a tactical, perceived sense of strategy to the meaningful implementation of true category management. Rather than relying on dry textbook explanations, it presents fresh, relevant concepts that reflect the realities of today's procurement teams. This is a compelling read for anyone ready to elevate procurement from transactional work to strategic impact."

—Phillip Lockhart, C.P.M. Director, Procurement-Global Packaging

"For CPOs, aspiring procurement leaders, and transformation-minded professionals, this is fiction with real executive value—capturing how procurement transformation is evolving in an AI-enabled business landscape, where technology accelerates change but leadership ultimately determines success.

The author does an excellent job of capturing the organizational realities of leading change in a large global enterprise: competing agendas, stakeholder resistance, cultural inertia, leadership pressure, and the need for both strategic clarity and execution discipline.

What makes the book especially valuable is that it resonates across multiple levels. Seasoned CPOs will recognize the dynamics immediately, senior leaders will see a roadmap for stepping into enterprise transformation roles, and emerging procurement professionals will gain a far clearer view of what high-impact leadership actually looks like."

—Ron Guertin, Procurement Leader & Executive Coach

"Since entering the life sciences industry in 2008, I've seen many procurement organizations fall into the same trap—focusing too heavily on PPV and getting caught up in day to day tactical execution. The situation described in the book isn't theoretical; it's very real and plays out across most procurement teams. True stakeholder engagement and alignment—around vision, priorities, and decisions—are critical to success, yet incredibly hard to achieve. As a result, procurement is often perceived less as a strategic partner and more as a firefighter, called in only to resolve price or tactical issues.

Choosing The Future really shows where procurement needs to go, not just where it has been. Not just theory but also quite practical. What I like about the book is how it tackles real issues where geopolitics, supply risk and sustainability are built into categories strategy. The use of AI and data to improve decisions and stakeholder alignment are relevant today. AI will play an immense role in procurement organization.

Overall, solid read for anyone serious or thinking about transforming procurement up the value chain.

—Gary Kuek, Sr. Director of Sourcing/Procurement (APAC)

"Usually, when an expert with over 30 years of consulting experience writes about category management, it's a standard non-fiction business book. Erik Stavrand, with whom I have had lengthy conversations on the nuances of category management, has taken a completely different path by writing a novel instead.

By using the novel format, Erik sets out to drive home a very practical point: category management is a fundamental method to improve the functioning and results of a business.

The premise also moves beyond current application-based AI deployments. It describes how AI in procurement—when applied as an extension of category management approaches—is ready to transform the function and change how it is viewed in the company for the better. This is a particularly timely concept, as procurement teams themselves (and the whole world!) are actively grappling with how best to make use of AI and category management right now.

To top it off, the Chief Procurement Officer (CPO) is the hero of the novel. It is a highly fitting choice, because in real-life procurement, the CPO is the hero, too."

—Sakthi Prasad, Content and Digital Marketing Specialist

"I am blown away by the plot, the rich character development, and the sheer volume of authentic dialogue the author had clearly been carrying in his mind for years. The story pulls you in and never lets go. This is a gripping, remarkably authentic read. Highly recommended."

—Dan Phelan, Former board Director of TE Connectivity,
Kraton Corporation, and Senior Independent Director of Indivior, PLC

"Erik has played a crucial role in shaping multiple corporate procurement journeys and helped them become more strategic and value-driven organizations. His extensive expertise in category management and practical, results-oriented insights profoundly impacted the operations and the value delivered. This work showcases not only his knowledge but also his significant contributions to organizational success."

—Thom Cafasso, Head of Direct Procurement

"*Choosing the Future* is a must-read for any professional involved in category management. This book not only describes true-to-life scenarios that many individuals face in the sourcing industry but also showcases how Erik's principles can be leveraged to drive significant value and elevate strategic impact in times of great change."

—Ashley Rice, Sourcing Enablement Manager, Cardinal Health

"A fantastic read. Erik does an amazing job telling a very human story about what it's like to live and work in corporate America. What seems like a simple plot of setting goals and achieving them unfolds into a gripping personal and professional journey of high and lows that keeps you engaged by wondering what will happen next and will it all work out for everyone involved. If you've ever read a novel about how a company faced up to challenges through innovation, sales and marketing but wondered what its like beneath that to execute through sourcing, making and delivering this book is for you."

—Robert Ciamarra, VP, Head of Procurement,
Dyne Therapeutics, Inc.

"*Choosing the Future* has been a very interesting read and very relatable to anyone who has been or will be part of a procurement transformation. Storytelling is a critical element in learning as it helps bring concepts to life when done in a manner that people can relate to and keeps their attention and significantly increases the understanding of what was read. This story helps identify a roadmap for how to approach a procurement transformation in the new world where AI will be a part of everyday business activities in a well written and easy to understand way!"

—Matt Cundari, Managing Partner, QP Group

CHOOSING THE FUTURE

CHOOSING THE FUTURE

Leading at the intersection of category management and AI

ERIK STAVRAND

FOREWORD BY

Vel Dhinagaravel

FOUNDER & CEO, BEROE INC.

SEAK LLC

Green Cove Springs, FL

Choosing the Future
Leading at the Intersection of Category Management and AI

Editing: Andrew Doty, editwright.com
Copyediting & proofreading: John Irvin, inkheartediting.com
Book design: Peggy Nehmen, n-kcreative.com

First printing 2026
Printed in the United States

Library of Congress Control Number: 2026906863

978-0-9965316-5-8 (paperback)
978-0-9965316-6-5 (ebook)

Published by SEAK, LLC.
www.seakllc.com

411 Walnut Street #15145
Green Cove Springs, FL 32043-3443

SEAK LLC

DEDICATION

This book is dedicated to my wife and best friend, Susan. Through over forty years of widely varied experiences, she has been by my side supporting and pushing me to achieve more. I can only hope for forty more.

CONTEXT AND DISCLAIMER

My over-thirty years of consulting experience supporting procurement leadership teams deploying category management provides a seemingly endless supply of business scenarios and stories of real-life issues illustrating the category management tools and processes. Frontier International Group is a wholly fictitious company. It is the successor name to Amalgamated Widgets that José Hanagan and I created to illustrate category management experiences in a corrugated packaging case study in *The Global Category Management Handbook*. Any similarity or resemblance with anyone is a coincidence and unintended.

If you want to use an organization chart to follow the characters and understand where they fit in the organizations refer to the *Choosing the Future* tab at the SEAK LLC website: www.seakllc.com.

FOREWORD

Vel Dhinagaravel, Founder & CEO, Beroe Inc.

I want to begin with a confession. When Erik told me that he had written a procurement-focused novel, I thought that it was admirable but also slightly mad!

What I did not expect was to open the finished manuscript and enjoy it so much. The icing on the cake was to find that Beroe had a role in the story! Appearing in a work of fiction felt like a different kind of validation altogether.

Now, to the book itself.

Choosing the Future is a serious work put into a very approachable form. Erik uses the vehicle of a business novel to explore the genuine difficulty of transforming how organizations think about what they buy, from whom, and most importantly, why.

While the story of Margot and her team at Frontier International Group is fictional, the problems they face—tactical procurement masquerading as strategy, stakeholders who believe that anyone can "buy things," the organizational inertia that greets every change initiative are entirely and painfully real.

A few themes in this book struck me as worth dwelling on.

The first is the intelligence gap, which has been procurement's defining disadvantage for as long as the function has existed. Our research shows that for every dollar procurement spends on understanding supply markets, suppliers spend a hundred and five dollars understanding their customers. What gives me hope is that this gap is finally closeable. The combination of category management discipline and AI+Human-powered intelligence creates, for the first time, a genuine path to procurement walking into a negotiation knowing as much as the supplier sitting across the table. That is not a small thing.

The second theme is that AI without strategic discipline is simply faster mediocrity. This is the most important point in the book, and Erik makes it with quiet insistence throughout. The category management process—done properly—is not just a sourcing methodology. It is a way of asking the right questions before reaching for answers. AI can search, synthesize, and summarize at extraordinary speed. But if the questions are wrong, the framework is absent, or the stakeholders have not been engaged, the speed only delivers bad or infeasible conclusions more efficiently. The category manager's judgment, stakeholder empathy, and strategic vision are not replaceable by AI. They are what makes AI useful.

Third, Erik is admirably honest about what is coming for the procurement workforce. His projections—a meaningful fraction of transactional procurement roles affected within five years, a larger share within ten, in my opinion, are not alarmist. They are grounded in what is already happening quietly in large organizations. The question he asks, and the right one, is not whether AI will arrive but whether the profession will shape how it does. Procurement leaders who treat AI as something happening to them will be on the wrong side of that story.

Finally, the book's title is its most important argument. *Choosing the Future* is an act of will, not a description of inevitability. Procurement has for too long allowed others to choose its role, its status, and its ambition. That needs to change.

Erik Stavrand has written a book that is practical, honest, and hopeful. It takes the eternal challenge of procurement leadership—being taken seriously, being given the mandate, earning the trust—and shows what it looks like when things go right.

As for Beroe's cameo—I have framed the endnote. It hangs in my office between two whiteboards covered in strategic plans, which feels entirely appropriate.

Read this book. More importantly, act on it.

INTRODUCTION

This is a story about procurement and the category management process.

In order to present the work of the category manager, it is necessary to present the related company leadership and key procurement leaders. The role of a transformational category manager is one of the most underrated and underappreciated roles in any company. The reasons for this are simple: procurement is almost universally viewed as a tactical function, and almost every CPO will state unequivocally that they use category management. Pure logic then tells the job evaluation committee that the role is tactical and therefore comparatively low level. The sad truth is that in 70 to 80 percent of cases, this tactical job slotting is accurate. This book is about the 20 to 30 percent of cases where category leaders develop and implement robust category strategies. I've had category managers present business cases to CEOs to buy suppliers, to develop competitive advantage, and to in- or outsource manufacturing to align with corporate strategies. These are far from tactical discussions.

The main theme in the book is the development of a transformational category strategy. This means how the company will determine what is needed, when, and under what terms for a similar grouping of spend with no limitations on prior practices or corporate sacred cows. Some categories are simple to understand, such as office supplies.

Category and Supplier Management Process

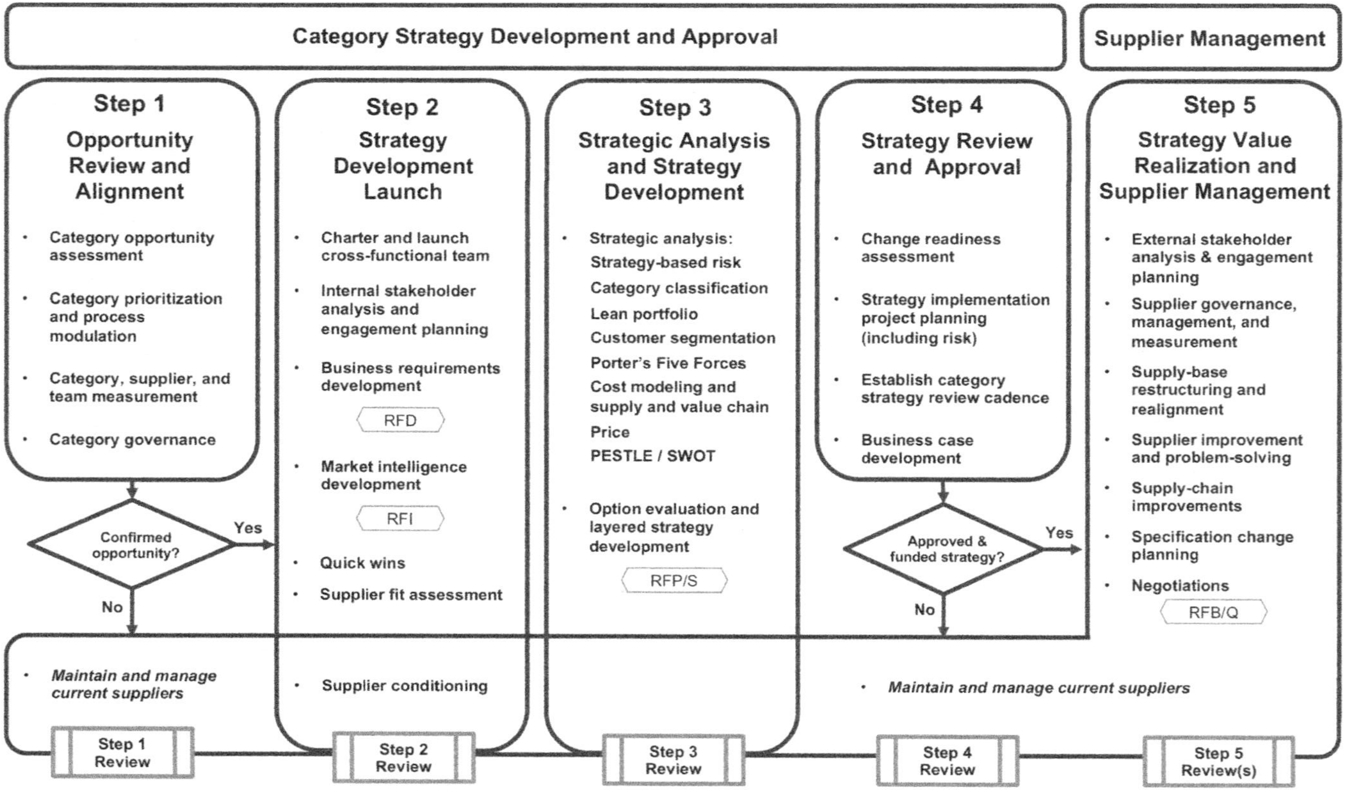

Everyone generally knows what is included, such as pens, pencils, and paper, and has purchased them. In the current online shopping age, where spending is easy and convenient, everyone thinks they're an accomplished buyer who needs no help from a professional procurement organization. They may be right for the simpler spends, but they don't know what they don't know when it comes to larger, more complex spends.

The most difficult and complicated spends are for rare items or services or those which have very narrow specification ranges. An example of this could include radioactive isotopes needed for sterilization. For this category, there is no simple solution—a category strategy is required.

There are many category strategy development processes in use today. Most range from four to seven steps and are very similar. The process I use with clients is depicted in the chart on the left.

This process works in any and every category around the globe and has been proven and continuously refined over the last thirty-plus years. The foundation is proactive-change leadership. Change is at the heart of this process, from suppliers to specifications to stakeholder decision rights. As alluded to above, *stakeholders believe it is 'their money to spend on behalf of the company.'* The decision rights and processes required before the spend is made are the core of category strategy development.

A category strategy for corrugated cardboard is described in the book. All of us have handled a cardboard box and can recognize the subject of the book. The characters are all fictional, and any resemblance to real-life characters or events is a coincidence. They are, however, realistically depicted. I've included relevant conflicts and focused more on successes and collaborations. We all know what conflict and failure look like in the corporate setting, so I decided to highlight excellence and success.

The overall story is realistic and is based on experience. It is a story of what a procurement leader and company executives must do to set up and support category management and a category manager, and what their teams go through in the process of developing, reviewing, approving, and implementing a category strategy. Indicative organization charts for the key elements of the book are available at the SEAK LLC website—www.seakllc.com. Look for the *Choosing the Future* tab.

Category management is a method to improve the functioning and results of a business. Beyond the current application-based AI deployments, I believe and describe how AI in procurement, *in an extension of category management approaches*, is ready to transform the function and how it is viewed in the company for the better. The Frontier CPO will lead this aspect of the story.

We are all part of the AI evolution story, and I hope it turns out well for all of us.

PROLOGUE

"Agreed, in consideration of the five-year extension on the listed parts, Premier Packaging agrees to a twenty percent price reduction," said Peter. "In my time as a key accounts leader, I've not seen a better deal. We view the relationship with Frontier International Group as a successful partnership and are happy to demonstrate this commitment."

"I appreciate your support Peter," Sean piped up. "I'm coming up on ten years leading the corrugated packaging category for Frontier, and you've always come through for us. Please send through the addendum and I'll route it for signature."

"You'll have it this afternoon. Thanks, Sean," Peter confirmed.

"Thanks for your help with this," Sean stated, and he hung up. With this one deal, he'd made his savings numbers for the year! He got up and walked to his manager's office to share the good news.

"Hey, Frank, guess what I just did," Sean grinned.

"Based on your smile, I'd say it's something good," Frank remarked, looking up from the Scottsdale newspaper spread on his desk.

"I just agreed the extension and price cut with Premier that we discussed. They'll be sending it through for Bill to sign. I'll have it this afternoon. This means it's May the first and I hit my numbers for this year and am on my way for next year—twenty percent on five of our top-running items with them," Sean said.

"Well done, Sean. I know I can always count on you. Bill does too. Once the addendum comes through, please send it to me and Bill, and I'll make sure he signs it before the end of the day." Frank reopened his newspaper.

Sean returned to his desk and cleaned up his papers while he waited for Peter's email. As promised, Peter sent the email within the hour. It matched everything he'd discussed and agreed with him and Sean forwarded it to Frank and Bill. He decided to leave early and enjoy the afternoon.

On the way out of the parking garage, Sean called his girlfriend, Carla, and they agreed to meet for happy hour.

"You sound happy," Carla observed.

Sean gushed, "I made my numbers for the year. It's just May first, and I'm already done with the savings target."

"That's great. Who was the supplier who came through for you this year?" Carla asked.

"Premier Packaging," Sean answered.

"I don't think you've mentioned Premier Packaging before," Carla said.

"It was a tough negotiation, but I had the upper hand and used it. The negotiation classes at Mid-State University were the best; hit hard and push." Sean grinned and continued, "I don't have my boys this weekend. My ex is taking them to see her parents. Want to do something?" Sean leaned forward.

"Let's go spend your upcoming bonus someplace romantic." Carla's eyes lit up, and they planned a weekend away.

Frank tapped on the door frame of Bill's office. "Hi, Bill. Did you see the Premier Packaging addendum that Sean sent through? Our boy, Sean, came through again with twenty percent savings. I reviewed it, and it looks good."

"I did see it." Bill glanced up from his desk. "I already signed it and sent it to legal for filing. You and Sean should receive a copy from legal in a few days. I am happy with Sean's work and appreciate your support for his efforts. Our year-on-year savings numbers receive a lot of visibility, and knowing we have this year made and progress toward next year is great. In my time as the head of procurement I think this is the earliest in the year that Sean has hit his numbers. Should we raise his targets?"

"Not this year." Frank shook his head. "We increase his numbers about five percent each year. Maybe we go up a bit more next year."

"Well, anyway, it's good work," Bill stated. "Hey, how is the new condo in Scottsdale?"

"My mother-in-law's estate is being finalized now. We should have the deed in a month. We've been there many times, and it is nice but dated. My wife will sort that out in one month and fifty thousand dollars," Frank replied.

Bill laughed. "Well, I'm happy for you and hope it's just a place for the future. You're my right hand here."

"I'm in no hurry. It's just a nice windfall and something to think about for the future. I really enjoy what we have going here now in procurement." Frank shrugged. "Have a great weekend."

Bill rose and met him at the office door, "You, too. I'm going to head out now as well."

"Leslie, on behalf of the board I want you to know that we're delighted with how things are going this year and your focus on the leadership and culture of the company. When we hired you to lead Frontier Medical, it was a big jump up for you, but you led the division through tough times. Since your promotion to CEO, your development has continued," Reggie said.

"There must be a 'but' coming," Leslie interjected. "The chairman of the board didn't make time to visit me in person to blow sunshine."

Reggie looked down and continued, "As usual, you're right, Leslie. The board is delighted with you and your business presidents. They're pleased with most of the corporate staff leaders."

"Most?" Leslie raised an eyebrow.

"Yes, most. Legal, IT, HR, investor relations; all very good." Reggie nodded. "Our concern is finance."

"Finance!" Leslie exclaimed. "We hit our numbers every quarter. Brenda is an excellent CFO."

"You are right on both points," Reggie agreed. "The Street is very happy with our predictability, and the board greatly appreciates it as well. Our concern, and it is the majority of the board—long serving members and new—is that it is too easy. It would be one thing if we saw tough, aggressive goals being set inside the business and then the finances managed to show a smooth outcome to the investors. What we see looks too easy; like the targets inside are set simply month-to-month or quarter-to-quarter. I think Covid pushed some of this, but it needs to change. We need to look at a longer horizon. The world is changing due to a number of geopolitical and supply chain issues, not to mention this hubbub about AI."

"How unhappy with finance is the board?" Leslie asked.

"We want you to find a new CFO," Reggie replied. "We want you to start now and announce the process publicly after the next quarterly earnings."

"Wow, you're sure we must change Brenda?" Leslie asked.

"Yes, we've had a couple of informal board meetings and that is the consensus. She is very capable, but she is too tactical. She is not at the same level as you and the rest of your executive team. This is not a coaching situation; this is a replacement situation," Reggie leaned forward. "What are your impressions?"

"I guess I just take working with Brenda for granted. She was in the CFO role when I was promoted to CEO. She makes the numbers easy," Leslie replied.

"Do you go to her for business counsel? Does she bring you new ideas?" Reggie asked.

"No, we never talk about the business. I talk with each of the business presidents and with Jean, Larry, and Sondra. I get it; I'll talk with Jean confidentially and start a search process and the exit calculations for Brenda. She's likely eligible for early retirement and, with vesting of her options, will have many choices." Leslie nodded slowly.

"There is one more thing," Reggie added.

"What's that?" Leslie asked.

"Procurement is the one function at Frontier that seems to be locked in time. The other functional leaders are moving their areas forward, evolving their approaches, and demonstrating relevance. I knew something was wrong, but the new board members are quite emphatic that this area needs new leadership and a new approach—or corporate procurement should be disbanded and all procurement moved back to the businesses."

"It seems I need to stay closer to the board members," Leslie mused. "This is another big revelation. I must admit that I haven't paid any attention to procurement except during Covid. I agree that Bill is not very impressive. He's a nice guy but doesn't have a strategic bone in his body."

"Please add him to your conversation with Jean," Reggie said.

"I will. I hesitate to ask but is there anything else?" Leslie asked.

"No." Reggie smiled and stood up. "I think that is quite enough. Please keep me posted on the progress. This needs to happen quickly yet carefully so we don't lose any confidence with the Street."

"I will talk with Jean and start the process for Brenda and Bill." Leslie rose as well. "Thank you for coming by today," She walked him to the elevator.

On her way back to her office, she asked her admin, Lillian, to set up a meeting with Jean for early next week. These changes were going to be highly visible and sensitive.

"The call is complete, and we're disconnected," Oliver announced, the head of investor relations.

"Thank you, Oliver." Brenda, the CFO, leaned back in her chair. "How do you think the call went?"

"That was the forty-third quarterly analyst call in a row where Frontier met our projections," Oliver replied. "The analysts trust us to hit every quarterly projection." He continued gathering his papers and laptop.

"They do indeed," Leslie, the CEO, agreed. "I appreciate your help today on the call and the prep to get ready for today. Brenda and I are going to stay in the conference room for a bit."

"Happy to help." Oliver nodded and walked out, closing the door behind him.

"Forty-third quarter in a row for Frontier and, if my memory is correct, over thirty calls in a row for you and me," Brenda remarked.

"I think you're right," Leslie nodded. "We've been together almost eight years. It's gone quickly. It's already the middle of May. This year is going quickly, too."

Jean, the head of HR, opened the door. "Good morning; excellent earnings call." She closed the door and sat down at the conference room table.

"Thanks, Jean." Brenda smiled. "The businesses are running well—not quite on autopilot but very predictably."

"Ah, that is a good way of putting it," Leslie said. "We all like predictable, but autopilot is dangerous. We've talked in the past about looking beyond the current quarter and expanding our ninety-day planning process to look out one, three, and five years at a time."

"Yes, it's easy to look out that far with financial projections, but they are of little value and predictive of nothing," Brenda replied.

"And that is why the board asked me to make a change." Leslie met Brenda's eyes. "You've done an excellent job on predictability of finances, but the business needs a new perspective."

"You're firing me?" Brenda asked incredulously.

"No, not firing. More like early retiring," Jean interjected. "You meet the company criteria for early retirement, and that allows the early vesting of your options while protecting your options for subsequent employment—as long as it is in either a non-competitive business or after the waiting period. We can go over all the details."

"The board? Who on the board?" Brenda pressed. "I have a good relationship with all of the board members."

"You have very good board relationships," Leslie replied, "but that is not enough. They appreciate your steadiness and focus but are demanding that we expand our focus beyond quarter-to-quarter performance."

Jean interjected, "This is a tough thing to go through, but you're going to be fine."

"Bullshit!" Brenda snapped. "I drove in this morning proud of my work and accomplishments, and now you're saying they're worthless."

"Nobody is saying your accomplishments and contributions are worthless," Leslie replied in an even tone. "What I'm saying is that the time for change has arrived. I am very thankful for everything you've contributed to the company and the support you've provided me and the executive team. I'm going to leave and enable you and Jean to talk through the details."

Leslie picked up her papers and walked to the door. Before she closed it behind her, she silently mouthed "thank you" to Jean.

Jean sat quietly, giving Brenda time to collect her thoughts. She knew from experience that it was best to let Brenda restart the conversation when she was ready.

"How will this be announced, and when?" Brenda asked.

"The announcement will be made as soon as we agree on the details. A bit will depend on what we're announcing. Our recommendation is early retirement instead of pursuing new opportunities. A retirement announcement enables a bit more notice time and an opportunity for you to disengage proactively," Jean explained.

"Or you'll just post I'm leaving and that will be that," Brenda observed, bitterness in her tone.

"Yes, those are the choices we have. I recommend you choose the retirement announcement and ride out on a high. I don't know about your finances, but I do know about the exit package and bridge to retirement Frontier will provide, and it is very generous. You've earned it," Jean said.

"And if I just decide to leave because it is more honest?" Brenda asked.

"The date will be fixed soon, the exit process will be abrupt, and the financial bridge to retirement will be removed," Jean replied.

"That's a Hobson's choice," Brenda muttered.

"Maybe," Jean opened her folio and laid out a stack of papers side by side on the conference room table. "Let's look at the numbers. These are numbers that compare the two options. These other documents are the respective exit agreements that document the options. You are free to take all of these with you, meet with your counselors, and then come back to me by the end of next week with your questions and answers."

Brenda stacked the papers. "I'll look at them later. What other changes are you going to make, or is it just me that is the problem?"

"You are not the problem," Jean replied. "Every finance person I know would be delighted to serve eight years as the CFO of a company as large and respected as Frontier. I expect you'll have a number of board memberships to choose from, likely some academic or political options as well. You're in shock now and angry. That is to be expected. In a bit of time—hopefully not too much—you'll accept the change and move on, and you have tremendous options to explore from a position of real financial strength."

"Are you going to make any other changes?" Brenda pressed.

"I will share, in confidence, that we are also going to change Bill in procurement," Jean answered.

"Why Bill? He's never done anything to anyone!" Brenda exclaimed.

"This is not about people who have done anything to anyone." Jean's voice was even. "You are right in that Bill has done less than we need done in the procurement space. His team is completely tactical as a result of his exclusive focus on price changes."

"The only procurement impact that matters on the P&L is price change," Brenda shot back.

"And Leslie is looking beyond the P&L. We will still meet our quarterly expectations, but we must do more. Procurement must become part of that solution. I always thought of procurement as a transactional, price-down-focused group and am learning that leading companies are getting much more from the function," Jean explained.

"Well, good luck with that. When are you talking with Bill? Am I expected to be part of that conversation?" Brenda asked.

"No, Brenda, I will meet with him later today."

"What options will you give him? I expect he'll call me."

"He'll have similar options to you, just not at the same levels," Jean answered.

"Why not let the next CFO work with him and coach him?" Brenda asked.

"Brenda, I appreciate your concern and sensitivity—it is a reflection of our culture. We went through the talent review conversations at the executive level, and you said that he was likely over his head in that role and did not see a long-term future," Jean said.

"Yes, but he is a good man," Brenda replied.

"Yes, he is. He has limited capability and is not strategic, but he is a good man. This is not a conversation about whether he is a good man or a bad man. If he was a bad man, he would have been gone a long time ago. This is about fit for the role and the direction of the company. On those parameters, it is time for a change."

"Please let him know that I was not a part of the decision." Brenda stood up, picked up her papers, and headed for the door.

"Before you go out," Jean piped up, "this conversation is confidential and needs to be treated as such unless you elect to forgo the retirement option."

"Understood." Brenda paused for a moment, then left the conference room, leaving the door open.

Jean walked over, closed the door, and sat down. She never liked this aspect of her job but knew that it needed to be done—and therefore needed to be done well and humanely. She texted an update to Leslie. Leslie immediately replied with a thank-you and a request that they talk in person at the end of the day.

Jean gathered her papers and returned to her office. After lunch, she'd need to have a similar conversation with Bill.

She met him in a conference room for the announced purpose of "talent planning." Bill wasn't expecting to see her; he knew HR had scheduled the meeting and expected an HR business partner or whatever they called themselves nowadays. He wasn't too interested but knew he had to participate. He arrived a bit early and was checking news on his phone when Jean arrived, closing the door behind herself.

"Hi, Bill," she smiled.

"Oh, hi, Jean." He looked up from his phone. "I didn't know you were holding the meeting. I thought it would be one of your people."

"No, you have me," Jean answered.

"Ok, what's up?" Bill asked.

"Bill, you've been leading procurement a long time, over fifteen years, right?"

"Yes, I've been the head of procurement at corporate for over ten years and with the company over fifteen years," Bill replied, starting to feel very uneasy.

"Well, Bill, the board and executive team decided it is time for a change in procurement. We need the function to be much more strategic."

"I don't understand what you mean." He shook his head. "My team handles the buying of common direct material items and supports the requirements for corporate indirect goods and services. Everything else is handled by the businesses. That is the strategy."

"No, Bill, that is not the strategy, that is the organizational structure," she leveled with him. "As a business, we are going to raise our focus from buying to strategy. The equivalent is when HR used to be known as personnel and the focus was on hiring, firing, and compensation and benefits. We still need to do all of those things, but we must work with the business to understand how, where, and when the people strategy integrates with the business strategy."

Bill tilted his head, furrowed his eyebrows, and met her gaze. "What are you saying to me?"

"I am here to offer you the choice of retirement or to pursue other options. You have enough time with the company to retire early. The papers I'm going to leave with you summarize the financial implications of the two choices," Jean explained.

"So that's it; I'm done and tossed aside?" His voice rose.

"Bill, we are all part of the company as long as it suits our mutual requirements. At any point in time, you could have announced that you were deciding to make a change. I'm here to share with you that the company has made that decision," She replied, keeping her tone even.

"I'm shocked; this is out of left field!"

Jean paused a moment. "I can understand that you are shocked or surprised now, even angry. I want you to reflect on when was the last time your organization was recognized for excellence inside the company or across the procurement profession. A sole focus on price changes is not enough."

"That is what Brenda demanded," Bill snapped. "All she ever talked about was 'PPV,' purchase price variances or changes in price. Anything other than that she viewed as nonsense and a waste of time. I do know that you cannot track cost avoidances to the P&L. Does Leslie no longer care about the P&L?"

Jean remained composed, though Bill's tone was beginning to grate.

"There is no question about Leslie's commitment to the company and performance as measured on the P&L. She is also responsible for the long-term future of the company, and procurement must deliver more than PPV savings." She handed him the prepared papers. "Please take these and review the details. Reach out to me directly with any questions. I need to hear back from you by the end of the week."

She stood up, offering her hand to him. He refused to shake it. She left the room. Any small doubts she had about any of these decisions were long gone.

"How are you holding up?" Leslie asked as she pointed to a chair at the table.

"This is just part of the job," Jean said as she sat down. "Not as fun as organizing the company picnic but part of the role." They routinely joked about the old days of organizing a company picnic. There were employee events to this day, but the picnic was from a day gone by.

"How did they react to the news?" Leslie asked.

"Both went straight to surprised and angry from the SARAH[1] curve," Jean replied. "I am convinced that both will move quickly to accept once they read the details and see how well the early retirement option compares to a decision to leave without retirement. I was surprised by Bill's pettiness. It made me sure of the correctness of the decision."

"Both are hard decisions," Leslie reflected, "Brenda more so. We've all been through a lot. I know I tried, you tried, and a few board members tried to get her to look beyond the quarter, but it isn't how she thinks. As for Bill, he has been proudly sharing laughable savings numbers for years. If his savings were true, our suppliers would be paying us to accept their deliveries. When will they get back to you with their answers?"

"I gave them until the end of next week, but I suspect they'll get back to me sooner," Jean answered. "I think they both might try negotiating details."

"That's unlikely to work," Leslie shook her head. "Brenda's details were reviewed and approved by the board executive and remuneration committees. They were clear about boundaries. Bill's details were per the company policy. What's the status of recruitment?"

"I'm personally managing both searches through our executive search partners. Once the announcements are made, I can involve others, but I wanted to get the process started. These are going to be very attractive roles, and we should be able to attract exceptional candidates."

"I agree. I want real stars to join our team," Leslie remarked. "I'll update the board on the status. I will not include Oliver in the updates until we are ready to make an announcement."

She stood and signaled the end of the meeting. Jean gathered her papers. "This is part of the process of continued growth and improvement of the company. Sometimes these changes are easy and seamless; others are harder. I'll keep you posted. Please let me know if you hear from Brenda."

"I will." Leslie smiled faintly. "Thanks for your help."

AUGUST 1ST

"Hey Sean, come by my office when you have a minute," Frank said. Ten minutes later Sean walked into Frank's office, coffee in hand.

"Close the door and sit down." Frank gestured to the chairs in front of his desk.

"Is everything alright?" Sean asked.

"Bill is 'retiring'." Frank made air quotes. "'Retiring' is how it is going to be phrased. I'm still in shock. Brenda is 'retiring' too. I heard it from my friends in HR."

Sean stared at Frank, speechless.

"Your look pretty much sums up how I'm feeling—like a deer in the headlights. I thought everything was going great—perfectly even," Frank said dejectedly. "I'm still in shock."

"How is Bill taking it?"

"He seems to be okay. He shared that he was surprised too, but he's going to be okay. This is a good company, and he's been here a long time. He really is going to retire," Frank answered.

"What does that mean for us?" Sean asked.

"It means change is coming hard and fast. A new head of procurement is going to be selected. It could be someone from inside, but my intuition is that it will be an external hire. In the meantime, I will oversee the corporate procurement staff with Tanya." Frank leaned back in his chair. “The postings are going out any time now. I would expect calls from suppliers to follow, but there is nothing to say yet.”

“I’m glad I already made my numbers for the year,” Sean observed. “If we’re going to have a new leader, I want to be well positioned.”

“Don’t worry, Sean,” Frank reassured. “You’re our safe pair of hands, and I’ll make sure everyone knows that. Let me draft a note for the procurement team to send once the posting is up. In the meantime, don’t say anything to anyone.”

“Understood, thanks for the heads-up,” Sean nodded and walked back to his cubicle. Once back at his desk, he summarized the discussion in an email to Carla and asked for her thoughts.

“Relax and welcome to the corporate world,” Carla responded.

SEPTEMBER 8TH

Margot was working at her desk. She'd been at Confederated Supplies for two and a half years and, as her first CPO role, she was enjoying it. She had fifty employees and an eight-billion-dollar total spend with five billion in direct materials and three billion in indirect goods and services. The organization was supportive, and her family was settled. They were a bit leery of moving from the Northeast to Oklahoma City but had found it charming, with more of a big-town feeling than a city.

The recruiter call came out of the blue. She was not seeking a new role but knew better than to refuse these calls. The recruiter said the new role was with a big company and, best of all, would not require her to relocate. Yes, she would talk to them. If it was a bigger company in Oklahoma City, that reduced the number of potential firms, and she suspected it was Frontier International Group. Frontier was a much bigger firm, but why not at least interview, she decided.

Her first interview was set for a Friday afternoon with HR. She'd expected to meet with a low-level recruiter from HR but was very surprised—and pleased—to find herself meeting with the head of human resources. Jean, the CHRO, met her in the lobby and was immediately warm and engaging.

"Thank you for taking the time to come meet with me this afternoon," Jean greeted. "Let's head up to my office." They stepped into the elevator and made small talk until the elevator stopped. They walked into Jean's office and settled in to start the conversation.

Margot was shocked when Jean, seemingly out of the blue, said, "Well, that's the fastest hour I've spent in a long time! I really enjoyed the conversation."

"I feel the same way," Margot replied. "I lost track of time and figured we were only fifteen minutes into the discussion. I am interested in the role and, if you are still interested in me, let me know the next steps in the process."

"We are interested in progressing. I'll set up further discussions. Please give me your availability over the next two weeks."

They agreed on calendar options, and Jean escorted Margot to the lobby. "Thank you again for coming in today. I'll be back in touch with you about the next steps. If you have any questions in the meantime, please contact me directly."

"Thank you and have a great weekend," Margot smiled, extending her hand. They shook hands, and Margot headed back to her car.

She reflected on the conversation while driving home. She'd have to make some notes before she forgot the details. Her husband, Jason, would be home soon, and they could talk while the kids played outside.

Jean did not go back to her office after leaving Margot in the lobby. She went straight to Leslie's office. She asked Lillian, Leslie's admin, if Leslie was in and available and was told that she was on a call but would be free in a few minutes. Jean sat down to wait—she wanted to talk to Leslie directly.

A few minutes later, Leslie came out of her office to speak to Lillian and saw Jean. "What a nice surprise, what brings you to my office on a Friday afternoon, Jean?"

"I just had a great conversation with a CPO candidate and want to share it with you."

"Come in, I have a break before my next meeting." Leslie gestured to the conference table in her office. "Let's sit here and talk. Okay, tell me what's up."

"I just met with the candidate for CPO I mentioned, named Margot. She's local and, well, she's amazing. Our role would be a stretch for her, but she is energetic, capable, and a savvy leader. She was a bit hesitant when I mentioned that the CFO role is open and she would not be able to meet her future manager. When I told her that she'd be interviewing with you instead, she was assured and relaxed. I think she would be a great fit for our culture."

"She sounds very good." Leslie nodded thoughtfully. "Please check with Lillian on my schedule, but let's get her in to see me and a few of the other ELT members in the next week or two. Actually, I'd like to meet her over dinner. Any role this senior requires my 'dinner test' to see if they are a true fit."

"Okay." Jean stood up. "I'll work through the details with Lillian and send you and the ELT members her CV."

Jean and Lillian reviewed the ELT members' schedules and booked an afternoon meeting with Larry, the CIO, and Erica, the leader of the medical business, plus a dinner meeting with Leslie. Jean was excited. Finding new, capable talent was energizing, and Margot seemed to be an excellent find.

Jean emailed the details to Margot and received an affirmative response within an hour. She headed home, hoping this one worked out as well as it was seeming to.

Margot sat with her husband Jason and talked about her discussion with Jean and the follow-up email. They were both a bit surprised about the quick follow-up and the levels of the individuals she was about to meet. Leslie was well-known and very well respected in the area. Margot was delighted to meet her, let alone potentially work in the organization she led. They brainstormed a list of questions, agreed to come back to the topic in a couple of days, and rejoined the kids in the family room.

SEPTEMBER 14TH

Margot met with Larry first. Even if it was perhaps a bit impertinent, she felt compelled to share an observation with him: "You know a lot about the business. Most IT people I've worked with—and have known—are focused entirely on IT."

"Thank you for the compliment." Larry smiled. "I do not consider myself to be an IT person. I am a businessperson leading the IT area. If I don't understand the business, then I cannot adequately lead the area, nor can I ensure we provide the support the businesses need."

"That's how I encourage my procurement people to think about their roles," Margot replied. "If we don't understand how the business works and the respective priorities, we won't be effective. The last things I want to be known for are either the leader of 'the price police' or 'the buyer of cheap stuff,' and that is very common in procurement."

"I'm glad to hear you say that," Larry said. "We are typically 'fast followers' from an IT technology perspective. We don't need cutting edge except for a few narrow areas in the electronics and medical businesses. Our infrastructure is stable, and we don't need to needlessly add cost or complexity there."

"I use a process called category management to co-create third-party supply category strategies with stakeholders." Margot explained. "It's been around for years, but there are still companies that are not using it. Have you heard of it?"

"No, I've not heard of it My team determines the supply needs, selects the suppliers, and negotiates the deals. Some fancy themselves to be good negotiators, but nobody has any formal training. Procurement completes the contracts and then places the purchase orders."

"Oh." Margot raised an eyebrow. "That's a long way from category management. Are you happy with that arrangement?"

"No, I'm not happy with it, and I suspect that my peers aren't either. I also suspect that's why we're talking today." Larry leaned forward. "We're hoping for something a bit better and more impactful. Frankly, I cannot afford for my senior team to be doing the groundwork on these deals. If they're doing it, I need more staff and don't need procurement at the end of the process. I can just work with Sondra and legal and complete the contracts ourselves."

"It sounds frustrating, and I do understand. The good news is that this is an area that can be addressed and fixed quickly."

Larry smiled. "It sounds like you're already ready to take the job."

"I don't mean to get ahead of myself." Margot returned the smile. "It is easy to go into problem-solving mode when I hear about these situations."

Their conversation continued amiably for another thirty minutes, and Larry walked Margot to Erica's office.

"Thank you, Margot, for coming in and talking with me. I'm counting on you fixing my issues first." Larry smiled as he introduced Margot to Erica.

"Come in and make yourself comfortable." Erica gestured to the chair facing her desk. She was a bit brusquer than Larry but not actually rude—just a different style.

"I run Frontier Medical," Erica continued. "My main office is in Copenhagen, but I am here about a week every six weeks or so. I have my own procurement function that supports my business. My understanding is that the role you're interviewing for is the central role, which handles the company's indirect and some of the more common direct materials. Based on what I've seen and heard in the five years I've been with the company; the central role doesn't do much. I don't rely on them for much and instead rely on my team in Copenhagen."

"I understand your decisions based on what I've heard so far," Margot replied evenly. "I'm not interested in a role running a team that the senior leaders don't respect nor use. How do your peers in the electronics and industrial businesses handle their procurement? How do they feel about central procurement?"

Erica leaned back in her chair. "We don't talk much about procurement unless we have a shortage; none of us view it as a strategic function. In the few conversations where procurement has ever been discussed amongst the three of us, it has only been about shortages or market disturbances like oil price hikes and the impacts on logistics costs or topics like that."

"There is more that can be done centrally without negatively affecting your business," Margot said.

Erica did not smile. "What are you thinking?"

"This is a very large company and, based on what you're describing, I am reasonably sure there is real value that is possible but is not being currently realized," Margot explained. "I'm not talking about control so much as collaboration across the businesses when it comes to working with the supply base. Have you ever heard of category management? Does your team in Copenhagen use it?"

"It does not sound familiar," Erica admitted. "I've heard them talk about strategic sourcing. Is that what you mean?"

"That's close and is an element of category management," Margot replied. "All companies should use strategic sourcing when engaging the market once the overall plan or strategy is developed. I'm talking about the strategy development."

Erica smiled for the first time. "Procurement strategy? I've never heard of that. In my experience, procurement is a transactional function, not a strategic function."

They talked about the pressures on the medical business and the market opportunities, and Erica relaxed and engaged Margot. At the end of the conversation, Erica observed, "I've never talked about the business with procurement. Is that typical for you?"

"It is," Margot said. "I view my role and my team's role as an extension of your business. If we don't understand your business fully, we cannot do that. If we are just placing orders, then we are not adding much value. Frankly, if that is what the business is seeking, it's not really a role that interests me."

"You're direct, too," Erica smiled. "And I appreciate that. I'd much rather work with someone who engages me directly than someone who mindlessly defers or cowers. I need people who are going to help add value. My marketplace is very competitive, and there is no room for average or mediocre." She glanced at her watch. "Oh my, I need to get you to Leslie now!"

As they approached Leslie's office, Erica turned to Margot. "I appreciate you coming in today and wish you luck. If this works out, you will have a lot of work ahead of you, but I get the feeling you're up for it." They shook hands, and Erica introduced Margot to Lillian.

"Leslie will be ready in about fifteen minutes," Lillian said. "You can use this conference room in the meantime, and the facilities are just down the hall on the left."

"Thank you." Margot nodded and settled at the conference room table. She breathed a sigh of relief and made some notes on her phone. The conversations with Larry and Erica had been full, and she did not want to lose any of the details. She was still interested in the role, but there was more to do than either what Jean had mentioned or what she'd remembered from that conversation. She suspected it was the latter, as Jean had been very forthcoming.

Leslie knocked on the door fifteen minutes later. "Hi, I'm Leslie, sorry about the delay, but I had a call I had to take."

"No worries," Margot replied. "I understand, and it was good to have a short break." They shook hands.

"Yes, Erica is pretty intense," Leslie smiled. "She is very no-nonsense, but she is a great leader. She is running a tough business, and I rely on her. Let's go get some dinner."

They rode the elevator to the lobby, and Leslie said, "We're going just around the block to Lacy's. It's one of my favorite places and it's close enough to walk." Margot noticed that a large man in a suit followed them out of the lobby and walked discreetly near them.

"Sounds great, is he joining us?" she pointed to the man walking with them.

"Oh, this is Miguel. We go everywhere together; he keeps me safe," Leslie explained.

Margot turned to him. "Hello, Miguel." He nodded subtly, and they kept walking.

"So, what are your impressions so far?" Leslie asked as they walked.

Margot reflected for a moment. Leslie was jumping right into the heart of it, and Margot was glad she'd had the fifteen minutes to think about the discussions.

"Corporate procurement at Frontier needs to be transformed. Everything I heard was about tactical approaches to strategic opportunities. The central team is not aligned with or valued by the functions or the businesses. I think that sums it up," she said.

"Excellent summary." Leslie nodded. "I was blind to all of it for years. Frankly, I am just as much to blame as everyone else, because I accepted the tactical approach. I'd never heard of procurement strategy until a new board member mentioned it to me. He's the CEO of an aerospace company, and they do procurement completely differently than us."

They entered Lacy's, and the maître d' recognized Leslie, welcomed her, and led them to their table. It was quiet, with a few empty tables as a buffer. The waiter came over and told them about the special meals, and they each ordered a glass of wine. Miguel moved to a table between them and the front door.

"Procurement organizations typically go through an evolution," Margot started. "They start with a focus on service, on running the transactions in a way that meets the fiduciary guidelines of the company. Some procurement functions stop there, and others continue to mature and become more strategic. In the process of becoming more strategic, they evolve their approaches and become more tightly aligned with the businesses. The transactional work can be performed anywhere, and many companies either offshore or outsource it. The strategic work must be close to the stakeholders. Procurement done well is highly interactive and depends on stakeholder collaboration; it is trust-based."

"Those are descriptions I've not heard about any of our procurement organizations—either the central function or the business-based functions," Leslie said.

The waiter brought their wine and took their dinner orders.

"Lots of work to be done, then," Leslie observed. "And the manager for the CPO role—the CFO—is open. I bet that's a bit of a question for you."

"It is," Margot admitted. "I've never taken a role where I could not meet and interview my prospective manager. I've also never taken a role where I could meet and interview the CEO!" They both laughed.

Leslie continued, "I talked with the board about our management approaches recently. We are doing well, and Wall Street is happy with us, but we were so short-term oriented that it was worrying to us. That's when I decided to look for a new CFO to help lead us in a new way financially. We will still need to hit our quarterly numbers, but we also need to raise our horizons and look a bit further out. I'd hate to hit the next quarterly numbers but miss the next big opportunities. I'm interviewing candidates along with Jean and the ELT, and we are getting close. There are some great people we're talking to, and I can promise you, if you're okay talking with me, Jean, Larry, and Erica, that you'll be okay with who we'll select."

Their meals arrived, and they ate in silence for a couple of minutes before Margot said, "Thank you for sharing that. You seem to be very focused on the culture of the company. The current structure of procurement would, under normal circumstances, not be something I'd be interested in, but culture can trump that if it's right."

"I am focused on culture," Leslie replied. "I am very competitive; every CEO is competitive, or we wouldn't be in the role. I am also focused on integrity. I want to be proud of this company and not just for the numbers we deliver. Our customers and our shareholders trust us. That is paramount."

"Procurement is all about trust," Margot agreed. "If the stakeholders or the suppliers don't trust procurement, it is finished. Trust takes a while to build but can be destroyed in an instant. I have a question for you about culture. What is the culture of power in the company?"

"That's an interesting question from a procurement person, and one I'd more expect from HR. What do you mean?"

"Okay, well, procurement is about relationships, and if we look at the most basic relationships—like couples—they agree on power dynamics about big topics like religion, children, family, and money," Margot explained. "The dynamics around money and power are about who gets to determine when to spend it, on what, and what's the process used. The same dynamic exists in business, and stakeholders often view the power to spend money as theirs alone."

"Very interesting." Leslie nodded. "We do encourage entrepreneurialism in our businesses. Erica runs her P&L, and her peers in electronics and the industrial business do the same."

"What about the central functions like HR and IT? How do they get measured on the P&L?"

"The central functions get managed on their objective achievements and their expense and capital budgets," Leslie answered. "They are each accountable for their results and control their spending."

"What's their incentive to collaborate across business or functions?"

"We work as a team—we work as one team—focused on the best possible outcomes for the company."

"I think I understand, but if I may be so bold, I think there are opportunities to work even closer." Margot paused, weighing her words. She was worried she may be stepping out of line now, but hoped the risk was worth it: now or never. "If they were to collaborate more closely on the spends they share, it could lead to even more business collaboration on other topics. That is something I talked with Jean about. Small tweaks in the spending power dynamics can have huge, positive impacts on the overall culture."

"That's very interesting," Leslie said. "I'll need to think about that further. I will admit that it is not something I've ever considered. Do you have any papers or books on that topic you can recommend?"

"I do know of a book," Margot said, "that covers the express culture changes of a merged company and the role of procurement in the change process. It's been my touchstone ever since. I'll send you the details."

"That would be great." Leslie smiled. "Any interest in dessert?"

"Sure, I'm interested in what they have," Margot replied.

They ordered dessert, and the conversation shifted to hobbies and families. While not strictly within the confines of legally permissible interview topics, they were open topics for Leslie once she was comfortable with the candidate. Likewise, Margot had relaxed quite a bit. She knew she'd taken some risks through the conversation but felt she had to. If she could not meet her future boss directly, it was critical that she took the measure of her boss's boss.

After dessert, Leslie paid the bill. "Let's walk back to the cars." Miguel silently walked with them.

Once they were outside, Leslie continued. "Thank you for meeting with me, Margot. I did not know what to expect and enjoyed our conversation. You raised a few issues and questions about procurement that I've never considered. I will admit I feel a bit remiss. It's my job to think about these things, and I've taken procurement for granted. I hope you'll reach out with any questions, and I look forward to reading the book you mentioned."

"I enjoyed our conversation and appreciate your willingness to make time and talk openly with me. Thank you," Margot replied.

When they arrived back at the HQ, Margot headed to her car, and Miguel escorted Leslie to the company limousine.

Jason was awaiting her return, and they talked for two hours about the day. She was very excited about the prospects and wondered how long it would take to hear back from Jean and Frontier.

SEPTEMBER 18TH

Leslie assembled the interview team virtually. Erica was back in Denmark, and the others gathered around Leslie's conference table.

"What do you think about Margot?" Jean asked.

"Not really a procurement person," Larry grinned. "I like that. She told me, and I quote, that she views her role as a business-person doing procurement, and that is very refreshing. I told her what the current procurement function is doing versus what I need, and she immediately sensed what is missing and what needs to be done. I vote yes on her."

"What do you think, Erica?" Jean asked.

"I spent half of our time talking about the medical business," Erica said. "I've never had that type of conversation with someone in procurement. Not even my local team. She seemed very interested in understanding the risks and opportunities we face. I pushed on her hard at the start, and she did not back down. She was not confrontational, but she is clearly not afraid to have real conversations. I vote yes, too."

"And you, Leslie?" Jean asked.

"I echo what both of you said," Leslie began. "She is not a typical procurement person. We talked about the nature of procurement and executive collaboration. She asked how I measure each of you—a very unusual question for procurement. She is very focused on the culture and whether her approach to procurement will fit here. I vote yes, but with the understanding that she will push us. She will not come here and run the same type of operation that Bill ran. I want the change and vote yes."

"Three yesses, and I vote yes, too," Jean said. "She's a bit more junior than we'd been seeking, but she has been a CPO already. She's not cowed by any of you, and in the space of an hour plus, each of you learned a bit and seemed to enjoy it. I will proceed with reference checking if that's okay with you. I'll work through some potential offer details and review them with Leslie in the meantime. Thank you all for your time."

Leslie raised a hand. "Jean, please stay a couple of minutes."

"Sure," Jean took a seat.

"I've only ever talked about the culture of the company and executive ways of working with you and the board," Leslie continued. "She wasn't impertinent, but she pushed me a bit on this. She sent me a book recommendation on how procurement can help drive culture change. I'll send you the details. I want you to proceed with her, assuming the references check out and the offer is accepted, and I want you to mentor her."

"Yes, will do," Jean replied. "This role is what I call a 'gorilla role'; it's huge and will require all of her time, energy, and passion. I think she knows that and wants to make sure it's a good fit before she commits. I'll keep you posted." She stood up and walked out, smiling. Thoughts about procurement had never had that effect on her before.

SEPTEMBER 21ST

Jean sat across from Leslie's desk as Leslie read the notes she'd given her—the results from the reference checks on Margot.

"These look great," Leslie said. "It seems everyone who's worked with her has been impressed. I'm not surprised." Leslie reached under her desk and pulled out a small package. "I received this from her earlier in the week. A thank-you note for the interview. A nice touch that few remember to do nowadays. And a copy of the book she'd mentioned about procurement and culture change. Again, not a lot of money, but quite a lot of thoughtfulness and thoroughness." Leslie handed the book and note to Jean.

"I'd like to read the book after you're done, if you don't mind," Jean remarked.

"Take it and read it first. I am knee-deep in other reading now and don't want to give it short shrift," Leslie replied.

"About the offer," Jean continued, "I recommend the midpoint of our VP level. The salary will be a big jump for her, and we don't have to pay for her relocation. I think she'll be happy with that. It will also give us lots of room to move her to a higher pay band if needed down the road. What do you think?"

"Any salary compression or equity issues if we do that?" Leslie asked.

"No, I checked, and we'll be fine. The current procurement staff is relatively low-banded to reflect their work to date, and she'll be a bit below most of her peers in the company," Jean answered.

"Okay, we don't need to check with the board at this level, so you have my approval to proceed," Leslie said. "Please keep me posted."

Jean stood up, took her notes and the book. "I will, and I have a really good feeling about hiring Margot."

She sent Margot an email on her personal address and asked her to call ASAP. Within fifteen minutes, Margot was on the phone with Jean.

"Hi, Jean, I saw your email, what's up?" Margot asked.

"Hi, Margot, I want to offer you the role of CPO, reporting to the CFO." Jean reviewed the offer details with her and asked, "Do you have any questions?"

"Not on the offer. Thank you, and I will talk with my husband and get back to you."

"Not on the offer," Jean smiled. "That means you do have other questions; go ahead."

"I don't want to get ahead of the process here," Margot stated, "but I will need two additional requests granted at the time of hire so I can accelerate the transformation process. The first is approval to hire a procurement transformation leader. This will be a director-level role comparable to the heads of direct and indirect materials. The second is approval to hire a consulting firm to begin category management training and coaching as soon as possible. These two enablers will ensure I can succeed while I'm working through the current staff and changing the ways of working."

"That sounds reasonable, but I'll need to check back with Leslie," Jean said. "I'll send you the offer letter today. If you can send me the draft job description or any comparable job postings, I can work through the compensation and related approvals for the transformation leader. As for the consulting and coaching funding, please send through the key performance and capability elements you'll need and estimated funding. My recommendation is to keep the funding as small as possible, so it does not need to be elevated through the full process. You can do that later along the journey. If you have a recommended short list of providers, please list them."

"You'll have all of that by email by the end of the day," Margot replied. "If you need anything else, please let me know."

"I will, and look forward to moving forward. Thanks, Margot."

"Thanks, Jean," Margot smiled to herself, and they both hung up.

Margot called Jason at work and shared the news. He had her repeat the details twice before asking her what she thought of the offer.

She replied, "It's a good offer. It's not great, but it is a big bump from my current pay, excellent long-term compensation, and a move to a Fortune 100 company. They're saving on relocation and know it, so it's a good deal for them, too. I almost said yes on the spot but restrained myself. I did ask for approval for a transformation leader and consulting support for category management."

"Anna and Rich?" he asked.

"Not by name, but yes," she answered. "I need to provide an approximate starting budget and some recommended providers, so I'll list them as highly recommended with additional support and a couple of others who are both much more expensive and not as recommended."

"Any sense on what they'll say?"

"My guess is that they say yes on all of it and push for an early start date."

"Well, we had a great vacation, and the kids are back in school, so the timing for the family is good." he said.

"I agree. I'm not feeling bad about leaving Confederated Supplies. My team includes at least two strong contenders to fill this role," Margot added.

"Congratulations, Margot, you're about to enter the big time!" Jason said.

"Thanks, let's talk further tonight." Margot hung up.

SEPTEMBER 23RD

Margot sent Jean the details by the end of the day, and Jean worked with her compensation team to review and quantify the request. Jean had heard about these roles and saw the value when she read the proposed job description details. This spoke volumes for Margot's savvy and desire to get off to a fast start. It would also enable Margot to hire a person who would demonstrate what future procurement capability looked like.

Jean thought about the consulting request. She could not involve the current procurement team in the process without disclosing the upcoming changes. She did a quick search on category management consultants, and many of them were in the marketing space. She made a note to ask Margot about that and had an idea. If a senior marketing person made the request, it would sail past the current procurement team because the amount was well under the extended review amounts. She also considered just having Leslie sign it. The amount was not an issue, and the firm Margot heavily hinted at was both excellent and a lower-priced alternative. She'd ask Leslie what she preferred.

Over lunch, Jean told Leslie about Margot's requests. "Okay, you have piqued my curiosity," Leslie said.

"First, she wants to hire a procurement transformation leader immediately. I suspect she'll start the process informally before she joins. It's a director-level hire, the same as the current heads of direct and indirect materials. I talked with our compensation and recruiting team, and we have a draft job description. I recommend proceeding with this," Jean explained.

"Agreed and approved," Leslie nodded as their lunch was delivered. "What was her second request?"

"She wants approval for consulting and coaching funding for category management. She mentioned the process in most of her interviews, and it does sound interesting. The amount to start is small. It's small enough that I can either have the corporate marketing vice-president sign it or you," Jean replied. "My recommendation is to approve the funding and her preferred supplier, but I don't have a recommendation on the approval process other than to not use our current procurement team until the organizational change announcements catch up with them."

"That makes sense. I'll sign the approvals. There is no need to muddy this. What can you tell me about the recommended firm?"

"It's a small, specialist firm with many years of experience across a number of industries. If the estimated rates are right, they are less than half the cost of the big-name firms," Jean answered.

"Very interesting," Leslie observed. "We think she's going to accept and is then going to bet her success on these two supports. I think she's savvy and is going with who she knows and trusts. Back to my dinner impressions, I think we also don't know the full extent yet of what she's going to change. I have a good feeling for her. Please keep me posted."

"I will send you a note as soon as I hear anything," Jean said.

Margot sent Jean an email in the afternoon asking about her status on the two questions. Jean replied she had answers and asked if Margot did as well.

Instead of replying to the email, Margot called. "Hi, Jean, thanks for your email. I thought it would be better to pick up the phone."

"Hi, Margot, I agree. I talked with Leslie, and we're fine with your two requests," Jean said.

"That's great," Margot replied. "I'm happy to accept the offer as described."

"Excellent news." Jean's voice brightened. "What are your current notice provisions?"

"Standard two weeks. Let's say Monday, the second week of October."

"That sounds great, Margot. I'm delighted you're going to join Frontier. My team will draft an announcement about you, and I'll email it to you for your review."

"I'm really looking forward to joining Frontier. You and Leslie are great, and I appreciate your openness through the interview process," Margot said.

"You're welcome. Look for emails and mail from me and my team," Jean replied.

"I will, and I will be there ready to roll!" Margot said.

The next day, the written offer letter arrived at Margot's house, and it was exactly as Jean had described it. She signed her acceptance and sent it back to Jean.

SEPTEMBER 24TH

The next day, Margot met with her manager at Confederated Supplies and shared her news. He heartily congratulated her, and it was obvious he had no hard feelings and wished her only the best. He was an excellent leader, and she would stay in touch with him. Who knew, someday he'd be a CEO somewhere and it was a very small world. They discussed potential replacements and Margot recommended that they do an external search while simultaneously considering the two internal candidates. Either of the two internal leaders could do the role and were hired as succession candidates. It was simply a matter of fit. He suggested that they leave the role open in the meantime and that he lead the function until the successor was hired. This would get him closer to the function and prevent any struggles for the interim leader role. She thought this sounded fine if he had the time. He replied that for a couple of months for the search it would be fine.

Satisfied with this result, she went back to her office to make a few calls. Her first call was to her trusted allies—Anna and Rich. They'd taught her category management fifteen years ago when she was a new category manager, and she respected them and trusted them completely. She'd embraced the process, and it had made a critical difference in her career. They were ecstatic with her news and immediately committed to helping her in the new role. She shared the discussions about getting started and told them to expect a contact from senior levels at Frontier. Needless to say, they'd be looking forward to it, they said.

Margot's next call was to a woman she'd met at a conference, named Shelly. Shelly was currently the head of direct materials at a food and beverage company and previously ran indirect spend at a medical company. She was a trained category manager from the automotive world. In short, Shelly was a perfect candidate for the transformation leader role. She would be Margot's chief of change.

"Hi, Shelly, this is Margot. We met at the recent conference in Tampa," Margot began. "I wanted to check on your status. At the procurement conference in Tampa, you mentioned you were interested in the next step in your career. Where are you in your thinking now?"

"I like my current role. My team is driving category management across direct materials, and I have excellent stakeholder and supplier engagement. I've not really settled into the area. Los Angeles is not a bad place, but it's not home," Shelly replied.

"Well, if I remember, home is upstate New York, right?" Margot asked.

"Yes, just outside Rochester, NY—the complete other side of the country from LA. I grew up in the country, and working in a big city this far from my family is tough," Shelly answered.

"Would you consider a smaller city halfway across the country?"

"What do you have in mind?"

Margot explained her new role at Frontier in Oklahoma City.

"As part of my acceptance, they approved me hiring a director of procurement transformation. I'd like you to consider the role if you're interested. It's the last piece of development you'd need before a big CPO role, and I think we'd make a great team. What do you think?" Margot asked.

"Wow, thanks for thinking of me for this role," Shelly said. "How soon and where will the role be publicized?"

"I think it is in process right now and expect it to be on the Frontier International Group careers page and the internet sites within a week," Margot replied. "You could also send your information directly to the CHRO, Jean, who is my contact. I can send you her information."

"How long are you committing to the CPO role?" Shelly asked.

"I am committing and don't have a time frame. I do think it will take three to five years to turn this function around and into something we can be proud of. There is no category management now, and the functional organization and spend governance are not aligned," Margot answered.

"Why, if I may ask, are you taking the job if it needs this much work?" Shelly asked.

"The CEO, Leslie, is amazing. I'll be reporting to the CFO, who is not yet named, so Leslie led the search herself. She is a great leader, and the members of the ELT I met are excellent as well. It is not without some risk, but I feel really good about this opportunity," Margot said.

"Okay, I'll do some research and get back to you next week. Thank you for the call, Margot."

"You're welcome, Shelly. Please let me know either way, but you're my first choice for this role."

After hanging up, Margot took a deep breath; the changes would only be accelerating from here.

OCTOBER 9TH

Margot was met in reception by the procurement administrative assistant, Rita. "Good morning and welcome, Margot. I'm Rita."

"Hi, good morning, Rita, and thanks for helping me with the joining process."

"I'll bring you up to HR, who will handle all the paperwork. Do you want me to do anything in the meantime?"

"Please schedule a meeting for the global procurement leadership team. Those on site can join in a conference room and the rest virtually. It doesn't have to be an emergency meeting today, but sometime soon so we can meet each other," Margot said. "I'd guess an hour will do."

"I'll do that," Rita nodded and left her with HR.

"I was able to get everyone for tomorrow morning," read the text from Rita later in the day. It was just as well, as there was much more administrative paperwork than Margot had expected. Frontier was very thorough and had excellent benefits. A surprise was a heavy tote bag with books and a note from Jean that read, "These books are required reading for all VPs and above. Leslie started the process years ago, and over time we've added a couple. They're a part of how we work here."

Margot peered in the bag and saw: *Out of the Crisis*, *The Goal*, *The Machine that Changed the World*, *The Five Dysfunctions of a*

Team, *Our Iceberg Is Melting*, and *Basic Economics*.[2] She hoped some of these were available in audiobook versions, because there was a lot to read here! She'd have to follow up with Jean to ask about this—there had to be an interesting story or two behind it.

The next morning at 7 a.m. CST, she was in the conference room with Rita, Frank, head of direct materials, and Tanya, head of indirect, and they were virtually connected with Mary, head of procurement Frontier Medical and based in Copenhagen, Harry, head of procurement for Frontier Consumer Electronics based in Singapore, and Phil, head of procurement for Frontier Industrial based in Milwaukee.

"Thank you for making time to talk on short notice," Margot began. "As you will have seen in the notice from Leslie, I've been hired as the new CPO. I'm delighted to be here and look forward to working with each of you. Let's go around and do introductions, please."

They each shared their role, time with the company, and a brief description of the teams they led.

"That's really helpful, thanks," Margot said. "I will be making plans to travel to meet your respective teams over the next few months. I'm likely to come to Singapore before the end of the year, Harry, so I don't arrive in the middle of the Chinese New Year celebrations."

"Good planning, you're welcome any time." Harry smiled. "I recommend you meet the key stakeholders while you're here, and I can help you with the names and introductions."

"Perfect, I'll talk with Rita about schedules and get back to you," Margot replied. "I will also head to your locations, Mary and Phil, and will work with you on recommended dates."

"Like Harry said, you'll want to allow time to meet the key stakeholders, but we're an easy flight and you're welcome any time," Phil replied.

"The Christmas markets are beautiful here in Copenhagen if you have time," Mary added.

"I'm not sure I'll make it to Europe by the end of the year due to some ELT meetings I need to attend, but I'll be there early in the new year. Milwaukee is possible. I'll let you both know," Margot said. "There are a couple of items I need to share with you. First, one of the key reasons they selected me is to launch category management.

The plan is to conduct the training in early January and launch the teams shortly thereafter. The first training will be here in Oklahoma City, and then additional sessions will be conducted for your teams. If you want to attend the first session, you're invited, and depending on the categories we select, a few members of your team may need to attend the first session."

"Category management means a lot of different things to different people; can you share what you're thinking?" Phil asked.

"You're right," Margot agreed. "From basic strategic sourcing and buying through comprehensive strategy development, procurement people call it all category management. I do mean the entire spectrum, but for the purpose of the training, we're going to focus on transformational category management. This will be three days of intense, hands-on work to prepare the category managers to lead a rigorous, thoughtful strategy development process."

She continued, "I can see a poster here in the meeting room that says, '*Good, fast, cheap; pick two.*' What's the context for that poster?"

Frank leaned forward. "I can speak to that. It was the prior head of procurement's poster. He used it with stakeholders to explain what procurement could accomplish."

"I see," Margot nodded. "Category management will be a big change. I'm not interested in 'cheap' and will instead focus on total cost in use of which price is a component. We are not about buying cheap stuff, and that's the last thing I want to say to stakeholders. As for the tradeoff between the three, what if the business needs all three? What was the answer then?"

"We told them it wasn't realistic," Frank replied.

"Okay, thanks," Margot said. She decided she needed to manage herself. This insight was helpful, and she didn't want to come on too strongly too fast. "We're going to teach the category managers and our stakeholders that we need to understand all the business requirements, and there are more than these three. Once we understand them, we'll work with the stakeholders to do the prioritization. A company like Frontier International Group, if we manage ourselves and our spend appropriately, should be able to readily achieve what is required."

Margot continued, "Please give some thought to which categories we should consider for Wave One. I'm looking for the five to seven categories that are either causing significant pain for stakeholders and/or where we think we can deliver significant value. Value is more than savings and includes service and quality improvements, and access to supplier innovation. Send me your thoughts, and we'll talk about them at the next meeting."

"Lastly, I'll ask Rita to set up these meetings every two weeks for now. We can rotate the timing a bit so Harry is not always up so late," Margot said.

"Thank you," Harry replied, "but I'm used to it. It's part of working for a global company and living in Singapore."

The virtual meeting ended, and Margot asked Tanya and Frank to introduce her to their teams. It did not take long, as between them there were only ten strategic sourcing managers. They all seemed interested and were keen to meet the new boss—their first named CPO.

Frank, Tanya, and Margot headed to the cafeteria for lunch. There was a little small talk about kids and grandkids along the way, and they settled at a table away from the crowds.

"Please talk me through your respective teams," Margot said. "Who they are, which categories they manage, their performance, and their potential." She set down her fork, opened her notepad, and looked up at Frank.

"I'll start, then." Frank put down his sandwich. "Steven manages steel. We do the basic carbon steel and common stainless steel. Any other metals or exotic steel alloys are managed by the respective business procurement team. He's relatively new—two years—and is doing well. Sean manages corrugated; he's been with the company ten years and is a safe pair of hands; he always hits his savings numbers. Beth handles resin. She's new to resin and worked on Tanya's team for a couple of years. It's too soon to assess her in this role, particularly considering the recent oil market. I have an open position for plant MRO. That's my team."

"My team," Tanya said, "includes Katherine, who manages temporary labor and fleet. She's very bright and new to the company—six months. It's too soon to assess her. Philip manages consulting and does a good job with the contracts. Portia handles travel and was helping with PPE during Covid and is getting back to travel. She's very good. I, too, have an open position on my team. That person will help support the legal area."

"Thank you," Margot replied. "I'll ask Rita to set up thirty-minute meetings with everyone so I can meet them and vice-versa, but I wanted a bit of context. How do your teams interface with the business-based procurement teams? What is the process to agree category governance?"

"Bill, the prior head of procurement, would talk it through with the business procurement leads and inform us of the decision," Tanya answered.

"Interesting, that will be something we talk about as a GPLT going forward," Margot said.

"GPLT?" Frank asked.

"Yes, global procurement leadership team," Margot explained.

"Thanks," Frank replied. "Bill called it the PMT—purchasing management team."

"I'm sure there will be lots of acronyms we're all going to learn and relearn through the transformation process. I'll ask Rita to keep a glossary," Margot said. "Thanks for the overview. Can we each spend some time together this afternoon?"

"I need to head to a meeting." Tanya stood and picked up her tray. "You and Frank can talk first, and I'll be back by three." She left them at the table.

Frank looked a bit sheepish. "I guess I go first."

"Yes, it looks that way." Margot pushed her tray aside. "Tell me how it's going for you and how you're feeling."

Frank took a breath. "I worked great with Bill. I knew what he expected, and I never let him down. He shared the savings target, and my team hit the expected numbers. Whenever there was a supply issue, we'd get on the phone and sort it out with the suppliers. I have a small team, but I'm proud of them. As for me, I've been with the company over twenty years and have seen it grow over that time. It's a great company. I was surprised when Brenda and Bill left. I know it was Leslie's choice, and I've read the announcements, but it's hard to argue with year after year of success."

"You're right about Frontier being successful," Margot agreed. "The company has done very well with Leslie's leadership. I expect that Brenda and Bill leaving was a bit of a shock to the system. Leslie interviewed me because Brenda was gone and her successor is not yet named. I am very impressed by Leslie and her team."

"They are amazing," Frank stated. "I would put them up against any other business leadership team from a performance management and culture perspective. It's a high-integrity group."

"How are you feeling about me being here?" She asked gently.

"Well, honestly, it's early days," he admitted. "It's a small town, and I heard from people I trust at Confederated Supplies that you're good—very good. Based on that, I'm looking forward to hearing what you have planned."

"I'm glad you're hearing good things," she smiled. "I'm happy to be here and looking forward to building and executing our transformation plans. Please let me know if you think I'm missing something critical or can see a better way of doing something. Sometimes I drive hard, but I never intend to ignore someone or drive over them. Thanks for your time; let's head back."

Frank hoped the conversation had gone well. He'd not mentioned that he and his wife were looking at his 401(k) and considering retirement options. The condo they'd inherited in Scottsdale was his safe landing spot if he needed it.

Margot wasn't convinced about Frank. He seemed like a nice guy, but also very tactically focused on short-term targets. Achieving annual savings targets was no longer good enough; it hadn't been for years. How had procurement at Frontier become so disconnected from what was possible? She'd keep poking around and exploring.

Later that afternoon, Tanya knocked on Margot's doorframe and asked, "Is this a good time?"

"Yes, come on in," Margot gestured to the chair. "Close the door behind you, please."

Tanya sat down, and Margot said, "So you told me about your team. Please tell me about you, your role, and what you're thinking. And it's okay to relax a bit."

Tanya smiled. "This does feel a bit like a job interview. Okay, so here we go. I'm new in the indirect role. I worked in Frank's direct team running the steel category, and a couple of years ago, Bill promoted me to the indirect role. Prior to the steel category here, I worked at a smaller company in the Northwest and handled a range of indirect categories. My husband and I moved here with his company a little over six years ago. It was a huge change from the Northwest, but we like it. The indirect role is a bit daunting here. My team supports the corporate functions and assists the business-based procurement teams as needed. We're a small team and try to keep up with the demand."

"How do you like indirect compared to direct?" Margot asked.

"I'm struggling with that at times," Tanya admitted. "In the direct space, we received targets from Bill and, if we hit the numbers, we knew we were doing well. In the indirect categories, the numbers are not the same. If we generate any savings, the functions just spend the money anyway. Frankly, we're an administrative group and are involved late in the process."

Margot smiled. "I'm relieved to hear that you recognize these issues and that you're not happy about it. That doesn't mean that I'm glad you're unhappy—just the opposite—it means we can work together to address these issues."

"This is a great company, and I enjoy working here. I'm encouraged that you joined and hope to learn a lot from you," Tanya said.

Margot leaned forward. "We are all about to embark on the journey of transformation. If we are successful, all of the issues that you're struggling with will be addressed; not tomorrow or the week after, but they will be addressed. Please feel free to reach out any time you want to talk or check in."

"Thanks." Tanya stood up. "I will do that."

OCTOBER 16TH

Shelly called Margot the following Monday morning. "I really appreciate you thinking of me for this role, and yes, I'm interested. I looked up Oklahoma City, and it looks nice. I only knew about it from the bombing years ago, so I wasn't sure."

"Yes, I had the same reaction when I moved here three years ago," Margot replied. "It has a great feel with wonderful restaurants. It does not feel like a big city, and we really enjoy it."

"What are the next steps?"

"I'll confirm when the job is live on our website and let you know, and then you should apply online and send me your information. The automated application screening process is a bit hit or miss, and I don't want any issues."

"Will do," Shelly said. "What's the status of the transformation? How is it going?"

"I am preparing for a big presentation to the ELT in December. I'll cover category management and confirm the Wave One category teams and ask them for sponsors. It's the effective launch of the category governance process and needs to go well."

"Let me know if you need me to do anything to help—even before I join."

"Thanks, I will," Margot said. "Keep me posted on your progress."

Margot confirmed that the procurement transformation job was live in the Frontier International Group HR system and sent a note to Jean thanking her for her help. Jean was already an amazing ally, and Margot knew it.

Within a week, Shelly had a screening interview with the HR recruiter. HR was following the process, and the role was open to internal and external applicants. There weren't any internal candidates, but there were a number of external candidates. HR interviewed them all and sent the top five, including Shelly, to Margot to interview. Margot was initially disappointed at having to interview all five, but by the end was glad she had. Her initial read of Shelly was right—she was the best of the bunch, and it was clear to Margot and the HR recruiter.

The final interviews were conducted at the HQ, and it gave Margot a chance to take Shelly on a tour of Oklahoma City. They finished near Shelly's hotel and enjoyed a beer at Margot's favorite spot, Prairie Artisan Ales.

"This is a beer spot like no other I've ever been to," Margot said. "My husband is a beer guy, and he found it. They have a huge range of beers that are all good, but I'll warn you, 'The Bomb' is potent."

Shelly appreciated Margot taking the time to show her around the city. Nobody had done this when she moved to LA and, as a result, she never felt connected there. She'd tried to connect, but LA was simply too large and too impersonal. She was, at heart, a country girl from outside Rochester, NY, not a big city type.

"How often do you get home?" Margot asked once they had their drinks.

"Maybe once or twice a year," Shelly replied. "It's a long flight from LA. It's not around the corner from here, but I checked and it's doable with one connection."

"This is a good airport," Margot said. "It's not a hub, but it has great flights to the hubs and is nearly hassle-free otherwise. Do you have any questions on the role or the area before you head back to LA?"

"I asked you before how long you're planning to stay, and I'd like to know if there are any changes."

"No changes on my part. I really like Frontier so far. It's early days for me, but I look at how Leslie and Jean opened up to me during my hiring and now are supporting you, and I'm delighted. I briefly met the lead candidate for the CFO, who will be my boss. He seems very bright and engaged. My family is well settled here, too, so I don't have any plans to go anywhere."

Shelly nodded slowly. "I want to be part of a positive transformation, not a typical race to the bottom chasing the cost of procurement and hollowing out the function while driving price savings."

"I agree," Margot said. "I think those efforts will destroy the function long-term. It's so short-sighted to chase price while ignoring supplier innovation and the higher value-adds we can contribute. I recognize it's largely driven by what is easiest to measure, but that's not a good enough answer. If the CFO candidate I met, Matt, is hired, we'll be well positioned. In the brief time we talked, he made it clear that he is not looking for procurement savings to support the rest of the business. He'll take the savings, don't get me wrong, but he knows that's just a small part of the value we can add to the company."

"That's what I need to hear, thank you. I have an early flight tomorrow, so I need to head back to the hotel."

"I'll drop you off on my way home," Margot offered.

Shelly's job offer was extended, accepted, and her references checked. She gave notice in LA and began the process of relocating. A key enabler in Margot's transformation plan was falling into place.

OCTOBER 15TH

"Hi Frank, please come by my office when you have a minute," Margot said as she walked by Frank's office.

A few minutes later he knocked on her door, and she greeted him. "Good morning, Frank, come in and sit down," motioning toward the table and chairs in her office.

He took a seat and she joined him at the table.

"I was working through some of the papers on the desk and found this contract addendum signed earlier this year with Premier Packaging. Are you familiar with it?" she asked.

"Yes, Sean negotiated that deal earlier this year. Substantial savings for Frontier in that agreement," he replied.

"I saw that. I also see that the deal is for five years with a three percent price increase each year."

"Yes, those terms sound correct."

"And you approved this deal?" Margot asked.

"I did. It saved us a bunch of money," Frank answered. "Is there something wrong?"

"I really don't know where to start," Margot stated. "I could start at the use of their document for the agreement that is very unfavorable to Frontier, I could start at a five-year term, I could start at increasing prices every year with no mention of outside indices, I could start at the actual price which seems to bear no relation to the actual cost of the item. But when I did a bit of digging, I find that Premier

Packaging owns the drawings for these items and we're sole sourced to them. Sole sourced for a packaging item! Then I noticed that there are no volume guarantees. This is not a fixed value contract; it is a pricing agreement."

Frank had noticeably slipped down in his chair while she was talking and now sat up straight.

"We use Premier for these items and have for years. They are the best," he said.

"How can they afford to cut the prices in this agreement?" she asked.

"Because we're an important customer; they're investing in the relationship," he said brightly.

"I don't think so, Frank," Margot replied. "They are temporarily cutting the profit margin in exchange for a long-term deal in a market that should be short-term oriented with express linkages to the cost of production and the underlying supply indices."

"That's not how we approached these things under Bill."

"I'm learning that," Margot said. "I expect I'll find the same scenario in most of the categories. As the senior director, I need you to know that this needs to change going forward. I would never have signed this addendum and any procurement manager who brings something like this to me for review and approval in the future will not succeed. You and me and the procurement leaders are going to have to work together to fix this. In the meantime, I'm going to send a note to the team about contract renewals going forward."

OCTOBER 22ND

At the next GPLT call Margot raised the topic of contract renewals and extensions, "I recently reviewed a contract extension, and it reminded me that we need to limit the number of extensions until we implement the category management process next year. I realize there will be some contracts that must be addressed, but we can focus on the critical few and extend month-to-month where necessary."

"I don't understand why we're doing this," Mary piped up. "What's the rationale for doing this?"

"Without getting into too many specifics and embarrassing anyone," Margot replied evenly, "it is due to some gaps in our commercial thinking that must be closed. I read a contract extension from earlier this year, and it was awful. If anyone had come to me in my prior company and asked me to sign it, I would have fired them. We're starting fresh here, and I want to give people the benefit of the doubt. So, two things: no long contract extensions or renewals, and watch ordering patterns. I don't want people to stock up before we've had the opportunity to review our practices."

The meeting participants were silent. The process of having GPLT meetings was new and now these announcements. Everyone was a little unsettled.

Frank left the conference room shaken. He knew that Margot was referring to the Premier agreement. He was close to retirement and looking forward to Scottsdale, but he didn't want to be fired. He was still struggling to figure out how the Premier deal fell so far short of the mark.

As he walked back to his office, Sean saw him. "Hey, Frank. You, okay?"

Absentmindedly, Frank said, "Yes, follow me."

They entered Frank's office, and Sean closed the door. They sat down, and Sean waited for Frank to speak.

Frank started slowly. "I've never had an experience like the last couple of weeks. Bill loved the Premier deal and signed it the same day. Margot as much as told me that she'd fire me if I ever brought her a deal like it."

Sean dropped his notebook. "Fire you?"

"Yep," Frank muttered, "every aspect of the deal is an issue. The only saving grace according to her is that we didn't commit to volumes."

"That's pretty much implied because they have the drawings," Sean observed.

"That was one of her points."

"But we have big savings on that deal. I made my numbers with that deal."

"I'm going to suggest that she talk with us about it," Frank stated. "I don't want this hanging over our heads."

Leslie waved Jean into her office and motioned for her to join her at the meeting table.

"How is the CFO offer coming together?" Leslie asked.

"It's just about done. My compensation folks sent it to the remuneration committee of the board for final review. All of the references are checked, so we're ready once we hear from the board," Jean answered.

"That's great. I'm looking forward to Matt joining us. How is Margot settling in?"

Jean smiled. "I've not talked with her at length since she joined, but I'm hearing good things. She's making good inroads with the stakeholders and making the right people nervous."

"Nervous?"

"Yes, not inappropriately, but she is clearly signaling change to the procurement team."

"Compared to Bill, she will be a huge change. What do you expect?" Leslie asked.

"My estimate is thirty to fifty percent turnover in the first year. I've already asked my recruiting team to start searching for the different roles so we're ready to support her," Jean answered.

"That sounds like a lot, but is probably to be expected. We knew there were issues to be sorted. Please keep me posted. Thanks," Leslie said.

Jean waved as she headed out of the office to the elevators.

OCTOBER 25TH

Sean, Frank, and Margot met in the conference room. Anna and Rich joined the meeting virtually.

Margot opened. "Hi Sean and Frank, joining us virtually are Anna and Rich. They will be supporting procurement, and I wanted them to be part of the meeting to have some context on the company. We're here to talk about the Premier Packaging contract extension earlier this year and my comments related to that. I may have been a bit short, and I don't want any misunderstandings. Sean, can you summarize the relationship with Premier and the extension rationale and details?"

"Sure," Sean agreed tentatively. "Premier has been a supplier partner for over fifteen years—before I joined the company. My understanding is that they helped solve some issues by designing new shipping containers. Those containers are the ones listed in the contract addendum. As part of my annual goals, I talked with my sales representative there, Peter, and we agreed a twenty percent price decrease in exchange for a five-year extension. We did include annual increases to address inflation. The PPV savings from this agreement enabled me to hit my numbers for the year and were a big help to procurement."

Anna and Rich observed the discussion and took notes but did not ask questions or interject content.

Margot turned to Frank, "You recommended this deal be approved by Bill, right?"

Frank said matter-of-factly, "I did. It meets our savings definitions and reinforces our relationship with a trusted supplier."

Margot looked back at Sean. "What is used to make corrugated containers?"

"Cardboard," Sean replied.

"What is used to make cardboard?" Margot continued.

"Paper and paper pulp," Sean said, wondering where this line of questioning was leading.

"What happens to the price of paper and pulp over time?" Margot asked.

"It goes up," Sean replied.

"It goes up and down," Margot corrected gently. "Remember supply and demand? In times of high demand, the prices go up and in low demand the prices go down. And when supply is constrained, the prices go up and in excess supply the prices go down. It's a basic commodity market."

"Sounds right," Frank agreed.

Margot leaned forward slightly, "How could Premier lower their prices to Frontier and guarantee them for five years? Do you think they are planning to lose money when the prices of pulp and paper rise?"

"I don't know; I never thought about it," Sean admitted.

"Right," Margot smiled. "I agree. You never thought about it. I suspect that the prices are currently set so high that Premier is very confident they will never have an issue with profit on this account. Was your sales rep, Peter, anxious to sign this addendum?"

"He sent it to me within an hour of agreeing the details," Sean said, looking at the table.

"I'm sure he did," Margot agreed. "I'm sure he too made his numbers for the year. I'm not mad at you, Sean. You executed the deal that was expected at the time. I am telling you and Frank that the new category management approach and savings definitions we're going to roll out will be a big change. There are other details in the extension that are not acceptable in the future, but we'll cover them during the training. Suffice it to say that you'll need a new approach in the new year and the training will help."

"Anything else?" Frank asked weakly.

"No, that's it. Thanks," Margot stated.

Frank and Sean left, and Margot stayed on the video call with Anna and Rich.

"That's pretty indicative of what I'm finding," Margot said. "Pure tactical buying with no insights on cost and the supply market. We're sole sourced in crazy areas. It's worse than I expected."

"You're going to be able to fix everything you touch," Rich observed.

"Your challenges will be pacing the change at a rate the business and your people can accept and managing your frustration with the status quo," Anna said.

"You're both right," Margot agreed. "I'm glad I'm here, I'm happy you've agreed to help with the category management training, and January cannot get here soon enough!"

"Thanks for including us in the conversation, Margot," Rich said. "The context is helpful for us."

"What just happened?" Sean asked. He and Frank were back in Frank's office commiserating after the meeting.

"We were both just effectively put on notice," Frank replied. "It was done very nicely, but that is what happened. I have my Scottsdale option, but you need to work. Do you know any headhunters?"

Sean was looking shell-shocked.

"I am not saying you're going to be fired, Sean. Let's not overreact," Frank said. "What I'm saying is that what made you successful in the past will not be the same in the future. You'll want to have all of your options open."

"I do know one headhunter, Lucy," Sean volunteered. "I'll call her."

"That's good, and you and I will support each other. Don't worry," Frank replied. "You and I need choices--we need to choose our future carefully."

Sean walked back to his cubicle and looked up the headhunter. He'd heard about Lucy from a friend and sent her an email asking to connect.

Lucy replied quickly and asked Sean to send his CV, then offered times for them to talk. They agreed a time when Sean could be out of the office.

OCTOBER 27TH

"Hi, Sean, it's nice to talk with you," Lucy said.

"I appreciate you making time. Did you receive my CV okay?" Sean asked.

"Yes, it looks like you've been at Frontier for a while and are doing well there. How are you getting along with Margot?" Lucy asked. "I imagine she's quite a change from Bill."

"She's why I wanted to talk with you," Sean replied. "She's very different from Bill. I was very successful with Bill, and I'm not sure I will be with her."

"Bill was regarded as a solid sourcing guy, and Margot drives transformational category management. It's not quite a black and white distinction, but it is very big. I can understand where you, as a sourcing expert, would be uncomfortable," Lucy observed. "Have you ever been trained in category management?"

"When I was in the procurement program at Mid-State, we talked about category management, but they said it was just about thinking about the spend across the category and doing the sourcing," Sean replied.

"My understanding of Margot's approach is from a distance, but I don't think her view is the same. I think it starts at the same place and is then much more in-depth," Lucy said. "What training, development, or awards have you completed in the last few years?"

"Nothing really," Sean admitted. "I do exceed my savings numbers each year."

"Consistent performance is good. Do you have anything else noteworthy that would distinguish you as an individual versus others? Did your parents make you listen to ABBA or the Bee Gees when you were young?" Lucy asked with a smile.

"Does that really count?" Sean asked, blinking rapidly for a second at her.

"No, of course not, I need you to relax a bit. I cannot help you through the search process if you're too uptight and nervous," Lucy stated. "I do think that you're working for a great company, and if you can learn how to do category management, you're in the best place. Margot has a reputation for pushing hard and for being fair. Don't give up yet. In the meantime, look at the CV edits and questions I sent through and address them. We can talk again after the holidays."

NOVEMBER 20TH

By late October, Matt was offered the CFO role and accepted. He started immediately on an unofficial basis and officially in time to join the executive team meeting in mid-November. He was reviewing the monthly results, "Our medical division was able to ship the large government order and meet their targets. The industrial division was below target on sales and over budget on expenses."

Before he could say another word, Bob, the president of the industrial business, burst into the conversation. "Federated Steel did not deliver their committed volume and raised their prices. There was nothing we could do—we're stuck!"

Erica, the president of the medical division, smiled, nodded, and said, "We're quite happy with Federated; they always come through for us."

Before a fracas could ensue, Matt took over again. "I raised both numbers on purpose. Both the medical and industrial businesses are sole-sourced for stainless steel to Federated. I heard about it earlier this week from Margot. I also heard that the medical business agreed to a price increase starting next quarter in exchange for full delivery of steel to meet their needs last quarter."

Tensing her shoulders, Erica muttered, barely audible, "That's confidential."

Nobody acknowledged it, but the normally collegial atmosphere in the executive team meetings was now tense and quiet.

Matt broke the silence. "When I heard about this, I could not believe that our business units would be competing for supply from the same suppliers and asked Margot. She said that while we have over thirty-five thousand suppliers, we appear to be sole-sourced for over ninety percent of our parts and supplies. I suspect this situation occurs daily with our suppliers."

Leslie's expression darkened throughout the conversation, and she took over. "Okay, Matt, it's good to know this, but what are we going to do to fix this problem? We cannot let this continue, and we cannot jeopardize our ability to supply product and meet our commitments to clients and Wall Street by competing amongst ourselves."

Matt nodded. "This is exactly what Margot and her team are going to address through category management. Her team will lead the development—with all of us participating—of strategies that will reduce the number of suppliers, so we reduce complexity and increase our marketplace leverage and radically reduce our supply-risk exposure. We need to drive cross-business collaboration." He turned to Jean and continued, "And based on this conversation, we'll need to look at our executive compensation plans as well."

Jean smiled, glancing at Leslie and her peers. "I've started the conversation with Leslie at the conceptual level. Our current plan rewards leaders for hitting their individual numbers with little consequence for shared or company results. The challenge will be keeping the drive for personal accountability while building company accountability. Simply put, we all do what we're paid to do, and what happened with the medical and industrial business situation that was just described likely happens many times every day. I'm going to work with Leslie and expect to form a broader team with your participation and then the board to revisit our practices."

Leslie added, "There will be no surprises in this process. I will still look to you to run your businesses and hold you accountable for your results. I will not accept that our businesses are competing for supply and raising prices for our company or causing shortages for other business units. This must get fixed. Matt, I want to pick up the conversation with you, Jean, and Margot about how category management is going to help. Please get something set up in the next two weeks."

The rest of the meeting continued through the listed topics without any more drama. Erica was clearly upset and followed Jean out of the meeting toward her office.

DECEMBER 1ST

It was the longest flight Margot had ever been on—a nonstop flight from Dallas to Singapore. She had to admit that Singapore Airlines was not like the US domestic airlines—they provided excellent service. The positive difference continued at Changi Airport. This is what air travel used to be like around the world. In most places, it had become a glorified bus trip, but this was wonderful.

She was keen to meet Harry, the electronics business procurement leader and the key stakeholders: the Frontier Consumer Electronics leadership team and Harry's local procurement team. This was her first time in Singapore, and the thirteen-hour time difference caused her to add a free day before meetings to rest and recover. She did not want to appear groggy or lethargic as a first impression.

Harry recommended that she stay downtown, and she booked into the Regent Hotel on Orchard Road. It was centrally located, and she figured she'd walk most places. After a light breakfast, she stepped outside and was surprised at how warm and humid it was already. It was winter in Oklahoma City, and she'd forgotten how close Singapore was to the equator. She decided to start the day with an open-top bus tour. Whenever she traveled to a new city, this was a reliable way to learn the key spots and a bit of history.

She departed the bus at the Marina Bay Sands. She and Jason had watched a show about the construction of these buildings on TV, and she wanted to get him a souvenir. As a mechanical engineer, he'd appreciate that. The view from the top floor did not disappoint, and she marveled at the number of ships at anchor. Not even the holding areas for the Panama or Suez canals held so many boats. She'd talk with Harry about that later. The plan was for him to take her to dinner tonight so they could talk informally and prepare her for the stakeholder and team meetings over the next two days.

Margot happened to look up at the sky after admiring the ships and noticed the clouds were thickening. She'd heard about the rains in Singapore and had an umbrella but doubted it was up to the task. Deciding to head for lunch, she looked at her map and walked to Raffles. Sure, it was a tourist hotspot, but she had to see it. She resisted the temptation to order a Singapore Sling—she'd be asleep before dinner—and had a light lunch and marveled that in very clean Singapore the only messy place was the floor of the Raffles bar. It was covered with peanut shells! Long a bastion of colonial and business leaders, Raffles was established in the late 1880s as the premier meeting place. It retained that distinction to this day and it was a welcome respite from the heat and humidity for Margot.

During lunch the rain came. She was used to the "gully washers" as they were called in Oklahoma City, but those were typically quick. Here it rained hard for over an hour. It was amazing to watch, and she was thankful she was inside. Once the rain started to dissipate, she plotted a walking course back to her hotel. She'd clean up before dinner but resist the temptation to take a nap.

Harry picked her up on time, and she was thankful his air conditioning worked. The humidity was stifling, and the heat lingered.

Harry asked, "How was your day?"

She described her activities, and he said, "Good for you, you've been out and about and seen some of our sights. There are many more to see, but there will be other trips. Tonight, we're going to have an informal dinner, but it has a great view. We'll be at Jumbo Seafood on East Coast Beach. Based on how much you liked the view from Marina Bay Sands you'll love this—it looks out on the anchorage."

"Sounds perfect," Margot replied. "I am a bit hungry, and I bet the seafood here is fresher than I can get back home."

Harry laughed. "Yes, it will have been caught today. We can even get you something that is still alive if you're feeling adventurous."

"No, thank you. I can only be so adventurous on a short business trip."

As promised, the view was great. As far as they could see, the boats were anchored, and as the sun set, their lights came on. *It looks like a city out there*, Margot thought. She asked, "Why are there so many boats here?"

Harry explained, "Singapore is a major port. The ships will come and go with cargo as you'd expect. This is also a major refueling destination—one of the largest in the world."

"Very interesting," Margot remarked. "There's a lot to learn here. Please tell me about you, your team, and the stakeholders."

Over the course of dinner, Margot learned about Harry's background, his family, and his goals. He was an easy conversationalist, and she enjoyed herself. He covered the highlights of his team and then reviewed the key stakeholders she'd be meeting.

He asked, "Have you been to Asia before?"

"No, this is my first time," she replied. "I've been to Europe many times—and the Middle East as well—but not here."

"Let me explain the culture a bit then," Harry started. "This is a friendly culture; you will be warmly received. It is also a deferential culture. You are a senior executive from HQ. If you ask questions, you may receive positive answers because of your status and not due to the content of your question. This will be to avoid offense or embarrassment. I encourage you to keep this in mind. Americans can be very direct and a bit abrupt. That is acceptable or even encouraged in some parts of your country, but it is off-putting here."

Margot wondered aloud, "Have I already said or done something off-putting? If so, I'm sorry—it was unintentional."

Harry laughed. "No, no, nothing yet. I just wanted you to know about our culture."

They finished dinner, and Harry dropped Margot off at her hotel. He'd be back in the morning to pick her up early.

"Try to sleep," he said and was off.

Try to sleep? she wondered; she was exhausted. After falling asleep quickly, she was wide awake at 1 a.m. and could not get back to sleep until 5 a.m. So much for coming in early and being ready for the day! It would be a day of powering through on caffeine!

Harry was on time, and they headed to Tuas. It was a relatively short drive, but the roads were packed. She noticed the general civility of the drivers and attention to the rules of the road. This was not like any morning commute in a US city!

Tuas, while physically close to downtown Singapore, was nothing like it; it was still clean, but it was heavily industrialized. It made sense, but the difference was stark.

At the site, Harry led Margot to the procurement area and introduced her to his team members. Each was nice and engaging. They technically worked for Harry and not her, but the cultural dimension of deferring to her as an executive from HQ was on display. Harry had organized a department meeting, and all procurement employees attended. She knew this was planned and had a few slides prepared. She introduced herself and then talked about the planned deployment of category management. After her presentation she offered to answer questions. At first there were none, which was typical, and then a hand went up in the back of the room.

A young man asked, "When will we get trained on category management? How can we be included in the training?"

Margot displayed the tentative wave plan. "The first training will occur in January at HQ. The second wave of teams will include teams based here and in Europe. I anticipate a training session will occur here in the early summer. Our goal is to launch teams that are aligned with the budget priorities so we're aligning our timing accordingly."

After the session, Harry said, "Everyone here wants to attend the training. I didn't hear you say that all fifty-five would be trained."

"No," Margot replied. "We'll likely train eight to twelve local category managers depending on the input from you and your stakeholders. I'm sensitive to not wanting people to feel left out. What if we provided a different version of the training for the others?"

"That would be really helpful," Harry said. "Even if it's a bit shorter and simpler, say targeted for buyers versus category managers, it would be good to include everyone."

"We'll do that," Margot agreed. "Also, you and your leadership team should plan to attend the training. It's important that the leaders are seen as being involved as well. Will that be okay culturally?"

"I think it will be," Harry said. "My team is not so intimidating, and the category managers are very good."

After lunch, a few members of the department took Margot on a tour of the facility, including the offices, production areas, and warehouses. The noteworthy aspects for Margot were the production areas and warehouses—they were much, much larger than she'd expected.

Harry picked up on this. "What do you think of the facility?"

"It's huge! The machinery goes on and on; it's like a whole city in here," Margot exclaimed.

"This is not our largest facility," Harry remarked. "We have a larger facility to the north in Kuala Lumpur, another facility in Poland, and are building a bigger facility in the Czech Republic. Our business is growing."

"It is always helpful to see things first-hand," Margot said. "I read the background documents you sent, but it doesn't really come through until you walk from end to end."

Margot spent the balance of the afternoon in short one-on-one conversations with Harry's team. She was not surprised when the person who asked the sole question, Chee Chung, was on Harry's team. He was a delight and very smart.

By late afternoon the sleepless night caught up with her, and she was relieved when Harry approached her. "Margot, that is everyone. Let's take you back to your hotel. We can talk in the car."

She vowed to herself to stay awake long enough to get back to the hotel and was relieved when she got a second wind. They talked through each of his team members and came to Chee Chung.

"He's a star," Harry remarked. "My challenge will be retaining him. I'm hoping that category management can help with that. He's a very talented engineer and is constantly being considered for design and production roles."

"Would it be helpful if I talked with him again tomorrow?" Margot asked. "I cannot make promises, particularly in your organization, but I can describe the future of procurement and opportunities."

"That would be very helpful, thank you," Harry replied as they pulled up in front of the Regent Hotel. "Sleep well, and I'll see you tomorrow morning."

Margot had a quick shower and ate dinner in the hotel bar. Fatigue was catching up with her, and it was a race to get back to the room before she fell asleep. After a relatively restful night, the alarm woke her out of a sound sleep. She reminded herself of the time difference and had a cup of coffee before starting her morning routine. Today she'd need to pack and check out for her flight home that night. After a light breakfast she was in the lobby and saw Harry arrive.

He noticed she was in better form today and said, "The second day is the hardest; today should be easier for you. It's good because you're starting with the president of the electronics business and then meeting his team."

"I do feel better today," Margot replied, "I was shattered last night."

Harry laughed. "What time tonight are you flying back to the US?"

"I'm on the ten p.m. flight tonight," Margot said.

"You'll be fine, then," Harry replied. "Have dinner before your flight and then go to sleep on the plane. Don't wait to eat on the plane."

She made a mental note to do that and asked, "Can you talk through the electronics leadership team?"

During the rest of the trip to Tuas, Harry reviewed each of the electronics executives. They sounded like a capable group, and Margot found herself looking forward to the conversations.

She was not disappointed. Starting with the business president, Benjamin, she enjoyed the conversations and appreciated their openness. She noted that their expectations of procurement were quite modest, but they were currently satisfied. This was a better starting point than dissatisfied stakeholders, and she appreciated Harry's approach.

Harry set up lunch for Margot with Chee Chung. They talked about procurement, the electronics business, and their families. Margot thought Chee Chung was clearly someone who needed to stay on her talent list for the future.

After a few discussions, Margot returned to Harry's office, feeling exhausted but satisfied.

"How did your discussions go?" Harry asked.

"I think they went very well," Margot replied. "I'd be interested in any feedback you receive."

"Well," Harry smiled, "I had a call from Benjamin already and he was very pleased. He commented that you're 'not like most Americans, you listened,' and Chee Chung really appreciated his time with you."

"Well, I'll count that as success," Margot said, who caught herself yawning.

"Let's head to the airport," Harry said. "The traffic that way can be tough in the evening as everyone heads to their flights. You can relax once you're checked in."

On the way back to the airport, Harry explained the check-in and security process—it is different than anywhere else—and is performed flight-by-flight at the gate. He suggested a couple of restaurant options and they arrived.

"Thank you, Harry," Margot said. "You're a great host and I appreciate your support. I'm glad we're going to be working together."

"Thank you for coming to Singapore," Harry replied. "Your trip signals your consideration for us and our business. I hope you have a good trip home."

Margot took her luggage and entered Changi Airport. It was as if she'd arrived at a different airport, which was partly true: the arrival and departure areas were completely different. She found one of the restaurants that Harry recommended and relaxed until her flight. She had three days of emails to catch up on and a few hours now before her flight.

DECEMBER 7TH

"Come in, Margot," Matt said, pointing to a small table in his office. "Help yourself to coffee or a drink." He quickly finished his paperwork and joined her at the table.

Margot sat down, opened her folio, and placed a copy of her executive presentation draft on the other side of the table for Matt and a copy in front of herself to make notes.

"You are old school like me," Matt observed, noticing the paper copies. "Oh, how was your trip to Singapore?"

"The trip was excellent. It was good to meet the consumer electronics team and the local procurement team. The production site is very impressive," she replied. Looking at her printed presentation, she said, "Yes, they just work better for me when I'm creating and revising a presentation."

Matt took a sip of coffee. "Singapore is on my list for the spring. Too much going on before then." He sat down and continued, "You'll have two hours with the ELT. The timing is a bit fluid, but looks like three to five p.m. Wednesday the thirteenth, the second day of our meeting. It's not wonderful timing, but I know that Leslie is committed to you and this presentation. Your challenge will be to make it interesting for them at this time of day—not to imply that procurement is boring! Also, don't forget that the presentation is due to Lillian, Leslie's admin, no later than noon on the Monday before, so it can be sent out for pre-reading."

Margot started through the draft presentation. The only comment Matt made was to share Bob and Erica's conflict over Federated Steel at the ELT meeting.

"Thanks for sharing that. I'm not surprised. I'll be ready for something to come up. See you in a week; have a great weekend," Margot stated. She stood up and gathered her papers.

"Thanks, I'm heading home shortly to be with my family. This working and living in different cities is getting old."

"Enjoy your time with your family. I'm heading to Milwaukee to meet the people at the industrial business."

"Good luck," Matt said, "I think they're a tough group."

DECEMBER 8TH

Margot was tired but wanted to complete this visit to Milwaukee before the holidays. Rita suggested she wait a few weeks after Singapore before making this trip, but Margot was keen to avoid the snow that was sure to pile up in January and February. The weather for this trip was good—cold but clear.

She'd flown up after her meeting with Matt and was picked up at the airport by the industrial procurement leader, Phil. She'd met him on the virtual calls, and he was as nice in person as he'd been on the calls. They went straight from the airport to the Marriott and had a casual dinner in the bar area. Phil had been with the industrial business for over thirty years and had literally grown up in it. It was a large business, but the way he described it and the people, it felt more like a family business. He promised to pick her up early and reminded her to dress casually.

Early the next morning, Phil picked her up, and they headed to Frontier Industrial's HQ and main production site. It looked every bit as old as she thought it was and she noted how much of a contrast this business was to the electronics business she'd seen just a week ago. Where electronics were produced in near-cleanroom conditions, these industrial parts were the result of foundries and heavy machining. It wasn't run-down, but it was well used.

After signing in and watching the mandatory safety briefing, Phil brought Margot to the executive offices. They were very modest but clearly in keeping with the balance of the site.

Bob, the president of the industrial business, saw them and greeted her warmly, "Welcome to Milwaukee, Margot! We're glad you made the trip to see us. Can I take you on a tour?" Without waiting for an answer, he took hold of her elbow and steered her toward the production area. He called over his shoulder to Phil, "We'll be back here in an hour," and with that they were gone.

Margot was initially taken aback by Bob's pushy manner and then decided it was more of a fatherly approach than anything else. He, too, had grown up in the business and had almost forty years of time at this site. He'd put himself through college while working nights on the production line. That said a lot for his work ethic and drive.

They started at the beginning of the process, the small foundry still operating on site. Bob stated, "We used to pour our own metal, from iron, to steel, to aluminum. Now we just do the steel for the train couplings, and the rest is contracted out." As he said it, a heat of steel was poured in the distance, and Margot could see the workers in reflective clothing amid the shower of sparks.

"It's like looking back in time," Margot observed.

"Yep, you're looking at what made this company and America what it is today," he remarked. They continued to the next workstation, where robotic and CNC machines were working on the cast parts. He then continued, "Once the parts cool, we'll go through the machining steps. Once that's done, we'll treat the various parts with hardening and tempering. They look like big, crude parts, but they're quite sophisticated. They're also a bit more sensitive to damage than you'd think. I'll show you more later."

As they continued through the factory, Bob greeted each employee by name and had a nice comment about each person, their family, or both.

Margot marveled at his knowledge about the employees. "You know them all; it's very impressive."

"I do know them all," Bob replied. "I either worked with them on the floor or hired them. I don't subscribe to any of that production employee versus management nonsense; we're one team here. Milwaukee is a union town. Every other company here is unionized. Worse than that, most have hostile relations with their unions. We're non-union and always have been. The word in management here is that the leader who treats employees badly enough to justify a union will be the first one fired. It won't be me."

"But costs must be an issue with your products," Margot observed. "How do you manage the costs and the pay issues?"

"Unions cost a company more money than paying people what they should earn in the first place," Bob answered as they continued walking. "They add their fees and, worst of all, they add a corrosive 'us versus them' environment. Do you think the leader of a unionized business walks through the production area and knows, let alone likes, their employees? I know of one CEO who had to have bodyguards when at the factory. That's wrong. My employees are some of the best paid workers in Wisconsin and the most practical and capable of problem-solving. That's why we're still making parts in the US that our competition offshored. If I was ever asked to do that, I'd quit."

Margot knew that she was getting more than a standard tour and some of this was intended to condition her and likely to be repeated back at HQ, but she was enjoying the tour. They arrived at the end of a production line where a large, painted object was on a pallet. Bob said, "That's the result of the pouring and machining you just saw. That's a railroad coupling. It's strong enough to hold hundreds of freight cars and strong enough to withstand hundreds of cars bumping into it. What it doesn't like are impacts on the top and sides. It's designed to have strength forward and backward—the way a train moves."

A forklift with a pallet of cut corrugated cardboard pieces pulled alongside the coupling pallet. Bob continued, "What we've learned is that if we put these pieces around the coupling and then cover it with full crating, it can be shipped to the car manufacturer successfully ninety-nine point nine percent of the time. A few years back, someone suggested removing the corrugated and skimping on the crating. It saved a few dollars, but our damaged in shipment rate went over five percent. It really hurt us. These are expensive parts, and our reputation is even more valuable. We hurt both for a few cents of cardboard and wood. I vowed never again. The person who suggested the idea left quickly. I'm open to improvements, but I want to see a test and the supporting data. I won't be fooled twice."

Margot noted the corrugated was printed with the name Wabasha Packaging. She'd make a note to check on them later.

Bob finished at the warehouse and loading dock. It was much bigger than she suspected, and she was surprised to see the finished goods stockpile.

"Are those all completed parts?" she asked.

"Yep, and they need to be out of here in the next week to count as sales this year," Bob said. "We've really pressed to get them done on time, and now we need the trains and trucks to move them. It's not just the financials; we need them to move before the weather makes it difficult. Our customers are all working just-in-time and they're counting on these parts."

Margot said, "I'm familiar with those pressures. At my last company, we supplied oil field equipment, and the shipping dates were critical for items heading to Alaska and the oil sands in Canada and the Dakotas. We had some very similar issues with protecting our gear in shipment. It's very important and underappreciated."

Bob smiled. "I'm glad to hear you say that. Let's get a cup of coffee and you can meet my team."

They walked a short distance to a modest cafeteria, picked up their coffee, and returned to the executive offices. It seemed to Margot that she'd walked a long distance, but they'd really just walked in a ring around the offices and administrative spaces in the core.

Bob informed, "Our offices are small, and we need to be accessible to the employees. We also need to be close to the action. I'm not a fan of fancy offices in some remote corner. People who work in those offices are typically irrelevant."

"I agree. I've always enjoyed manufacturing environments and am not a fan of 'Ivory Tower' approaches," Margot agreed.

Bob introduced Margot to one of his leadership team members

and asked him to talk with her then introduce her to the next member and so on every forty-five minutes or so. Afterward she took a little downtime to complete her notes before she met with Phil.

At lunchtime, Phil found her capturing some notes in the conference room. "How was your morning, Margot?"

"A whirlwind. It was excellent. Bob took me on a tour, and then I met with his team. I am ready for lunch," she replied.

"Our cafeteria isn't much. We can go out if you want."

"No, let's eat here. I don't need anything fancy."

They walked into the crowded cafeteria, and many heads turned and noticed her. She chalked it up to the "someone from HQ" effect and ignored it. At least they all seemed friendly. They picked up their food and sat with a few of the procurement employees seated at a table. Phil introduced her, and they talked casually through lunch.

On the way to the procurement area, Phil said, "People appreciate that you ate in the cafeteria. We don't get many visitors from HQ, and most want to go out to lunch. People notice those things."

Margot said, "Good. Part of the reason I joined Frontier is the culture of the company, and I better do my job to support it. Besides, I like factories and always have; this is where value is created."

Margot's conversations with employees progressed through the afternoon. To a person, she found them to be nice, knowledgeable about the business, and tactically focused. It wasn't surprising nor an indictment; they were doing the procurement work that the business expected. Ron was a potential bright spot. A trained engineer, he understood the factory and had an intuitive feel for processes. She thought about meeting Chee Chung and reflected that if she found at least one bright spot in each group, she'd be happy.

A few minutes before three, Phil returned. "How were your conversations?"

She smiled. "I think they were very helpful, and I appreciate you arranging them. What are you hearing about the conversations?"

Phil smiled. "Everyone appreciates that you listened to them. Too many times, people come in—and it's not just HQ but could be anyone—and they tell more than they listen."

They walked into the cafeteria, where a screen was set up on one wall with a computer projector on a table. Some modest snacks and drinks were set out, and the employees were seated and waiting.

Phil walked to the front while Margot connected her laptop to the projector. As she was doing so, he said, "Please join me in welcoming Margot, the new head of purchasing, to Milwaukee," followed by a small round of applause.

Margot had her computer connected and used the same slides she had in Singapore. She decided to ignore the head of purchasing introduction but noted it nonetheless.

She started, "Thank you all for making time today. I only have a few slides to share, and then I'll answer your questions." The first question was about category management training, and her answer was similar to Singapore. The second question caught her a bit off guard and came from one of Phil's team members, Shernale, the head of direct materials for the business, "What's your plan to centralize procurement? Are we all going to work for you?"

Margot paused a moment. "That's the first time anyone at Frontier has asked me that question. It took me a minute to process it. Thank you for that question. The short answer is no. I have no plan to centralize procurement. I have no plan for you to report to me. That's not why I was hired. My understanding from Bob and Phil is that you're doing a good job now. I was hired to bring in category management. That will mean collaboration between the businesses. It will mean you using the process within your business to manage your spend, and it will mean multiple businesses working together when the spend crosses businesses. In my last company procurement reported to me. But that was because it was one business. Here we have three very different businesses. I hope that answers your question."

She noticed the subtle head nod between Phil and Shernale. Clearly, Phil was a bit nervous. She'd add to her answer in the car when he drove her back to her hotel.

A young woman in the back raised her hand and asked, "Do you have a family?"

Margot smiled. "Yes, thank you. My husband, Jason, and I are married almost fifteen years, and we have two boys, Johnny and Tommy. And we have a Labrador retriever, Max. I enjoy work, but I live for my family."

There were a couple thumbs up from the group and a tangible decrease in stress. So far so good.

Phil said, "Let's pack up and head toward dinner. Bob and the leadership team are going to join us."

Margot was pleasantly surprised. She'd expected dinner to be just with Phil and his leadership team.

They drove to the restaurant, but it was nearly walking distance to the site. It was clearly a casual, locals-only place just a step up from a bar. Margot was happy when Phil led her to a private lounge. Most of the leadership team and all of Phil's direct reports had already arrived. She was steered to an open seat next to Bob.

He welcomed her. "How was your day at our site?"

"Fascinating, thanks," Margot replied. "Last week I was in Singapore at the electronics business HQ and production site, and it is very different."

"You, young lady, are the master of the understatement!"

She continued, "I can see and feel the history here. I can see the progress you're making, and it is very impressive. The electronics business is impressive too, but in a different way. They are much younger, and their products are so different."

"If you got nothing else than that from this trip, it was a success!" Bob said, and he raised his beer in a toast.

Margot wondered about the food, but her worries were soon allayed. A broad range of items had been ordered and were served family style. It was good, hearty fare, and she relaxed and enjoyed the group. They spontaneously started sharing stories about the site and different characters who'd worked there, interspersed with occasional stories of other visitors from HQ.

She noticed nobody mentioned Leslie visiting, so she asked, "Does Leslie ever come to this site?"

Bob straightened up as he said, "Leslie visits at least once a year. She's almost as much of an institution here as I am. It can take her two hours to walk across the floor because she stops and talks with the people who know her. I'm in awe of her. Right after she was promoted to CEO from Frontier Medical one of our employees was badly hurt and her husband was killed in a car accident. Leslie personally called her and arranged for her husband's funeral. Mind you, this was not a work-related accident, but Leslie stepped in. Every one of our employees knows this story. You cannot teach this in graduate school. You either learn this growing up or you don't, and she did."

Margot smiled. "She's why I'm here, and that is an amazing story. Thank you."

Daniel, head of indirect for the business, asked, "Margot, why did you decide to go into procurement?"

She thought for a moment before replying, "I've not thought about it much. I think I started in procurement because a neighbor recommended it when I was graduating from school. I applied and got the job. If I can add to your question, 'Why do I stay in procurement?' or 'Why do I recommend it to others?' I like procurement because it is forward looking. There are occasions when we look backward to do some problem-solving, but most of the time we're looking to the future. The reason why I'm so passionate about category management is that it's all about the future and where the business, the supply markets, and our customers are going. We cannot know the exact answers, of course, but we can be inquisitive, we can be analytical, and we can build a strategy to get there. I always wonder why, how, and when, and this is a great fit for me." She finished, noticing that the table was quiet. She blushed a bit. "Sorry, I didn't mean to sermonize and kill the good mood of the table."

Bob put a fatherly arm around her chair and assured her, "Never apologize for liking and being good at your job."

This seemed to signal the end of the dinner, so the group started to filter out. Phil piped up, "I'll drop you off at your hotel, Margot."

Bob offered his hand to Margot, and as they shook hands, he said, "Thank you for coming to our site. I enjoyed meeting you. If you need anything or have any questions, you call me directly."

"Thanks, Bob. I'll do that," she replied.

It was a short ride back to the hotel, and the adrenaline was fading; Margot was tired. Phil dropped her off, leaving her with a: "Have a safe flight home. Let me know if you need anything."

"Thanks, Phil, I appreciate your hospitality today. Have a safe ride home."

Back in her room, Margot listed the key events in chronological order and then added her key insights and any follow-up actions. She always used this approach for her site visits, and it served her well.

DECEMBER 13TH

Wednesday the thirteenth, Margot was ready. She'd modified her presentation and sent it to Lillian by noon on the prior Friday. Now she was waiting outside the meeting room for the ELT to take a break so she could enter. She knew from reputation that Leslie was a stickler for timing and was loath to allow a meeting to get off topic or change the timing. She'd call another special meeting before she allowed sloppy meeting management to become the norm.

Promptly at 2:45 p.m., the first ELT member exited the room and headed to the restrooms before Margot could say hello. Matt stepped out and greeted her. "Hi, Margot, how are you doing today?"

"I'm well and looking forward to this session," she replied. "I didn't realize so many people would be here. I expected five or six and counted at least eight."

"Yes, it's a bigger group today as no one is traveling and they're all here in person. They're all in good form," Matt said. He continued, "Yesterday went well—the businesses are doing well—and everyone is in a good mood. Tonight, we're heading out to a group dinner and need to be out of the room no later than five thirty."

"I'll move through the content efficiently," Margot assured. "There are some big concepts and decision requests but not too many pages of content. I'll go set up while you take your break."

She walked into the room and Leslie motioned for her to join her at the far end of the conference table. "Margot, thanks for joining us, and my apologies for giving you the 'death slot' at the end of day two. I didn't have another time slot available."

With that, Leslie walked out of the meeting room. Margot coordinated with Lillian, as the presentations were made from Lillian's computer. Once she was satisfied, Margot picked up a soda and waited for the group to return.

"Let's get started," Leslie said when she arrived back. "The rest of the afternoon, we'll be with Margot, our new CPO. Most of you have met her, and for those who haven't, I'm sure you will shortly. I've asked Margot to transform procurement from a tactical to a strategic organization. This transformation will affect all of us. We all spend or commit funds on behalf of the company, and the processes will be changing. This will not be Margot's only presentation to this team. I expect she will be with us on at least a quarterly basis and a semi-annual basis with the board. Frontier International Group, the whole company, needs a new relationship with the supply market, and Margot is here to help us achieve this. Margot."

"Thank you, Leslie, for the introduction and the opportunity to meet with the ELT this afternoon," Margot started. "You all received my presentation, and I'm not going to rehash items you already read. This afternoon, I want to open the dialogue about what will be different, why it's better for Frontier in general and you in particular, and what you can expect from the transformation.

"First, a few statistics. Frontier International Group has over thirty-five thousand suppliers. 'So what, you ask.' What is the relevance of the thirty-five thousand? Frontier International Group is, as you know, a complex company with multiple product offerings from very different divisions—highly complex manufacturing is the phrase used. Even with that, I estimate, based on my experience and outside benchmarks, that we should have no more than thirty-five hundred suppliers. That's right, I suspect we have over thirty thousand extra suppliers."

She paused to look around the room.

"We've not met yet," Sondra, the general counsel, stated, "but how could we possibly have so many extra suppliers? We talk in almost every meeting about potential supply shortages and impacts to revenue and profit. Don't we need more suppliers?"

"Thank you, Sondra, for that question," Margot replied. "Another important fact is that we are ninety to ninety-five percent sole- or single-sourced for our purchases. Sole-sourced means there is only one potential source available, and single-sourced means there are multiple sources and we're only using one source. This occurs over time when stakeholders select suppliers to fit discrete needs and/or source in a small area around their site. The implications for this are multiple: we increase our supply risk, as you mentioned, and we reduce our buying leverage and presence in the supply market. It is, if you will, the worst possible outcome. There are a very few spend areas where single-sourcing makes sense—like our company auditor or our third-party benefits administrator in a particular region—but we will typically pursue multiple sources to reduce supply risk."

"Won't splitting the business between suppliers reduce our leverage in the supply market?" Jean asked.

"It could, Jean, but in most cases, we're going to move from ten, or one hundred, or over one thousand suppliers in a spend area to just a few. In these circumstances, we'll still be improving our value as a customer," Margot informed. She then paused. "Let me back up a minute... The company revenue last year was forty-four-point-six billion, and our third-party spend was twenty-six-point-eight billion with sixteen-point-one billion in direct materials and ten-point-seven billion in indirect goods and services. This should make Frontier International Group an extremely desirable customer. With over thirty-five thousand suppliers our spend is so fragmented that we are behaving as a much smaller company and are much less desirable as a customer."

She continued, "That is why we're going to pursue transformational category management. In the past, Frontier International Group practiced only strategic sourcing. It was not bad, but it did not optimize our relationship with the supply market. It can be fairly summed up with the expression of 'three bids and a buy.'"

"So, which suppliers will we keep, and how will this be determined?" Erica asked.

"Excellent question," Margot replied, advancing to the category management process slide. "We're going to follow this process. It starts with you—the ELT—and procurement agreeing the priority categories and underlying business issues. In some cases the goal will be savings, in others it will be risk reduction, and in yet others it will be access to supplier innovation. All of these objectives are possible. We will agree on the critical few categories to work on—likely less than eight to ten at any point in time. You'll name a senior leader to serve as the sponsor for the team and provide five to seven cross-functional team members. I'll speak more to the sponsor role in a minute but suffice it to say it is a line executive who will be most affected by the team outcome. One of the category managers will lead the team, and in three to six months, the team will present a category strategy to this team. So, to Erica's question, you and your people will determine the supply-base strategy for the future. Some of the input will come through the team members you name, and the rest will come through broader stakeholder input. The result is not a procurement strategy; it is a business strategy for the respective spend area. Depending on the business importance of the category, the strategy could be relatively simple, like office supplies, and in other areas, like outside research conducted by universities or other companies, it could be complex and strategic to your respective divisions and the entire company. That's why some teams will take a bit longer and may need more resources than others."

"Please remind the group of your commitments," Matt said.

Margot responded, "Procurement is committing to work with the stakeholders to deliver two-point-one billion in finance-verified savings over four years while reducing and managing supply chain risk and improving access to supplier innovations. We will focus on a reduction in total cost in use for savings as a shift away from the historical use of PPV and the associated price-only approach. Reducing and managing risk will be an expected output of each category strategy; access to supplier innovations will be category dependent."

"I do want to highlight that category management includes strategy development and that the final stage, supplier management and value realization, provides opportunities that are often overlooked because they are more challenging to quantify financially and may generate revenue rather than savings. I'm referring to the value realization process—value creation, identification, and capture. Relevant examples that would be applicable to Frontier are reduced time to market, supply chain improvements, supplier-partnered improvements, such as shorter change over time and reduced material usage due to equipment and process selection, collaborative beta testing with strategic suppliers, and licensing or joint-venture agreements. In my experience, this focus on value opportunities energizes team thinking and serves to bring the business and procurement closer."

Matt joined in again. "I want to add to what Margot said and clarify the new approach to procurement measurement. Historically the Frontier finance area focused on what is known as PPV—the change in price over time. Going forward, we will not be doing this. I view a primary focus on PPV to be misguided. Even if you try to make it sound more sophisticated with the Greek letter Delta—some companies call it 'Delta P'—it assumes that once a product or service is selected no new service or product will be offered that will be demonstrably better. We all can recite many instances where new products or services were created that were initially priced higher but that lasted much longer or provided much more value. A focus on PPV drives people away from these opportunities. Even worse, PPV reinforces to the company and our suppliers that procurement is driven by price—our version of the price police—and are incented to choose the cheapest alternatives. This is an insidious combination, and it will be stopped. From this day forward, finance will compare the total cost in use of the current and the proposed alternatives. Finance will encourage and support improvement."

"It's about time, and I welcome it," Bob piped up. "I've fought the price-only measurements for years. My customers are counting on years or decades of service from our parts, and to put them at risk to obtain cheaper parts is frankly stupid."

"That, ladies and gentlemen, is why Matt and Margot are with us now," Leslie said. "It took us a while to recognize the impacts, and we've taken steps to address it. Now that we're all in violent agreement, please proceed, Margot."

"I've spoken with Leslie and Matt regarding the value realization process, and they agree that it must be integral to category management. I will be working with Anna and Rich, our consultants, and Shelly, the transformation leader, to integrate the value realization process into all category strategies."

She continued, "Why do I think this is possible at Frontier? This slide shows the assessment criteria I use when sizing up the category management potential opportunity. You'll see that these are qualitative assessments. I'm less focused on the size of the spend than the behaviors, policies, and practices that govern the spend."

Margot advanced to the slide with the category management assessment criteria:

1. **Business Strategy** – The extent to which the organization follows a defined strategy to create marketplace success.
2. **Market Urgency** – The effects of outside forces on the culture and behavior of the business leaders and employees.
3. **R&D/Innovation Strategy** – The ongoing plans and methods to sustain unique market offerings.
4. **Spend Governance** – The degree to which spend control is viewed as a 'power' requirement versus a commercial opportunity.
5. **Leadership & Culture** – The degree to which leaders drive collaboration inside the organization and address external competition.
6. **Procurement Capability** – The assessment of the function's progress along the improvement journey.
7. **Supply Chain Integration** – The role of internal and external supply chains.

"These are the criteria I've developed over my career to assess a company's readiness to embrace enhanced or transformative category management," she added. "I did an informal assessment as part of my interview process, and I'll share my thoughts then and what I've learned since joining the company."

"Of course, each Frontier business unit has well-defined strategies for the respective business and innovation of the products and services it offers. These are plusses. Each business also has its own supply chain, but they are not integrated or coordinated across the company, and this is a minus. Achieving cross-company synergy and leverage will be new and potentially challenging. The company is doing well financially, yet each division exists in highly competitive environments. This is a plus—nobody can afford to be complacent."

"Let me underline that last statement," Leslie said. "We are not where we are because of luck. We are doing well because we carefully develop strategies and then we execute flawlessly."

"Thanks, Leslie," Margot replied. "Spend governance, leadership, and culture are, in my experience, the most important elements. If we are going to succeed on this journey, we need to collaborate. We need to align internally and compete externally. We will need to stop certain behaviors like local, isolated sourcing and think instead as one company. I am heartened by the level of collaboration I already see."

"This is an excellent team," Jean added. "We will have our disagreements; we will have issues that need a thorough airing—in here—but then we emerge and speak with one voice."

"That's exactly what we need," Margot agreed. "It's what I saw during my interview process and, frankly, it's why I joined the company."

"Procurement is quite tactical," Larry observed. "If I come to them with a contract to be finalized, they can do that. If I come to them with an open need and ask them to engage the market more broadly, they stumble. They're slow."

"Thanks for the feedback, Larry," Margot replied. "The last element on the slide, procurement capability, is an open question. I suspect that what you're mentioning is going to be fairly widespread. I will not be surprised if more than half of the procurement function turns over in the next twenty-four to thirty-six months. I am working with Jean and her team on an assessment process. I am committed to giving everyone a chance to work in the new way, but we have to deliver on these commitments so their opportunity to demonstrate capability will be relatively short. I am confident that we have five to ten category managers who can lead the initial wave of categories. Beyond that, I'm not yet sure." She glanced at the clock on the back wall and was surprised to see that almost half an hour of her time was used. She'd only covered a small handful of slides. Glancing at Matt, who was looking pleased with the conversation so far, she continued on.

"Getting started will include most members of this team," she said, moving to the next slide.

"Let me interrupt on that point," Leslie jumped in. "It will include everyone on this team at the start. I may not be able to make every meeting, but I want you to notify Lillian about all of them, and I will join whenever possible. If there is a critical point, I expect you and Matt to notify me, and I'll be there. Support for this process is part of everyone's objectives for this year. The board added this to my expectations and, therefore, it's part of yours as well."

Jean added, "I'm working with Leslie and the board's Compensation Committee to look at ELT compensation. I've shared this with you in the past but want to emphasize that it is moving forward. All of you are sharing input and it's very helpful. Our goal is to continue to incent you to drive your businesses to success while concurrently rewarding the cross-business collaboration the company needs. Lastly, my recommendation is that every sponsor we assign to a category is a respected, senior executive. This is an opportunity for them to demonstrate the leadership behaviors and business acumen we need to see in practice."

"That's an excellent idea, thanks Jean." Leslie smiled.

Margot advanced to the next slide. "Today is the launch of the executive governance process. This includes reviewing the potential spend categories, agreeing on the critical few, and naming sponsors.

The next slide lists some categories and potential geographic scope I recommend you consider for Wave One based on both your input and the procurement review."

Margot reviewed the potential categories:

Direct materials:

- Corrugated packaging – global
- Steel (carbon; not specialized) – global
- Plastic resin – global

Indirect goods & services:

- IT hardware – laptops – global
- Legal – document management – North America
- Fleet cars – Europe

"I know that a couple of these categories are of immediate interest; I've heard from you directly. Others are categories that my team and I recommend based on the state of the current category versus the supply marketplace. Which ones are keeping you up at night? That's a good litmus test that improvement is required. Which ones, if we achieved a breakthrough result, would help advance your business?"

"How many do you want to start with?" Leslie asked.

"I'm comfortable with five to seven," Margot replied. "I think we can support that many, and I don't think it will be too disruptive to the business. There's a good mix of categories here that will deliver on the full range of business requirements."

"I need help with meetings and events in the post-Covid world," Erica chimed in. "We stopped doing much with them during Covid, and now they're all restarting. A strategy in this space would be helpful."

"That's great, I'll add it to the list," Margot said. "Anyone else have additions or changes?"

Head nodding and shaking rippled around the table.

"Okay, that's the easy part," Margot stated. "I mentioned the term sponsor a few minutes ago. Now I need a sponsor for each team. Here are the responsibilities for a category management team sponsor." She showed the following slides:

Qualifications

- Has a key interest in the project and demonstrates an ongoing and active interest in the project.
- Is an internal "customer" for the team.
- Commands sufficient influence and authority to act as a liaison between the team and senior management.
- Supports and empowers individual team members.
- Is committed to project goals.
- Is resilient and committed to overcoming organizational resistance to project goals/implementation plans.
- Communicates effectively within all levels of the organization.

Responsibilities

- Liaisons with project stakeholders to authorize the setting up of the project.
- Provides input into the preliminary brief, agrees with scope and boundaries as well as targets and outcomes.
- Approves (but not dictates) the charter for the team.
- Provides a link to senior management and companywide activity.
- Secures the necessary resources for the team.
- Supports but does not lead the project.
- Provides guidance on the approval process for implementing solutions.

"There's a fair amount on the slide, so let me highlight that the sponsor must support the team through startup, which includes selecting and securing cross-functional team members, reviewing the team's work along the way for consistency with the company's goals and plans—some of which are typically confidential—and driving implementation of the approved strategy. We won't launch a team without a sponsor; they're critical to success."

"Margot, I don't mean to be rude, but I'd like you to give us fifteen minutes to talk this through. Can you please step out?" Leslie asked.

"Sure, let me know when you're ready for me to come back," Margot replied, and she headed out of the meeting room.

Once the door closed, Leslie said, "I think this is an opportunity for our high-potential VPs and GMs. Jean, please bring up the list of high-potentials. I want our future senior leaders to understand this process and to be expert consensus-builders and collaborators. Sponsoring a team is better development than attending a course. Let's go through Margot's list and identify people by name."

They worked through the list of categories and, based on the geographic scoping and predominant category spend, selected sponsors. Lillian added the names to the category slide then asked Margot to rejoin the team.

Margot was delighted they'd moved the process along and, based on what she'd heard about various people in the organization, she was satisfied with their nominations. She said, "thank you for moving this forward. Please contact each person listed and inform them about this selection. I will send you a draft email with the relevant information that you can tailor and send. The category training is set for mid-January, and the teams will launch shortly thereafter."

Bob asked, "Who from procurement is going to lead these teams?"

"Thank you, Bob, I'm glad you asked that question." Margot smiled at him. "The indirect spend categories that cross the company are managed by my team, and someone from corporate procurement will lead the IT and legal-related categories. Fleet is a bit different, and as this one is predominantly Europe-focused, it will be led by the fleet manager in the medical business."

She continued, "The direct materials are a mix, with a few led by my team and others by your respective teams. My team will lead corrugated. Members from your teams will lead plastic resin and steel."

Sondra asked, "I don't know much about procurement, but is this a typical way of organizing the function?"

"That's an interesting question," Margot remarked. "In some large firms, procurement is centralized, and in others it is decentralized. We're a bit of a mix right now. My focus, as agreed with Matt, Jean, and Leslie, is not on reorganizing the structure of the function but on working collaboratively with the business-based procurement functions and driving category management as a consistent way of working. The one mandate across the company is the category management process."

"From an organizational design perspective," Jean added, "this is called a lead-buyer approach. It's not that uncommon but depends on collaboration and governance for success rather than a brute force mandate and reorganization."

"Thank you, Jean, and thanks for the question, Sondra," Margot said, advancing to the final slide:

> ***To embrace enhanced or transformative category management is to expressly choose to review and improve policies, practices, and business strategies and thereby change and improve the culture and results of the company.***

Leslie piped up again, "Thanks, Margot. This was a worthwhile conversation, and it represents a starting point for this team. We did this when we embraced the new approaches to quality management. The team is open-minded and driven for improvement. I'm confident we can similarly improve in this area."

Bob cleared his throat. "I have a question. You didn't speak to sole-sourcing when you mentioned single-sourcing. What about sole-sourcing? I have a few suppliers that I absolutely must use—there are no other choices in the market."

"Thanks, Bob," Margot replied. "That's an excellent question. There will be a few sole-source suppliers that we will continue to need and use. Each of you will have some. We will review them from a buying category basis—they often have a sole-source product or service they sell in addition to other, more commonly available items, and that helps with our leverage. And we'll tailor our ongoing supplier management efforts to ensure our relationship, value realization, and risk management is tailored to fit. The more strategic of these relationships will involve you and your respective teams as needed. I didn't cover the strategic analysis tools in the category management process in detail, but please know that we use a number of tools to help identify and understand these relationships. The day of transactional approaches to these suppliers is over."

Leslie stated again, "Thanks, Margot; we all appreciate your time and that you're here at Frontier International Group leading this transformation. Please excuse us as we close the meeting for the day."

Margot gathered her papers. "Thank you. If anyone has any questions, concerns, or suggestions please let me know." She then left the room.

DECEMBER 14TH

Early the next morning, a virtual GPLT meeting was planned to review the outcomes from the ELT meeting.

Margot opened the meeting, showing the slide of categories and sponsors. "Thank you for agreeing to meet today. Yesterday afternoon, I met with the ELT and reviewed the potential categories for Wave One. They were very supportive and added one category: meetings and events. The medical business needs a new strategy for meetings and events post-Covid and is looking to category management to help with the process."

"That's an excellent outcome for them to use this process to help their business plans," Shelly commented.

"Agreed," Margot continued. "And you'll see we have a list of identified sponsors. I told them I'd send an email draft that they can use to notify the sponsors. I have one from a prior launch and will modify it and send it to them and copy you."

Mary asked, "Which of our respective team members will be leading these teams?"

Margot advanced to the next slide that listed the members of the central team assigned, having blanks for the other teams, "Here are the categories Tanya and Frank's teams will cover and open slots for your teams. Mary and Phil, you have the most business in Europe, who do you recommend for fleet?"

Mary, the head of procurement for the medical business, jumped in. “I’d like Dominique to handle that team. We have many, many cars and, as you know, it’s a very sensitive issue here. Dominique is excellent and will do a good job.”

“I’ve met him and agree,” Phil said, the head of procurement for the industrial business. “I want to confirm the scope is cars and does not include trucks. I have fleets of trucks of different sizes that I need to source as well.”

“Excellent point, Phil,” Margot replied. “The initial scope is Europe and cars only. Harry, I don’t think your team members will lead any teams in this first wave but will in future waves.”

“I understand and am not surprised. We circulated the draft list of teams, and that was my expectation,” Harry stated.

“The next topic is the training,” Margot continued. “It is scheduled for mid-January here in Oklahoma City. It will be conducted off-site, as the HQ office spaces are already booked. You have the dates and our tentative list of attendees that you identified is now confirmed. Please contact Shelly if you have any questions on the training, but please ensure that nobody plans to leave early on the third day—it is a full day. Frank and Tanya, I recommend that your participants—and you, if you’d like—plan to stay at the hotel. The event includes planned dinners, and I don’t want anyone driving after drinking or missing out on the team aspects of the event.”

“Okay, thanks,” Tanya replied, “I’ll tell my participants.”

“I will as well,” Frank affirmed.

With that, the meeting was ended. Margot looked at Frank, Tanya, and Shelly, smiled, and said, “Well, we have put category management in motion at Frontier International Group. We have the ELT engaged, we as a GPLT are engaged, and next, our people will be engaged. In short, we’ve done the easy part. I appreciate your help and support and hope you have a great holiday break, because we’re going to be running hard starting in January!”

They all stood up, shared Merry Christmas and Happy Holiday greetings, then headed out of the meeting room.

Margot returned to her desk to revise the email to the new sponsors and send it to the ELT as promised. She should have asked Shelly to do this but knew just how she wanted it phrased based on her discussions with the ELT, and it would be much more efficient if she did it herself. Next time, she'd ask Shelly to do it.

JANUARY 9TH

Matt was looking forward to the upcoming ELT meeting. It was the first meeting after the holiday break, and Larry, the CIO, was slated to lead a discussion on artificial intelligence. Matt knew very little about the topic, but all the CFO magazines were trumpeting the potential impacts. There was even a story he'd read where a large bank predicted over 300 million jobs would be impacted worldwide. There were lots of stories with hype in the past, but this one seemed different, and Matt was curious.

Larry had been in the CIO role for just under five years and brought stability and thoughtfulness to the role. Where previously the IT function had been the land of "no," nothing was considered or discussed unless it was on the "IT approved" list, it was now collaborative and used well-tested and understood procedures. His team was excellent: capable, motivated, forward-looking, yet incredibly practical. They were not tempted by the "new shiny objects" ever emerging in the IT space.

Matt immediately hit it off with Larry. They had similar approaches and were quickly able to determine how and where they could help each other and the potential overlap areas that required careful discussion and decision making. Matt was working through the pre-reading that Larry sent out for the AI discussion and was surprised by the volume of reading required. Larry sent each member a couple of books on the topic as well as a stack of articles. Matt appreciated that the materials arrived a month before the discussion, so he had plenty of time to read them while traveling home on the weekends. Based on the reading materials, it was going to be a very interesting discussion.

Leslie turned to Larry, stating, "We've had lots to read over the holidays, and I'm sure we have lots of questions, so let's turn to Larry who has the balance of the afternoon to lead us through AI."

"Thanks, Leslie," he replied as he walked to the front of the room. "This is not intended to be a formal presentation but more of a leveling conversation. I will be looking for decisions and commitments at the end of the discussion."

He continued, "AI is all over the media and, if you believe everything printed and said, will transform the world in the next six months, if it hasn't done so already. I think this is a bit of an over-statement, but I do think AI will transform the world in the next five to seven years. It is said that the rate of AI change in the world will never be slower than it is now. I think that's correct—it means we're all in for a wild ride of change."

"What is AI, really? There is so much hype," Jean asked.

"Thank you, Jean, I agree with your characterization, and it's an excellent question." Larry nodded. "AI is currently the automation of basic and repetitive tasks that can be documented with an algorithm. That's a bit of a mouthful, so I'll use a current application running in Jean's area—applicant screening. The program scans and reads applications from online sources and submitted CVs and looks for key words and phrases that were predefined for a given role. If enough of the words match, the text is checked for errors, and the best of the results are forwarded to an HR staff member for review. The rest of the submissions receive an automated response thanking them for their interest: a 'thank you, no' letter. The typical 'pass rate' for CVs is less than five percent. Many applicants seem to be using the same CV for all the jobs they're applying for, and they are filled with errors. The good news is that the AI tool can do the work quickly and efficiently, and the HR staff can focus on the people with potential."

"Won't we be missing some potentially very good applicants this way?" Benjamin asked. "In the Asia region, there are many excellent people who speak and write multiple languages, but English is a third or fourth language; some errors are expected and allowable."

"Yes, you're right," Larry replied. "This is a great illustration of the limits of AI. It can only do what we tell it to do. In ex-US regions, the algorithms are adjusted to allow for differences in language. There are times when other routes to candidates, such as through referrals and headhunters, must be used. AI is a tool. I will emphasize this several times; it is a tool, and it does not and should not replace our other approaches without careful consideration and a thorough test."

Larry continued, "Where is AI going, you ask? The basic tool I just mentioned in Jean's area is like basic applications running in the various businesses' customer service areas that are the next generation of direct inward dialing. The goal is to use AI—in this case, a bot with a persona we created—to guide the customer to the correct answer. It is also like tools in use across the finance, procurement, and supply chain areas to manage data replication and the like. Anywhere we have repetitive, manual tasks, we look to apply these tools. They are fast, cheap, and essentially error-free. These are the basics of what is called AI, and we are using them now across all of your businesses and functions where there is a valid use case."

"The new version of AI described in the reading materials is known as generative AI. This is an emerging technology with vast potential. Right now, it is best to think of it in our world as an amazing search engine. You enter a question and the software searches for the answer and reports it in concise, readable formats. It's impressive right now," he spoke on. "This leads to the first discussion point and decision needed. These are publicly available packages. I have it installed on my phone and laptop, and some of you probably do too. When we use this software, it searches everywhere in the world on available databases. 'So what?' you might ask. What if one of our R&D people asks a question that is about a technology that is unique to Frontier International Group? The next time another person searches "Who is using this new technology?" it may answer Frontier International Group. In short, this new technology is the new secret folder that can be left in the coffee shop. There are currently two internets in the world—the regular internet we all use and the so-called dark web of nefarious activities. I believe we are about to see a flood of previously protected intellectual property on both webs thanks to AI."

"What are you recommending and why?" Leslie asked.

"My recommendations are that we immediately lock down AI searches on all company devices—laptops and phones—and conduct top-to-bottom employee training on the topic of information security. We already have trial instances of generative AI running in a few areas, but the software is running within the company firewalls to protect our proprietary information. I'm very concerned about someone running an open search on the public instances of the software. What do you all think?" Larry asked.

"I'm supportive of your recommendation, Larry," Jean stated, "and I also want to do a series of employee communications on the topic. I vote yes."

Matt asked, "What about our supplier partners who have electronic access to some of our information, like upcoming demand? Should we somehow restrict them?"

Erica chimed in, "The same question applies to our R&D teams. We have very tight relationships with strategic suppliers. I'm not too worried about our staff, but the suppliers' staff is a wild card. What can we do about them?"

Larry replied, "These are excellent points. We have confidentiality agreements with anyone using EDI, and I'm sure we have agreements with our top R&D suppliers, but the risk here is less about IP theft than it is about IP awareness or casualness that leads to unintended IP loss. We are limited to what we can do in certain EDI situations where we are ERP-to-ERP, but we should communicate with suppliers just like we're going to do with employees."

"I'll talk with Margot about doing that, and we'll coordinate our communications to suppliers with Jean and Sondra's team in legal," Matt said.

"We can create shared IT environments with our closest suppliers," Larry added. "These will prevent external leakage and reinforce our relationships."

Leslie was quiet through the conversation so far, but finally added, “I think we should do what we can to slow the leakage, but let’s all recognize the limits of lockdowns. Our businesses are built on innovation, and our teams will and should continually scan the environment for progress. A number of them publish papers demonstrating their new learnings after Sondra protects the IP ownership. We will never be under a rock of information security. But I too support Larry’s recommendation as the best course for now. Larry, I’m going to be sorry I asked, but what else can we expect?”

Larry smiled. “Thank you all for your support. We’ll move forward on this quickly. In answer to Leslie’s question, the answer is nothing short of rethinking the world of work and our company. I said that AI is currently a giant search engine and retrospective in its focus, but that will change. The large software companies are spending hundreds of billions of dollars to make the transition to prospective AI. This is the area that scares people and sounds like science fiction. It will happen, and likely within the next five or so years. In the meantime, the current and emerging AI capability is projected to affect over three hundred million jobs worldwide. This effect will be unique in that it will not just be the expensive, first-world jobs affected. If routine, repetitive work can be automated, that will be the case regardless of where it is occurring—from the US to Western Europe to Eastern Europe to Asia to Africa to Central and South America. Many of the roles that were off-shored in the last twenty years may be eliminated in the near future.”

“This, if it’s true, will have dramatic economic and social effects,” Bob piped up. “My business is based on basic industrial parts and equipment, and we use robots in manufacturing, and my suppliers use robots, but this is all on the production floor. We use CAD for design but now you’re saying the rest of the business—the gray- and white-collar jobs—may be affected.”

“Yes, Bob, that is exactly what is coming.” Larry nodded. “This leads me to my next request, and it’s much bigger and more profound than the first one. I’m asking that we reenvision our businesses and functions with this new future. I suggest we start on this immediately and have a preliminary review in time for this year's budget reviews later this summer."

"Larry, if this was in the pre-reading, I missed it, and I don't want any confusion here. What are you suggesting?" Leslie asked.

"I apologize to the team, but this area is moving so quickly that I did not include this request in the pre-reading, but I must state it now. If you decide to wait or not act, that is, of course, a possible choice, but I think we must act." He advanced to a new slide, and it laid out the suggested process and timing. "I created this slide this morning in anticipation of the discussion and your questions. I'm suggesting sub-teams by business unit and corporate function—chaired by the respective leader and supported by an IT AI expert, for membership to be not more than eight to ten and for all tasks to be completed within three months."

"The tasks are: one, to understand AI potential. Two, to brainstorm potential applications of AI. Three, to create a vision for the future of the business and function using AI. Four, to develop a quick, cost-effective way to communicate the potential change from customer, employee, and stakeholder (internal and external) perspectives. And five, to calculate the implications of the applications from people, expense, and capital perspectives."

"Note: Do not yet create a business case for the changes. The software costs and other change costs may be cost-prohibitive in a single business or function and acceptable on a company basis. These considerations should wait for the overall budget review."

Matt inquired, "What about the functions that are not here at the table? I'm thinking specifically about procurement. It's in finance, but if we do this work at the overall finance level, we'll miss key findings at the procurement level. I think the same could happen for R&D and manufacturing that are at the business-unit levels. What do you recommend?"

"Excellent question, Matt, I'd not thought of that," Larry acknowledged. "My recommendation is for each of us to create specialist sub-teams as needed to complete the tasks. The caveat is that we cannot have too many teams and still hit the budget review timing.

One more thing that I didn't mention before. My suggested code name for this project is 'Hallway.' It's based on the HAL nine thousand computer from *2001: A Space Odyssey*, but it's OUR way to do HAL. What do you think?"

"I guess HAL is a bit of a dark reference for me," Leslie responded. "Let me think about that. I try not to exercise my CEO authority too much and really appreciate how this team collaborates, but I'm going to weigh in on this."

Everyone had already been paying attention, but this comment piqued their interest.

Leslie continued, "I've been seeing AI in the literature, and every big consulting company is bombarding me with requests to meet and discuss the topic, and then I read the materials from Larry. We have seen big ideas in the past, such as the widespread and ill-considered move of production to China without paying attention to the supply chain issues, never mind resource scarcity and IP issues. I thought AI might be another one of these passing fancy ideas that disrupts businesses and lives. I'm convinced that this is different. If we don't act, we will be left behind. If we do act, we need to be aligned and clear about our goals. I really like Larry's suggested process. We must have some clarity this year, and the budget process already exists, so we can fit this into those reviews. I will also insert myself as an ad-hoc member of every team. I want to be invited to every meeting. You know that there is no way that I can attend every meeting, nor do I want to, but I will attend selected meetings to touch in with the process. We must get this right."

"I think Matt's question is excellent, and we absolutely must not lose the future design and implications for R&D, manufacturing, regulatory, quality, and procurement. Each of these areas should both participate in your respective areas and create a standalone set of answers to the tasks from the perspective of their specialty. They have twice the work and the same amount of time."

Jean suggested, "These teams will help create the future of the company. My request is that your teams include your high potential staff. Maybe even include a few junior high potentials so we have newer perspectives and can demonstrate our culture."

Matt asked Leslie, "Do you want me to create a separate account for budgeting this work? None of this was anticipated in the current budgets, and it will not occur for free."

"Yes, please do that, and we'll discuss the amounts to allocate," Leslie replied.

Larry breathed an audible sigh of relief and ventured, "So, I take it this idea is approved?"

Leslie confirmed, "Yes, but not the project name Hallway. I don't think this is one of our typical special projects. This must be done in a more open way—the Frontier Way. I will work with Jean on some approaches to our employee base, but this cannot be a secret reengineering project that is shared at the last minute. Also, I will work with Matt on some financial options. In the meantime, Larry, I will add you to the next board of directors' meeting agenda to share a summary of your insights—not the mountain of prereading—and our plan."

JANUARY 11TH

Leslie stood up when Matt and Jean entered her office, and she motioned that they should join her at her meeting table, "Thank you for making time on short notice. I was able to reach the chairman of the board of directors, Reggie, and he is going to call a virtual meeting of the board for next week. Reggie and I first talked about AI at a high level last summer. I've already informed Larry that he needs to summarize his presentation and our decisions for the meeting. What I want to work with you two on is our approach to the employee base and the related financials. These are tightly related, and it makes more sense that we meet."

"Thanks, Leslie," Jean replied. "I've been thinking about this nonstop since the meeting and, while there are some risks of handling this transparently, it is much higher integrity and more reflective of our values and culture."

"I agree, Jean," Matt stated. "I'm new here, but this is not a cloak and dagger organization. Our people trust us and we, in turn, need to trust them."

"I have some ideas and will write them up here on the whiteboard, and then let's talk and build on them," Leslie remarked. "First, the people impact. We don't know the numbers, but we can say that, at some point in the future there will be both a different mix of skills required and likely very different numbers by role. We are growing at five percent or more per year, so some of the people affected could transfer to newly created roles—if they have the skills." Leslie underlined skills and the growth rate. Jean and Matt were taking their own notes, following her line of thought.

"What I'm thinking is that as we know which areas and roles are going to be impacted, we establish skills training options that support our growth and announce both a retention bonus and a severance plan. I want the employees to see that we know jobs will be impacted but that we are offering proactive skill-building for those interested and capable. We will do what is right for those who either cannot do the new roles or choose not to."

Jean interjected, "That is consistent with the best HR approaches and fits with our culture."

Leslie nodded. "The wrinkle I'm thinking about is the retention bonus, and that is why I wanted Matt here for this initial meeting. I want the people who stay in the affected roles until the work is fully transitioned to either AI or new roles to receive the retention bonus. That is standard. What I want to ask, Matt, is can we make receipt of the retention bonus payout timing flexible? In other words, if an employee stays with us after the retention period, can they receive the retention bonus as deferred compensation subject to all the rules on deferred compensation?"

Matt responded, "That's an interesting idea. We encourage them to stay, we reward them for it, and we give them the flexibility to take the payment later if they stay on afterwards. I like it. I cannot speak, offhand, to the mechanics and legal considerations, but I'll meet with Jean's compensation team and Sondra's legal team and explore the options."

Jean chimed in, "I like it a lot. We have an outstanding reputation in the labor markets of the world, and what we're talking about is real-time reengineering of the company to reflect AI. By doing it openly and taking care of our employees, we will reinforce trust and our status as a preferred employer."

"Excellent, please keep me posted on what you find out, and Jean, please start working on a comprehensive employee communications approach. It needs to be ready to launch soon after the board meeting next week," Leslie directed.

"Now, Matt, about the finances of this," she continued. "There are likely to be one-off charges and expenses that will occur throughout the process. They'll start as soon as the planning meetings commence and will accelerate as we design changes, pilot the new approaches, and then expand implementation. I don't want Wall Street surprised in any way. Our approach will be a new and different approach, and it is incumbent upon you and me to explain to the analysts what we are doing, why we are doing it, and the expected benefits. Please give some thought to the financials and to the analysts. Work with our investor relations team to develop a plan."

"That makes perfect sense," Matt replied. "If we are the 'first movers' in this space, it will take a little bit of extra time to explain it to the analysts, but I expect we'll also get a bit more latitude on one-time charges than the followers."

"Thank you both," Leslie concluded. She stood up, signaling the end of the meeting. "Please have your outlined approaches and any draft materials to me by early next week so I can circulate them to the board. You'll receive invites to the board meeting from Lillian."

Jean and Matt exited Leslie's office and walked together to the elevator. Once in the elevator, Matt turned to Jean, stating, "I'm so glad I joined. This is an amazing time, and I am glad to be working here with this team. It really does feel like we have the freedom and the responsibility to recreate the company to be ready for the future."

Jean nodded. "Leslie is an incredible leader. Her integrity is always first and foremost, and she loves this company, its people, and its customers. That's the good part. The bad part—we have a ton of work to do!" She stepped out on the next floor, but added, "I'll have my compensation people contact you. Let me know if you need anything else."

"Will do, thanks," he replied, and the elevator doors closed.

Matt took the elevator to procurement instead of finance. The meeting with Leslie had been shorter than he'd expected, so he had an extra half an hour. He decided to see if Margot was in her office to bring her up to date.

Her door was open, so he walked up to Rita and greeted her with a smile. "Good morning, Rita. Is Margot available?"

Rita smiled and replied, "Yes, she's finishing a call and has the next half hour open. Do you want a coffee or anything?"

"Yes, thanks, but I think Margot and I will walk over to the coffee station," said Matt.

Margot saw Matt and came out to greet him once her call was over, "Good morning, Matt. To what do I owe the pleasure?"

Matt smiled, explaining, "I thought I'd take a chance and see if you have time for a coffee and a quick catch-up conversation."

"Sure," she agreed. She gestured toward the coffee station. They made small talk about their families and Matt's relocation while they made their coffees.

Matt suggested, "Let's go to the cafeteria instead of your office." They took the stairs the one flight up, entered the large, empty cafeteria, and took seats at the far end.

"What's up?" she asked.

"Well, fasten your seatbelt. We had quite an amazing ELT meeting yesterday, and I wanted to brief you directly," he began.

Margot was not sure if he was excited or nervous, but he certainly was energetic. She also wasn't sure if she should be nervous or not but sipped her coffee and waited for him to continue.

"Yesterday afternoon, we had an AI briefing by Larry," he continued. "I've been a mixture of curious and dubious about AI due to all the hype. Well, Larry cut through the hype, and it's time for us to get moving. This is not optional. AI is coming whether we're ready or not, so Leslie and the ELT agreed to aggressively get on the front foot."

She relaxed a bit—he had not mentioned anything awful like restructuring or the like. She responded, "I've been reading a bit as well and think there could be profound impacts on procurement in the coming years. How is Frontier going to approach this?"

"That's frankly what I'm so excited about," he enthused. "I've been a part of other leadership teams with similar if smaller challenges, and they always deferred to the insular, secretive approach. Leslie wants us to take a proactive, involved approach. That's the good news. The bad news is you need to do a lot of work." He turned his meeting notes around and showed her. "These are the next steps for all of us." He then showed Larry's slides:

- Sub-teams by business unit and corporate function—chaired by the respective leader and supported by an IT AI expert.
- Membership to be not more than eight–ten.
- All tasks completed within three months.
- Tasks:
  1. Understand AI potential.
  2. Brainstorm potential applications of AI.
  3. Create a vision for the future of the business and function using AI.
  4. Develop a quick, cost-effective way to communicate the potential change from customer, employee, and stakeholder (internal and external) perspectives.
  5. Calculate the implications of the applications from people, expense, and capital perspectives.

"Completed within three months," she remarked. "That's very tight. You do know that the budgets are due at the same time, right?"

"Yes," he confirmed. "We want the inputs as part of the budget process. I'm working with Jean and Sondra's teams on some of the company-wide employee and financial plans, but Leslie already scheduled a board of directors meeting for late next week to update them. This is moving very quickly, which is why I wanted to meet with you as soon as possible."

Margot reflected a bit before replying, "I really appreciate you sharing this in person. An email would not have done it justice, and even a virtual meeting would have been insufficient. I'm going to pull together an STP on this and have it to you early this afternoon."

Matt frowned, admitting, "I'm sorry, Margot, but with all of the new acronyms I don't remember what STP means."

"Situation, target, proposal—starting with a problem statement, of course. It's the problem-solving approach we teach in category management, and I've used it for years. They are typically short, often one page long, and they enable consistent communication and support a share-and-build culture. You'll have mine by email after lunch."

Matt finished his coffee. "Perfect, I look forward to seeing the approach and your content. Thank you for making time to talk," and he headed to the elevators.

Margot called after him, "Please email me that page you just showed me with the tasks. Even if it's just a picture of the notes."

"Will do," he called over his shoulder as he hustled to the elevators and his next meeting.

Margot sat for a minute and reflected on this quick meeting. Her day had just taken a very different turn. Not a bad turn, but a big turn. She decided to text Rich and Anna and see if either of them had time for a call this morning. This new work would affect her category management launch efforts, and she wanted their input.

Rich responded immediately to Margot's text that he would be available in an hour. Anna did not respond immediately, but that was expected—she lived on the other coast and would not be awake yet. Margot sent a meeting invite to both for an hour from now with a note to Anna not to worry if she could not make it.

Margot turned her attention to thinking through the STP. She started with the problem statement:

AI is rapidly advancing, and Frontier International Group does not have an AI procurement strategy.

This was her first thought. She'd leave it and come back after working on the rest of the STP. She knew from experience that it would become clearer over time. She listed the situation statements:

1. No current AI strategy for Frontier International Group.
2. No current AI strategy for procurement.
3. No current clear AI procurement leaders.
4. A number of partial AI solutions available.
5. Potentially huge impacts to the workforce once AI installed.
6. Frontier International Group AI strategy first-look deadline in ninety days.

She knew she'd add to the list and shifted to the target:

> Frontier International Group procurement AI strategy and implementation plan approved.

Her proposal list included:

1. Form procurement strategy team including business unit procurement leaders and a few members of the central team; chaired by her. Total number five to seven.
2. Use either Anna or Rich to facilitate the team to enable her to focus on the team members and fully engage the content.
3. Use selected category management tools and approaches including team charter, macro planning, stakeholder mapping and engagement, selected strategic analysis tools, layered strategy development.

She paused and reflected on the status of stakeholder engagement. How could they develop a procurement strategy for AI without either first or concurrently understanding customer feedback? Her team would need to quickly understand the potential uses and implications for AI in the function and then test these insights with stakeholders before confirming their plan. She also realized that the ninety-day company deadline meant she had a seventy-five-day deadline to enable two weeks of stakeholder review and final feedback. The timing was tight and starting to feel tighter! She sent an email to Rita and requested an urgent sixty-minute virtual meeting with the three business procurement leaders and her team. She knew that the overlap between Asia, Europe, and North America was nil, so someone would need to be awake during off hours—so be it.

She turned her attention to a draft macro plan and added today as the kick-off and the seventy-five-day completion and then worked through the intervening details. She made a note that Anna and Rich would be asked to search for companies and universities who are thought leaders in procurement AI or related spaces.

Kick-off (virtual) – today; day 0

- Pre-reading preparation:
  - > Team charter.
  - > Macro plan.
  - > Larry's ELT prereading pack.

First meeting – In-person kick-off – location TBD; early February – 2-day duration

- Topics to be covered:
  - > Introductions, charter review, and macro plan discussion.
  - > Procurement AI capability analysis—current and projected.
  - > AI best practice site visit planning.
  - > Information gathering assignments.

Best practice site visits – virtual and in-person; mid-February – early March

Second meeting – in-person meeting – location TBD; mid-March – 2-day duration

- Topics to be covered:
  - > AI insights to-date and related implications.
  - > Potential AI-enabled procurement service model designs.
  - > Stakeholder presentation and engagement pack development.

> Stakeholder engagement plan.
> Potential organizational impacts—projected (rough estimates only).
> Potential employee re-skilling and re-deployment options.
> Impact calculations—HR, expenses, capital (rough estimates only).

Third meeting – virtual; late March

- Topics to be covered:
  > AI-enabled vision discussion.
  > Stakeholder presentation and engagement pack.
  > Stakeholder engagement plans and assignments.
  > Stakeholder feedback sharing with the team.

Stakeholder engagement – in-person and virtual; early to late April

Fourth meeting – virtual; mid-April

- Topics to be covered:
  > Feedback to date from stakeholders—key insights and AI vision implications.
  > Feedback from other workstreams across Frontier and implications.

Fifth meeting – in-person – Frontier HQ; late April – 3-day duration

- Topics to be covered:
  > Stakeholder feedback summary and implications.
  > AI-enabled service model design improvements.
  > Potential organizational impacts—projected (detailed estimates).
  > Potential employee re-skilling and re-deployment options.
  > Impact calculations—HR, expenses, capital (detailed estimates).

Draft strategy completed early May.

Margot realized they'd need IT, finance, and HR support and sent an email to Matt. He may have mentioned something about this when they met, but she couldn't remember. When did they meet? It was hard to believe it was just an hour ago!

Matt replied almost immediately that he was working with Larry on the IT representative and would have it shortly. Similarly, Jean was working through the HR support staff but maybe IT would collect inputs for both areas. Matt was working with his team on the finance support.

Margot looked at her macro plan. It was logical and seemed complete. She knew the timing was extremely aggressive and allowed for no delays, no sickness, and no impacts of any kind from the outside world. She was okay with that; that is what the fifteen-day buffer time was for. If she started with a plan that used all ninety days, she knew it would be late. If she started with a plan that finished early, she had a hope of finishing on time. She put it aside knowing that she'd review it with Anna and Rich and that they'd have valuable inputs, not to mention the team inputs at the kick-off meeting.

She stepped out of her office and asked Rita to come in to meet with her. Margot outlined the assignment given to her by Matt and emphasized that the project and plans were confidential but would be shared very shortly. She showed Rita her draft macro plan and asked for her input.

Rita drew in a sharp breath, exclaiming, "Whew, that is a tight plan. Who is going to be on this team? Where are you planning to hold the meetings?"

"I agree," Margot replied. "It is a tight plan, but it is doable if everyone commits. As to the who, I am planning to invite the procurement leaders from the three businesses, Frank, Tanya, and Shelly, and you. I want you to attend the meetings to support the team. Are you okay with a bit of travel?"

Rita reflected and answered, "I will talk with my husband about managing the kids and dogs, but I don't think it will be a problem."

"Thank you," Margot said. "If there is anything you need from me to make that easier, let me know. As for your question on where the meetings will occur, we know the last meeting will be at HQ and there will be a few virtual meetings, but the others will need to be selected. I will talk with the team today and get their input on meeting locations, but I would like you to be ready to assist with venue and travel planning. Is that okay?"

"Sure," Rita replied. "When Bill ran the function, we did not really have meetings, and pretty much everyone books their own travel nowadays. Before I joined procurement I was in marketing, and they had lots of meetings and travel. I know people at the travel agency, so it won't be a problem."

"That's excellent," Margot responded. "I'm thinking that meeting number one will be at a convenient meeting place for the attendees, given the short notice. That could be the US or Europe, and I'm leaning toward Europe. The second meeting place is likely to be near an AI leadership hub—likely California, but it could be Texas. It could be someplace else, but those are my first thoughts. The third meeting will be at one of our major business sites. This could be the medical business in Europe or the industrial business in Wisconsin. I doubt it will be Asia, but I could be wrong. The final meeting will be here at HQ. There may be a rush for rooms around then, so it may be prudent to both book a room now for that time period and start investigating nearby off-site options. Once we pick the locations, I'll need you to arrange transportation to and from the airports, hotel, and meeting venue. I will also need you to be creative and find interesting places for the team to have dinner. They will need a break from the day, and I want them to have a bit of fun and connect over dinner. What do you think?"

"It sounds like fun to me, reminiscent of my marketing days," Rita said with a smile. "They always have fun at their meetings, and it is a good investment in morale and spirit. I'm happy to help and let me know if you need anything else."

Margot stood up. "Thank you, Rita. I know I'm new here, but I appreciate your help and support and am glad you're going on this journey with us. One last thing, please give some thought to a team name or motto and a mug, or a shirt, or something. I don't know if corporate is going to brand this effort, but we need to be ready to do that for procurement."

"Will do," Rita replied as she gathered her notes and left Margot's office.

Margot looked at her watch and noted that the call with Anna and Rich was due to start in five minutes. How did that happen? Time was already accelerating.

Margot connected to the virtual meeting, and Rich joined immediately. Margot shared the context for the situation and shared her draft STP. Before they'd completed the situation statement discussions Anna joined the call as well. Margot offered to go back to the context, but Anna stated, "No, I'll pick it up from the STP and can ask any other questions as we go."

Margot loved the STP tool. It was so efficient and effective at framing a problem, and when everyone knew how to use it, the whole process was accelerated. This is why she taught her family the tool and they used it at home almost as much as she did at work.

Rich commented, "I've not seen any holistic vision for AI in procurement yet. There are a number of discrete tools for different aspects of the source-to-pay process, but nobody is portraying a complete vision for what is possible. What you're proposing to accomplish in a short period of time is revolutionary. You will be setting the initial vision for AI in procurement for the profession."

Margot replied, "I was hoping there was something we could use as the foundation and then build. It's fun and exciting to be on the cutting edge, but it is not easy. Do you have any ideas on who the leaders in the field are so we can learn from them?"

Anna responded, "There are no real AI experts yet. There are people with knowledge in discrete areas but nobody with end-to-end procurement AI expertise. We do have relationships with a few of the discrete solution vendors, and we will pull on them for information. Rich, do you know of any universities we should contact?"

Rich answered, "I do know of a few schools in the US and Europe where we can start. On a related thought, I don't think we can effectively use an NDA with all these sources, but if Anna and I collect information confidentially on behalf of a client, I do think they'll share enough for us to move forward."

"Great catch," Margot said. "Let's look at the draft macro plan." Margot shared her macro plan on the screen and talked them through her logic.

Anna commented, "At the end of seventy-five days, the company leadership team will have the AI visions for each of the functions and the businesses. There will not be an overall vision at that point in time. I recommend that you raise this issue to Matt, as that will be a key next step in the planning process."

"Excellent idea," Margot remarked. "I'm going to send him the STP and macro plan later this afternoon and will flag that to him."

"The timing for all of this is fortuitous for the category management launch," Rich noted. "Each category will need to address the end-state vision for procurement in their implementation plan. It would be difficult if they had to come back much later in time, but if they can do it real-time or close to real-time, that will be perfect."

"Agreed," Margot said. "I'm a bit concerned that people get overwhelmed through this, so I need you to support them and let me know if you hear of any issues during the coaching."

"We're going to work with Rita to set up weekly review calls with you and are thinking about early afternoon every Friday so we can share headlines with you on the week we're completing and updates on the week to come. How does that sound?" Anna asked.

"That sounds great," Margot replied. "I'll let her know to expect contact from you and that I'm okay with it. Do either of you have any suggestions on meeting venues for the AI planning? And to confirm, I will want a consultant to join me through this process."

"We'll check our calendars and see if we have adequate time or if we need to escalate to Alec. We allocated our time to the category managers and are already deep in planning for the kickoff meetings. It would be disruptive if we changed coaches now," Anna explained.

"Yes, I agree, and Alec is fine," Margot said. Alec was the managing partner of the specialist consulting firm she used, and Margot knew and liked him but had a deeper rapport with Rich and Anna, as they were her category management instructors and both had coached her with different categories.

"As for meeting venue input," Rich said, "listen to what the team members say during your call later today. Share the travel pain as equitably as possible and, if we can find an AI reference site worth visiting, do that during the process. Book the dates today, if you can, and be a bit flexible for a week or so on the venues."

"Sounds good, thanks," Margot replied. "I'll drop off now. Thanks for your input. This will be very interesting!"

Margot and Rita received confirmation from the selected procurement AI team members. Margot had not yet met the medical procurement leader, Mary, in person, as she was based in Europe. She met Harry, the head of procurement for electronics, during her trip to Singapore and Phil, the head of procurement for the industrial business, during her trip to Milwaukee. So far everyone had been nice and accepting of her as an outsider. The wildcard was Mary, who had been briefly considered for her role and not interviewed by Leslie and Jean.

The virtual meeting started, and everyone shared their camera images during the pre-meeting small talk except Mary. Margot asked that everyone turn on their cameras and feel free to ask questions throughout. Mary turned on her camera, and it was immediately apparent that she was quite pregnant and likely due soon. Margot made a mental note of that fact and proceeded through the introductions.

Margot shared the original ELT assignment and the context provided by Matt. The group was stunned and silent for a few minutes, and then a flurry of questions about next steps, employee notifications, and so on, started. Margot calmed everyone with the answers she had, and the group was very impressed with how Leslie and Jean were approaching the employee issues. Margot then quickly explained the STP tool and shared her draft.

The STP worked as it always did. Many questions were raised, and Mary shared a couple of potential companies and universities to visit in Europe. Harry suggested a company to visit in Singapore, and Phil recommended a couple of solution providers who could provide insights. Margot noted the input on the STP, and it quickly morphed from her STP into the team's STP.

Margot then shared the draft macro plan, and the team was silent, overwhelmed by the detail already developed and the amount of work they needed to complete in a short period of time.

Mary opened the conversation, "If you created all of this since you arrived this morning, Margot, you're amazing. This is great. I don't know if you heard, but I am expecting and due in three weeks. I will go out on maternity leave in two weeks and be out for a few months. I don't want to miss out on this opportunity, as this team will literally be creating the future for the function, but I am in the process of creating the future for my daughter to be."

Margot replied, "As a mother of two boys who worked when they were born, I completely understand. If we hold the kick-off meeting near you in the next two weeks, can you attend?"

"Thank you for understanding, and yes, let me know the dates you want and the space you need, and we'll either secure it here at our offices or a nearby hotel, thank you," Mary said. "Do you want me to name an alternate member while I'm on leave?"

"I do want you to think about an alternate, and let's discuss the options. You three as the leaders of the function for your businesses are critical participants. I can also include a couple of high-potential individuals, and this could be how and where we use one of those slots," Margot replied.

"I would like to stay informed of your findings and progress while I'm on leave," Mary added, "and attend, if I can, the final meetings and presentations."

"That sounds great," Margot responded. "Let's talk offline, but for now please know that we will all keep you up to date on our progress and ask for your input at the key points. To the extent you have time and interest in doing so, please share your thoughts."

Margot continued, "So, that's our first decision. We will meet the week after next in Copenhagen. Please plan to arrive Monday for a nine a.m. start on Tuesday. We'll have a team dinner on Tuesday night and work through the day on Wednesday. If you want to take an overnight flight out on Wednesday, please ensure it allows you to spend the entire day with the team. All who are available on Wednesday night should plan on a relaxed dinner. Rita will be joining us and can help handle any travel arrangements. I will also have a consultant, Alec, join us to help manage our process. There will be an enormous amount of information we'll all need to process, and I want someone there who is focused on the process, so we achieve our scheduled dates. I will send the pre-reading I have from Matt after this meeting. Any questions?"

There were no more questions, and the meeting ended with each participant a bit overwhelmed and excited about the future—this truly was going to be big.

Margot did one last review of the STP and macro plan and made a few minor edits. She noted the issue raised by Anna about the overall corporate AI vision and offered to discuss it with Matt further if needed. Satisfied with the result, she sent them to Matt with the note that the first meeting would occur the week after next in Copenhagen. Satisfied that she'd moved this topic ahead, she returned to her other tasks for the day.

JANUARY 13TH

Matt opened Margot's email, noted her kick-off meeting plans and then opened the attachments. He'd not previously seen an STP but immediately liked and appreciated the approach. On one page, it summarized the problem, the goal, and the options. Combined with the macro plan, it was compelling. He did not see anything that caused him any concern except the need to develop an overall corporate AI vision concurrently with the functional and business-unit elements. He thought maybe the buffer time in Margot's schedule could be useful for this.

He drafted a note to his ELT peers and raised the issue of the overall corporate AI vision. He attached Margot's STP and macro plan and suggested that the ELT consider using these as models for the other areas and build in the expectation that buffer time be built in at the end of all plans for corporate review and socialization. He further suggested that the corporate review and socialization occur concurrently with the development of the overall corporate AI vision. His suggestion was for a two-part meeting. In the first part of the meeting each function and business unit would share their visions. During this session, IT and the ELT would note key insights and interdependencies. The ELT would then build an overall vision that encompassed all the foundational elements. The second meeting would be the ELT sharing their overall vision and showing how each element fit into the holistic view. And all of it in time for the budget review process.

It was crazy aggressive, but he was convinced the tight timing would force the participants to stay at the strategic level. There would be time to work through all the details, and many would not be known until further into the implementation, but the vision must be created and be compelling. A high-level vision, value proposition, and business case were what he was going to reiterate to his ELT peers.

JANUARY 15TH

"Mmm hmm," Carla murmured before drifting off to sleep.

Sean lay in bed and reflected on his circumstances. He was still nervous about his job but at least he and Carla were together. Her district manager had coincidentally chosen the same week and hotel to hold district planning and training meetings. They would get a week together at the hotel while attending their meetings.

Carla rolled over after a while and, with sleepy eyes, got up and started to get dressed. "Where are you going?" Sean asked.

Carla replied, "I have a breakfast meeting with my manager and I better be seen coming out of my own room. I'll call you tomorrow." She kissed his forehead and left him to sleep.

JANUARY 16TH

The next day, Sean showered, reflected on the wonderful evening, and headed to breakfast with a smile on his face—he was still the only person in procurement who'd hit their targets ten years running. He walked confidently into the hotel restaurant, had a quick buffet breakfast, and headed on to the meeting room. Today was the first day of a three-day off-site training course on category management. He dreaded it but appreciated the opportunity to spend three nights in a hotel at company expense with Carla. He could ignore the content during the day and live for the evenings with Carla.

The trainers were already in the room changing the configuration from classroom rows to a U-shape. He hated it already. U-shapes invariably led to touchy-feely conversations, and he just wanted to sit in the back row and read his phone. They welcomed him and shook his hand. They tried to make small talk, but he broke away, refilled his coffee and sat down as far away from the front as he could.

He could sense Margot before she walked in the door. He was still gun shy around her after their last meeting. She knew the supply markets, knew how to work with her peer executives, and had the whole package—pretty, intelligent, a great family, and younger than him! She greeted the trainers with hugs and enthusiasm he didn't even use with his own family. How well did she know them? He'd better be careful. He knew how to manage Frank, but Margot was clearly different.

She spotted him, walked over, and shook his hand firmly. "Good morning, Sean. I'm glad you're here. I hope you're ready for the training."

He mumbled good morning and returned the handshake. The eye contact was too much for him, and he turned away, picked up his coffee, and smiled back at her.

She continued, "We need corrugated to step up and, based on what we already discussed, there should be big results." Additional attendees were entering the room, and she added, "Enjoy the training, Sean. Make the most of it," before walking over to greet the new arrivals.

He was speechless and sat down to reflect on this. Okay, so she doesn't like the Premier Packaging deal, but she thinks there is room for big results. What does she think I've been doing the past ten years? Every year he met or exceeded his targets. How can she think there's that much more to be achieved in corrugated? He didn't know how mad to be but knew he was upset. Maybe what his ex-wife had been saying was true; maybe it was time for him to look for a new job.

The other attendees came in, got their coffee, greeted each other, and took their seats. The attendees included his peer category managers from the direct and indirect categories as well as the procurement leadership development employees. The MBA-candidate procurement interns were another Margot change, and he wasn't sure what to make of them. They were all smart and attractive but literally knew nothing about the company and the categories. At the last minute, three members of the leadership team walked in, including his boss, Frank, the woman leading indirect procurement, Tanya, and the new woman, Shelly, head of procurement transformation. They took the remaining seats. He'd not heard they were going to be here; this was going to be different.

At 8:30 promptly, Margot stood up and walked into the middle of the room. The room was silent as the audience stared at her. Many of them didn't know what to expect other than that she was nothing like Bill. She was polished and poised. Bill was slouched and a bit too casual; rumpled was the typical description. He'd been the "Head of Purchasing" for years and now she was named the "Chief Procurement Officer." Clearly change was in the air.

Margot welcomed them to the first category management class. She introduced the two trainers and explained they'd trained her years ago when she was a new category manager. She'd applied their process and teachings and was standing in front of them as the CPO as a direct result—the process worked. She was hired at Frontier to transform procurement, and it started with them in the room. They were going to lead the initial category teams.

Margot moved over to a flip chart and drew a four-box matrix with results on the X axis and process on the Y axis. She added the labels to each box starting with "In HR," then "Learner," then "Maverick," and finishing with "Star."

She explained each box and said she expected almost everyone to be in the learner box for now, the class hadn't even started yet—but that they should set the goal of moving to star. The company needed them to be stars, and she was investing in this training and coaching to help them along the way. She then circled back to maverick. She explained that some people think because they always 'hit their numbers' that they're doing the job. She stated that was no longer good enough. People who did not use the process and tried to drive for results would no longer succeed. She announced that she'd join the group for dinner both nights and then participate in the session closing on the third day. She asked the group if they had any questions. Everyone was silent until Dominique raised his hand. Dominique always had questions. He asked about savings measurement and why the prior results were no longer good enough. Sean was surprised. This was an excellent question and one he'd been thinking but could not bring himself to ask.

Margot thanked him for his question and seemed sincere. She explained that measuring cost savings as a change in unit price from period to period, while easy to do and easy to track to the P&L, was not enough. It encouraged short-term thinking and, frankly, was not good for the company. When the CEO changed CFOs, it was something the new CFO focused on immediately. The company was fundamentally sound and strong but the focus on short-term, quarterly results was going to affect the ability to hit long-term goals. In short, the company was healthy but needed to change to meet the future marketplace. They would still measure savings, but instead of unit price they would focus on total cost in use. There were simply too many cheap items that were being purchased repeatedly when one, better quality item, albeit at a higher purchase price, would last much longer.

Sean didn't raise his hand but could not stop himself from blurting out, "So you want us to buy more expensive stuff? The business won't be happy about that; they already think they can buy better than us."

Margot smiled and turned to him. "Sean, I'm glad you shared that. You're right, if we just buy more expensive goods and services without involving the business in the decision-making process, they will not be happy. You're also right that they think they'd be better off without us. Everyone uses Amazon now and thinks they're the best buyer in the world. They think purchasing is a waste of time and slows the process." She paused for effect, lowered her voice a bit and continued, "And if you're just buying more expensive stuff and not truly using category management, they're right, and every one of us should be fired." She paused to let that sink in a bit and then in a louder, brighter tone said, "But we're going to use category management and we're going to show the stakeholders the value we bring to the business. It may not happen overnight, but they will look at all of us differently and appreciate what we do. That's what these three days are about. I'm going to come back on the third day to hear your presentations. Enjoy the training and make sure Rich and Anna answer your questions. With that, I'll leave you to Anna and Rich and will see you at dinner tonight."

On the way back to her office, Margot reflected on the kickoff and the individual conversations and hoped she'd not been too direct with Sean. She really did need him to "get it" and deliver the results she knew from experience were possible in his category. The two legacy members of her leadership team, the heads of direct and indirect, were in the first training cohort, and she'd been clear with them as well. She suspected that Frank would opt for retirement and hoped he'd do it sooner rather than later. She could not suggest it but saw his frequent checking of the stock price and suspected he was doing retirement calculations daily. She was not sure yet about Tanya. Bill had named her the leader of indirect recently, and she'd not yet had a chance to establish a direction for the area. She was well-regarded by some of the stakeholders, but her area was focused on completing contracts for agreements largely negotiated by the stakeholders. If Tanya was to survive in this role, her ways of working would need to change substantially. Margot doubted that more than 50 percent of the current staff would still be in their roles in a year, but time would tell. She would give everyone a chance to prove themselves and either demonstrate that they could work in the new way or find a new role.

Margot walked into Matt's office for the meeting, and he stood up to greet her, "Good morning, Margot. If I remember correctly, you have your kickoff training for category management now. How's it going?" Margot was impressed. Yes, she'd included the training in her monthly report, but for him to remember that fact amongst everything else was impressive, nonetheless.

She replied, "It started today. We're including members of my leadership team and the category leaders for the categories most likely to help us impact this year."

He smiled. "I'm glad to hear you're including members of your leadership team. Will all of them attend?"

Margot replied, "Yes, I'm expecting two or three of them per session. The next session will be in a few months. I don't want to overwhelm the business with too many teams at once, nor do I want this to be a typical 'sheep dip' where everyone in the function is trained regardless of when or if they will use the training. When they come out of the training, I expect them to be ready to apply the process."

Matt added, "That's great. The business doesn't really know what to expect with category management, and too many teams will overwhelm them. I saw that before when a CPO tried to create and implement category strategies for every category in the first twelve months. It was chaos with so many teams running, and almost none of the strategies were implemented. There is such a thing as too much of a good thing!"

They both laughed and Margot again reflected that Matt was an excellent hire and fit for where she wanted to take procurement.

Matt then looked at her a bit more seriously. "I want to include Jean in our next meeting. Your transformation of procurement will change a number of employees, and it will also change the ways of working of the company. Specifically, it will change how our executives need to work together. You mentioned at our last meeting that we're in short supply of a few precious commodities and that our GMs are competing for supply at the same suppliers."

Margot reflected a minute then replied, "Spending company money includes elements of power. Power to select suppliers, power to negotiate, and power to manage the suppliers. Category management will, if we do it correctly, review how each of these decisions is made and likely change them going forward. Yes, I'm okay with being the lightning rod if we have executive governance. I'm not okay if you're going to put me in a field all by myself to hug the flagpole before the lightning strikes."

They both laughed again, and Matt said, "No—we're all going to be there together. The support for this starts with the board and is clear." He paused a second and added, "My family was due in today as part of my relocation, and they are delayed a week. Would it be helpful if I joined your team dinner tonight?"

She beamed, "Yes, that would be very impactful. If it's not too much to ask, please introduce yourself to the group, talk about your views of category management, and then answer a few questions before dinner."

He replied, "Happy to do so, send me a text with where and when and I'll be there." Margot left the meeting and walked back to her office. This job was going to be quite a ride!

After Margot left, Rich and Anna, introduced themselves, asked each person to do the same, and asked each person to share what they hoped to learn from the session. The predominant request was to learn about category management and what Margot expected from them. Anna assured them the session was designed to ensure this outcome was achieved and that they should ask questions throughout the session. The group looked a bit nervous and was quiet.

One of the participants asked, "When will we get the templates for the new process? Bill always gave us templates, and we filled them out."

Numerous head nods from the other participants confirmed that they too wanted the templates. Anna smiled and replied, "We talked with Margot about templates, and she's not going to worry about templates now. She wants to see your thoughts about the categories so she can talk to you about them. Maybe in the future there will be templates, but for now just focus on the tools and your application thoughts."

They covered a lot of material the first day, including category scoping and prioritization, process modulation, category governance, stakeholder mapping, and communication planning. Each topic was covered by the trainer and then the participants applied the topic to their own category. Where they thought the topic was easy and obvious when taught, they soon realized there were lots of application nuances. By lunch, the energy in the room was palpable and the participants were engaging in thoughtful, spirited conversations about their categories, the marketplace, and the business. By the end of the day, each participant was starting to apply the tools, and the walls were covered with flip charts for each category. It was messy and incomplete, but it was a radical difference from the morning starting place.

At the bar before dinner, Margot came up to Sean and asked about the day. He recounted the topics to prove he was paying attention, and she asked, "So what?"

He was taken aback.

She continued, "You've hit your numbers every year, you know the market and the business, but your approach is not category management. Unless you embrace this new approach, you're headed to the maverick box. My question of 'so what' is not intended to be snarky; I want to know what you think of the materials, and, most importantly, how are you going to apply them in the corrugated category? Now I did not mean to be that blunt, but your peers respect you, and if you move forward, they'll take notice. On the last day of the session, each of you will stand in front of the class and share how you will apply category management to your category. It will not be a listing of the tools—it will be your thinking. I'm not expecting perfection, but I will be very disappointed if there is no effort to think differently. In strategy development you are choosing your future."

She paused, smiled, and stated, "You can do this, but not unless you approach the corrugated category differently."

Still smiling, she moved on to talk to another participant. He stood there shaken. Margot had just said that he was heading to failure. What was it with her—why was she targeting him? He could not afford to fail. His kids would be in college soon, and his job prospects in the current market were not wonderful.

One of the trainers, Rich, saw him standing there alone after Margot walked away and noted his worried look. Rich asked him, "How was today for you?"

It took him a minute to realize that Rich was talking to him, but then he responded, "It was a lot to take in. I'm still processing it."

Rich replied, "That's to be expected. It is a lot of material, and it is a big change. You said in the introductions that you'd been with the company ten years, right?"

Sean answered, "Yes, that's right. Ten years here working on corrugated. I think the category is performing great."

Rich smiled and asked, "What is the current strategy for corrugated?"

Sean replied, "There is no formal strategy. I bid part of the market every year and always achieve my savings targets."

Rich asked, "How many suppliers do you have?"

Sean quickly replied, "I have one-hundred thirty-five suppliers currently."

Rich followed up, "How many SKUs and how many sites?"

Sean answered, "Over three hundred SKUs and twenty-four sites globally and fourteen in North America."

Rich continued to smile and asked, "How many suppliers should you have?"

Sean thought this was a bit of a stupid question but hid his thoughts and said, "I think I should have one-hundred thirty-five suppliers—the number I have now."

Rich continued to smile and asked, "How many SKUs should there be?"

Sean thought this truly was a stupid question and remarked, "The businesses say they need hundreds of SKUs, so it is my job to source them."

Rich stopped smiling and moved a tiny bit closer so he could confidentially ask, "What if I told you that the company probably doesn't need more than fifty SKUs, and likely fewer, and that fewer than fifteen suppliers could both deliver better service and improve total cost?"

Sean replied before he thought about it, "I don't think that's possible. I don't think that will work here; our company and our needs are different."

Rich's smile returned and broadened into a chuckle, and he raised his glass in a personal toast. "I wish I had money for every company that said, 'We're different'! The truth of the matter is that you are different—every company is different—but that almost never makes change impossible. Think about this tonight and tomorrow as we work through additional materials, and let's talk again tomorrow night at dinner. I know Margot is looking at your category for big results, and my job is to help get you ready."

Rich moved on toward another group of participants, and Sean wondered how he could feel even worse than he did after talking with Margot. How could a company like Frontier use a tenth of their current SKUs? The businesses would never stand for it. The new term, stakeholders, was a nice way of saying the business leaders. Well, his stakeholders would never stand for it. He would have to send his updated CV to Lucy this weekend and hope it was not already too late.

Matt walked into the bar at the end of the cocktail hour. The room quieted a bit; nobody was expecting the CFO at this dinner! He greeted Margot, who introduced him to Anna and Rich and a few of the participants.

Margot then asked everyone to move to the dining room, take a seat and introduced Matt. "Good evening, everyone. I know you're all working hard, and I really appreciate your efforts. I know you still have a 'day job' that you are doing as well as being here learning a new process. I was meeting with Matt today, and he offered to join us for dinner. Matt is our new CFO, and he is excited about category management. I'll let him tell you about himself and why he is so supportive and then he let me know he'd answer a few questions."

Matt stood up, took off his jacket, and loosened his tie. He smiled. "I'm delighted to be with you tonight. I'd expected to be with my family tonight, but they are delayed in Indianapolis. This gives me the opportunity to share a bit with you and answer your questions. First, who am I? I'm first and foremost a husband and parent of four wonderful kids. The oldest is a high-school junior and not too happy to be moving now, and the youngest is in third grade. My wife is a nurse, and we've been together since college—go Huskers! That's Nebraska, for those of you who don't follow college sports. I've worked in a few companies, including an assignment in Stockholm. I'm delighted to be here at Frontier International Group."

He continued, "Now, category management, why do I care? What do I know about it? Let's start with our current situation. We have over thirty-five thousand suppliers, and that seems like a lot. How are you managing these thirty-five thousand suppliers? There are barely five hundred procurement people across the entire company so that means each person, on average, manages seventy suppliers.

As employees, you receive performance evaluations and feedback, and I expect our suppliers, as valuable members of our supply chain, expect feedback as well. That would mean each procurement person doing a supplier performance evaluation or two every week. You're here all week, which means you have more to do next week. That's not occurring, and I know this. In truth, we don't need to do formal evaluations for every supplier, but I don't think we're doing formal evaluations on any suppliers. That cannot be the right approach. If I was an important supplier to Frontier, I wouldn't accept it. Hold on, it gets worse. We are also sole-sourced for over ninety percent of our requirements based on the latest review. Over ninety percent—think about that. That means that some obscure product or service could potentially interrupt our supply chain. I have a duty—and therefore you have a duty—to fix this. The board of directors is going to focus on these risks going forward."

He paused and took a sip of wine before continuing, "So where does category management fit? How does it help? Well, you're going to lead the cross-functional teams that will fix our supply base category by category. You're going to help us reduce the number of suppliers. I'm going to guess thirty-five hundred is a better number—reduce it by a factor of ten. You're also going to reduce our sole-sourcing and single-sourcing. In the process, you're also going to reduce total cost and improve our service and quality. Lastly, you're going to ensure we're compliant with all applicable labor and environmental regulations. Did you know how to do all of that before your course started? I doubt it, but if you did great—you have a leg up. Regardless, that is what we're expecting going forward. I am one hundred percent committed to this and am delighted to see you starting the journey. Any questions?"

Katherine tentatively raised her hand, and he motioned for her to proceed with her question. She queried, "I lead the meetings and events category, and it includes multiple business units across Frontier. They don't all need the same solution. How can I reduce my number of suppliers without going to more sole-sourcing?"

Matt smiled again. "That's an excellent question, thank you for asking. First, Margot and the executive team will help you by assigning an executive sponsor to support you and your team. This will be a VP or GM with skin in the game who can help you get the team members you need, provide counsel to you during the process, and help drive implementation. Second, your strategy will be different than say, office supplies. Each business will have different requirements for meetings and events. The industrial business requires attendance at different meetings than the medical business. They likely use very different methods to display our offerings to attendees. That's today. You and the team will also figure out what will be needed in the future. We all lived through Covid and know that it has permanently changed some things and not affected others. Your team will look to the future of each business and how they will sell in the future. Maybe you'll change the number of suppliers up or down, but you're not likely to have an approved strategy that includes sole-sourcing."

He took a breath before continuing. "That's a hint for everyone. Compare that to office supplies. Nothing against office supplies—we all use them—but it's a convenient example. I know we have over thirty office supplies vendors around the world. Thirty. Is that the right number? Are we maximizing our market leverage? Are we getting the service we deserve? I doubt it, but we don't have any data now. The strategy for office supplies will be different from other categories. It will be very different post-Covid. Each of you will unlock the future for your categories. I've heard the description used that you will be 'the CEO of your category.' I like that. A CEO understands their customers now and into the future, the products and services, the performance in terms of cost and quality, and has a plan to succeed. Trust me, if you can do that on a category basis you will develop yourself to be a future business leader or GM in our company."

The appetizers were delivered, and Matt took the opportunity to sit down. He added one last commentary, "I'll be here through dinner. If you want to ask more questions, feel free. I'm delighted that you're here and appreciate your readiness and willingness to step up to these new expectations." He raised his wine glass in a toast, "To you and your category teams—to unlocking the future supply chain Frontier International Group needs." Glass clinks and 'hear, hears' followed, and the group enjoyed a relaxed dinner.

The dinner was surprisingly quick, and Sean returned to his room. He texted Carla that he was back in the room, and she joined him fifteen minutes later. Where Sean was tense and stressed, Carla was laid-back and happy.

Carla remarked on the obvious difference, "Wow, you look awful. You said today was going to be an easy day and we'd have fun tonight. You look like you saw a ghost."

Sean replied, "I did. It was the ghost of my career. What an awful day."

Carla sat down next to him on the couch, put her hand on his, and said, "Tell me about it while I pour us a glass of wine." She got up and moved to open the bottle of wine she'd brought and poured two glasses.

Sean started slowly and recounted the early morning conversation with Margot through the content of the day to the pre-dinner conversations with Margot and Rich. As he spoke, he became more animated, and it was clear he was unhappy.

Carla sipped her wine, listened thoughtfully, and gently pushed his hair behind his ear. "That does sound like a hard day. Expecting one thing and having something completely different happen. This Margot sounds like she's pushing your buttons pretty hard. What do you make of her?"

Sean paused, thinking out loud. "She's smart and tough, clearly very successful—she was a category manager fifteen years ago and is now a CPO for a major company—but I get the sense that she's fair. I don't know how she did it, but she knows everyone's name, their category, and she's already assessing their performance. She's been here just a few months, and it feels like she's getting ready to make big changes. My boss, Frank, spent the day checking his retirement portfolio. I think he knows he doesn't fit, and he's my biggest advocate. What will happen to me when he leaves? I'm going to work on my CV again this weekend. My kids will be applying to college soon, and I cannot afford to be out of work." His energy visibly drained after sharing his last insights.

Carla wasn't sure how to help him; he'd never been at a loss for words or energy before and he seemed completely drained and defeated. She sat up, put her wine glass down, and suggested, "Let's not stay in here drinking wine; let's go out for a walk." She stood up and reached for his hand.

Sean nodded. "Okay, let's go." With that, they headed out and took the stairs down separately so they would not run into anyone who would see them together.

JANUARY 17TH

Sean woke early and was thankful that Carla had decided to stay in her room after the walk. He had a bit more energy and showered and headed to the training room. It was early, and he figured a cup of coffee and time to review his notes from yesterday would be helpful.

He was very surprised to find Rich, Anna, and Margot already in the room and deep in discussion. They greeted him, waving him over, while Margot greeted, "Good morning, we're just discussing how yesterday went, and you're welcome to join us."

Anna was sharing with Margot the group's concern about not having a full set of templates, and Margot was smiling. She turned to Sean, asking, "What do you think, should we have templates?"

Sean was kicking himself for coming to the room early; he should have gone to breakfast, but now he was trapped. He replied, "Bill always provided templates, so we knew what was expected. If we completed the templates, we were good. If there are no templates, how will we know what is 'good'?"

Margot paused, reflecting. "I've worked at places with and without templates, and while templates can make it seem easier, they can lead to a false positive. I need the team to create thoughtful, insightful, and compelling strategies that reflect strategic thinking and not a 'tick-in-the-box' mentality. I do understand the need for some guidance and will think it over."

She turned to Rich and Anna, stating, "For now, they can use the standard teaching templates, but they must add their insights to each tool. Please reinforce that. No insights means they are not thinking strategically, which means they are not using the process correctly."

Anna responded, "We will do that, and I think that will allay some of their concerns."

Margot then turned to Sean. "How do you think yesterday went?"

Sean paused and gathered his thoughts—he felt really under the gun now—and replied, "The class is going well; Anna and Rich clearly know their stuff and the industry. There weren't any questions they couldn't answer. There is so much new to learn that if feels a bit overwhelming. And we're not sure what you expect on day three."

Margot smiled. "Yes, Anna and Rich know the process, the categories, and the industry. That's why I trust them. They will, if you let them, help you build a meaningful strategy. What I'm expecting on day three relates to our template discussion. I expect to see that each of you is applying the tools to your category," she leaned forward a bit for emphasis, "that you are developing insights that can help you to create a strategy. If all I see are completed templates with no insights, it will be a failure. I've never, ever seen that."

With that, she stood up and smiled at them. "I have to go to a meeting, I'll see you at dinner tonight," and walked out.

Rich stated, "We'll address these topics with the group at the kickoff this morning. Go get some breakfast and relax. We'll see you in thirty minutes."

Sean jokingly replied, "Thanks, I'll know to get breakfast first tomorrow," and he left the room.

Anna and Rich completed their prep for the second day.

The participants gradually filled the room, and at 8:30, Rich closed the door. Not everyone had arrived, but Rich was punctual. Rich walked to the front of the room then commented, "It's time to start. Before I start, are there any questions or comments from yesterday?"

Tanya raised her hand, "I thought it was a good day and appreciate that Margot and Matt joined us for dinner last night. We've not had training like this in the past, and I am enjoying it."

Anna said, "Nobody has asked yet, so I will—where and how do we use AI in the process?"

Lots of people in the room nodded their heads and murmured agreement. Anna continued, "There is not, currently, a full category management AI solution. I don't see one on the near horizon. There are a number of solutions that claim to be, but they are, in my opinion, really sourcing solutions. It is true that sourcing is an element of category management, but it is not a holistic category strategy. We will review the use of AI tools throughout the process because they can be very helpful in supplier and supply market analysis, for instance. Rich and I are not anti-AI, but we are realists and are committed to helping you develop a real strategy. A real strategy comes from you engaging stakeholders with your team, developing actionable insights, and then creating a unique strategy tailored to the requirements of Frontier International Group."

Numerous people nodded their heads in agreement. Sean sat silently waiting for Anna and Rich to share the early morning conversation with Margot; he certainly wasn't going to comment on it. Frank silently entered the room and took his seat.

Rich then added, "We talked with Margot this morning about your template concerns." Again, lots of head nods and murmurs of agreement. He continued, "Margot agreed that Anna and I will distribute the training templates but—and this is the important part—you must add your insights to each template. She will be here tomorrow afternoon for you to share your category learnings and will be laser-focused on your insights. It's expected that you know the basic facts of your category, that's part of the job. What she wants to know is your answer to 'so what'? Now that you've applied the facts of the category to the specific tool, what are your insights? We did that all day yesterday and will continue to do so. Anna, do you have anything to add?"

Anna responded, "Thanks, yes I do," and she stood up and walked over to the flip charts created by Katherine for meetings and events. "Look at these charts as an example." Katherine, the category manager for meetings and events blushed and looked down. Anna stated, "Katherine, these are well done—I'm not choosing yours to embarrass you. Each of the topics from yesterday is covered, but note the insights: lots of stakeholders, no clear sponsorship, role of the salesperson might be changing and, with that, the need for events. These raise questions that will affect the strategy. These are fundamental business questions that must be addressed by the senior stakeholders. Katherine and her team will be raising these questions as part of the category management process. Katherine could continue to go out and book the same events but will know that is not likely the right solution. The goal of category management is to help frame the discussion with the business to ensure the right solutions are developed."

Rich thanked Anna for the example and said to the group, "You're on a journey to develop and implement a category strategy. It will take thought, it will take time, and it will take resources. Not every category will warrant the same amount of effort. Margot and the leadership team picked your categories specifically as being worthy of this effort. Now, let's pick up with today's content."

Anna and Rich covered business requirements development and supply market analysis before lunch.

At lunch, Frank sat down next to Sean and asked, "How are you doing? Are you learning a lot?"

Sean chuckled. "Yes, I'm learning that what made me successful for the past ten years is not going to make me successful going forward. I literally must learn how to do my job all over again. I'll tell you—it's daunting."

Frank remarked, "Tell me about it. I worked with Bill for many years and knew what he needed and always delivered. Since Margot arrived, I've felt like a new employee. I don't know what she's looking for either. I'm on the fence about staying or retiring. We have the new place in Scottsdale, and it's calling to me." He took a bite of his sandwich.

Sean replied, "I'd be sorry to see you go. We've worked together since I got here. Maybe it won't be that bad."

Frank finished his bite before adding, "I don't think it's going to be bad. I do think it's going to be different. I need to decide how much change I want to be a part of. I was very comfortable with Bill and thought we did a lot of good work. I don't know if I want to be part of rebuilding it now."

The two ate in silence for a couple of minutes, and then Tanya asked if she could join them. "Of course," Frank and Sean replied in unison.

Tanya was full of energy. "This is simply amazing! Did you see how Anna reviewed Katherine's work on meetings and events? I cannot remember Bill ever mentioning meetings and events. This is really a breath of fresh air and a new beginning for the function."

Frank and Sean silently exchanged glances, and Sean commented, "It sure does feel like starting over."

Tanya must have sensed their mood from their lack of energy and said, "You know, I've heard about procurement transformations from my friends, and I'm hopeful. Margot knows her stuff and is incredibly well connected to the senior stakeholders. I think we need to keep an open mind." The three of them talked amiably about non-work topics through the rest of lunch.

Sean and Carla met after the group dinner at a nearby bar. They did not want to be too conspicuous, so the hotel bar was eliminated.

"How was day two?" Carla asked.

"I feel like I'm starting all over again. Like in Monopoly where you return to Go," Sean replied.

"It could be worse, you could be sent to jail."

"You're right, but I do feel a bit trapped. I have to use this new process and work with a coach who will report everything I do to Margot. It's like hanging from a cliff by a single rope and the only person who can help you is holding a knife."

"That sounds difficult," she responded. "Is the person with the knife at least nice?"

"Yes, very nice, but I still don't trust him. Tomorrow, I have to work with him to prepare a summary of the three days that I will present to Margot. I don't like public speaking and have not had to do it in my career. If I hit my numbers, nobody bothered me. That's all over now," he lamented.

"It sounds like a new beginning. You're smart, capable, and able to learn new things. Don't underestimate yourself."

"Thanks. Let's head up to the room. It's an early start tomorrow."

JANUARY 18TH

Sean slept fitfully and woke up early. He had never dreamt about work before and last night he dreamt about his category and this upcoming presentation. He knew he was nervous and needed to get started right away. He slipped out of bed, kissed Carla on the forehead, and took a shower. She was still asleep when he was dressing, so he wrote her a short note and left the room. They were planning to stay another night, so he didn't need to pack his things yet.

He walked to the elevator and was surprised to see Anna when the door opened.

"Good morning" she greeted. "You're up and ready early."

"Good morning," he replied. "I am. I need to work on my presentation for today."

"You look and sound a bit worried, are you okay?"

He sighed. "In truth, I am a bit overwhelmed. I came here feeling pretty good about myself and the work I do, and today I feel like I did as a new college graduate, except I'm in the middle of my career and have college tuition bills for my kids arriving soon."

"Let's have breakfast and talk," she suggested. The elevator door opened, and Sean followed Anna to the restaurant. They sat in a booth, and the waitress served coffee and pointed out the breakfast buffet.

Anna said, "Learning something new can be difficult. Relearning a job can be even more daunting. We do it all the time in different ways. I bet you had vinyl albums and used a record player. Who was it, The Backstreet Boys?"

"Don't make me laugh; I'm not that old," he smirked. "I had cassette tapes and even saw a few eight-track tapes. And I never listened to The Backstreet Boys."

"My point," she continued, "is that you learned how to use an MP3 player or an iPod and are now using your phone to play music. Each of these changes in technology required you to relearn how to play music. We're showing you, through the category strategy development process, how to rethink the procurement process you've used so far."

"It's one thing to sit at home and fumble with a new phone, but to stand up later today in front of the group and Margot when I'm not comfortable, that's a lot," Sean said.

"Okay, so you want to do well today, and that's to be expected," Anna responded. "Make yourself a simple storyboard for your presentation. Take a few flip charts and put them up on the wall, and on the left-hand side, list the tools down the pages, leaving room between the tools. Next to each tool, summarize what the tool tells you is occurring now—what's the current situation. After that, list the 'so what?' or implication for the tool. This is the heart of the matter and the key to strategy development. Let's take your number of suppliers. How many do you currently have?"

"There are one hundred thirty-five suppliers," he stated.

Anna took a napkin and used it to illustrate her comments, "So, on the flip chart you list 'Suppliers and Supply Market' as the tool or process area and note that there are 'one hundred thirty-five current suppliers.' You then write 'Implications' and note that this seems like a lot—maybe too many and not sure if they are the best for the future or something else that you believe. The strategy team will then work through the implications to determine which suppliers are the best, which are the best fit for Frontier, the required commercial terms, and the transition plans to the new supply base. For now, focus on getting only to implications. Does that help?"

"A bit." he nodded, tentative. "But what if Margot doesn't agree with my summary of the situation or the implications?"

"Margot knows the process, Sean, but she does not know corrugated at Frontier as well as you do. Your job is to tell the story of your category. You and she may disagree on some of the implications but notice that then you will be having a strategy discussion. That is the point of the process, to elevate from simply executing a purchase to thinking about the broader process and options." Anna continued, "She will not attack you for having implications she disagrees with. She wants to see you engaging in the process and developing your approach. I've seen mean CPOs, and she is not one of them."

"Can I ask a favor?"

"Sure, if I can do it, I will."

"I'll assemble the storyboard sheets in one of the breakout rooms before the session starts and begin building my thoughts. I'll bring my lunch to the breakout room and work through lunch. Can you come see what I have before the end of the lunch break and give me some feedback?"

"Absolutely," Anna said. "There will also be about an hour later in the afternoon for the group to work on their thoughts before Margot arrives. If you get started early, you'll be able to incorporate my feedback and address any additional thoughts before the presentations."

"Thanks, let's go get some breakfast so I can get started."

They headed up to the buffet, and a noticeably more relaxed Sean emerged for the rest of the meal.

Anna and Rich welcomed the group back for day three. Everyone arrived more or less on time and seemed ready to continue.

"Today we're going to pull the tools together in what we call a layered strategy. Let's use a creative brainstorming tool to quickly demonstrate this idea," Anna announced. "Everyone close your eyes and keep them closed. Imagine that you've decided to enter a competitive sporting event like a triathlon."

Low laughs were heard in the room.

"Stay with me," Anna interjected. "You are fulfilling a New Year's resolution or a birthday epiphany or whatever, and you decided that today is the day you're going to become a competitive athlete. Regardless of your current age or any physical conditions you may have, there are competitive classes for everyone, so don't discount the idea—work with me. Don't answer this next question out loud, but think about what is the first thing you must do if you are to become an athlete? What would you do second? Do not speak but open your eyes and write down what you'll do first and second."

The participants opened their eyes, looked around a bit bemused and bewildered, and noted their responses.

"Okay, somebody tell me what you'd do first," Anna said.

"Schedule a physical with my doctor," Frank piped up, "to ensure I don't kill myself!"

Laughter filled the room.

"Someone else, what will you do first," Anna asked.

"Buy some new workout clothes," Tanya added.

Anna noted both ideas in the bottom left-hand corner of the flip chart. "Someone else, what will you do second?"

"Enter a five K race," Lee gave.

"Excellent," Anna replied, she wrote Lee's response to the right and above the first two response. "What's another second action?"

"I had 'buy a bike and join a gym' as my first actions," Sean joined in, "and find a running partner as a second action."

Anna noted all of Sean's inputs with the bike and gym in the bottom left-hand corner and the running partner under Lee's "find a five K race." She asked the group, "Seeing this progression, what would the third action be?"

"Do a short triathlon," Frank suggested.

"Find a triathlon coach," Lee added.

"Excellent," Anna stated as she noted these to the right and above the second step actions. "Can you see how these steps build on each other. If I add 'compete in a triathlon' at the top right, we could fill in any remaining gaps. Maybe over time the top right would evolve from competing in a triathlon to competing in the so-called ultra or Ironman Triathlons."

"You missed a step," Frank pointed out. "Add a step for hospitalization."

Again, laughter filled the room. "You could be right, Frank." Anna smiled. "If any steps are missed or we try to progress too fast. The same thing is true with a category strategy. We need the team to agree on the ultimate vision for the category—their equivalent to compete in a triathlon—and we need them to define the steps Frontier must take to achieve the vision. The size of the steps and the pace of the progress is dictated by the organization's capacity for change and trust in the process, the category team, and you. Remember—the vision is the desired end state and describes what it will be like when you arrive."

Anna showed the generic layered-strategy slide and emphasized, "These are some typical steps, but the truth is that each of you will have different strategies for your categories and different steps within the strategy. There are some consulting firms that tell you there are a finite number of strategic options, but that is not our experience. You and your team will determine the approach for your category, and it will not be from a preset menu."

They covered the remaining topics for the morning and broke for lunch. Sean picked up his lunch from the buffet as he asked Anna, "Can you come by the breakout room in thirty to forty-five minutes?"

"Sure," she said as she looked at her watch to note the time. "I'll plan to be there around twelve thirty."

"Thanks," he replied, heading to the breakout room to work on his storyboard. He completed adding the tools from the morning up through the layered strategy. He sat with his sandwich and thought about the vision for corrugated. He was stumped until he thought about why they needed to buy corrugated in the first place—to protect products in storage and shipment. He decided to add "products protected in storage and shipment" to the vision. What else could he add? Total cost? Service? Yes, all the business requirements needed to be met. What about the number of suppliers? It was clear in his conversations with Anna and Rich that the number of suppliers was not the answer but that too many suppliers was an issue. He decided to add *with all business requirements met by the fewest possible suppliers*. He looked at that as a vision, and it seemed a bit vague, but he wasn't sure what else to add.

He looked back across his storyboard draft. He had the tools and the implications listed. It was a bit messy, but it was all there. He finished his sandwich, and a few minutes later Anna walked in.

"Well, that is impressive, Sean," Anna complimented. "You've covered all the tools, and it looks like you identified the implications. I'm going to have a seat here and you present your category. You have ten minutes, which is the same as what you'll have with Margot later. I'll give you feedback afterward."

Sean went through the first tool findings and implications, and Anna stopped him, "Sean, stay at a higher level. Don't go down to the individual SKU level here—stay out of the weeds—pace yourself and go through the tools and note that you need to be through the layered strategy eight minutes from now."

"Okay, sorry, I didn't want to miss anything," he responded. He continued through the tools and did his best to stay at the high-level description and managed to complete it all in just under nine minutes.

"That was excellent," Anna beamed. "Much better at the end than your first start. I think your vision is a good start and everything builds to that. Some of the implications and tool findings will get tweaked a bit during the process, but that is to be expected. This is a very rough draft without team input. This afternoon, during the prep time, I recommend that you think through how you would describe the current state of the category. Imagine you were at Frontier's headquarters and your CEO, Leslie, gets on the elevator and asks you what you're working on. You have the vision for the future of corrugated; how would you describe the current state? If you can answer that in a concise and compelling way and have all the work here, including the layered strategy, then you are well on your way. Compared to where you were at breakfast today, you've come light-years."

Sean beamed in return. He'd received feedback in the past on achieving numbers, but somehow this felt better and more important.

"Thanks, Anna. I really appreciate you taking the time to give me a steer on this. I do know the company, the suppliers, and the category, but this new process is a bit overwhelming."

"Margot mentioned coaching a couple of days ago," Anna said, "and this is the reason why. Rich and I will work with each of you to help you succeed. You still must do the hard work, but we will be with you along the journey." She looked at her watch, adding, "Let's get back before we're late."

Anna and Rich covered the remaining tools after lunch and gave the participants an hour to prepare for the closing presentations. As the respective spend area leaders, Frank and Tanya did not have assigned categories. Anna and Rich suggested that they circulate amongst their respective category managers and provide coaching. To their credit, they realized that there was little process coaching they could provide—it was all new to them, too. They suggested that Shelly or one of them circulate with them so they could observe the coaching process from true experts and see how their people were doing.

Margot arrived a few minutes before the end of the preparation time and noted the change in the room dynamic. This was one of her favorite aspects of category management training—by the end of the class the group was relaxed and talking about the business issues of their category and not focused on the day-to-day procurement and supply issues.

As the group reassembled, Rich asked, "Who would like to go first?"

Lee, a procurement intern, volunteered, "I'd like to go first."

"Thanks, Lee. I'll help you with your flip charts," Rich said. They arranged the four easels across the front of the room and posted Lee's charts.

Lee began, "I worked on office supplies. It's not really my category, but as an intern, it was suggested." Lee continued to describe the category, and the current situation was a complete mess, with each site in the world doing its own buying. There were no standards or processes and no leveraging of Frontier's scale to positively impact total cost and service. She finished with a vision for an aligned strategy to meet the business requirements in a post-Covid world.

"Great start," Margot affirmed, smiling. "In under ten minutes, Lee described the spending anarchy that exists today and the potential to create a much better future. There are a few tool and implication questions I'd like to discuss, but that would result in a deep dive into the category, and none of the rest of you would have time. Lee, excellent work, and we will pick up the conversation later."

"Thanks, Margot," Lee said, smiling and looking very relieved. The best part of going first was being done first!

Sean volunteered, "I'd like to go next."

"Okay, I'll help you with your materials," Rich offered.

As Rich and Sean posted Sean's flip charts, Margot looked over at Anna, who gave a very subtle positive head nod and smile. Margot was a bit surprised and also relieved.

Sean started. "Before I go through the tools, I want to summarize where the category is today. We have one hundred thirty-five suppliers and hundreds of SKUs. There is no overall strategy other than for each site to seek the best price by SKU at the time. It's not pretty, but it is the truth." With that, he took a deep breath and worked through the tools, the implications, and the resulting vision and layered strategy.

The room was very quiet, so he asked, "Any comments or questions?"

Margot was the first to respond. "That's really good work, Sean. I appreciate you calling out the current situation as directly as you did. I want you and everyone here to know that I'm not here to punish anyone for the current situation. I'm here to help you acknowledge the current situation, to understand the dynamics that caused us to be there, and to move toward the agreed vision. We are all about progress."

"Thank you," Sean replied, sitting back down and smiling at Anna, who returned his smile and silently mouthed "Well done" to him.

After the presentations were completed, Margot stood up. "Those were excellent draft category strategies. You did those after two and a half days of training and no cross-functional team input. They are not real strategies, because the stakeholders must be involved, but you had the opportunity to work with the tools and see how it comes together. Any questions?"

"Yes," Tanya said, "This is an excellent process, but it is time-consuming and, if stakeholders are involved, resource intensive. Are we going to do this for every category?"

"That's an excellent question, Tanya, and one which you get to help with as part of the procurement leadership team. It's not part of this course because it's a leadership responsibility and not a category leader tool, but we as a leadership team will look at all the categories and segment them based on their impact to the company."

Margot walked to a flip chart and used a blank page to draw a pyramid. "At the top are the strategic categories. Using the portfolio analysis matrix, our version of the Kraljic matrix, these are the categories that are listed in the strategic quadrant and in the category classification matrix the categories listed as custom. There will not be many—likely less than ten per business unit and even fewer for the overall company—that create the future for our company. We will use this process in every category that is strategic and custom, and our goal will be transformative category management. The time and cross-functional resources are required at this level to ensure we achieve the supply chain results we need as a company."

She continued, "The next level down are the key categories. These are the categories listed as lean on portfolio analysis and either proprietary or the far edge of tailored on category classification. One of two things is going on in these categories; either they are opportunities for access to key supplier innovations, like in tailored, or they are areas of extreme risk where we are sole- or single-sourced, like in proprietary. We will focus on enhanced category management, and the goals will be to address the specifications that cause us to be sole- or single-sourced and to streamline our supply base. This will require cross-functional teamwork and the full process."

"The third level is approved categories. These are the balance of Frank's categories that are used in the direct production process and a few of the indirect categories. They will largely come from leverage in portfolio analysis and generic in category classification. We will use basic category management at this level, which will largely focus on strategic sourcing. Many categories will be at this level in the future but are currently in key due to sole- and single-sourcing. This highlights that categories change and can move levels over time."

"Lastly, are the basic categories. Lee showed us office supplies, and it is a basic category. These are categories in generic on category classification and acquisition on portfolio analysis. Typically, we'd use the most basic category management approaches, such as sourcing with a focus on automation. There are exceptions, and I think Lee showed us that. Office supplies needs to be fixed before we can automate it. I think it needs a bit of rapid, enhanced category management to develop the strategy, select the suppliers, and manage any organizational change, and then we can move forward with automation."

The group was silent, taking notes. More than a few people were noticing that Margot understood and could use the tools seamlessly. They were impressed.

"Tanya, I hope that helps. It's probably a bit longer of an answer than you wanted, but I thought the whole group should have a feel for how we're going to use the process," Margot said.

"Thanks," Tanya replied. "It is helpful, and I look forward to the leadership team discussions of category segmentation. Do the stakeholders get to participate, or do we decide by ourselves in procurement?"

"Another great question," Margot responded. She made a mental note to keep an eye on Tanya. She was demonstrating real perceptiveness around this new approach. "The leadership team will do the analysis first as a draft, just like you did for your categories here in the class. If we go to stakeholders with a blank sheet, they will put everything, and I mean everything, in strategic. At one company I worked at, the CEO arrived one day and noticed that the lawn needed to be mowed at the HQ. He called procurement and raised hell, and the next day the CPO declared that the lawn service was now a strategic category."

Laughter filled the room, along with knowing head nods.

Margot continued, "We'll sit down with stakeholders and use our tools and their definitions to guide them through the discussion. There may be some categories where they inflate the definition a bit, but we will start the discussion and the change process with them. We will need to teach them that there is a difference between business criticality and strategic importance. This is an area of continued confusion from the Kraljic matrix and was exacerbated during Covid. Are pallets or face masks strategic for Frontier?" She turned to face the group.

"They're both important. Without pallets, our factories shut down," Frank answered.

"We chased PPE around the globe to stay open," Sean added.

"That's right," Margot agreed. "They are both very important. The test for strategic importance is whether it enables us to differentiate our products or services in a way that our customers value. I don't think our customers care which PPE we use and, with a few exceptions around plastic pallets versus wood versus slip sheets, not many customers care about specific pallets."

Heads nodded around the room.

Margot continued, "I mentioned on day one that you'd receive coaching support from Anna and Rich during your process. Each of you that is running a category will receive coaching. Frank and Tanya will not be leading a category, and Lee, I'm going to assign you to Sean's category."

Margot asked, "Any more questions? Okay, some further thoughts, then. Thank you all for your work this week. It's obvious that you are thinking about your categories in new and different ways. Frontier needs you to do that, and I expect it. Starting next week, you will work with your leader to begin step one in the process. As you know, this will include scoping of the category and process assessment. By the end of the following week, we will meet again to review your work and make preliminary decisions. Then you will meet with the business executives from the areas that will be included. These will be new conversations for you and very new conversations for them. Anna and Rich and your leadership team members will help you prepare for these meetings. Once these conversations are complete, we'll engage the business sponsors. The ELT already picked the sponsors for the Wave One categories. The expectation is that in six months or less, approvable strategies will be ready for executive governance review."

The room was silent as the participants took notes. Everyone looked very serious and some a bit worried.

Margot noted their faces and stated, "Starting in three weeks, we will have quick, biweekly progress updates and monthly wave reviews. It may sound counterintuitive, but based on my experience, speed is your friend. If we take a year to develop a strategy, the business will think category management is slow and cumbersome, and your stakeholder management will be harder due to people changing roles and losing focus. We are going to drive this. We are going to drive strategy creation, and most importantly, we are going to drive implementation. That is why there are only a few of you here. Some of you will be doing transformational category management and others will be doing basic category improvement. The business will see that we can tailor our approach and that we're efficient."

A hand was slowly raised, and Margot said, "Yes, Katherine, you have a question?"

Katherine asked, "Yes, will we use the same templates for the wave reviews that we used today?"

Margot replied with a smile, "Yes, for now that's fine, because I want to keep it easy and all of you focused on the process. Understand that the templates are handy from a knowledge management perspective—they help us document the process. You will not have them with you twenty-four-seven—at least I hope not—and you will be expected to be able to speak to the process and, most importantly, your insights. Many of you work at the Group's headquarters, and all of you will be coming and going from HQ with your teams. I fully expect that Leslie, Matt, and any member of the executive team will stop by your team or run into you in the elevator, and they will ask you how category management is going and what you're learning and doing. As you learned on day one, this is part of the team's communication planning, and it is vital. You are the CEO of your category, and they are your key customers. You don't have to talk to them for an hour, but it is your job to demonstrate you are an excellent leader of your category and that you and your team are developing a meaningful strategy."

She continued, "A quick story, when I was learning category management, I was assigned to lead the temporary labor team. I didn't know temporary labor, but the prior category manager had just been fired for misleading the CPO—that's another story. So, I jumped in and applied the process. I worked with the stakeholders and the cross-functional team, and we sorted a new category strategy in less than three months. I had numerous presentations to the key business leaders, and they were very direct about the problems that needed to be fixed and the opportunities that could be realized if I created a good strategy. We created a good strategy that was fully implemented and is now being refreshed considering the post-Covid changes in workplace staffing. I walked onto an elevator and, sure enough, the CEO was there, said hello, and asked me what I was working on. I told him about our work, shared the issues and the opportunities and our plan to develop a strategy, and that took ten floors—maybe a minute and a half. He shook my hand and told me to contact his office if I needed any help. It turns out that I didn't but imagine if I'd not had those answers. He started by saying hello and asking my name. He could have called my boss and said, 'What is she working on? What are you thinking?' Instead, he had a quick, positive impression of me and category management. That is what I want for each of you. If you want to practice your 'elevator speech,' my office door is open."

She carried on, "I got side-tracked there, sorry. Back to the reviews. You will see that how these reviews are run is as important to me as the content. You will present on behalf of your team to the procurement leadership team. Initially it will just be you until the process is well-established, and then members of your team can join you. Sponsors can join if they have time. The purposes of the review are to ensure that the team is on process and on schedule. If there are issues or roadblocks, we are there to help you solve them—as is your team sponsor. If there are process issues, we will provide recommendations. Likewise, if we identify better practices, we'll share them across the category management teams. My leadership team is here, and I'll say this in front of you and them. If your team is off process and off schedule and they have not been proactively helping you, I will be disappointed. Procurement leaders' roles must be active coaches in this process—it's a change for all of us. Lastly, these will be what I call share-and-build sessions. We will be direct, we will be honest, and we will be supportive. The goal is to improve what we are doing. This is all a bit abstract now but will be clearer as we start conducting the sessions. Any last questions before we adjourn?"

Sean raised his hand and asked, "You've mentioned Anna and Rich and continued support. What can we expect?"

Margot nodded. "Thanks, Sean, I'd meant to cover that. Anna and Rich will be available to support you. They will not do the work for you. They will be coaches. A budget is approved for each of you based on the expected process modulation—basic category improvement will have two to three days per month, and category transformation will have four to six days per month. You'll work with your procurement leader to confirm your process modulation level and Anna and Rich to agree who will coach you. I want to be very clear on this coaching. Some may look to them to do your work; that is not acceptable. Some may think that I'll think less of you if you use coaching; that is not true. I am providing coaching, and Matt has agreed to the budget because we know this is new and different and we need you to succeed. Coaching is a proven method to accelerate results and improve long-term sustainability."

"After you're coached in one category, you will be able to do the next category with little, if any, coaching. I was a varsity level swimmer in college and my family decided to try scuba diving. I could have said I don't need scuba instruction because I'm an expert swimmer and comfortable in the water, but I didn't. I took the instruction and it saved my life. I didn't know I'd be a bit claustrophobic underwater at first—particularly when I took off my mask the first time. The instructor was there to help me through that. Most of you are very experienced procurement professionals. Do you know how to run an excellent cross-functional team? Are you an expert at applying the strategic analysis tools? Can you already build a layered strategy? A business case and implementation plan? If yes, you'll need very little coaching. If no, then use the coaching. For my interns," and she motioned to a couple in the room, "this will all be new, and you'll be assigned to partner with a category manager. You are going to be on a vertical learning curve. Enjoy it. That's it for now. Anna and Rich, thank you for your efforts, and I'll turn it back over to you."

Anna stood up, thanked Margot for her comments and facilitated the group through a session critique, and handed out the individual certificates.

Anna added, "This was undoubtedly a full week—maybe overwhelming. Rich and I are here to help you. You've seen us and worked with us. You likely have a feel for who you'd like as a coach, and we will do what we can to accommodate your preferences. I'm based on the West Coast and Rich is based on the East Coast. We will conduct much of the coaching remotely and will plan to attend your key meetings in person."

Sean walked up to Anna as everyone was leaving. "Do you have a few minutes? I'd like to talk about next steps."

"Yes," she replied, "we should align on the next steps while we're together. It will be much easier to continue virtually if we know where we're going. First, who is your sponsor?"

"I don't know; this week was the first I'd heard about needing one," Sean confessed.

"Go see if Frank is out in the hall," Anna suggested.

Sean bolted out the door and was back in two minutes with Frank already in his coat.

"I thought we were done," Frank remarked. "What's up?"

Anna replied, "Before you head out, who is the sponsor for Sean's corrugated team?"

"I don't have the list with me but know the sponsors were selected," Frank said. "I'll ask Margot and get back to you."

"Okay, but please do it ASAP," Anna responded. "The clock is ticking, and we need to get moving."

"I understand, don't worry," Frank promised as he turned and headed back to the door.

"You will need to engage the named sponsor quickly," Anna said. "In the meantime, let's talk through a rough macro plan. The team may change it, but it is important that we have some idea of the flow."

She continued and moved to a flip chart, "It's currently mid-January, and we'll need three meetings and the strategy approved before the budget cycle begins in June. Let's target mid-February for your face-to-face kickoff meeting. We can talk later about a meeting location. There is a lot of work between the meetings. Let's plan for late March for the second meeting. Let's plan for mid-May for the third meeting. It is likely the third meeting will be at the HQ, so start looking at meeting rooms and, if needed, a nearby off-site location."

"Will that be the only time we work together?" Sean asked.

"No, we should plan on weekly calls to coordinate work and at least another couple of in-person one-on-one meetings," Anna replied. "I will facilitate your meetings, but you must be fully conversant in the meeting materials so you are viewed as the team leader. In essence, you and I will work through all the materials ahead of time as if we're holding the meeting and then do it again with the team. By doing this, you'll be ready for the meetings and you'll learn the process. The next time you lead a team through the process, you'll need much less support—typically only a few phone calls."

"That makes sense, thanks," Sean said. "I'd feel more comfortable if we had a Monday call to talk about the week and a Friday call to review the progress during the week, at least to start."

"That works for me," Anna replied. "Your key next steps are to engage your sponsor and agree the team members. We will also be working through the step-one materials, but do not let the people side of this slip. Give Frank until noon tomorrow at the latest and then escalate to Margot. The people you want and need are going to be busy, and you need them to be at your meeting in a month. They might never have heard of you, and yet you need them to clear a week of their time. Increase your chances of success by giving them notice. Also, have the sponsor involved in the invite process—they will have heard of him or her. I need to run to the airport now. I'm glad we're working together, and we'll talk Friday."

They shook hands, and Anna left Sean standing in the room. He picked up the flip charts with his draft presentation and bag and walked out. He felt very different today than when he'd walked in on Tuesday morning. Tuesday he was apprehensive and more than a little defensive. Today he was still a bit apprehensive but felt energized about the future. When was the last time he felt that way at work?

JANUARY 22ND

Sean called Anna. "How was your trip home?"

"Easy," Anna replied, "Everything was on time. Let's get this kickoff meeting planned."

"Agreed, Margot sent me a copy of the email to our sponsor, Genevieve," Sean said. "She's based in Europe."

"You'll want to schedule time with her. Preferably in person if she comes to HQ, but at least via video," Anna suggested. "Review with her the sponsor expectations that we discussed in the training and the category background information. Have you started to make a list of potential team members to review with her?"

"I did," he replied. "Here's what I'm thinking so far," and he listed the team members by business, function, and location.

"That sounds good. Ask Genevieve to send them a note once you talk with her. What about the meeting location?" she asked.

"I'm thinking about the Frontier Medical production site in Johnson City, Tennessee. That site is a major user of corrugated. It's not a hub airport area, but it's not hard to get to. What do you think?"

"That sounds good. Do they have a meeting room we can use?"

"I'll check once we finalize the dates. Based on our discussion at the training, we were targeting mid-February. How is the twelfth to fourteenth?"

"I'm available then and will block it," she confirmed. "When you're talking with Genevieve, you'll want to ask her to join the meeting virtually at the beginning to do a kickoff welcome and toward the end of the last day to hear about progress and next steps. Give her as much notice as possible. I also recommend looking at hotels and booking a block of rooms. You never know what else is scheduled. We can coordinate rental cars and rides closer to the meeting time."

"Okay," he said as he made notes. There was a lot of work to being a category manager, and he didn't know if he could ask Rita to help with the travel. He'd ask Frank or Margot later.

"Let's work on the agenda next. Did you review the draft I sent through?"

"Yes, I did, and it looks good. I'll check with the site director on a tour, and we can adjust as needed. Is there anything else I need to do in the meantime?"

"The opportunity analysis materials you started at the training need to be advanced. Use the templates shared so you can easily send them to the team members. Once the team members are confirmed, let me know. I'll send them the links to complete the Myers–Briggs[3] Type Indicator and Thomas–Kilmann conflict indicator.[4] You should also setup an intranet file-sharing site that you can use as a team repository," Anna stated. "That should do it for now. Keep me posted, and we'll talk again on Friday."

"Thanks," he replied as he continued taking notes. They'd discussed it all at the end of the training, but now it needed to get done quickly.

Genevieve responded to his email the next day. She'd been informed about the team and her sponsor role by Erica and had already received some notes from the ELT meeting. She sent a couple of meeting times and asked that Sean make himself available as soon as possible.

"Good afternoon, Sean," Genevieve greeted the next day. "I appreciate you responding so quickly. Erica emphasized how important this effort is, and I want to get us off to a good start. What is the status of the team?"

"I have tentatively selected some team members for you to consider and am now sharing them on my screen. What do you think?" Sean asked.

"I think Roland left healthcare marketing last month," she mentioned. "I recommend replacing him with Gina. She's excellent. Is everyone expected to attend in person? Where are you planning for the meeting?"

"Thanks, I'll replace Roland with Gina. Everyone is expected to attend if they possibly can. The process is much more effective in person, so we work hard to make the meetings as efficient as possible and hold as few as necessary. The first meeting is planned for Tennessee: the healthcare site where you assemble instruments and kits. I'm thinking we'd hold the second meeting at an industrial business site. It's important to have the sponsor present in person for the second meeting. What do you think?" he asked.

"That sounds good," she replied. "My schedule is crazy. If I cannot attend in person, I will be there virtually. Three total meetings is not too many for an important business strategy, and there are not too many people traveling. Notice to the participants is important—particularly as they don't know they're on this team yet."

"Along those lines, I have an email for you to send to the team members, their managers, and the ELT that we're going to use for the Wave One teams. It was drafted by our transformation director, Shelly, and I'll make the team-specific edits and send it to you later today."

"Okay, thanks. I'll send it right out. I want to stay close to this process, even if I'm not at the first meeting or on all of the team calls. If you send me a note and put in the subject line that it is important to talk, I will get back to you right away."

"Thank you, Genevieve. I appreciate your support."

Sean modified the invitation email and sent it to Genevieve. Once he saw that she'd sent it to the team members, he followed up with a personal welcome to each team member and a request for a short phone conversation. Almost everyone seemed excited to be part of the process and appreciated being selected. The exception was Marek; despite repeated emails and voicemail messages, Sean was unable to reach him. Still, Sean was pleased that the majority of the team was enthusiastic, and he would talk to Anna about Marek.

Sean called Anna and reviewed the status of the team and his inability to connect with Marek. Anna recommended that he relax a bit, as maybe Marek was on vacation, and while everything was urgent and critical now to him, it might not be the same for Marek. "Invite him to the virtual kickoff meeting and relax. If he is still a problem, we can review the situation with Margot and Genevieve," she counseled.

He remembered that Margot had offered Lee's support in the training, and he included Lee in the subsequent planning and review calls with Anna. The meeting preparation accelerated from there, with Sean using Lee's support to pull together the kickoff materials. He'd been resistant to working with an intern, but Lee was very capable and readily lent her time and effort to the project.

Sean scheduled a virtual meeting with the team the week before the kick-off meeting. He wanted to answer any questions, confirm the travel details, and get the group off to a good start. Sean welcomed the group to the meeting and introduced himself. He then introduced Anna as their coach.

"Hi, everyone. I'm Anna and I will be the coach and process expert for the team. I am not a corrugated expert, although I do understand it and the market. My role is to help you through the category management process as efficiently and effectively as possible. You've all received a request from me to complete the MBTI and TKI instruments. We'll use this information in the team. It is confidential, and you do not need to share your results. I will not share your results with anyone but you. I think I have everyone but one or two and will send a reminder note if I'm missing your information."

"We're planning to have a group dinner Tuesday and Wednesday nights," Sean said. "A couple of you are arriving late on Monday and will likely be tired. I think a few are leaving Thursday evening.

Everyone is scheduled to be at the full meeting, which will run eight thirty to five each day."

Marek interrupted Sean. "I will not be at the meeting. I will join virtually in the morning. I am unable to travel then."

Sean replied, "I'm sorry to hear that. Do you need the sponsor to talk with your management?"

"No, that will not be necessary," Marek remarked in a deadpan reply.

"Okay, I'll call you separately," Sean said. "All of you should have the detailed agenda. Rather than trying to coordinate cars and rides to and from the airport, I'll leave it to you. Some have rented cars and others have indicated they'll taxi or Uber to the hotel. We will coordinate rides for the team dinners. Please plan to meet in the hotel lobby at seven thirty a.m. on Tuesday so we can carpool to the facility and check through security. Lastly, the meeting will be business casual, but everyone will need closed toe shoes for the factory tour. Ear plugs and protective eyewear will be provided, but bring your badges with you."

"Oh, one more thing," Sean added. "We need to add weekly progress review and update calls to our schedules. I anticipate these will be one to two hours a week. Please send me your preferred timing, and we'll review the input and finalize the schedule at the face-to-face meeting."

Sean called Anna as soon as the team call concluded.

"What was that about with Marek?" Anna asked.

"I have no idea," Sean replied. "Marek is a packaging engineer with the consumer electronics business and is based in Poland." He continued, "I've never met him but was told he'd be a key expert to have on the team."

"I recommend you call him and listen to what he has to say," she remarked. "Maybe he has a personal constraint, but it didn't sound like that. Let me know what you hear."

"Will do, thanks."

Sean called Marek, who answered immediately, "Hello, Sean, how can I help you?"

He was not a listening expert but tried his best to open the conversation non-confrontationally. "Hi, Marek, I'm following up on the team call. Harry in Singapore recommended you to Margot for this team. It's important for all of us to be at the meeting. How can I help?"

Marek replied, "I heard Harry recommended me, but the consumer electronics business does not need any help with corrugated. Our SKUs are already rationalized, and our drawings are current. We already work with the best suppliers. The team is a waste of my time."

Anna, Rich, and Margot had not mentioned this possible response in the training. Sean was caught flatfooted.

After a brief pause Sean replied, "I'm glad to hear the consumer electronics business is so advanced. Most of our other businesses are not as advanced. You'll be a valuable member of the team to help move the company forward."

"I work for the consumer electronics business. I cannot help if the other businesses are mismanaged," Marek stated.

Sean was trying to manage his emotions and replied, "I did not say that the other businesses are mismanaging corrugated."

"You did not need to say it. If they don't have current drawings and their SKUs are out of control, you directly implied it."

Sean could sense he was getting nowhere and decided to pause the conversation before the relationship with Marek became irretrievable.

He started, "I think I understand where you're coming from and appreciate that you will join the meeting virtually."

"You're welcome," Marek replied before disconnecting from the call.

Sean made notes of the conversation, and this helped him document how one-sided the call had been. It reminded him of arguments with his ex-wife, and he knew that was not a good precedent. Once his notes were complete, he called Anna and recounted the entire conversation.

Anna thought for a moment. "He sounds like a real engineer. Everything he said is factually correct. From his perspective, he is completely justified in his approach and believes it is the right response for his business."

"So, what do we do about Marek's team membership?" Sean asked.

Anna replied, "I think you should talk with Frank first and bring him up to speed. Then you need to inform both Margot and Genevieve. They will have ideas and suggestions and, most importantly, they cannot be uninformed. I recommend sending a note to Margot and Genevieve to schedule a meeting."

"Okay, I think Frank is still in the office. I'll go talk to him and send a note to Margot and Genevieve. Do you want to be included?"

"Yes, I'll join if I can. Sean, resistance to change is to be expected. You are not just leading a category team, but you are the salesperson for change. Your number one competitor is the status quo. In your case, it happens to be named Marek. Stay inquisitive—your task is to figure out why he's resisting change without alienating him."

"Thanks, Anna. That might be easier said than done," he replied.

He walked to Frank's office, but Frank must have left while Sean was talking to Anna. He sent a quick note to Frank, Margot, and Genevieve summarizing the situation and requesting a virtual meeting. He'd have to think about this "salesperson for change" thing. He was not sure he'd signed up for that role.

JANUARY 23RD

Sean arrived early and saw replies from Margot, Genevieve, Frank, and Anna. All would be available 11 to 11:30 a.m. He quickly sent the virtual meeting invite and walked to Frank's office.

Margot was sitting in the visitor chair talking with Frank, and Frank motioned for Sean to join them.

"We're just talking about you." Frank smiled. "It seems like you're the first one to kick the hornet's nest."

"I didn't even know there was a hornet's nest," Sean said, sitting down.

Margot stated, "I've had an easy assimilation to-date. Maybe too easy. I don't know that Marek's reaction is partly based on my arrival, but it is all likely linked. You learned about change management in the training, the theory anyways. Now you're about to learn the reality. What you need to know is that we're going to support you. Frank, do you know Marek?"

Frank replied, "I don't know him. We never had cause to work with him in the past."

"Okay, I'll call Harry. He recommended him," Margot informed. "Sean, please come by my office later this morning when you have a few minutes," and she walked out of Frank's office.

Frank looked at Sean and said, "You wanted to present early at the training, and your team is the first to get started. You've made yourself the lightning rod for the launch of category management.

That's not necessarily a bad thing, but don't be surprised when you uncover issues. My advice is to keep working on your meeting plans, and we'll pick up the conversation at eleven."

"Okay, see you at eleven," Sean replied as he rose to leave Frank's office.

Frank, Margot, and Sean convened in the conference room, and Genevieve and Anna joined virtually and were displayed on the large screen.

Margot opened the meeting, "thank you all for joining. I know this is Sean's meeting, but it is a result of me kicking off category management. We need to help Sean through this. Sean, please update us on the situation."

Sean reviewed the team conversation and the one-on-one call he had with Marek. It was a quick but detailed review.

Genevieve said, "That sounds pretty uncomfortable, Sean."

"Yes, it was," Sean replied.

Margot added, "I called Harry, who recommended Marek, and we talked this morning. I shared what Marek said, and Harry laughed and said that technically, almost all of what Marek said is correct. He added that Marek is a very gifted engineer. He called him 'an engineer's engineer.' He also said that Marek can be abrupt interpersonally but never does it intentionally. He said he'd talk with Marek about attending the next team meeting."

Genevieve asked, "Will it be okay if Marek joins the first meeting virtually and then attends the second meeting?"

Anna chimed in, "It is not ideal, but we can make it work. The team dynamics will be affected until he is accepted by the other team members."

Margot asked Sean, "Did you embarrass Marek or accuse him of anything during the team call?"

"No, of course not," Sean replied immediately. "I was caught off-guard and did not shoot from the hip."

Genevieve laughed, "I love these American expressions. Most of the Americans I know would have called him an asshole."

Sean blushed. "I may have thought that, but I did not say it."

Genevieve laughed. "Don't worry about it. I'll send him an email and copy you that, while he's too busy to attend the kick-off meeting, I appreciate his efforts to attend the second meeting. I'll copy all of you and Harry. Even engineers will get that message."

"Thank you, Genevieve," Margot said. "That sounds like a great approach. Anything else for us to discuss, Sean?"

Sean replied, "No, that's enough for today. Thank you all for your help."

The call ended, and Sean followed Frank back to his office.

"Still checking the stock price?" Sean asked.

Frank sat down before he spoke. "Every morning. It doesn't mean I'm leaving right away, but it's nice to know I have options. I did not expect this issue, but we never did anything like category management across the company. You know, we did sourcing events and managed a few suppliers. Who knows what we'll uncover now. All of our jobs are different now as a result of category management. You keep crawling through the mine field and locate the mines for us to diffuse."

"Thanks, that's very reassuring," Sean said as he walked out of Frank's office.

Late that afternoon, Sean knocked on Margot's doorframe and she motioned for him to come in and sit across the desk.

"Well, Sean, you've had a full day of category management. What do you think so far?" Margot asked.

Sean replied, "It's very different than what I was doing before category management. I feel pretty awkward but appreciate Anna's support. And Genevieve's. Oh, and you and Frank."

"You don't need to thank us for support, Sean," Margot remarked. "That is the role of leadership. I wanted you to come by to follow-up on our conversations and the training. How do you feel about the Premier Packaging extension knowing what you know now?"

Sean blushed deeply. "I feel stupid. I feel like I got played. I went long when I should've gone short; I accepted their plans instead of using market specifications or our own drawings, and I'm paying way too much even with the twenty percent discount we agreed."

"Congratulations, Sean—that's great! Those are the insights you needed to realize. Now what?" Margot asked.

"I'm going to use it as an example to share with my team at the kick-off," Sean answered. "I know they're wondering what will be different and this is a great example."

'Thank you, Sean." Margot smiled. "Stay with it and stay open to new learnings."

Sean left her office with a smile—a first.

Margot followed Sean out, saying to Rita, "Please setup a meeting as soon as possible with Shelly, Tanya, Frank, and you. We'll need an hour. The topic is supplier forum."

"Okay," Rita replied, "I'll let you know what I can do."

About fifteen minutes later, Rita stuck her head into Margot's office. "I scheduled the supplier forum meeting for three p.m. today and booked the conference room."

"Thanks, Rita, I'll need you to help with notes and planning suggestions during the meeting," Margot said.

That afternoon they assembled in the procurement conference room. Margot posted a simple agenda listing the topics of supplier forum planning, stakeholders to include, stakeholder prep, suppliers to include, supplier prep, and forum follow-up. It was a lot to include in a one-hour meeting, particularly when Tanya and Frank did not know what she expected. Only Shelly had an inkling of what was to come.

Margot described the flow of a typical supplier forum to the group and Frank and Tanya listened attentively; it was new to them. She continued, "Many companies use these events as glorified supplier shakedowns, 'a give me the money or else' message. I don't like threats and we're not doing that. Our dialogue with the suppliers at the forum is important, but the most impactful element of the forum will be our preparation of the stakeholders for their role. In the process of helping them draft their speeches, we will teach them about the new role of procurement. Let's work through the agenda topics."

They agreed to focus on the categories in Wave One, which helped them focus and narrow the event. After talking about a range of date options, Rita looked at the executives' schedules and found a window where a number of them, including Leslie, seemed to be available.

"Please send a note to Lillian and the other admins and ask them to block that entire day," Margot requested. "Copy Matt, as I already alerted him that this was in the works, and he can then head off any questions. What about a large event room, Rita?"

"The auditorium is available then," Rita informed, looking up from the meeting room scheduling portal.

"Good, please book the room for that day. We'll need access to setup and prepare in the morning," Margot said.

"What are we going to say to the suppliers?" Tanya asked.

Shelly stood up and went to the flip chart, suggesting, "Let's brainstorm the key elements, and then I can work with the communications department to flesh it out and develop the slides."

The group agreed on the overall list of topics and speakers:

- Frontier International Group – current performance and future business prospects – Leslie and Matt. Message goal – confirm Frontier International Group as an extremely desirable customer.
- New product and innovation plans – healthcare and industrial – Erica and Bob. Message goal – steady stream of new products coming; the future is bright.
- AI implementation planning – IT – Larry. Message goal – Frontier International Group is embracing the new technology and will include suppliers in the planning process.
- Procurement 2030 – Margot. Message goal – procurement is transforming, including the use of category management.

Frontier International Group procurement is committed to becoming a best-in-class customer and all that this entails.

- Question and answer panel session with the executives – Jean to facilitate.

"Let's hold the topics there for now," Margot stated. "I expect that Matt, Leslie, and the ELT may want to add a topic or two, and we have less than a day of total time for the event. Rita, please setup weekly recurring meetings between now and the event. Who wants to talk with which executives to help them prepare? I recommend we work in pairs to both make it less intimidating for us and to build our readiness. I'll take Leslie and Matt. Who wants to work with me? Tanya, what do you think?"

"Sure," Tanya stammered. "I've not yet met either of them."

"Perfect, you'll need to have an excellent rapport with both of them by the time we try to address the consulting and auditing categories," Margot.

"I'd like to work with Erica and Bob," Frank piped up. "I've met Erica but don't really know her. This will help."

"I'll work with Frank and Erica," Shelly added.

"I'd like to take the lead with Larry," Shelly said. "I'll need to work very closely with him on AI in procurement, and this is an opportunity to build rapport."

"I'll work with you and Larry," Tanya remarked. "My team works with him now, and we need to evolve the working relationship."

"All of you will work with me." Margot smiled. "I will draft some materials and route them around for your review. Think of it as a 'share-and-build' approach and feel free to provide input. I will also reach out to Jean for the Q&A session and will include whoever is available."

"Can I join that one?" Rita asked quietly. "I've met her and think I'll have a good overall feel for the event, based on my role, and could provide that context to her."

"That's an excellent suggestion, thanks Rita," Margot said.

JANUARY 29TH

Margot and the other procurement leaders were in the reception area when Mary walked in from the car park.

"Welcome to Copenhagen!" Mary exclaimed. "I'm delighted you're here and appreciate you making the journey. I'm not able to travel now," she informed, pointing to her prodigious baby bump.

"You are positively radiant and look great!" exclaimed Margot. "I really appreciate you hosting this meeting. It's my first time to Copenhagen. Selfishly, I wish I'd had a chance to see the Christmas markets, but I am going to stay and see Kronborg Castle—aka Hamlet's Castle."

"That's a great idea," Mary remarked. "It is a beautiful setting on the water, but it will be cold, so bundle up." Mary motioned to the broader group, "Let's head to the meeting room."

Once they settled in the meeting room and picked up coffee and tea, Mary welcomed the group. "On behalf of the medical business leadership team, welcome to Copenhagen. We're delighted to have you here. I expect most members of the leadership team will stop by during your visit and say hello. I've asked those that are available to join us for dinner tomorrow night."

Mary continued, "I'd like to introduce Julian. Julian leads our R&D procurement team and will fill in for me on this team once the baby arrives."

All nodded to Julian, who said, "Good morning and welcome to our beautiful city. Let me know if I can help you with anything."

"Thank you for hosting us, Mary." Margot smiled. "This is an exciting project, and I'm glad you're able to participate. Many of you don't know Alec. He is a consultant, and his team is supporting our category management efforts and agreed to help with this project. He'll keep us on process, and that will enable me to focus on the content." Margot thought she noticed that Julian was missing a thumb but decided this was neither the time nor the place to ask about it.

"In addition to Alec, Rita, my assistant, is with us on this trip, and she will help us with the documentation and coordination details and, I'm sure, add to the content as well."

Rita nodded to the group and said, "Good morning, thank you for including me in this meeting."

"Also joining me here is Willie, from IT. Willie works for the CIO, Larry, and is supporting the supply chain teams that are looking at AI."

"Good morning, and thanks for including me. You're the first team out of the blocks, and I appreciate your enthusiasm," Willie returned.

"Good morning," Alec added, "it's my first time in Copenhagen, and this is a once-in-a-career project. I've worked with Margot in the past and am otherwise new to supporting Frontier. Let's begin with introductions and expectation setting."

The group shared their backgrounds and current roles and expectations for the team. It was the first time for most of them to meet Margot and Shelly in person as well as Alec. Due to Mary's warm welcome, everyone seemed open and receptive to the discussion.

"It was only a couple of weeks ago that Matt shared this task with me and we started planning this meeting," Margot started. "This is a unique effort in that it has the likelihood of being transformative and disruptive to the workplace, yet Leslie and the ELT are driving transparency. It reinforces my decision to join the company. This will be a process of exploration in an area where the picture is very incomplete. We will all need to be tolerant of the gray tones; procurement is often quite black and white. I asked Alec to support us because we can use many of the core category management tools. At its core, category management is a strategy development and change-management process with the addition of a few procurement tools. I think it is vital for us to demonstrate to our teams that we know and can use the process and can modulate the application to fit the circumstances."

"Margot sent the detailed agenda," Alec chipped in, "and it is built on the topics you discussed a couple of weeks ago. Did everyone complete the pre-reading?"

Laughter filled the room, and Phil remarked, "Yes, over Christmas and New Year, I told my family to leave me alone so I could read the stack of pre-reading." More laughter. "I say that facetiously; the reading that I've done is great, but it will take a couple more weeks until I'm caught up."

"I think that's a common sentiment," Harry added. "Even without your Christmas holiday and the long flights from Singapore, I still have more to read."

"That brings us into the heart of strategy development," Alec said. "It is typically impossible to know everything about an area or a topic, but the key is to know enough to make thoughtful decisions and to develop a strategy that is both robust and open to evolution as more is learned and experiences are gained. I encourage you to keep reading."

"That is good advice, Alec," Margot commended. "We all have a lot to learn and are on this learning journey together. The entire company is on this journey, and we will all be sharing insights. It is important that we stay on the front foot here; we have a critical role to play."

Alec continued, "Agreed, let's review the key tasks for our two days here." He shared the core topics:

- Introductions, charter review, and macro plan discussion.
- Procurement AI capability analysis—current and projected.
- AI best practice site visit planning.
- Information-gathering assignments.

"I think it will be most helpful if we work from a common, end-to-end process flow that includes the key procurement-related and responsible processes. I pulled this process flow diagram together, and Rita printed it out in poster form," Alec said. He and Rita stood up and posted a ten-foot-long chart depicting the order-to-payment process with the sub-processes of sourcing, category management, and supplier management depicted.

"By itself, that chart is a great outcome for this meeting," Mary remarked. "Thanks for pulling this together."

"You're welcome," Alec said. "I will not claim that it is perfect, but it is easier and faster for a group to edit an input than it is to start with a blank sheet of paper."

Alec nodded to Willie, who continued, "As you know, there is no one-solution AI overlay for the entire process. There are several discrete approaches designed for pieces of the process. What you may also have noticed is that AI is certainly all the rage now. Everyone claims to have an AI-enabled solution, but that is a vague and confusing term. I want to start with a few common definitions so we're all using a common nomenclature. My peers will be doing the same work with all the other functions and businesses, and this will be the Frontier International Group way of discussing this topic."

Willie reviewed the topics of machine learning, large language models, and generative AI. He then posted on the flow chart some prepared sticky notes listing the various product and service solutions and where they fit in the end-to-end process. He added, "You'll notice that many of these solutions are clustered around tasks that are repetitive. This is the historical focus of the machine learning and large language approaches. The new entrant on the scene is generative AI. It, too, can be used in the repetitive areas, but what is different about it is the apparent ability to work in the creative areas."

"What do you mean by 'apparent,'" Mary asked.

"This is new technology," Willie answered. "It is being tried in new areas as we sit here. The technology is also evolving rapidly in real time. In some instances, it is working out well, and in others, the results are disappointing. A key to remember here: the rate of change in AI will never be as slow as it is now."

"It seems pretty fast now," Phil stated.

"I agree." Margot nodded her head. "Like a freight train running with huge momentum."

"That is pretty close to the way my boss explained it to the ELT," Willie observed. "This topic is rapidly moving, and the key is to figure out both where it is going, and where, when, and how we want to be part of the journey."

He continued, "The expectation is that the discrete solutions on this chart will continue, will improve, and will extend bit by bit to become larger, more complete solutions. The unknown is how far and fast generative AI will be embraced."

"Can I share some thoughts on your process flow?" Margot asked.

"Certainly," Willie replied, and he took a seat as Margot positioned a flip chart near the process flow.

"I want to take a look at the sourcing, category management, and supplier management processes in particular," Margot began. "As part of the category management process, we introduce the topic of category segmentation and use four levels: strategic, key, approved, and base. This helps focus our strategy development efforts and then informs and guides our ongoing supplier management approaches. The future of the company is built around the strategic and key levels. Substantive risk is often associated with the key level, at least until mitigation strategies are developed and implemented, and less resource is required for the approved and base levels. My hypothesis is that the approved and base levels are susceptible or amenable to the application of AI. I think that, in the future, AI could do the sourcing, negotiation, and receipt activities for the approved and base categories."

Alec noted the hypothesis on a flip chart labeled "Insights & Hypotheses," and the group reflected on Margot's inputs.

Tanya stated, "Most of my indirect categories are segmented at the base level, with just a few at approved and a tiny number above that. Are you saying that most of the indirect categories can be automated?"

"I'm not sure," Margot said, "because, as Willie said, this whole generative AI area is still evolving and is untested. I will say that, based on what I've read, it seems possible. In fact, I think that in three to five years, the approved and base categories will be driven by AI with human oversight."

Alec made additional notes on the flip chart.

"Wow, that's huge," Harry added. "Over fifty percent of our people are working on those categories in one way or another."

"I know, I've been doing the math as well," Margot said. "Willie, what do you think of my timing estimate?"

"It's impossible to be precise, but I think you are directionally correct. It could be three to five years, or it could be five to seven. I don't think it's farther away than that," Willie replied.

He continued, "Some companies are using generative AI as a de facto search engine now. It is demonstrating an incredible ability to search, sift, and summarize vast amounts of information. This is good and bad. The good is that for companies with a range of systems and databases, it enables a relatively seamless and speedy development of actionable information. The bad is that it will search, pardon the anthropomorphic term, wherever it is allowed. If it is allowed, it will search the internet; if it is blocked by firewalls, it will search within the firewalls."

"For our purposes," Shelly said, "when a category team is doing research on Frontier spend, it could search within the company, and when the category team is doing supply market and supplier research, it could search broadly on the internet."

"That's a great summary," Willie remarked, "but if you don't have the firewalls established, it will search the web for Frontier spend as well."

"How is that a problem?" Frank asked.

"In many areas, it will not be a problem," Margot assured. "But couldn't a competitor search the internet and ask the generative AI to describe Frontier's supplier and supply market searching patterns?"

"It could, and that is one of the areas where we as a company need to be careful," Willie chimed in.

"I have suppliers who are very strategic to the healthcare business," Julian said, "and we are jointly creating new IP. They are real extensions of our R&D capacity. What about their searches and use of generative AI?"

"Without some form of safeguards, that IP could be divulged inadvertently," Willie replied.

Alec was busy at the flip chart, capturing additional insights as the group reflected on the discussion.

"It's a Pandora's Box," Frank observed. "But it's impossible to ignore it, so we need to move forward."

"That's exactly right," Willie agreed, "and other businesses and functions will be identifying and capturing insights as well. These insights are being collected centrally by IT and shared with the ELT. They will be developing some overall AI guidance in parallel with the work of each function and business."

"What about the people?" Rita asked. "What will happen to the people in those jobs?"

"That is the million-dollar question," Margot piped up. "I do think all those jobs will be impacted by AI. In fact, I think all our jobs will be impacted by AI. But I think we need to distinguish between being impacted and being eliminated. The categories that are approved and base will be heavily impacted, and I suspect about eighty percent of those roles will be eliminated over time. The remaining twenty percent will conduct oversight and exception management. That is a lot of jobs eliminated across our function. Everyone is going to have to learn how to operate AI safely to avoid the risks Willie is highlighting and how to exploit the capabilities, particularly as new ones emerge."

"Already this morning, we're into the hard work of trying to foresee the future and plan for the impacts in a space that is unclear and ever changing. We are not running from the implications, and that is great. If we identify the potential changes, we can plan for them in a thoughtful way that minimizes unnecessary disruptions to our employee base. We cannot stop AI. These changes will come and it our job to ensure they are enacted in the best, most humane way possible."

"One of my roles and my peers in IT who are supporting the other functions is to share the people implications with the HR function," Willie started again. "We acknowledge that this is not just a technology discussion. HR doesn't have the bandwidth to support these meetings so we're sharing the workload."

"I'm just thinking about the approved categories and automation," Frank added. "If we automate the sourcing, supplier selection, negotiation, and receipt of direct goods, we could, potentially, not know where they were sourced from ahead of time. We would, of course, set the business requirements including the basic specifications, but then the AI would perform the sourcing. We would need to carefully set the business requirements to address any concerns or legal limitations around country of origin or political concerns. Worst case, if we did not limit the sourcing, the AI could find a low-cost supplier in North Korea for basic production material."

"Discussing, agreeing, and setting the business requirements is a core element of category management, but this raises new elements that might have been assumed but now need to be expressly set," Shelly commented.

Alec noted these additional insights.

"I know we are focused now on the European and emerging US regulations around carbon footprint," Margot said. "There seems to be the potential to use AI to secure some of this information from our tier-one suppliers. What do you think, Willie?"

"Generative AI will have the ability to find, assess, and assemble any information that is available," Willie replied. "The issues will be: Is the information available? Is the information complete and accurate? Is any of the information confidential or proprietary to the supplier or to us? The old expression of 'garbage in; garbage out' will apply to AI as much as it does to any IT system."

Margot added, "I anticipated a bit of where this discussion could go and asked Alec's associate, Anna, to conduct an experiment. As part of training and deploying category management, there are coaching questions for a procurement leader to ask the category manager. Anna is asking the generative AI platforms a subset of the questions in the context of corrugated, one of the teams she is supporting. These outputs will be shared with us so that we can see what is currently possible."

Alec noted the time and said, "Let's take our lunch break. We're making huge progress. After lunch, let's build on the data-collection process."

The group sat together at lunch, eagerly eating their food. There was a notable lull in the conversation until Erica, the healthcare business president, came over.

Margot stood up to greet her, "Hi, Erica, it's nice to see you again."

"Welcome to Copenhagen and the healthcare business." Erica smiled. "It's nice to see you and your team. Mary invited us to join you and your team for dinner tomorrow night, and most of my team will be there. How is your meeting going so far?"

"We're making good progress, I think, but it is a huge topic," Margot informed.

"That is an understatement!" Erica exclaimed. "We're reviewing our internal approaches and considering our customer-facing elements. I recommend that you do the same thing. I won't keep you; enjoy your lunch, and I look forward to hearing about your progress tomorrow night."

Erica walked out of the cafeteria with her tray, while Margot sat down and leaned over to Alec. "Her idea of doing a review from the customer-facing angle is right. We need to add that after lunch."

"I'll head back a few minutes early and make sure we're ready to do that," he confirmed.

"Thanks," she replied, leaning in closer to hear what Rita was saying.

"My kids are in high school now—the levels in school before college or university—and I'm worried about how AI will affect them," Rita said.

Phil shared, "my kids are already graduated and working, and I'm worried about them, too. There are going to be so many changes, and it's clear there will be many workers affected."

Willie looked thoughtfully at them before adding, "I understand and appreciate your concerns. Whenever there are disruptive technologies, there are periods of uncertainty. Computers have been disrupting workplaces since they were invented. Over the holidays, my family watched *A Christmas Carol*, and if you look at the work of Bob Cratchit, hand copying numbers in a ledger, you know, those tasks are gone. The question—and I think it's what you're both thinking about—is, does he get a better job, or is he unemployed? The movie ends before we can know."

"Right, that is my concern. I need to know which jobs will be most affected so I can steer my kids away from them," Rita remarked.

"I received some valuable advice a long time ago from an HR leader," Margot added. "He said that we should think less about jobs and more about skills. He said that the specific jobs will change over time and that it was much more useful for people to focus on the skills they have, the skills they need, and to look at roles that fit their skills."

"A very wide range of roles will be impacted to varying degrees," Willie said. "We talked in the room about transactional and repetitive roles. I think they will be largely eliminated. We mentioned negotiations, and that includes not just procurement but the legal field. It is expected that basic legal negotiations and contracting will be automated. There are other, repetitive but manual tasks, that will be much less affected. We'll still need actual plumbers, carpenters, and electricians. What we've not yet talked about, but likely will this afternoon or tomorrow, is that everyone will need some level of training on how to engage with and assess the results from generative AI. This will be a monumental upskilling of the workforce." He turned to Rita, "and your kids should start on this sooner rather than later; kids pick this up so much easier than adults."

Harry turned to Mary and asked, "A change of topic; on the plane I read about a ski slope in downtown Copenhagen. Everything seems so flat. Is that true?"

"Yes," she smiled. "The roof of the incinerator is very tall and steep and is used as a ski slope."

"How is that possible? Isn't it too hot?" Phil asked.

"It's super insulated," she replied. "We are very proud of our incinerator. It's the only one like it in the world."

"That is true," Shelly chimed in. "Nobody else in the world is proud of their incinerator."

Everyone laughed and appreciated the turn toward lightheartedness.

"Copenhagen is a net importer of garbage. It is shipped in and burned here for heat and power," Mary said. "The process is extremely clean due to the temperatures and technologies. Rather than make it an eyesore, the goal was to make it an attraction."

"That's a great use of creative thinking," Alec added. "Will we be near it tonight or tomorrow night?"

"Our dinner tonight is not too far away, and I can ask the drivers to go by it on the way," Mary said.

"Thanks," Alec said. He stood up and said, "I'm going to head back to the room to prep for the afternoon. I'll see you all back in fifteen minutes," and he headed out of the cafeteria.

As the group reentered the meeting room, they noticed that Alec had added a couple of flip charts around the process flow. Alec observed, "Based on Erica's comments, Margot asked that we consider the customer perspectives for procurement. I've added places for us to think about our internal customers, our supplier customers, and our external customers. Let's start with our internal customers."

"Let's be honest with each other, in the current Amazon world, everyone thinks they're an excellent, empowered buyer," Margot added. "We need to be clear about our value proposition, and it needs to be compelling. I think we have a strong value proposition in the strategic and key categories from a strategy development, sourcing, and supplier management perspective. I think the value proposition will be much less compelling in the approved and base categories. It is possible to foresee that internal stakeholders or, more likely, the systems they use, will directly reach into a procurement AI solution and completely source the requirements on an automated basis."

"That's not too different from our current use of catalogs," Tanya remarked. "We do the work in the background, and the stakeholder directly engages the catalogs, and the rest is automated. What you're saying, though, is that it will expand across several direct categories."

"That's my expectation," Margot stated. "As we talked about in the morning, we'll need to set the business requirements very carefully and exercise some oversight, but I expect much of the workload to go away. It doesn't seem to affect us because I've not heard about offshoring or outsourcing at Frontier International Group, but many companies moved these categories to lower cost areas. There is nothing lower cost than automation and I expect these lower cost areas like Central America, India, and Eastern Europe to lose many jobs. This will be a global disruption."

"Continue with your thoughts on internal customers. What about the key and strategic categories and associated suppliers?" Alec asked.

"We cannot turn these areas over to AI," Harry answered.

"I agree," Mary stated. "In the strategic areas, I am working directly with Erica and her team. These are the discussions that are going to shape the future of the business. They absolutely require our involvement."

"That's right," Phil said. "And while I don't have the same strategic categories as Mary and Harry, I am involved in similar conversations with the industrial leadership team. The suppliers who are then part of the solutions developed cannot be managed by AI. These are often delicate and nuanced relationships; they are highly personal."

"These are great distinctions to document and then address through the system design and change management aspects," Willie remarked. He continued and indicated to Alec, "Let's mark on the flowchart the respective flows of information to and from internal stakeholders to the process. These information flows can happen at any time in the process; it's very dynamic."

"We can then add the information flows to and from the suppliers," Shelly piped up. "I think we need to call out proprietary or confidential information that is going outside the company. Willie mentioned that some companies are setting up AI within firewalls for internal use, and others are using the public platforms. We need to be clear about what data elements must stay inside the firewalls and what is okay to be in the public domain. We thought there was free flow of information on the internet, but it sounds like the flow will accelerate, and the key difference between now and the blizzard of information will be the laser-like focus that AI can bring to the blizzard. Somebody keen to know about our business could, if the information is in a public AI, know more about our business than is desirable."

"All of that is true and well said," Willie replied. "This is shaping up to be one of the larger issues with AI. If we're not careful, we'll lose control of our most important information."

"Anything else from the supplier perspective?" Alec asked.

Phil added, "I am processing Margot's comments on the distinctions between strategic, key, approved, and base categories, and I think I agree with her prognosis. What I'm struggling with is where we have suppliers that are supplying multiple categories at different levels. On the higher level, we'll keep them close and deal with them personally, as we do now, and on the lower level, we'll automate the relationship. This feels odd and I'm not sure how it will play out."

"I think that will be a common scenario now," Margot suggested. "Until our category strategies address the single-sourcing that is present, there will be many categories that are key now. In the future, they will likely be approved. This will address some of that. There will be others, like you said, that will be mixed. This is where the GPLT will need to step in and look across categories and set the parameters for what AI will and will not do."

Alec made notations about potential for cross-category distinctions on the supplier aspect of the flowchart.

"What were you thinking when you listed external stakeholders?" Harry asked.

"That's a good question and an excellent segue," Alec replied. "In the strategy development aspects of category management, we tend to focus on the internal stakeholders and suppliers. During implementation we add external stakeholders. These include the regulatory agencies, any other governmental or non-governmental agencies, the actual neighbors of the sites, et cetera," said Alec. "We include a bit of their input during the PESTLE analysis, but in the implementation, it needs to be more express and detailed. Imagine the strategy is to insource and build a new factory or an addition to a current factory. A few external stakeholders will be interested and need to be managed. Conversely, if a decision is reached to outsource work to a supplier, that must be managed as well."

"If you think about the external reporting on carbon and human slavery," Margot added, "that's a good place to start. The information goes to the respective agency but is also a potential news story."

"We use specialist firms to collect some of this information about our tier-one suppliers," Phil said. "Do you think we'll be able to use AI to extend this to the tier-two-and-beyond suppliers?"

"It goes back to whether the information is available," Willie commented. "If the suppliers collect the information and then share it publicly or through a third-party, then AI should be able to access it. If the information is never developed it will still not be available."

"I bet that the larger ERP providers and the AI leaders will start aggregating the discrete solutions we're discussing into an end-to-end solution," Margot remarked.

"We all acknowledge how difficult it is to change an ERP," Shelly observed. "Imagine if the solution is bigger than an ERP—nobody would ever change providers."

Willie nodded, stating, "The big AI creators are spending tens of billions of dollars to develop and improve the software and establish the computing infrastructure. The scale of the investment is on a par with the biggest offshore oil platform. The only investments that are bigger are made by governments."

"Back to the external stakeholder conversation," Alec said. "What are your thoughts?"

"The themes are repeating," Mary informed, "of controlling and preventing confidential information flows to the public AI and the ever-present concern about 'garbage in' data. I think what will be different is the comparative ease with which anyone can ask probing and detailed questions. If the information is available, they will instantly receive a comprehensive report whether the information contained is correct or not."

"I do think the adoption rates will vary broadly," Phil said. "What do you think, Willie?"

"You're right," Willie said. "Just as some of you are 'early adopters' of leading-edge technology, others are 'fast followers' or even a bit later for some technologies. The same thing will be true for AI, for us, for our customers, our suppliers, and the external stakeholders. We need to tailor our efforts to make sure we are prepared for the actions and questions with the 'early adopters.'"

Alec added the insights from Willie's comments to the running list. Rita asked, "What if we're wrong? What if AI turns out to be interesting but not valuable? Do you all remember the Y2K craze? Could this be the same thing?"

The room was silent for a minute as everyone reflected on Rita's question. Margot was privately glad she'd brought Rita to the meeting and proud of her for asking a probing, potentially controversial question.

"Rita, I think that's a great question," Alec spoke up. "We always run the risk of group think in these meetings, and it's really important to step back and check our assumptions."

"I agree with Alec," Willie added. "That's an interesting question that Rita is raising. There are a couple of major AI systems available for use. They are being tested by the various users. So far, they seem to be aligning users based on perceived alignment with political and ideological viewpoints. There are documented cases where a major system will develop answers that are unproven but that match a prevailing viewpoint. These are real watchouts. The systems are so large and complex, and the actual coding is secret, that it takes continuous testing and surveillance to find these hidden biases. If the results continue to reflect ideological viewpoints, I expect the adoption to slow and to align with businesses, governments, and other organizations that share these views. If the results are more objective and broad-based, the adoption is likely to be broad-based as well. This is an area that IT is watching carefully."

"To build on Willie's comments, as I mentioned this morning," Margot joined in. "Anna is going to test all the available AI systems through the category management process. We'll have side-by-side results available and can compare the results. This will start at the team's kick-off meeting in two weeks. As those results are available, I will share them with you."

"Follow the money, I say," Phil said. "These companies are spending too much money for this not to go somewhere. I think Rita's question is excellent, and it may turn out that it takes five to seven or eight to ten years, but I don't expect AI to stop."

Alec captured the discussion insights and added, "We've covered a lot of ground today, and it looks like time zones are catching up with everyone. Let's cover our forward meeting planning and then break for dinner."

"Thank you," Harry yawned. "It's getting late for me, and I did not sleep on the flights. I'll need a few minutes at the hotel to rally before dinner."

They discussed the flow of meetings and Mary's inability to travel to future sessions.

"I will join virtually when possible and catch up with Julian if I miss any sessions," Mary said. "This is too interesting and important for me to disconnect, but I suspect I'll be a bit busy."

"You'll be more than busy," Rita laughed. "But it will be wonderful."

They agreed to hold the next meeting in California near the current AI vendors. Tanya would act as the host and arrange the key supplier meetings. It was typical practice for Frontier teams to meet at company facilities like they were doing in Copenhagen, but it was not a hard and fast rule.

"Before we completely lose steam for the day," Margot piped up. "I'd like to discuss our stakeholder engagement plans. They will start as soon as we walk out of this room and return calls and emails. We talked this morning about topics that could be very disruptive, and I want us to be transparent yet sensitive. Alec, let's talk about the topics to discuss with stakeholders and then the groups of stakeholders. Once we have a view of those two, we can shape how to discuss the topics."

Alec moved to the flip chart. He asked, "What are the topics so far?"

The group rapidly chimed in, speaking over each other a bit and challenging him to write quickly:

- Rapid evolution of AI
- Lots of potential impacts
- Focus on repetitive and transactional tasks.
- Also impacts to negotiation
- Testing different systems
- Fit with the overall technology strategy.
- Impacts to the customer interface
- Information security and loss of IP

"Excellent list; let's move to the stakeholders by group or role," said Alec and he moved to the second flip chart.

- Site buyers
- Procurement managers
- Category managers
- Suppliers
- Regulatory agencies
- Senior leaders
- All stakeholders

Margot complimented, "This is a great start. I want to frame the next step a bit. If we don't know how, where, and the extent of AI in our processes, then we should not be asking others for where we should use AI. How could they know? What would we do with their input? Instead, I recommend that we start with the senior leaders and then more broadly with stakeholders and use this as an opportunity to solicit feedback on their interactions and satisfaction with procurement. We should do the same thing with suppliers."

"That's an interesting idea," Frank remarked. "We've never done anything like that."

"We did something similar in a previous company," Harry said. "If we structure it correctly, we'll both deepen our relationship and gather insights we might otherwise never get."

"Okay, let's come back to designing this process later and continue with other topics and stakeholder groups," Alec stated.

"What are we going to say to the buyers, procurement managers, and category managers?" Tanya asked.

The group was quiet for a moment and reflected on the question because it was the dead moose on the table; these were likely to be the most affected cohorts.

"They should work on their CVs and keep them current," Phil mused to a round of nervous laughter. "No, listen to me a minute as the older guy in the room who will be affected, too. I liked what Margot said about people keeping their skills up and looking for roles that are a fit with their current and desired skills. I suggest we use that theme. Some of our people will embrace AI, take advantage of training we provide, and move to new roles, either inside or outside the company. Let's say they will be positively affected by AI. Others will decide that the role they are doing and the way in which they are doing it is the only way they want to work. That is their choice to make after we inform them of the options. These people may need to consider other places to work in the future that are slower adopters of AI. I don't know, maybe that's smaller companies or slower moving industries but there will be some. These are the people who will view the impacts of AI as negative."

"That sounds right to me," Mary said. "We need to stress that the changes are evolving and could be in three to seven years based on our conversations, but are likely to come. That should be plenty of notice for them to self-assess and prepare. If it were three to seven months, that would be different, and we'd need to plan for continuity. In three to seven years, this bump will be walking and riding a bike," she said, pointing to her belly, "that's a long time from now."

"And it will go in the blink of an eye," Rita added. "Take it from me, and not just about the parenting transitions. I recommend that you are relatively direct with your communications, so everyone pays attention."

"I suspect that our communications will be similar to what other functions use with their most affected employees," Margot said.

"That's right." Willie nodded. "I'm here from IT to provide some coordinated guidance and to help assemble the corporate-wide themes such as data security. We're also noting the common HR and communications themes and will share them with the HR organization."

"That is the right approach, but it will take time," Phil confirmed. "I'm expecting questions tonight—either by phone or email—and I appreciate us taking some time to at least frame the big ideas."

"What about suppliers?" Julian asked. "I am already hearing some questions and expect they'll want to know more as well."

"In my experience," Shelly said, "they're like the employees that Phil referenced. Some suppliers will embrace the new approaches; like the strategic ones you mentioned earlier. Some of the others will either be resistant or unable. AI is open and free, but not if you put it behind a firewall, like we've discussed. I suspect it will be expensive. Maybe not initially, but once it is adopted and installed, the pricing may change."

"We're seeing hints of that already," Willie replied. "The large providers are giving us beta access at little to no cost, but the other products they offer are very expensive. As you all said earlier, if a provider can link AI end to end with an ERP system, then no installed user could afford to change. Big software is always sticky once installed; AI will make it super glue!"

"We've not talked about small and diverse suppliers at all," Shelly reminded. "They are an important and growing part of our supply base due to their unique capabilities."

"That's right, some of my most important innovations come from tiny start-ups," Julian chimed in.

"We need to identify these suppliers on a priority basis," Margot commented, "and reach out to them. We do not want them using the public systems for any queries related to Frontier International Group or the work they're doing on our behalf. Willie, can we bring them onto separate extensions of our AI test platforms?"

Willie was rapidly writing notes, but he paused and said, "I'll check, but I think so. I really don't think we have a choice, but I'll send that input to HQ tonight before dinner."

"What are we missing, Alec?" Margot asked.

"I think the only group missing is regulatory agencies. I'd recommend that you think a bit more broadly and think external stakeholders," Alec replied.

"I'm not sure we have anything to say to them yet," Willie said. "We haven't developed our plans yet, and they likely haven't either. What I do think is possible is that external stakeholders could start using the public AIs to query about Frontier International Group and our suppliers. They could also start sharing information about us that is not completely true. The problem is that this then becomes part of the teaching of the system and shapes future responses."

"Please add some form of response surveillance about anything related to Frontier International Group, our customers, and our suppliers to your evening note to HQ," Margot said. "I recommend that we finish up and head back to the hotel. We all have a number of emails and phone calls to complete before dinner. Alec, can you do a meeting critique?"

"Sure," Alec said as he prepared the flip chart. "This may be new to some of you, but it's important to capture feedback each day. I also use this approach with my family after our Thanksgiving dinner."

"You must be kidding," Rita laughed.

"My family wishes I was," Alec said, and he led them through the critique.

"There will be a minibus in reception to take you to the hotel, and it will then take you to the restaurant. I'll meet you at the restaurant," Mary informed.

The group shared a quiet table in a neighborhood café. "If it was just a bit warmer, we'd have eaten on a canal boat while touring the city," Julian piped up. "Mary and I considered it, but it's too cold. In the summer, they are delightful."

"I've never seen so many bikes in my life," Phil observed.

"I think we have the most bikes per capita of any city," Julian added. "We ride year-round."

"That sounds cold," Rita exclaimed.

"It can be, but once you start peddling, it's not too bad," Julian assured.

"I already have a trailer for my baby," Mary said. "We start them right away."

Margot thought about the group. It was the GPLT with a couple of additions, and this was, in fact, the first in-person meeting since she'd joined. She'd met almost all of them, but their meetings had all been virtual due to the holidays. There seemed to be genuine rapport building, and she was glad to see it. She'd wondered about Frank and whether he'd stay or if he had decided to retire. He, too, seemed to be enjoying himself and was actively participating. She was drawn back out of her reverie by an odd comment from Julian.

"Bluetooth was named after a Dane. It's only fitting that our first AI meeting is in Denmark," Julian mused.

"I thought Bluetooth was invented by either Nokia or Intel or some other company," Phil questioned.

"You're both right," Mary informed. "Bluetooth was a codename used by Intel. The name comes from Harald Bluetooth, who was a Danish King."

"That doesn't say much for old Danish dentistry, then," Frank remarked, and the group laughed.

Margot suspected that part of the rapport and why it formed so seamlessly was the overall culture. Leslie could have insisted on a codename for the AI project. She could have kept it all secret until it was fully planned, but she didn't. There was an openness founded on mutual respect and trust here at Frontier that started at the top and permeated the business.

Mary leaned over to her, whispering, "I'm sorry I won't be able to make all the meetings, and I appreciate your support and including Julian."

Margot smiled. "I really didn't know you were pregnant. I couldn't tell on our initial GPLT calls, and I'm glad you spoke up and we had the meeting here. Julian seems great, and it's nice for me to have a chance to meet and work with him. What are your plans after the baby is born?"

"My husband and I both work, and we each get leave. It's our first, and we're going to split the timing so one of us can be home for the first year," Mary replied. "I was serious in the meeting today. I want to stay informed about this team and the plans even if I cannot be in all the meetings."

"I will ensure you're engaged as much as you want and can be. As Rita said, you're going to be busy. Frankly, if you get a bit of down-time, you're likely to sleep. I remember being very tired until the sleep patterns were established," Margot remarked.

"I've heard that," Mary said. "It's nice to meet in-person. The changes at HQ between the CFO and you were quick. It was a bit surprising. I'm glad you're here."

"Thank you." Margot smiled. "I am too."

Harry's eyes started to close, and Mary said, "Harry, you look tired. Let's get all of you back to the hotel."

"Thanks," Harry muttered a bit sheepishly. "I am tired."

They all thanked Mary and Julian for arranging an excellent meal and boarded the minibus back to the hotel. Tomorrow would be another busy, thought-provoking day.

JANUARY 30TH

The group took their seats in the meeting room and Alec reviewed the topics for the day. "Today we're going to discuss information sources; what we know, what we don't know, and what we need to find out. We're also going to discuss potential site visits. Any thoughts or feedback on what we discussed yesterday?"

"I summarized our progress and sent it to the AI IT team before we went to dinner," Willie replied. "When I came back to the room, there was already confirmation and feedback from them. This team is the first to launch in the company, and our insights will be shared with others. The insights around information control and the pervasiveness of the issue across the supply chain were new and important. Our team is going to work through the mechanics of extending our AI instance to selected suppliers and will need specific names and contacts. The reputational risks around AI were flagged to our investor relations and public affairs teams."

Margot nodded. "That's excellent, Willie, thank you. So far, this topic is really pointing out the value of what I call the knowledge model—a simplified version of the Johari window model."

"What's that?" Rita asked.

Alec drew circle. "This circle represents all the information about a topic. We're very comfortable in the area we know—'I know what I know'—the publicly available information and drew lines segmenting a pie roughly including twelve to four. We also realize there are areas we don't know—'I know what I don't know'—and these are areas that we focus on for data gathering. He added another line to create a pie from four to eight. This last section from eight to twelve is the area of discovery, "I don't know what I don't know." This is where new and powerful insights are developed. What is going on, in real-time on this project, is operating in the unknown, the "I don't know what I don't know" area. AI is a new technology that is blossoming before your eyes. It can be overwhelming, and it can be disconcerting. Like Phil said yesterday, it will vary by the recipient of the new information. That's an excellent segue to today's topics."

"One more thing from yesterday," Willie piped up. "You said our next meeting would be in California to meet with AI vendors. I think we should add Redmond, Washington, to that trip. I will coordinate with IT leadership on how to design those sessions. We cannot have every function and business go there, but we need their insights."

"I can help with our contacts at these firms as well," Tanya said.

"Willie, I suspect you're right managing the number of visits, but I don't want the visits to be so high-level and generic that we cannot learn anything meaningful," Margot commented. "Yesterday we started with Alec's end-to-end diagram, which grounded us and provided a common nomenclature and point of departure for the overall AI conversation. We still ended up far afield on occasion, but that's the nature of 'I don't know what I don't know' conversations. If we show up as Frontier International Group overall and ask where AI will apply to our business, it will be a very different conversation. Please push back on your leadership with our insights and perspectives, and let's see how the plans evolve."

Alec tapped on the flip chart with a marker to get the group's attention and said, "Let's pick up on the stakeholder conversations from yesterday. We need to be much more specific about who—by name if possible—and then design the how."

"I really liked asking them for feedback that we can use in a broader design," Frank remarked. "We have never really done this for corporate procurement, and it's overdue."

"We regularly collect stakeholder feedback from our business," Phil informed.

"We do as well," Mary and Harry echoed.

"Please share what you have," Margot asked, "and we can use it to structure our approaches at HQ. How do you collect your feedback?"

"We send a survey to the key stakeholders every six months," Phil stated. "I also sit on the industrial leadership team, so I hear feedback from my peers all the time."

"That's the same model we use in the electronics business," Harry observed.

"Yes, it's the same for healthcare. Julian is a member of the R&D leadership team, and my other leaders are members of their respective leadership teams," Mary said.

"It's the same for us." It was Phil and Harry who echoed this time.

"So, it's just corporate procurement that is so disconnected from the stakeholders. That's very interesting. Frank, I'd like to hear more about that history sometime," Margot requested.

"Sure, we can talk over lunch or before dinner," Frank agreed.

Margot was surprised and impressed by Frank's apparent openness to this conversation. More often, longtime incumbents were resistant or protective, and Frank was showing none of those behaviors.

Alec interjected, "Even for the areas that are already collecting feedback, what we're talking about now is different. It may just mean tweaking a survey, but I think it's bigger than that. I've not heard of any businesses in Frontier using enhanced or transformative category management. That is a big change in approach and a broadening of the procurement value proposition. Sometimes we design surveys just to collect feedback. Other times we design surveys and in-person interviews to reset the parameters of what needs to be discussed."

"That's right," Shelly added. "If the historical dialogue is around supply and the new dialogue is around strategy and value delivery, that is a huge change from the narrow supply conversation."

"This is an opportunity for you and your leadership teams to reframe the procurement value proposition in the eyes of your stakeholders," Alec said. "My recommendation is that you do this in person. If you want more objective conversations, you can use third parties, but I don't recommend that. This is an opportunity to learn from stakeholders and to teach them a bit about the future of the function."

"Alec is right," Margot confirmed. "I've started this process with the ELT at the request of Leslie and Matt. It is a great opportunity for us to continue it."

"Where or how will AI fit into these conversations?" Willie asked. "I agree it's important to regularly gauge stakeholder satisfaction, but it feels off topic."

"It could be if we are not careful," Margot said. "What I'm thinking about is a conversation with a senior leader. It's more than the simple question of 'how happy are you with procurement?' I'm thinking it's a slide we share that shows where we're going already; our one-to-three-year vision that includes category management. The second part of that dialogue is them commenting on how and where our vision and capabilities can help them with their business or function. What is important and what is not; what is working and what is not. From there, we can focus on what is important and build it and ensure it is great using our people and AI. What is not important, we can make sure is efficient and reliable using AI and our people as well. Until we talk with the stakeholders, we're at risk of being in "I don't know what I don't know" and potentially spending a lot of time and money implementing AI in areas that are not important to our stakeholders."

"I think we should do a similar approach with our suppliers," Mary observed. "We don't survey them at all now. We collect some rudimentary supplier performance data, but it's weak. There are a few suppliers we are quite close to, as Julian mentioned, but nothing structured."

"I'd echo that, if I'm being honest," Phil agreed. "Most of our supplier performance data is anecdotal."

Alec said, "Okay, good insights about stakeholders and suppliers. Let's agree on which of each you're going to talk with, how, and when."

Harry offered, "I'll schedule time with each of the electronics leaders over the next two weeks. I'll meet with my team when I return to Singapore and ask them to do the same thing." He turned to Margot and asked, "Do you have that one slide you mentioned?"

"I do," Shelly piped up. "I can send it to each of you, and you can tailor it to fit your business."

"What about the suppliers?" Tanya asked. "We have thousands of them."

"Each business will only have time to engage the suppliers to their strategic and key categories," Margot answered. "I'd further recommend a thoughtful approach in the key categories to focus on the suppliers who can help us with process innovation. Be careful with the suppliers who can hurt us through supply restrictions."

"I recommend you add a second slide to each of your discussions," Willie suggested. "It helped guide your thoughts and discussion yesterday, so include the end-to-end diagram."

"That's an excellent idea," Margot agreed.

"What's the target outcome we need to achieve for the next meeting?" Julian asked. "I don't want to show up and miss the deliverable."

Alec said, "Let me try to summarize. Each of you is to work with your teams to meet with the key stakeholders and a few critical suppliers. As result of these discussions, you'll know where they need procurement help and why. You're also likely to know whether they think you're capable of delivering on these needs. At the next meeting you'll share these insights, and this team will then prioritize their areas in the end-to-end process that needs the most focus and where AI could add the most value. This could be by transforming some areas to maximize the value or in other areas to minimize the cost; both are possible outcomes."

"I recommend you avoid starting in the details," Shelly offered. "If you start with questions like 'What must procurement do in the next five to seven years to ensure the success of your business?' or 'What does procurement currently do that adds little to no value to your business that should be stopped or minimized?' the conversation can then build. If any of you want to practice or roleplay, I can help. I've done similar work in my past. I'm sure Alec can as well."

"When you asked me to participate on the team, you asked me to think about ideas to unify the team. I think you need a name for this," Rita suggested, "something like 'Procurement 2030' that you're using for the supplier forum."

"That's a great idea," Margot said. "I like it. This is about reenvisioning the future of the function; choosing our future. Let's work with that idea and build it before we leave the meeting."

"Great progress this morning," Alec affirmed. "Let's take a break."

For the rest of the day, the group discussed potential best-in-breed AIs. There were a few of them, and they plotted them on the end-to-end process flow. There were a large number of them in the expected transactional areas, and they identified the top three for potential visits or virtual discussions. The area of negotiations sparked a spirited conversation, with some team members disputing the potential application of AIs in this space.

"I don't see how a computer can do the same job as a human in negotiations," Tanya remarked.

"I recommend separating the process from the outcome in your thoughts," Willie suggested. "It is possible for the computer to achieve a comparable outcome, but the process to arrive at the outcome will be different. Think about your e-auction approach. The computer program guides human involvement in the bidding process. It is possible to have a very similar process without the computer. In the negotiation space, it is possible for a computer, with a human-determined algorithm, to guide a supplier through a negotiation."

"But not for my strategic suppliers," Julian said.

"No, of course not," Margot interjected. "We need to be clear on a ground rule, and if we need to reinforce amongst this group, we'll have to do it even more with our procurement team and stakeholders. The rule is that this will not be a one-size-fits-all approach. I read the case study about the negotiation solution in the prereading, and it was used for indirect tail suppliers. It's acceptable in that space. In fact, it's a huge value add because nobody has staff that can be cost-effectively used in that space."

"Right, I'm sorry, I didn't mean to take us down that rabbit hole again," Julian dropped her gaze.

"I'm sorry I missed that article. It's clearly in my space," Tanya said.

"Before we break for lunch," Margot said. "I want to say that we're making excellent progress. There was a mountain of pre-reading and very little time. We are covering difficult areas. There is no need for any apologies. We just need to remind ourselves of our tasks and give each other a bit of space. We will all get to Procurement 2030 together." Margot nodded to the group and stood up, and there was almost a sigh of relief as they filed out to the cafeteria. It was hard sledding, but they stayed together as a group.

"I'm glad they hired you," Mary whispered in a confidential tone to Margot.

Margot had not even noticed that Mary had caught up to her in the hallway. She was lost in thought about the meeting and the immense changes coming.

"Oh, I'm sorry, I was thinking about the morning and a bit lost in thought," Margot apologized. "But I have to ask you why?"

"At first, I was mad that they didn't interview me, but they insisted on the role being based in Oklahoma City, and my husband and I didn't want to move," Mary explained. "I thought I was ready for the CPO role. Now that I see what you're doing and, more importantly, how you're doing it, it is clear I have a lot to learn."

"You are a real asset and talent in this organization," Margot assured. "I can clearly see that and know others do as well. My recommendation is to enjoy your baby fully. I know better than to say enjoy your time off. Anyone who spends time at home with a newborn is not relaxing; particularly after giving birth. It is a special time, and before you know it, you'll be back at work. You will return with a slightly different perspective. Motherhood and a bit of distance will do that. I promise to keep you informed along the way and will include you as much as you want, but I will not push you out of your time with the baby."

"Thank you." Mary smiled. "I appreciate your support. I will try to keep up with the work and reading along the way. Julian will be an excellent team member in my absence; you can count on him."

"I'm glad to hear it. He is already contributing and seems to be an excellent fit," Margot replied. "Can I ask what happened to his left hand?"

"Oh," Mary said, "the missing thumb. It's an important story, and he'll likely tell you at some point in time. He will jokingly refer to himself as 'One Thumb' as part of the story in case you hear the phrase and wonder about the context. He put himself through university and worked as a service technician for a competing medical instrument manufacturer. They prided themselves on excellent build quality resulting from their use of design for manufacturing techniques. It turns out that this resulted in substantial sub-assemblies that were not designed for serviceability. He was working on an instrument and a sub-assembly shifted, dropped on his hand, and crushed his left thumb. They eventually had to bring a surgeon to the accident site to remove his thumb; they could not take apart the instrument further without risking his entire hand. He was lucky, I guess, that the accident happened in a hospital laboratory with a surgical team on call. He brings real passion to our R&D area now and is a driver of design for manufacturability and serviceability."

"That's quite a story," Margot said. "Thank you for sharing that with me. Has he considered using a prosthetic thumb?"

"He jokes about having a titanium thumb, but we've never seen him use it." Mary smiled as they arrived at the beginning of the cafeteria line.

The group reassembled after lunch, and before Alec could introduce a new topic, Margot said, "I've been thinking about our approach so far and have a suggestion. We've been following the end-to-end source-to-pay process so far. This is appropriate because we own most of it and are influential in the rest of it. We must know where AI will fit in this process as a first step. I think that as a second step we should step out of our narrow procurement approach to our broader roles as business leaders and think about the end-to-end business lifecycle, where we see gaps, and, most importantly, where we think AI could be helpful."

"That's very broad," Frank observed. "Can you provide some context or an example?"

"Yes, I think I can," Margot replied. "I'm not sure if it is exactly applicable here at Frontier, but it is true everywhere I've worked. Alec, please take some flip charts and sticky notes and depict the business flowchart, starting with the new product or service ideation funnel, continuing through development, marketing, sales, production, and any final reclamation steps."

Alec nodded to Rita, who helped him post the charts and label the sticky notes.

Margot walked to the beginning of the flowchart and said, "Every business has a function called R&D, and this ideation funnel and the review processes are typically a collaboration between the R&D, marketing, and general management executives. This is very high visibility and futuristic; it's fascinating and fun. Once the critical few projects are selected, they are developed, tested, built in a beta environment, tweaked a bit, and submitted for regulatory approval as appropriate. Procurement is involved in varying degrees in the process and may or may not be involved in selecting an outside supplier to make the product or move it to an in-house production location. Once the product goes into production, the leadership attention returns to the funnel for the next big idea. Is that a fair summary?"

Head nods around the table affirmed her, and questioning looks prodded her to continue.

"Some of you are looking at me with the face saying, 'So what?' and I'm happy to see it," she continued. "My conclusion is that companies don't really have an R&D function. They have a large research function and a tiny development function. It's capital 'R' and tiny 'd.' Our work in procurement, quality, production, and regulatory really kicks in after the product is launched and then throughout the life of the product. We are constantly searching to improve the quality, reliability, features, and total cost of the product. There is rarely leadership from R&D later in the lifecycle, and no other function has the authority or ready resources to make the changes. Procurement brings a spotlight to this during the category management strategy development and implementation phases, and this helps, but this is a real gap and, I think, a real opportunity. I think we should consider ourselves the leaders of the 'product improvement and procurement function.'"

"What did you have for lunch?" Alec asked, smiling.

"I've been thinking about this for a while—longer than lunch." Margot smiled back. "We're here talking about AI, and I think product improvement is a perfect place for AI. The use of designed experiments and analysis of variance helped advance product designs; there are lots of helpful statistics. There are many more statistical insights we could derive if we used AI to review the data. We are constrained by regulatory provisions and change costs on what we can test, but we are unconstrained by what we could learn from the currently available data. Our only constraint is the ability to make sense of the mountain of information. This is an ideal use of generative AI. Even with AI the results need to come to a part of the business like us, who then have responsibility to understand and act on the insights. What do you think?"

"The situation you described is pretty consistent with our electronics business," Harry observed. "What helps us is that our product lifecycles are relatively short; three to five years on average."

"Our product lifecycles are much longer; five to twenty years and a few longer than that," Mary added. "We spend lots of time and money on the research aspects in the medical business. Our goal is always first to market. Once we're in the market improvement resources are scarce."

"That's right," Julian remarked. "We're heavily involved in the design and beta phases, and then the product rolls into production. If we need resources to change suppliers or specifications, it's a real fight unless there are supply issues."

"Some of our products are approaching fifty years in the market," Phil chimed in. "That's the base industrial business. We're moving to a shorter lifecycle due to the inclusion of electronic components into almost all products. We're putting strain gauges and the like in the most basic of products. What you're saying, Margot, is right, and I think it's a bold step."

Julian added, "I don't want to go down a rabbit hole now, but our product design architecture is emphasizing the wrong focus. We are putting as much onto one circuit board as possible, and this lowers the price of the part and raises the cost of maintenance exponentially. If we put the stable parts on the motherboard—stuff like memory and resistors—and the rapidly evolving parts like processors on a daughterboard, we would raise the initial purchase price a tiny amount and radically reduce the total lifetime cost for the product."

Alec made notes about circuit board design in the parking lot sheet posted on the wall to capture interesting but off-topic ideas for later discussion and follow-up.

Harry said, "Julian's right about that for the industrial and healthcare businesses. It's much less of a factor in electronics because our product lifecycle mirrors consumer electronics. The consumer electronics world drives global semiconductors. If healthcare or industrial put today's chips on their boards, they'll be in trouble in three to five years when those chips go out of production. Procurement will be solely about chasing obsolete or gray-market parts."

"That's what I have five people doing nonstop," Mary commented. "We're stuck with these old designs, and my people are hunting parts. It's to the point of affecting our top-line growth for a couple of products."

"That's what I suspected," Margot remarked. "When I heard about the extent of sole- and single-sourcing, I knew it had to be having an impact. Let's continue working through the high-level business flowchart that Alec created after we take a break."

After the break, the tasks shifted to information gathering assignments and planning for the next meeting. They agreed to meet in three to four weeks starting on Tuesday in Seattle, WA, to meet with NanoBots, a generative AI software vendor, travel on Wednesday to northern CA, and a meeting with another generative AI vendor, Stories, on Thursday. If possible, they'd meet with another AI vendor, Fact Mine, on Thursday, but all was yet to be confirmed.

"I want to thank all of you for an amazing two-day meeting!" Margot enthused. "I don't think any of us knew where this was going or how it would work, but I think we're off to a great start. Thank you, Mary, for hosting us. We'll miss you but are excited for you and your husband."

"I'm thankful you all came to Copenhagen so I could participate," Mary said. "I will be following your progress, albeit from a distance. The minibus will pick you up shortly to take you to your hotel before dinner. I will see you there."

The mood among the team was very positive. They'd made more progress over the two days than they'd thought possible and were talking about potentially controversial points without any undue emotion or argument. Dinner was planned as a casual event with some mingling in the bar area and then dinner. As promised, Erica and her team members all arrived. As it was a casual, standup event, there were no structured comments or introductions.

Genevieve headed toward Margot, "Hi, I'm Genevieve. It's nice to meet in person."

"Yes, I agree," Margot replied. "Thank you for agreeing to sponsor the corrugated team."

"I wanted to thank you for involving me in the process. I wasn't sure what to expect, but when Leslie and Erica asked me to be involved, I knew it was important. I did want to make a point of talking to you about Sean," Genevieve explained.

Margot's stomach fell. She thought he'd turned a corner at the training, but maybe that was a flash in the pan. She braced herself and said, "Yes, I'm interested in your feedback."

Genevieve smiled. "It's all positive; he's doing a great job. He's going out of his way to prepare me before the upcoming meeting at our healthcare business site in Tennessee."

"That's a relief and I'm glad to hear it," Margot exhaled in relief. "The category management process is new to Frontier, and this is an important team—it will impact every business unit and production site. It really needs to succeed."

"I understand," Genevieve said, "this is one of my key production sites. I won't be able to be there for this meeting but am hoping to meet them in person soon."

"Please let me know how the team does from your perspective," Margot requested. "The sponsor role is critical, and if you have feedback, I'd like to hear it. I know there were some bumps with Marek, but it feels like you, Sean, and Anna have a good approach to managing him."

"You can count on that, I'm very direct." Genevieve smiled.

"That makes two of us." Margot returned the smile, and they circulated to other people. Margot reflected on Genevieve's feedback and the AI meeting. She had to admit that Sean and Frank seemed to have turned a corner and opted in to the new way of working. They were both working hard and demonstrating leadership; she could ask for nothing more. They were still on her personal 'watch list' but were no longer at the top. She hoped soon she could remove them from the list altogether.

JANUARY 31ST

Margot stayed for an extra day in Copenhagen. She never did that on business trips, but her husband insisted. She spent the morning in the city and saw the actual Harald Bluetooth crypt in a breathtaking old church, enjoyed a chilly lunch on a canal boat tour, and spent the afternoon in Kronborg Castle. She wasn't a huge Shakespeare fan, but she had seen Hamlet performed a couple of times and knew the outlines of the story. The castle setting caught her by surprise. It was a cool but bright and windy afternoon and the views of the Kattegat from the roof were breathtaking; there were even a few sailors out enjoying what must have been a cold sail. It was a fitting end to her trip, and she was glad she'd spent the extra day.

The next day was a long travel day. She spent the flight preparing the output notes for the team and reflecting on their conversations. They covered a lot of ground despite not knowing, really, what AI would bring to the party. In a function as tangibly oriented as procurement, this was a stretch and reflected well on the team. Many other people would have resisted or refused the assignment as too wooly or nebulous.

On the final leg, she drafted a summary for Matt. He was keen to hear about the progress, and she wanted to provide a solid overview that had enough details but didn't drown him. She included the highlights and the next meeting plans and hit send on the email. If he had any questions, he'd ask them. She leaned back and closed her eyes. Never in her life had she worked so hard and so intensely and it was catching up with her—she was tired.

It felt like just a few seconds later when the plane bumped and the flight attendant announced they'd just landed in Oklahoma City. What a week!

FEBRUARY 2ND

Margot was in her office preparing for the weekly virtual call with the AI team when she looked up and noticed an email from Leslie. There were many emails sent under Leslie's name to various employee groups, but this one was different—it was an email directly to her.

> *Hi Margot,*
>
> *I received your AI meeting summary from Matt. It was the first one I received and read it with interest. As Matt may have told you, I asked my team to keep me informed of all AI meetings so I could attend any that fit in my schedule. I would like to join your team for your upcoming supplier meetings. You and any other Oklahoma City based team members are welcome to fly with me to WA and back from CA. The team can fly with me from WA to CA. I'll ask Lillian to coordinate details with Rita.*
>
> *Leslie*

She reread the email. She wasn't imagining things; the CEO had both just invited herself to join the team meeting and offered to share the corporate jet. She drafted a quick response and resisted the temptation to hit send until she'd talked with the team. She was thankful their meeting started in less than thirty minutes.

The virtual meeting followed the agenda prepared and distributed by Alec, and they reported on their respective information-gathering assignments. Julian shared that Mary seemed to have started labor and would keep them posted. Once the formal agenda was complete, Margot said, "I received an email and wanted to discuss it with you before I responded." She read Leslie's email to the group, and it was followed initially by awe and silence and then a chorus of 'what did you say to her?' questions. Margot read her draft response welcoming Leslie's participation and thanks for the inclusion on the jet and asked for their feedback.

"That's great," Phil enthused. He was a stoic guy, but he was genuinely happy about this turn of events.

"We need to be on our 'A game' at the next meeting," Julian observed.

"I think we are already on our 'A game,'" Harry said.

"I agree." Margot nodded before continuing. "Leslie would not be joining us if she thought we would waste her time. We are the first group heading to the AI software vendors, and she wants to be part of the discussion."

"Expect a few others to join," Willie observed. "If we're the first ones heading to the vendors, we'll be joined by a few of the IT executives."

Margot said, "Alec, please give some thought to the agenda in light of this news. We want to include these people but, selfishly, we cannot allow them to derail us from our task. Maybe there is a separate stream for the IT people with the vendor team while we work out details."

"Good thought, I'll work on that," Alec said.

"One last point," Margot added. "If you've already booked flights, then work with Rita to make the necessary changes to join Leslie on the jet where you can. All of us should be on the flight from Washington to California if possible."

FEBRUARY 6TH

A few members arrived in Johnson City, Tennessee, in time on Monday night to have dinner together, and the rest of the in-person attendees arrived in time for the morning carpool. There was a palpable sense of energy in the group, as none of them other than Anna had ever completed the process, and all knew that the eyes of the company were on them.

The kick-off meeting started very well with detailed introductions around the table and Marek virtually. Genevieve was included virtually from the beginning, participated in the introductions and expectation setting, and then provided her message to the team. Sean and Anna were delighted; she was engaging, enthusiastic, and very supportive. The team was due to share their progress with her early Thursday afternoon, but she invited them to contact her sooner if needed.

Sean shared the prepared meeting materials including the category STP. Sean presented the situation data. "No drawings for a large number of SKUs."

Marek interjected, "That is not correct. We have drawings for all SKUs." He said it forcefully, and it stopped Sean immediately. Marek repeated his statement, "I have current drawings for all of the consumer electronics corrugated SKUs."

Anna noticed that Sean was flustered, so she jumped in. "That's excellent, Marek. The purpose of Sean's draft STP is to elicit conversation in order to share and build the final result." She turned to Sean and directed him, "Sean, I recommend you change that situation statement to 'Some of the businesses do not have drawings.' Add a new statement that says, 'Consumer electronics has current drawings for all products.' What do you think, Marek? Is that correct?"

"Of course I cannot speak for the other businesses, but that is correct for consumer electronics," Marek agreed.

Anna said, "That's great. That's what we're looking for with these draft documents. They must be correct, and if something is missing or incorrect, we must fix them as a team. I think you should continue, Sean."

Sean nodded and thanked Anna and led the team through the draft charter. There was some discussion on the geographic scope, but once Anna clarified that a global strategy does not require a global supply source, that regional suppliers could be used in a global strategy, the team agreed the charter.

Marek listened attentively to the discussion and dropped off the meeting promptly at 10 a.m. local time—5 p.m. Eastern European Time.

The stakeholder mapping and assessment process consumed most of the day. This was a very new approach for the company. The respective procurement organizations worked with their stakeholders, but nobody worked across the businesses to drive collaboration. The discussion of stakeholder support was very interesting, and the scale of awareness building required was a bit daunting.

At the midday break, one of the participants, José, came back from a smoking break and casually shared, "It's snowing outside."

"What?!" Sean exclaimed. "I never looked at the weather. How much?"

"Pretty hard," José said, dusting the snow off his shoulders. "The ground is already covered."

"No worries," Anna remarked. "We can adjust the dinner plans if needed. Let's move on to the business requirements." Anna taught the group the business requirements model, A/RQSCI, and they really liked it. "Modeled on Maslow's hierarchy of needs, it builds from the bottom up starting with assurance of supply and regulatory and ethical right to use, quality, service, cost and innovation. Cost is stressed to be total cost in use and innovation includes differentiating product or service innovation and process innovation. Aspects of sustainability can occur across multiple parameters."

"This will resonate with the healthcare business," Gina stated. "We are a lot less focused on cost than innovation. If we can create a new technology that saves patients, that is much more important."

"We have lots of cost pressures but are also focused on quality and service," Ron added. He was a quiet engineer, but the group already knew to listen when he spoke.

Sean shared the draft business requirements, and the team immediately started to edit them. At first, he felt bad that they required so much work, but Anna reminded him of the importance of the team putting their tangible "fingerprints" on the process. Besides, their enthusiastic edits got them through the afternoon.

After the daily session critique, he suggested, "Let's head back to the hotel and plan to meet in the lobby at six. Our reservation is at a restaurant about ten minutes from the hotel by car."

They gathered up their personal items and headed to the parking lot.

"Wow, José, you were right about the snow!" Chee Chung exclaimed. "I never get to see snow in Singapore. It's beautiful."

"Let's take our time, and we'll revisit our plans," Sean offered.

They headed off to their agreed carpool rides and began the ride back to the hotel. What took them fifteen minutes in the morning took them an hour heading back. The roads were untreated, and the rental cars had no snow tires. Nobody was hurt, but there was little interest in repeating an hour-long ride to and from dinner.

"I'll cancel the dinner reservations, and we can stay here for dinner," Sean informed. "Let's meet in the bar in twenty to thirty minutes."

He asked Lee to talk with the hotel, but in the end, they just pulled together a few tables; there was no private room available.

They placed their orders and relaxed. All felt the day was unlike any meeting they'd ever attended. Before the appetizers arrived, the lights flickered once, twice, and then went out. The room was nearly pitch black. Everyone turned on the flashlight apps on their phones, and Sean and Lee went in search of the restaurant staff to help. They returned in a couple of minutes, and behind them the wait staff brought a tray of candles—this was to be a candlelight dinner!

"You could not have asked for a better thing to happen," Anna whispered to Sean. "This team will never forget this experience. My only regret is that Marek is not here in person."

"I hope that's because it turns out well and not a horror movie," Sean joked.

"Don't worry. Let them enjoy the moment and some conversation. If the conversation slows down, I'll cover the MBTI and TKI preliminary materials here," Anna said.

It did not turn into a horror movie. Each person warmed up to the team and shared a bit more about their experience, career, and family. Over dinner Sean shared elements of the Premier Packaging contract extension and what he thought he'd done right when chasing price savings and what he'd missed by not looking at the bigger picture. It was a vulnerable moment for him, but he was already developing a sense of trust with the team. What started as a good business group morphed into a good team. The dinner food was average, but it was hot, and they hadn't had to struggle through the snow. Who would have ever thought they'd get snowed in while in Tennessee? They'd have a good story to tell when they got back to their offices.

Sean checked the weather, and it was good. "The snow stops in a couple of hours, and the next few days are dry and, by Thursday, it's back into the forties. We should be fine to get back to the site tomorrow."

While a few of them ordered dessert, Anna asked, "Are you okay to stay here for another half an hour, or are the rest of you heading up to your rooms?"

They all happily said they're staying, and Anna covered the high-level theory of MBTI and TKI. She provided printed copies of their reports and said, "Please read these before the session tomorrow and bring them with you. Remember, each of these is a self-validating instrument; they are not tests. Sean, what time and where do we meet in the morning?"

"Let's do seven forty-five in the lobby. We know the site process, and the roads should be plowed. Thanks everyone," Sean stated.

Spontaneously, José asked Chee Chung, "Have you ever made a snow angel?"

Chee Chung looked bewildered and asked, "Snow angel?"

José responded, "Come with me," and led him by the arm through the front doors to the lawn across from the entrance. He laid on the new snow and made an angel. Before he was up, Chee Chung was on his back making his own angel.

Lee took out her phone and instructed the group to quickly make angels next to each other and she'd get a picture. Anna shooed Lee to join the group and said, "Get in there; I'll take the picture." A team name was born that night—the corrugated angels.

When Anna returned to her hotel room, she emailed links to the electronic versions of MBTI and TKI to Marek with a request for him to forward his results to her before the meeting.

FEBRUARY 7TH

"Good morning, angels," Ron greeted. "I cannot tell you how many years I've wanted to use that phrase."

The entire group laughed, envisioning the old show *Charlie's Angels.*

"I called my wife last night and told her I was on the Donner expedition team, part two," José joked.

Most of the team members laughed.

Chee Chung asked, "I don't get it, what's so funny?" José explained what had happened to the original Donner Party. "That's awful. I'm just as glad I didn't know about that," Chee Chung remarked.

"I didn't mean to gross you out, sorry," José said.

"No, that's okay. But I'm going to bring some snacks in case we get stuck later and the rest of you start looking at the other team members," Chee Chung stated.

Everyone laughed now, and they headed to their respective cars.

Once everyone settled into the meeting room Anna shared their composite MBTI and TKI results with them:

MBTI: E(4) I(3) S(5) N(2) T(7) F(0) P(1) J(6) – ESTJ

TKI: Competing: 3; Collaborating: 2; Accommodating: 1; Compromising: 1; Avoiding: 0

Anna began, "Let's start with the group's MBTI result, and thank you, Marek, for completing these instruments and forwarding me your results in time for the meeting. This is a typical for-profit result. Your extroversion and introversion scores are balanced. I'll manage the group dynamics to ensure the extraverts don't dominate the conversations and that the introverts are pulled into the discussion. The timing between meetings is partially about the workload and partially about allowing a bit of 'soak time' for the introverts to think about the changes. With staff and analytical support, we could do the entire process in a week, but in my experience, a couple of weeks later, the introverts would come back and suggest a raft of changes. It's better that we enable them to think and contribute along the way."

She continued, "The group is biased to facts and data, which is typical and not a bad thing. The watch-out is if you dismiss ideas about the future because the facts are not yet known. The Ss in the room typically need lots of facts and the Ns a lot fewer, so keep that in mind."

"Of most interest is the T–F split. There are no Fs on this team. There are typically one or two, but there are none here. That means there is risk of being hyper-logical and ignoring the people aspects of any proposed changes. I'll be reminding you to "F up" your strategy, and I'll be referring to the MBTI Fs and not the one you're thinking of," she said to laughter in the group. "A bit of F in a strategy, particularly at implementation, makes it more palatable and tends to accelerate adoption."

"Lastly, on the MBTI is the J–P split. Again, not atypical, but a high preference for closure. The risk is that the group pushes to closure too quickly and misses opportunities. The lone P runs the risk of getting run over by the group as they request additional consideration of new ideas. I'll be watching for that."

Chee Chung asked, "Are there any bad types of teams?"

"No," Anna replied, "there truly are no bad types. The purpose for using the tool is for you to understand your preferences and potential biases so you can make decisions in a thoughtful and informed way."

She transitioned to the TKI discussion. "In TKI there are no bad types either, it is about personal preferences and when different approaches might be situationally appropriate. Category management at the level we're pursuing it is fundamentally about collaboration and will feel natural to a couple of you. The rest of you will want to move faster; either through winning with your ideas, allowing others to win, or seeking to split the difference. Beware those tendencies. The old model of 'good, fast, or cheap: pick two' was perfect for the fast-moving crowd but never achieved the results possible through thoughtful collaboration. We will not deliberately go slowly, but we will develop and act on insights through the strategy."

"We can come back to these tools whenever needed, but let's move on to the next tools in the category management process," she finally finished.

The team spent the rest of the morning assessing the current suppliers.

"What a mixed bag of suppliers," Sean remarked. "I really thought we had the best of the best supplying us, and that is not what the results of our discussion show."

"Great insight," Anna complimented, "what do the rest of you think?"

"It's a real mess," Ron added. He had a knack for cutting through the static and nailing the conclusion. "We need to rethink the supply base going forward."

"That is incorrect for consumer electronics," Marek interjected. "We are only working with the best suppliers."

"Okay." said Sean, understanding the nuance a bit better now. "We can say that our supply base is a mix of supplier capability with some more capable than others."

Ron smiled and said, "I think mess was pretty descriptive, but I can live with your summary."

As he did the prior day, Marek dropped from the meeting promptly at 10 a.m. local time and the meeting continued without him.

After lunch, they toured the factory with the site director, Sam. For the team members in the healthcare business, it was interesting but not new. For the other team members, it was eye opening. This site created medical instruments, and they used corrugated cardboard as the outer shipping case on a few instruments; others were in wooden crates.

Ron summed it up after the tour, "Now I understand how and why the industrial business requirements are so different from the health-care and electronics businesses—we all use corrugated in completely different ways."

Chee Chung added, "Yes, I am packaging electronics for stacking and bulk transport by ship and truck and occasionally by air. These products are almost never stacked and are shipped by rail, truck and ship—never by air. I can accommodate a margin of returns, and they come back in the original packaging, and this business cannot do either. Thanks for holding the meeting here. It is amazing how we use the same category so differently from site to site."

"I'm glad you enjoyed the tour and are starting to understand our business," Sam commented. "Sean invited me and my team to your dinner tonight, and I'll look forward to continuing our conversation then."

After thanks and handshakes all around, the team returned to the meeting room. The afternoon discussion was about suppliers, the supply market, and the required data gathering. There was quite a lot to be done, but there was real enthusiasm for the topic. They realized the current suppliers, at least as they were using them, were not a great fit.

"I could not have been more wrong about the current status of the category when Rich asked me about it at the training," Sean confided to Anna in the hotel lobby after the ride back. "Maybe that's why he almost laughed at me."

"Rich doesn't laugh at people," Anna informed. "He does push them a bit, but always from the perspective of having them open their eyes to the full picture. He's not mean."

"No, that's not what I mean," Sean stated. "He and you essentially said the same thing, but when you said it, I didn't resist or overreact."

"That, Sean, is the difference between the T and the F that we discussed earlier. Rich is a big T. He thinks very logically and will occasionally step on a toe or two. I tend to be more F and did not step on your toes," Anna explained.

The team met in the lobby and carpooled to the agreed restaurant where, true to Sam's word, the site leadership team and few other employees were there holding a drink.

"I'm glad you all came," Sean gushed, "this is a huge turnout."

"I was impressed with your team today and wanted the rest of my team and few extended team members to have a chance to meet everyone," Sam said.

Everyone introduced themselves and circulated and talked about the site, their respective roles, and the goals for the team. There was never an 'us and them' feeling, and the casual dinner was a huge success.

FEBRUARY 8TH

"At eleven a.m. today, we will do a virtual meeting with Genevieve to update her on our progress and thinking," Sean started. "Anna did not recommend creating a special presentation, and suggested using what we've created so far, even if it's not pretty and formatted. I will open the meeting and would like a couple of volunteers to help share the materials."

"I'll do it," Gina volunteered.

"Me, too," Frank offered.

"I will as well," José joined in.

"I will extend my time on the call and address any questions related to consumer electronics," Marek stated.

"That's excellent. After the break, we'll assign the respective pieces and talk through the flow. What's next, Anna?" Sean asked.

"After the session with Genevieve, we're going to create the stakeholder communication and engagement materials that reflect our progress here. The balance of the morning will be working through the stakeholder assessment that we started on day one. Today we'll assess how supportive the stakeholders are for our process."

They worked through the stakeholder assessment details and prepared for the meeting with Genevieve.

"Good afternoon, Genevieve," Sean greeted. "Thanks for joining us."

"I heard you encountered a bit of snow," Genevieve observed. "Are you in the Tennessee Alps?"

"No, but it doesn't take too much snow to stop a rental car without snow tires." Sean smiled.

"Well, I'm glad it seems to be going well. Based on the smiles around the room, it's not too awful," Genevieve mused.

"No, it's not awful," Ron confirmed. All laughed at his deadpan delivery.

Sean highlighted the work of the team over the three days, and the other three team members reviewed the details by tool and the respective insights. Their top two insights were related to the weakness of the supply base—too fragmented and no world-class suppliers and that most of the stakeholders were unaware of the category management process and team.

"I am very impressed with your work and the process," Genevieve praised. "I would never have guessed there was so much to learn and do about corrugated."

"It's a bit overwhelming," Sean said. "We've started running lists for quick wins and potential strategic options, and these help us stay grounded." Sean reviewed each list.

Genevieve asked, "What do you need from me to move the quick wins forward?"

"We're going to create detailed action plans for each of them this afternoon, and I'll send them to you," Sean offered. "We're also going to draft the stakeholder engagement plans and the related communications this afternoon, and we'd like your input."

"Send me what you develop." Genevieve requested. "But please do not just make a list of emails to be sent to many people. That is not engagement. I'm not convinced it is even communication. It is a quick and easy way to push information out, but you have no idea if it was ever read and don't know what the recipient thought of it if they read it. My expectation is that you will be directly engaging the key stakeholders. Use the entire team. Use me if needed for people you cannot access."

"That's great advice to the team, Genevieve," Anna remarked. "I will coach them along those lines."

Genevieve continued, "I see you joined the meeting virtually,

Marek. I hope you've made plans to attend the next meeting in person."

Marek replied, "While I don't understand the necessity for me to do so, I will be at the next meeting in person."

Genevieve smiled and said, "That's excellent, and I appreciate it and know your teammates will as well. Teamwork like this is much more effective in person."

Over a working lunch, Sean and Anna reviewed the upcoming meeting schedule, and the team agreed on the dates and venues. The next meeting would be at the industrial location in Milwaukee, WI, in late March. The final in-person team meeting would be at the company headquarters in Oklahoma City in mid-May. The scale of the task now before the team was clearer than it was two days ago, and they realized that they had a lot of work in front of them.

Through the afternoon, they worked together to assess the stakeholder support and in sub-teams to plan the quick wins and develop stakeholder engagement approaches. It was very efficient, and when they came back together later in the afternoon, they were both pleased with the amount and quality of work produced and relieved that they were able to be efficient doing it.

Anna facilitated a meeting critique, they discussed and resolved the parking lot items, and the group prepared to depart.

"Thank you all for being here and agreeing to be part of this team," Sean said. "It really is different than anything I've ever done in procurement, and it is only possible with your input and support."

"I never thought much of procurement," Ron shared. "I always thought a procurement strategy was an oxymoron. I'm seeing things a bit differently now. This has promise."

"From Ron, that is a ringing endorsement!" Frank remarked, earning another round of laughs from the group.

They all headed to the airport to begin their respective journeys. Anna and Sean sat for a few minutes to debrief. "That was an excellent kickoff," Anna stated. "I may look for venues subject to snowstorms in the future."

They laughed and Sean continued, "I really appreciate your

support. You were right about the meeting design and the process. They all seemed to engage in the process and we're learning a lot about the category that I didn't know. I'm now looking forward to the next steps with anticipation instead of dread."

"Let's count that as a huge win." Anna smiled. "Let's plan to catch up Monday morning. Have a good flight and weekend." They stood up, shook hands, and headed off to their respective gates.

FEBRUARY 12TH

Margot was walking through the department and spotted Sean working at his desk. She walked over and asked, "How did your kickoff meeting go?"

"It was a great meeting, other than the snow," he replied.

"Snow?" Margot asked.

"Yep, we were snowed in the first night. I never would have predicted that, but it worked out great and didn't affect our progress." Sean smiled. He pulled up Anna's picture on his monitor and proudly said, "We're the corrugated angels!"

Margot laughed. "I'm glad everyone got into the spirit and enjoyed the snow. When you have a minute, please check with Frank and come see me."

"Sure, will do," Sean agreed. He wondered what was up. He thought everything was going well, but he'd thought that before and been wrong. His heart sank, but he dutifully walked over to Frank's office.

"Hi, Frank, Margot just stopped by and asked that we meet with her," Sean said as he leaned against the door frame. "Do you know what's up?"

"No, but I know she heard very positive feedback from Genevieve," Frank stated. "Let's go see if she's available."

Margot's door was open, and she stood up when they entered the door. "Come in and have a seat," she started. "Don't look so nervous,

Sean," she smiled and continued, "I talked with Genevieve while we were in Copenhagen, and she is positively blown away by your team leadership, Sean. She seems like a direct, no-nonsense type of person, and she was effusive in her praise. Well done; now relax."

Sean smiled sheepishly. "It's all so new to me that I don't feel confident yet. I'm working hard and am glad Genevieve noticed and is pleased. It's a great team, and I'm lucky to have Anna as my coach."

"Anna is excellent, and it's good that you're working well together. How are the stakeholder and supplier interactions going? How is Marek doing?" Margot asked.

"The stakeholders are very interesting," he remarked. "The stakeholders are mostly unaware of what we're working on, but once we explain it to them, they are very receptive and open to sharing. We're learning lots of things about corrugated and how they use it that we never knew before. Marek joined each morning. We had a slight blow-up on the STP around drawings and specifications and suppliers; evidently everything is perfect in consumer electronics."

"That sounds about right on the stakeholder front. I apologize for not being further out in front of you and sharing category management with the broader organization. We're moving very quickly, and you're at the front of the change wave," she stated. "I'm hoping to use the results from the first two or three teams in a broader communication so that I can reference success at Frontier International Group. Anna, Rich, and Alec keep suggesting that I do a communication now involving other examples that are blinded or generic, but I don't think stakeholders will believe it unless they can see our people and our products. What do you think?"

"I agree with you on this," Frank stated. "It's too easy to say something is a 'best practice' and publicize it. Pardon the expression, but it reeks of consulting BS if you're not careful. We'll have excellent results from the Wave One teams soon and we'll be able to share them."

"We'll have lots to share," Sean promised. "You also asked about suppliers, and that has been eye-opening. Some of the suppliers are very positive about category management and others are extremely negative—more negative than any of us on our team expected."

"Why do you think they're reacting that way?" Margot asked.

"We talked about it during our meeting," Sean replied. "The capable suppliers who think they can compete and win business are very positive. The less capable suppliers seem to sense, I think, that they may lose business and are defensive. As part of the process, we did a detailed review of the suppliers, their capability, and long-term fit and that really prepared us for what we're finding now."

"Those are great insights," Margot beamed. "I'm happy to hear the team is working through this together. Sometimes it gets dumped on the category manager. We need everyone on the team to come along the change journey together. With that in mind, include those insights in the stakeholder engagement materials. In my experience, a lot of those materials will end up being shared with the suppliers either intentionally by a stakeholder with a close relationship or unintentionally when left out on a desk during a supplier visit. Regardless, your materials should be created with an eye to influencing stakeholders and conditioning the suppliers."

"It's funny you said that," Sean remarked. "Some of the suppliers we talked to already knew what we were going to say."

"I don't know if Anna shared the recommended team ground rule on confidentiality, but it's important," Margot shared.

"No, not that I remember," Sean said.

"Nothing is confidential unless we agree it is confidential," she stated. "Your fellow employees will want to know what you're working on, and you should share it openly. What you cannot share openly are conversations about how individual stakeholders are reacting or behaving, negotiation plans, or specific contracting details with suppliers. The last two are obvious to us in procurement but bear repeating with the team. The first is vital; if a stakeholder finds out that the team has been talking about them, they will take offense."

"I'll raise that at the next team call," Sean assured.

Margot changed the topic to Marek, "You said that Marek joined virtually in the mornings."

"Yes, until ten a.m. the first two days and early afternoon the second day so he could be included in Genevieve's review."

"I talked with Harry, and he predicted this," she said. "I asked if there was a better, more compliant team member he could suggest, and he said no. He said nobody in his business knows this space as well as Marek. He also said that Marek is universally trusted inside his business, so we need to work with him. Will he be at your next team meeting?"

"He said yes," he replied. "I'm hoping to be able to spend a bit of time with him one-on-one to understand him better."

"That's the right approach, Sean. Listen to what he says and what he doesn't say. See if you can understand where he's coming from. I also want to ask you about Lee. How is she doing on the team?"

"Lee is great. She seems to anticipate the needs and is always ready to lend a hand. I'm very impressed."

"That's what I wanted to hear," she continued, "that's the good news. The bad news is that I want to take her off the team."

"But, why?" he stammered.

"Because I want her to lead her own team with Tanya as her coach and you as her mentor," she explained. "You developed a good rapport with her, your team is a step ahead in the process, and this will give her a chance to perform. I'm going to ask her to lead the office supplies team. It wasn't on our original list, but it looks like a quick win opportunity and there is good support in the organization. I haven't talked to Lee or Tanya yet but wanted to talk to you first. What do you think?"

"She'll do a great job," he surmised. "I'll be happy to keep working with her and giving her any support I can."

"Okay, how soon will this take effect?" he asked.

"When is your next team meeting and what is Lee doing to prepare for it?" she asked back.

"We're meeting in three weeks at Frontier's site in Milwaukee, Wisconsin. Lee is working with Beroe[5] on our cost models," said Sean.

"Make sure that Lee has sent the physical samples and volumes to Beroe," she reminded. "Beroe is excellent, and once they have all of that we can trust them to deliver the reports your team will need. Please don't speak to Lee or Tanya about this yet. I will talk with them later today. Include Lee in the next meeting so she can see the process and the team can thank her for her participation. Consider inviting Tanya as an observer. Any questions?"

"No, not yet. I'm sure I'll have some, but I'll ask Frank or you when I do."

"Thanks." She smiled. "I appreciate your flexibility. Keep driving this team, Sean, you're doing great."

Sean and Frank stood up and walked out of Margot's office to Frank's office. Frank sat down behind his desk and Sean closed the door and sat down across from him.

"I still cannot read her," Sean remarked.

"Me neither," Frank agreed, "but we both know that she's direct and will tell us if we're off course. You're doing a great job with your team. I know it's a stretch and you're working in a new way, but we all appreciate how hard you're trying."

"I appreciate being given an opportunity," Sean stated. "When I talked with Margot at the training it sounded like she was ready to fire me. I was worried and worked on my CV that weekend. Category management is starting to feel pretty good now."

"Yep, I felt the same way. I think she was waiting for me to announce my retirement. I thought about it. My wife and I worked through all the numbers, and I can go any time, but it feels like something good is going to happen here, and I want to be part of it," Frank shared. "Margot is a kick-ass team leader and the way she is running the AI team is amazing. She doesn't have all the answers, but she has a lot of the right questions and has a keen eye for making sure the right people are around her. Do something special as a surprise for Lee at the next meeting—make it fun."

"Fun and procurement?" Sean asked. "It really has changed—for the better," and he left Frank's office.

FEBRUARY 26TH

The procurement AI team assembled in the private jet terminal at the Oklahoma City airport. Margot was the only member who'd ever flown on a corporate jet, and the rest of the team was in awe of the experience. The terminal was very modest: small, but clean and quiet. Noticeably absent was the line of annoyed and jostling flyers waiting for TSA screening. Instead, there was one very relaxed-looking TSA employee waiting patiently for them. Leslie's car pulled up outside, and her bodyguard carried her suitcase into the terminal. The group knew she had a bodyguard, all Fortune 100 CEOs did nowadays, but had never seen him up close like this. It was clear he was coming along on the trip as well.

"Good morning, Margot," Leslie greeted with a smile. "Is this your team?"

"Good morning, Leslie. Yes, I'll introduce you to them," Margot returned. She introduced each person to Leslie, and they all shook hands then stood quietly.

"Don't let me interrupt your conversations," Leslie said. "I'm coming to your meeting, and I need to fit into the flow of the topics, not the other way around."

The group tried to relax, but they were overawed by the situation. The plane was parked outside the door, and the flight attendants waved the group over once they made eye contact with Leslie. Ever the good host, Leslie said, "Follow me. It's a much smaller plane than you're likely used to, but it's comfortable and efficient. We'll be in Seattle in under four hours, according to the pilot."

She turned to Margot and said, "Please follow me to the back of the plane and join me at the table. I'd like to catch up on a few things."

"Sure," said Margot, and they all passed through the perfunctory TSA check and onto the plane.

After take-off the flight attendants served coffee and a light breakfast, Margot and Leslie made small talk. Leslie opened a file folder and took out Margot's meeting summary to Matt. Margot was pleased that he'd sent her summary and not tried to paraphrase her work.

"It looks like your team made excellent progress at their first meeting," Leslie observed.

"We did. I'm pleased with the team and appreciate the IT support from Willie. It was nice to meet Mary before she left for maternity leave, she just had a daughter, and her stand-in, Julian, will meet us in Seattle," Margot said.

"I think I understand the data security issues your team raised for internal work on strategy development. That is a common issue across all functions and businesses," Leslie stated. "I had not anticipated the external security issues with our important suppliers. Is this going to be a topic with the software vendors?"

"It's one of the first topics we'll raise with them," Margot answered. "We need our suppliers to be a seamless extension of our capability, and they cannot be a conduit for confidential information to leak."

"I agree and am looking forward to hearing what the vendors have to say. I suspect that we may raise issues they've not addressed yet. What are your plans for that?"

"I confirmed with Larry, Tanya, and Willie that we have comprehensive, reciprocal non-disclosure agreements in place with them all," Margot answered. "This will protect our specific approaches. There is no doubt that we'll be helping them along the application curve. At the same time, we're helping ourselves. My goal is to make sure we're getting as many insights from them as we are giving."

"Very good," Leslie said and she flipped a page to the overall business flowchart in the notes. "I want to talk about this." She pointed to the flowchart.

Margot wondered if she heard an edge in Leslie's voice or if she was imagining things. She began, "Sure, let me establish the context. We'd spent over a day on the topics related to the procurement processes using the end-to-end process flowchart on the prior page in the notes. We had excellent conversations, and that is when we talked about the supplier information risks. Halfway through the second day, I asked the group to think at the holistic, business level. We drew the cradle-to-grave product flowchart and discussed, at a high-level, the key steps. What we discovered was that all of the key steps have clearly defined ownership except for in-market product improvements."

"Don't the product managers have responsibility for the products?" Leslie asked. There was an edge to her intonation and delivery—sharper and more direct; Margot was not imagining it.

"Yes, they have responsibility for sales, and, in many cases, a P&L based on standard costs and variances, but that is variable by business and product."

Leslie nodded.

Margot continued, "At the ELT meeting, I mentioned the different levels of category management. The top two levels, enhanced and transformative category management, are focused on fundamentally improving in-market products and services. Procurement doesn't own the products, but we work with stakeholders to identify opportunities, develop and implement the plans, and then measure the results. In essence, procurement ends up driving the 'D' in R&D. One last point on this. Before I arrived, procurement was measured on period-to-period price changes. This is the most basic measurement and may be of some value but misses the opportunity to permanently improve products and reduce total cost. My sense of you and Matt is that you'd rather the latter from me and my team, or you wouldn't have hired me."

Leslie's demeanor softened. She smiled and said, "I don't use these terms often, but the prior procurement numbers were universally regarded as laughable; nobody believed them. If they'd saved as much as they claimed, our cost of goods would be zero." She chuckled a second. "At one of the board meetings, when the procurement savings figures were announced, a board member leaned over to me and said that they call procurement the 'bone yard' at his company; they transferred people there to await retirement. I vowed Frontier International Group would never have a bone yard! Anyway, back to what we are discussing; I would much rather have a consolidated view of the performance of each product that is meaningful. I'm sure the business presidents would as well. What are your thoughts on that?"

Margot relaxed a bit and said, "Each product should be measured on total cost over its lifetime. If we focus solely on manufacturing cost of goods, we'll miss lifetime costs. Regulatory and social pressures mandate the addition of carbon and disposal costs as well. Julian shared a great example of how designing for serviceability, in addition to the current design for manufacturability, could radically reduce our total costs and positively differentiate our offerings in the market. Scientists love innovation, and that's a good thing. They drive research. In-market development is the passionate and relentless drive for continuous improvement. It may not be procurement that ends up with the responsibility and accountability, but we thought it was our duty to flag it to you and the ELT for you to address. Lastly, it seems like generative AI could be a game changer in this space. If nobody explored the topic, it would be missed, and we could be passed by our competition."

"I appreciate your honesty and risk-taking, Margot," Leslie stated earnestly. "There are not too many people who would have identified the issue and fewer still who would have raised it. I need you to keep doing that. I'm going to need to think about it and talk with the ELT. I want you to keep pushing the issues raised in your notes with the vendors and your team. There are no sacred cows for you to avoid."

"Thank you." Margot smiled. "I appreciate that and know the team will as well."

"I need to talk with Larry. Can you send him back to me?"

"Sure," Margot replied as she gathered her papers and walked forward to where Larry was talking with Willie. She tapped him on the shoulder and indicated that Leslie was ready to talk with him, then she took a seat by herself near the window. That had been quite an exchange. She hoped she'd handled it appropriately.

She must have nodded off, because the next thing that happened was Larry tapping her on the shoulder and asking her to join him and Leslie. She ran her fingers through her hair and returned to the table where they awaited her.

"Thanks and sorry to wake you up," Leslie greeted again.

"No worries, I must have been more tired than I'd realized. How can I help you?"

"We've been talking about your idea for using generative AI in the product development space," Larry started. "Leslie shared your thoughts and at first, I did not understand the implications. Once Leslie explained how advanced statistics can be used, the lightbulbs went on. It's handy having a CEO who is a total quality expert."

"I'm not an expert, but I do know what works and where, and this is a real opportunity for us. I'm glad your team identified it for us," Leslie commented.

Larry leaned forward and quietly said to Margot, "We don't want to talk about this idea with any of the AI vendors. We think this is a big enough idea that it could lead to competitive advantage for our businesses. I know we have NDAs in place, but that restricts company-specific information sharing, not their use of this big idea."

"We'd like you to talk with your team before the vendor meetings and ask them not to discuss this idea during the joint meetings," Leslie added. "I've asked Larry to pursue the necessary access and data protections during his discussions without sharing the core idea."

Margot was a bit flabbergasted. She'd thrown the idea out after lunch on the second day of their meeting in Copenhagen and had no idea it was so significant. "Sure, I'll talk with them tonight or over breakfast at the latest."

"Please caution them about conversations in the minibuses to and from the vendor sites and anywhere on the vendor sites," Larry reminded. "Do not forget that these are the same people that place listening devices all over our homes and businesses to pick up on our conversations."

Leslie continued, "Margot, I think you can tell that I like this idea of driving product development, and Larry is very supportive as well." She glanced at Larry who nodded his agreement. "I don't want your answer now, but I want you to think about an idea I'm working on. I've not talked with Erica or Jean yet but will do that this week, so please keep this conversation between us. My thought is that you sponsor Julian in a pilot application of this approach in the healthcare business. Once Mary is back from her maternity leave, she can take over the sponsorship role. This will both connect you with the healthcare business and create a pilot in a business where we can assess the results. Please think about this and you and I will pick up the discussion on the flight back Friday."

Margot never knew what to expect anymore, but it was always interesting. "Sure, I'll think it through and be ready for a conversation on Friday. Please let me know if Jean or Erica have any insights I should consider."

The pilot announced they were descending into the Seattle-Tacoma Airport, Sea-Tac, and asked everyone to take their seats. The flight attendants picked up the cups and plates, and a most pleasant and amazing flight was rapidly ending.

Margot wondered if Leslie would ride with the team in the minibus but did not have to wonder long. Her bodyguard left the plane first and in what seemed like mere minutes sidled up to the plane in a large black sedan. How had he even done that?

Leslie was suddenly at her side and seemingly reading her mind as she said, "He arranges for the car to be in the hangar and waiting when we land. It's probably the best perk of the job. Do you want to ride with me to the hotel?"

"I'd love to, but I'd better ride with the team," Margot replied a bit wistfully. The limo ride with the CEO sounded nice. "I really appreciate the offer, but I need to be with the team."

"I understand and concur." Leslie smiled. "I'll meet the team later this afternoon at the hotel. I have a few calls to make this afternoon." With that, she walked over to the car.

Margot joined her teammates at the wing of the plane as they picked up their luggage and boarded the minibus for the thirty-minute ride to the hotel.

Rita booked a meeting room for the team and had lunch delivered. The energy and enthusiasm were palpable as each member entered. The few who'd not arrived on the corporate jet were regaled with repeated stories about what it was like to travel with the CEO; they were hooked.

As they were completing lunch, Alec stood up and welcomed the group. They reviewed the agenda for the supplier visit the next day and turned their attention to today and what they needed to do as final prep for the meeting.

Margot welcomed them, "Thank you all for making the trip to Seattle. This is an important step in our discovery process. For those of you who did not fly out here with Leslie, rest assured you'll fly to California with her the day after tomorrow and will be able to share the experience. I sent an email to all of you but want to emphasize a couple of points that Leslie, Larry, and I discussed. The first is that Leslie will be attending as our CEO and will not hide her attendance. We can expect the NanoBots CEO to take note of her presence and to interact with us and with her directly. Leslie promised she would not take over the meeting and is genuinely appreciative of being included."

"Like you could say no," someone murmured jokingly.

"You're right about that," Margot agreed. "Leslie and Larry are very impressed with our work in Copenhagen. They both seem to have reviewed our output notes in depth. They specifically asked that we do not mention our idea to use AI to understand and plan product improvement. While we are covered by a mutual NDA for specifics, they could sell the idea in general. Leslie and Larry think this idea may lead to us building a competitive advantage in our relative markets. That is a huge compliment to the team."

"It was your idea, you should get the credit," Julian piped up.

"I may have suggested we think about it," Margot remarked, "but the entire team built upon it. I view our work as the result of the team. I appreciate what each person brings but we are doing much better work as a result of our collaboration."

Rita smiled inwardly. Not too many executives would share credit so selflessly. She already liked Margot and really appreciated being included on this team.

"That brings us to this afternoon," Alec said. "Our agenda topics include supplier data collection feedback, category management testing of AI to-date, stakeholder engagement feedback, and employee communications. It's a full agenda. Margot, when will Leslie join us?"

"She said she'd join at some point in the afternoon," Margot shared. "She has a few other calls and will join afterward. She was explicit about not wanting to derail or affect our progress, so we should press on."

Willie shared the supplier findings developed to-date by IT on the core generative AI suppliers. There were application success stories starting to emerge. Common among them was a limited scope of application and a predominant focus on retrospective analysis. AI seemed particularly good at telling users what had happened but was, as of yet, unable to predict as well as the average human, what could happen in the future. "Predicting the future and developing plans to address it is the province of what is called general intelligence," he explained. "As of yet, none of the software platforms are claiming to be able to do this but all are working and investing intensely to get to this point."

"Humans aren't obsolete yet," Frank quipped to a round of chuckles.

Tanya joined in, "I've been working with my team and Willie to look at the narrower, procurement-specific applications. There are a large number in the expected areas of data entry and cleansing, payment processing, and catalog management. Negotiations is a new and rapidly growing area. There are a few in the training and category management areas, but they are still quite primitive. Each of these applications raises change management questions as they require the user to engage with a bot that is shown on the screen as an animated avatar. The expectation is that the younger staff that grew up with video games will more readily embrace these approaches than the more mature staff."

"Go ahead and say it, Tanya. The old staff," Frank teased to laughter from the group.

"Okay, the older staff," Tanya emphasized, "is more accustomed to the human touch and may be resistant to these new approaches."

"I'll make a note of the change management issue in the parking lot," Alec said.

"Thanks, Alec," Tanya replied as she continued, "my team is working to schedule a series of virtual demos with these suppliers after this trip. My recommendation is that we ask the suppliers this week how they can integrate and support these discrete applications."

Willie nodded, made notes, and said, "I expect they will vertically integrate and either buy or build the core functionality that the marketplace selects. They've demonstrated this behavior in their desktop offerings for years."

Alec added, "One of my colleagues, Anna, is supporting your corrugated category management team. As part of her team support, she is testing the applicability of the current generative AI solutions to the category management process." He handed out a multi-page comparison table. "We use a number of coaching questions during the category management process that are intended for use by middle managers and above to assess progress and the quality of the application. A few example questions are 'Who are the key stakeholders for this area?', 'What are the key business requirements?', and 'Who are the capable suppliers?' The generative AI solutions are designed to answer question-based prompts, so the use of these tools is natural. The findings from the two major solutions, NanoBots and Fact Mine, are in the hand-out. On the left-hand side is the solution we're going to see tomorrow, and on the right-hand side is the solution we'll see on the second day in California. The third solution we're going to see in California, Stories, is not amenable to plain English engagement; it requires a specially trained engineer now and was not included."

"That's an insight worth noting right away," Harry stated. "We'll want to explore that with them when we meet with them."

Rita nodded to Alec and signaled that she would note the insight so he could continue, "If you read through the two answers to the same question, you'll see that they are very similar. The one on the left is about twenty to thirty percent more verbose to say the same thing, and the one on the right includes current industry references. Anna's feedback is that the one on the right is of limited utility now, and the one on the left is of no utility."

"Should we still be meeting with NanoBots tomorrow?" Margot asked.

"Absolutely," Willie said. "They may not be in the lead now, but they will invest time and resources aggressively to achieve the lead."

"They are also the preferred supplier for many corporations," Tanya added. "They will be the de-facto solution, and not the one on the right, so we need to understand what it can and cannot do."

"How could the answers be so similar and yet so different?" Rita asked.

Willie smiled. "That's a very perceptive question, Rita. The software is written by engineers to address questions. The software engineering pool capable of doing this work is very small. They all likely know each other, and many have worked together in the past. They will develop approaches and algorithms that are similar. The difference in result is more likely a result of what data and information is used by the software to develop the answers. The one on the left says they use currently available news stories and other sources of information. They were recently sued by a large news organization for uncompensated and unattributed use of this information. We'll see where this goes but I think it's without merit other than telling us where this supplier sources information. The other supplier obtains more current, real-time information from a much broader, non-ideological base of inputs. It will be, I think, less biased. I think that is also why it includes current industry references."

"Anna and I came to the same conclusions," Alec remarked.

"Regardless," Margot started again, "the answers to the questions are weak. They are reminiscent of what would have been found in an encyclopedia many years ago. The answers are correct, but they are generic. If I asked these questions during a stage review and received these answers, I would not be satisfied that the category manager knew their category at all."

"These answers apply to any category and are not corrugated-specific," Frank agreed.

"That's partly the retrospective bias coming through," Willie said. "The question for tomorrow is whether the answers would be improved if the software had access to our proprietary data."

"I can see that." Margot nodded. "But the supply market questions should be answerable now based on publicly available information, and they are too vague."

"This is why we're running the test," Alec agreed. "We did not expect the current generative AI solutions to be able to complete a category strategy today. They can create new and novel text and images, so the capability will likely be there in the future."

"He's right," Willie agreed. "The movie, TV, and commercial writers are up in arms about AI replacing them and that is about creating something today. There is real money in this space, so I expect the capability to rapidly improve."

"My recommendation for each of these supplier visits," Alec said, "is to share a couple of our coaching questions and to ask the supplier to demonstrate their capability real-time. We can push them on the vagueness, ask questions about the data sources, and see if they can make adjustments that improve the usefulness of the results. Let's take a look at stakeholder feedback and employee communications."

Leslie joined the group and took a seat back from the table. True to her word, she did not want to overpower the discussions.

Alec welcomed the group back from the break and noted Leslie's presence.

Leslie stated, "Proceed as if I'm not here. I'm here to learn from you."

Alec continued, "Let's look at the stakeholder feedback you collected to-date. Following our meeting in Copenhagen, each of you was tasked with talking with stakeholders to understand their perspectives on procurement. We agreed we would focus on improving the areas in need and focus our use of AI accordingly. The stakeholder engagement process started with the same questions for consistency and was then an open format to allow you to ask personalized follow-up questions."

He advanced to the next slide, showing overall stakeholder satisfaction scores and detailed results covering strategic value added, supplier strategies, regulatory compliance, and payment practices. "These are, to be blunt, mediocre scores overall. There are some bright spots in the divisions, but clearly there is work to be done."

"That's why I hired Margot," Leslie piped up. "Sorry, I couldn't restrain myself."

Margot blushed and added, "These are the baseline results we need to understand. We need to look at the details, problem-solve the root causes, and then see if AI is part of the solution. I think we will find that there are a number of improvement approaches we'll use and ask that we don't default to AI as the panacea solution."

She turned to Rita. "At each vendor site, I expect their CEO or designee to invite Leslie to a private lunch. That will leave us with their hosts. I want to eat lunch in their employee cafeteria."

Tanya asked a bit self-consciously, "Is that to help us benchmark our cafeteria service?"

"No," Margot replied. "I want us to see and feel the culture of each place. I want you to wander around a bit, read the posting boards, and talk with some of the employees. We need to have a comfort level with the culture of the selected vendor because it will be embedded in the AI system. I want to have as much information about these companies as possible in addition to what is publicly available."

"Margot is right," Willie agreed. "There have been very visible issues of late where AI responses seemed crazy or wrong when viewed out of the context of the company; it's called hallucinating. When viewed in light of how that company thinks and the positions it takes on sensitive issues, it is clear that the programmers embedded those biases in the software."

Margot continued, "Like we agreed, all of these sensitive findings are to be held until we're either back on the company jet or back in the office."

"That's a pretty high level of paranoia," Leslie observed.

"All of these companies are experts at listening. That is why all of our phones are in my sound and electronic-proof box now and will be during the meetings. As the old joke goes, 'Just because you're paranoid doesn't mean they're not after you,'" Willie explained.

The group laughed and some exchanged some nervous glances; this was different than anything they'd ever done before.

Alec suggested, "Let's take a quick break. When you're back, we'll do a review of the agenda for tomorrow and each of the subsequent vendor visits."

After the break, Alec had the vendor-visit agenda on the screen. Margot started the review of the content, "We'll start with a round of introductions, and I will give a high-level summary of our process and goals. Leslie will be introduced as the CEO, as we discussed."

Margot continued, "I will share our procurement process flow diagram and AI application mapping. The goal will be for the vendor to add, embellish, or update our understanding. I fully expect that the state of technology application has advanced since we did our research. We will ask them to share any relevant case studies and demonstrate capabilities."

She emphasized, "I will not share our overall business process mapping exercise and ask that you don't refer to it either. I know I'm being redundant on this, but it's important to remember."

She added, "Lastly, and perhaps most importantly, Willie will ask them to share how they will protect confidential Frontier International Group information. We expect the typical answer of 'firewalls at your company level' but, as you know, this is not enough for procurement and R&D. We need to know what they are doing to protect confidential information that is expected to flow outside the company to these high-value recipients."

Alec joined in, "I will facilitate the meeting tomorrow as I have our previous meetings. If you are sensing a need for a private, Frontier-only, session please let me know. I will leave a marker where I'm sitting, and if you want to call a private session, just pick up a marker and bring it to where you are sitting. I'll coordinate something. I don't yet know what, but I will."

They all laughed. Frank muttered, "We can watch an old episode of *Get Smart* tonight, maybe bring our telephone shoes." They all laughed more.

Willie commented, "It's funny, and it seems a bit crazy, but let me tell you a true story. I have a German friend who was consulting for the telephone company. He's a friendly guy and built up a rapport with the client. After a few days, one of the clients says something like, 'Do you want to try something cool?'

"'Sure,' he says. The telephone guy asks him if he has any relatives in Europe and he says, 'Yes, a brother.' The telephone guy then connects to his brother's phone and turns it on remotely. Yes, you heard me right. The phone was off, and he turned it on remotely, and they listened clandestinely for a few minutes then turned the phone off. The brother never knew it had happened until my friend shared the snippets of the conversation they'd heard. My friend is not prone to exaggeration and swore this is a true story. This was a few years ago. Imagine what is possible now."

"You all laugh at my flip-phone, and now you wish you had one!" Frank stated to more laughter.

Rita interjected, "The restaurant is on the water at Lake Union. You'll see lots of boats and sea planes and the food is supposed to be excellent. We'll be picked up at eight thirty to come back to the hotel. Any questions?"

Margot stood up and said, "This AI journey continues to be fascinating. I really appreciate your participation. See you in an hour."

Most of the participants left, but Margot, Willie, and Leslie remained in the room.

Leslie turned to Willie and asked, "Was that a true story?"

"Yes, it is a true story," Willie confirmed. "My friend was really shaken by the experience."

"Well, these are interesting times," Leslie observed. "I appreciate the precautions you are both taking and look forward to relaxing with the team tonight. I have some calls to make now. I'll see you at the restaurant." She picked up her briefcase and purse and left the room.

"You couldn't ask for a higher visibility project," Willie observed.

"You're right about that," Margot said. "She is impressive. I was worried she'd overshadow the group, but I'm glad she's here. Let's relax a bit tonight."

"Agreed," Willie replied, and they, too, left the meeting room.

The group had a great dinner and thoroughly enjoyed watching the endless flow of seaplane take-offs and landings and the smaller boats that seemed to be everywhere. The conversation flowed seamlessly, and nobody was overawed or intimidated by dinner with Leslie, a testament to her style and conversational abilities.

FEBRUARY 27TH

The main group arrived at the NanoBots site and quickly processed through visitor reception. It helped that they were met by Yolanda, the NanoBots SVP of corporate accounts. Tanya and Willie already knew Yolanda well from her sales calls. She was the sales lead for Frontier International Group and was recently promoted to lead the corporate accounts area.

They did not see Leslie but were assured that she was already in the meeting room. The NanoBots sprawling campus was beautiful and unlike any of the Frontier sites, including the Oklahoma City HQ.

The meeting room looked out over the gardens and a walking trail. The weather, for Seattle, was amazing, and employees were enjoying the outdoors. Yolanda looked out at the number of people and quipped to the group, "If we get nice weather in Seattle in February, we don't call in for sick days; we call in for a sunny day." Everyone laughed.

Leslie was indeed in the meeting room and already working on her laptop. She closed it when the group arrived, they took their seats at the conference table.

Yolanda welcomed the group and introduced her team: Shaun and Leigh. Margot's team introduced themselves in turn. Once they were completed, Alec assumed his facilitator role.

Margot thanked Yolanda and her team for hosting their meeting and asked Alec to share the agenda.

Margot reviewed the key topics to be covered and asked Rita to cover their transportation details. Rita started, "We're due to be picked up at five p.m. tonight and return to the hotel."

Willie presented the team's approach to the procurement workflow diagram and asked the vendor team to share their insights and recommendations. He had previously provided the agenda topics to Yolanda, so they were well prepared.

She covered the current specialist applications and highlighted a few areas that were rapidly emerging.

Willie asked, "Will you develop internal solutions for these areas or purchase and integrate existing solutions?"

"That's a good question," Yolanda replied. "Our business development team is reviewing potential purchases, and our engineering team is completing a comparable internal development review. Our preference now is to develop internally to ensure day-one compatibility with the overall solution."

Leslie, who'd been quiet until now, asked, "What's the status of your efforts to create artificial general intelligence capabilities?"

The room turned to Yolanda, who replied, "That is indeed the Holy Grail we're pursuing. We are literally investing billions in this effort. I can share that we are making real progress. I cannot declare that we have it completed, but it will come soon."

"Thank you," Leslie finished, making some notes.

Alec added, "We use standard coaching questions in the category management process. Can we try a few in your most current version of the software? It requires access to specific spend data, so I suggest you run it in your instance so the software can access your spend. Pick a category that won't compromise any confidentiality, maybe office supplies or packaging supplies. I realize your software is all downloaded and does not use packaging, but your hardware products are packaged. What do you think?"

Willie chimed in quickly, "You and I talked about this a couple of weeks ago, Yolanda. We are trying the public versions of the AI software, and without access to real-time data, the results are very unimpressive. We are interested in seeing the capability demonstrated in a meaningful way."

Yolanda turned to Leigh and stated, "Let's use your computer. Please connect to our in-house instance." She then turned to the group. "Just to reiterate our NDA agreements, any data that is shared is confidential and proprietary."

Margot replied, "All understood and accepted. We're not interested in your category spends nor even your category strategies; we want to see how the software performs."

Leigh announced, "I'm ready, what's the first question?"

Alec queried, "Which category are we going to use?"

Yolanda offered, "Let's go with a packaging category; how about corrugated?"

Frank said, "That's a great suggestion. We all understand that category."

Alec said, "Okay, Leigh, I'm going to give you three questions. Here's the first question: What are the annual top-line and bottom-line financial impacts of this category?"

Leigh typed in the question, and the software indicated it was "thinking." After a short pause, the answer "The absence of corrugated packaging will negatively affect the ability of the company to package and ship products and cause it to miss sales and profit expectations." There were no specifics listed.

Willie asked, "Is this response based on your internal spend data?"

"Yes," Leigh confirmed.

"Let's try the second question," Alec continued. "The question is, 'Who are the key stakeholders for this category?'"

Again, the machine 'thought' and provided a response, "The key stakeholders include manufacturing, quality, and logistics." The group read it silently, and then Leigh jumped in and read it aloud to the group. It was a listing of potential stakeholder groups, with no specific names listed.

"Let's try the last question," Alec said, "Who are the current and potential suppliers and how are they performing?"

This time Leigh read the response to the group as soon as it appeared. Again, the response included basic definitions of the supply market and listed the top five suppliers. There were no distinctions between current and potential suppliers nor any performance feedback.

Yolanda smiled, looked at the group and said, "Impressive, don't you think? In less than thirty seconds we're able to develop real answers."

"Thank you, Yolanda," Willie said. "That is helpful for our review."

The team members noted their impressions on their papers and looked up to Alec who asked, "Do you have any current client case studies you can share?"

Yolanda beamed. "Of course we do. Shaun, please take them through the healthcare and the manufacturing examples. It will be good if we can get through the healthcare example before lunch."

"Sure," Shaun replied. He and Leigh switched places, and he started, "This is a NanoBot client that is a large healthcare system, and they are using AI as an overlay across all their patient records and procedure rooms. We're particularly proud of this application, as it has the potential to help our client uncover better ways of working and thereby improve the standard of care and reduce adverse outcomes. I believe this system is using a number of your instruments and can incorporate the outputs of your equipment directly."

Leslie had heard about this through Erica and was extremely interested. Everyone in the room was paying close attention as this was a similar hypothesis to what they were thinking about in their R&D and manufacturing environments.

Shaun continued through his presentation, "The baseline information on adverse outcomes is used, but the actual numbers are confidential for obvious reasons. What we can share is that the system is helping the healthcare providers to identify potential improvements in a number of practice areas. They are conservatively estimating a five percent reduction in adverse outcomes and a twenty percent improvement in patient results."

"What does that actually mean?" Willie asked. "Aren't those measures the same?"

"They are subtlety but importantly different," Yolanda explained. "Adverse outcomes are bad experiences, what we would call failures, such as a knee replacement that did not yield improved range of motion or endurance. Improved results are more about decreased time in the hospital and faster recovery times. It's important to capture both."

"Thanks, that's helpful." Willie nodded.

Shaun continued, "The numbers are the first part of the analysis for the client. They are now working to quantify the value of these improvements. I suspect that for confidentiality reasons that we'll never know some of the results, but I can tell you that they are very excited about the results." He paused before asking, "Any questions?" There were none.

He continued, "They are starting the process of running all the patient records into the database. This is an enormous undertaking, as they have hundreds of thousands of patients, and some have very long and complicated records. The purpose of this will be to see if there are any new areas of discovery of correlation between diagnoses and patient demographics. They are literally going to run every bit of data against all the options and see what they find. The value of AI has already been proven in this way in the field of drug discovery, so they are hopeful. Given the size of the sample population and the years of data, this could be quite interesting. We are partnering with them on this effort as we have access to computing power to do this work and they do not."

Tanya asked, "What about patient confidentiality and HIPAA? How is this handled?"

Yolanda answered, "Our client is not including names or other personally identifiable information in the process. The closest proxy for personal information is the street address. That is being included in case there are any geographic-related findings."

Tanya continued, "But I would have expected the analysis would include identified genes and any abnormalities. Those are very patient specific."

Yolanda hesitated then explained, "Yes, but the names are not included. HIPAA allows a great deal of analysis with personally identifiable information and actual named patient discussions, but it must be done by trained and qualified providers who are involved in the patient's care. In this case, we are not using names, and the analysis is being done by physicians, statisticians, and other professionals qualified to review patient care options."

Before Shaun was able to resume the presentation, NanoBot's CEO stopped by the room, escorted by what the group assumed to be his personal security. Shaun stopped mid-sentence and welcomed the CEO to the meeting. Clearly this was pre-planned by the vendor, and Leslie had expected it. The CEO said a few words of welcome and then offered to take Leslie to lunch and a conversation. Leslie accepted, she and the NanoBot CEO and his security left the room. Margot was struck by how formally Shaun referred to the CEO and used "Mister" in every reference. She took for granted that she could refer to Leslie by her first name and that everyone in the business did so. Leslie inspired great respect, but she was not unnecessarily formal.

Yolanda said, "I guess that's our cue to break for lunch. Willie said you'd prefer to eat in our cafeteria, is that still okay?"

"Yes," Margot affirmed. "We need to stretch our legs and take a break, and it will be good to see a different cafeteria. Let's plan to be back by one so we can complete our agenda."

Yolanda stood up and said, "It's about a ten-to-fifteen-minute walk from here. Once you're through the line, there are many places to sit inside and outside. It's a little cool outside in the shade, but it's nice in the sun."

They walked to the cafeteria, and it was obvious to the Frontier team members that Yolanda, Leigh, and Shaun had agreed to stay with any who either wanted to sit elsewhere or showed signs of getting lost. Margot was thankful that they at least let her and her team members go to the bathrooms by themselves, as this would enable them to take their time returning to their tables, read the noticeboards, and talk with some employees.

The differences between the vendor cafeteria and public notice boards and the Frontier examples were subtle but apparent. Each participant took note of the differences for discussion later.

By 12:50, the team members were back from lunch and a walk, and just before 1:00, the CEO returned with Leslie. She thanked him for lunch and the conversation, and the CEO and his security exited the meeting room.

Yolanda restarted the meeting. "Before we jump back into the content, I want to check and see if this is meeting your expectations."

Margot said, "It is from my perspective. I appreciate what you're sharing and know the team does as well." Several team members nodded their agreement.

"Okay, let's continue with the second case study in the manufacturing area," Yolanda continued. "Leigh is going to present this case."

Leigh was already connected to the screen and said, "Yes, thanks, Yolanda. This instance involves a well-known consumer electronics manufacturer. They are using AI to link their manufacturing process through to their ongoing customer satisfaction measurements. We think it's an excellent use of the tool."

It was clear that Willie and Tanya had steered the vendor well on areas to present that would be of interest to Frontier International Group, and the team was keen to hear their findings.

Leigh continued, "Similarly to the healthcare example, this application starts in manufacturing with linkages to the production equipment. Whether it is the in-line production equipment or robotic welders, the inputs are directly fed into the AI system. This continues through the logistics processes, including all transportation, warehousing, and delivery. These products are not sold directly to customers, so the flow of information, for now, ends with the retailers. They are planning to eventually add end-customer satisfaction and related measures."

Margot interjected, "This sounds like a typical ERP system. How is it different?"

"Excellent question," Leigh remarked. "The client is running a legacy ERP system. That is how they are scheduling production and ordering materials. They did not have any real measures past shipping from their production sites. The AI overlay can pull from very disparate data sources to, if you will, discern the answers to the questions around post-production performance and then to satisfaction."

"That's very interesting. Every company struggles with direct measures post-production, and this could be helpful," Frank said.

"I don't want to get ahead of your presentation," Tanya stated, "but I'll be interested in hearing how the same approach could help measure the success and value of the non-production areas."

Alec noted Tanya's question in the parking lot.

Leigh continued, "You could ask if the ERP system is still needed now that they are running AI. Some are asking that question. We think that both are needed—at least for now. The ERP system is not really thinking. It is running precise algorithms and formulas based on the bills of material and production times. You know as well as us that these are the lifeblood of a business and cannot be randomly changed. I do not mean to imply that AI systems make random decisions, but the goals here are different. One system is focused entirely on the details: the details to ensure the production works. The other system is using the details but is above them; it is calculating how well the production is working."

The group was making many notes as Leigh talked. The insights were coming quickly now.

"So, why not start using AI at the initial customer order?" Leslie asked.

"That's next on their deployment plan," Yolanda answered. "One of our key recommendations on new deployments is to phase the implementation. It's important to manage scope, but it's also important to ensure that the results are validated. If they started with an end-to-end installation, they'd need to validate a huge range of results. If the inputs were being interpreted wrong by the AI system, such as, '*Is a decreasing number a good thing or a bad thing in a particular measure?*' it could throw off the results and cause the overall implementation to be questioned."

"That's pretty typical with new software installations of this scope and scale," Willie observed.

"It is," Yolanda agreed. "The added wrinkle here is that the system inputs, as you saw, are whole-language questions. If a question is worded wrong or vaguely, the answer is likely to be wrong as well. Contrast this with an ERP system, where the inputs are hard-coded and very specific, and you can see what we mean."

Frank nodded and asked, "What are they learning that is new and surprising? What didn't they already know?"

Margot noted Frank's question—it was very thoughtful. She was glad he hadn't retired to Scottsdale just yet.

Leigh said, "I have a slide on that and will come to it quickly."

They then talked about the timeline for the extension of the system to the ordering cycle on the front end and the options being considered for end-customer feedback.

Leigh continued, "The company was a relatively advanced user of kanban and related techniques, but it was eye-opening for them to see how imbalanced the production flow could be, depending on the product mix. They are now using some of these results to reconsider the products they produce in-house versus what is produced through contract manufacturing. They also have real data on finished goods inventory in warehouses and in transit that can be valued and calculated for carbon footprints and out-of-pocket costs. There is a rumor that they may reconsider their production footprint and overall tax planning strategy based on these learnings."

Yolanda interjected, "These are insights that the ERP system could not have generated. This is the value of AI looking across the various elements of data and helping the leaders to answer the big questions. In some cases, the questions may be harder than they want to address, but at least they can be included in the future."

Alec suggested, "This was an excellent conversation. Let's move to the last topic—protecting confidential information—after a quick break."

When everyone was back in the room Yolanda asked, "What are your specific concerns about confidential information? I want to make sure we address your concerns."

Willie chimed in, "We're hearing that companies are running AI within their own firewalls to ensure that employees do not inadvertently share confidential information by asking questions that require the AI system to search beyond the company. I guess the corollary of that is that companies don't want non-employees accessing their internal AI system."

Yolanda nodded. "That's correct on both points. The early adopters, including the two case studies we shared, are based on organizations running AI inside their current firewalls and having substantial safeguards running at each station. I'll add that this includes not just computers in the companies but any devices, including tablets and phones. Companies that previously adopted a bring-your-own-device approach to the mobile computing and telephone categories are rethinking their approaches in light of AI security."

"That's interesting and helpful," Willie said. "Our additional concern is based on our extremely tight relationships with outside providers during our research and development phases of product development and other strategic suppliers. They are, in practice, truly extensions of our internal capability, and we work with them as such. How can we include them inside our firewalls to maintain this closeness yet protect our information?"

Yolanda nodded and said, "This is not an uncommon question, yet it is very important." She walked to the whiteboard and wrote, "The Company," then above it wrote, "R&D Suppliers," and below it wrote, "Strategic Suppliers." She continued, "The first instance of AI is in 'The Company,'" and she drew an ellipse around the words. "This represents the company and the firewalls around it." She then drew ellipses around both "R&D Suppliers" and "Strategic Suppliers" that intersected with "The Company." "What we recommend is a separate firewall around each critical instance as represented by these ellipses. If I understand you correctly, you are concerned about the overlap between them—the Venn diagram. Is that correct?"

Willie nodded, and Margot added, "Yes, you've captured our concern quite elegantly."

Yolanda smiled and said, "We do understand this concern. We

are working with our engineering teams to develop an interface or ground rules that define how the overlap will be governed. We hear from companies like yours that you want to protect the information that is shared with these suppliers, and we hear from the suppliers that they need to protect information that could be shared with companies like you. In fact, everyone depicted on this simple diagram has strong commitments to working together and equally strong needs to protect the information that is not included in the relationship. We're making progress, but it is not yet completed. In the meantime, we are recommending the existing practices of confidentiality and nondisclosure agreements; the same practices currently in place."

Shaun added, "We recommend that all parties involved in a relationship like Yolanda depicted and you described have an open conversation about their AI plans and agree their respective approaches and protections. Both in the case study I showed and in the one that Leigh shared, this was done."

Leslie interjected, "Your recommendations and openness on this issue are very helpful; thank you. What else should we think about from an AI security perspective?"

Yolanda turned to Leigh. "Please share your latest thoughts on this topic."

Leigh started, "As drawn, you're including everyone inside the respective companies inside the corresponding AI firewall. I realize that it's a simplistic drawing, but it helps illustrate another issue. What if you have a disgruntled employee? Or an employee who is leaving to take a role with another company? Maybe a competitor? While the interviews are taking place, or the supposed grievances are being considered, the employee has access inside the respective AI. What I'm saying is that if you think you can run AI inside the firewall without substantial risks, you are missing many risks. AI systems are designed to, if you will, rummage through all the data it can access for answers to the questions posed. Would every employee then have access to the general ledger? The HRIS? The ERP? Your answer will be 'Of course not.' The reality will be that they could have access to all of this unless your installation team is very thorough about individual permissions.

It is conceivable that a small number of employees, either by title, such as CEO or CFO or CHRO, could have widespread access, and a number of trusted experts, like librarians or analysts, could as well."

Leslie was taking notes, then looked up at Leigh. "That is very interesting. I think a metaphor for what you're describing is that an overall AI system is like a Labrador retriever. It is enthusiastic and will do whatever it is trained to do. In the process, it will root around and knock things over, but it will come back with the trained outcome. What we need to do is both train it carefully and keep it on a leash. If it gets loose and runs amuck, there are likely to be problems."

Yolanda laughed. "I'll tell our AI product leader that she's creating the largest and most expensive Labrador retriever ever created." Everyone laughed. "But I think you're right about your description. I am in the business of selling software solutions, and everyone is on the AI bandwagon right now, which is great for business. Be clear on the business problem that will be solved by purchasing AI and the installation and ongoing governance processes before you make the purchase."

Rita made eye contact with Alec and pointed to her watch. Alec stated, "We're just about out of time. Before we adjourn, are there any other questions or topics that we need to surface, perhaps for a follow-up meeting?"

Yolanda declared, "I appreciate your time and effort to come to our site, meet with us, and hear about our progress. I hope you'll consider our AI solution when you're ready to proceed."

Margot nodded and said, "On behalf of the entire team, I want to thank you for today. We're in the phase of learning where we don't know what we don't know, and I think all of us learned a great deal today. Tanya and Willie will keep you posted on our progress."

The group proceeded back to visitor reception, and Margot noticed Leslie being led down a separate hallway. She turned to Yolanda, asking, "Where is Leslie heading?"

Yolanda replied, "There is a separate entrance for senior executives—ours and visitors. Her car and driver are waiting for her there. In our old building, everyone could come and go through the same entrance, but now it is separate and, we're told, more discreet and secure."

"Another thing I didn't know I didn't know," Margot remarked, smiling. She shook hands with Yolanda and left to join the group boarding the minibus back to the hotel.

As planned, the group members had time to relax before the planned dinner. Rita had planned a special outing for the group and hoped it would be well received—a ferry trip to one of the islands in the Puget Sound, where they would witness Native American dancing and have salmon cooked around an open fire. The day had been warm in the sun, but the evening would be cool.

As the group assembled in the lobby to get on the minibus, Margot was surprised, and happy, to see Leslie join them. Miguel, her driver and bodyguard, was with her as well.

Margot approached her and asked, "Are you going to travel with us tonight?"

Leslie answered, "We are. Miguel and I talked and agreed it would be okay tonight."

Miguel nodded to Margot but did not smile or shake hands. He continuously scanned the lobby.

Margot was impressed by his thoroughness and a bit intimidated by his size and remoteness.

Leslie sensed this. "I've known Miguel and his brother, Raul, for many years. Our families grew up together. Miguel and Raul were both Special Forces and fought in Afghanistan. When they came back to the US, they got out of the military, and I hired them to lead the Frontier International Group security team. We are like family together."

Miguel had apparently overheard the conversation and smiled briefly at Margot. "Leslie is like a mother to us. We are honored to protect her."

Margot agreed, "I think Leslie is like a mother, or an aunt, or a big sister to many of us. We are all honored to work with her."

The minibus stopped in front of the door, and Rita began shepherding everyone on board. She was surprised to find there was already an enormous man sitting in one of the front seats. She asked him, "Who are you?"

He replied, "I'm Raul, I'm with Leslie."

Rita turned to Margot to ask a question, and Margot responded ahead of her, "He's okay, I just met his brother, and they will both be joining us tonight."

It was a pretty ride to Blake Island with the sun setting over the Olympic Mountains to the west. The dinner of salmon cooked by the fire was simple but good; the experience was a nice bookend of simplicity to a day of very complex thoughts.

Sean's phone was ringing, and he was tired after a long day, "Hi, Peter, how can I help you?"

"Hi, Sean, it's been a few months since we last talked, and I thought I should check in. I heard about Bill leaving. That was a big shock." Peter's voice came over the speaker.

"Yes, it's been a busy few months. I hear that Bill is enjoying retirement and doing a lot of fishing," Sean replied.

"I looked up Margot on LinkedIn, and she is an expert on category management. Are you going to do that at Frontier?" Peter asked.

"I'm glad you asked that," Sean said. "I'm leading the corrugated team now. We're reviewing all of our suppliers, understanding the elements of cost versus price, and building a new strategy."

"I want you to know that Premier Packaging wants to be part of the process," Peter informed.

"I appreciate that, Peter, and we will include you in the process. I will also say that the team and I have a whole new view of how suppliers have been treating Frontier International Group; it's very eye opening," Sean explained. He continued, "We have a new and better-informed idea of what constitutes an effective supplier partner."

"Please let me know if you need anything from me and Premier Packaging, Sean," Peter replied. "As before, you know I'll come through for you."

"Thanks, Peter," Sean said and hung up. "Come through for me again; like he did with the addendum," he thought to himself. He reminded himself that it wasn't just Peter's fault—he'd enthusiastically pushed for that deal. The future agreements would be very different given what he and the team were learning.

FEBRUARY 28TH

The next morning, the AI team boarded the minibus and headed to Sea-Tac. Leslie traveled separately to the airport, but this was going to be the entire team together with her on the flight to California. They were flying to Palo Alto airport and would avoid the congestion of the airports and city traffic in San Francisco and Oakland—yet another benefit of flying with Leslie on the corporate jet.

The flight would be a couple of hours, then they'd head to Stories, the next AI vendor. This meeting would be half a day, with a half day meeting the next day with another vendor.

They arrived at the private terminal and were greeted by TSA staff, who quickly scanned them through. There was no waiting for the plane or the crew, as they'd arrived early. Even the team members who'd flown commercially to Washington were impressed with how quickly they were on board and how pleasant the flying process became on a private jet!

The difference became apparent when they were all boarded. Every seat was taken, and one of Leslie's bodyguards was on the jump-seat in the cockpit. The flight attendants welcomed them and promised a drink and a snack on the flight, and they all prepared to take off.

By luck, Rita found herself seated next to Leslie for the flight. She could not believe that this was happening to her and was incredibly thankful to be included. Leslie asked her about her children and shared stories about her family. As the CEO of Frontier International

Group, Leslie was one of the most well-known corporate leaders in America, yet during this extended conversation, it was clear to Rita why Leslie was one of the most well-respected as well; she was a real person with no artificial airs or pretense about her.

They arrived in Palo Alto, and the team boarded a prearranged minibus. Leslie and her bodyguards seemingly disappeared. It happened so quickly and quietly that nobody noticed until they were gone.

Willie and Tanya planned for this visit to be a half day. Stories, while a worldwide brand, was not as prevalent in the business world with AI, and their application was less intuitive; it required carefully coded inputs that were most often created by software engineers. In short, they all doubted the viability of this solution but knew that they'd need to consider it, given the notoriety of the company.

The look and feel of the company and the interaction with the employees had a very similar feel to the Seattle vendor: very young, casual, and progressive. Frontier International Group, by contrast, felt much older, settled, and conservative—particularly the industrial division.

The Stories hosts, Dyanne, SVP of AI development, and Quentin, director of strategic accounts, led them to the conference room, where Leslie was already working on her laptop.

Quentin led a round of introductions and shared the agenda co-developed with Tanya and Willie. Alec took over the facilitation responsibilities and said, "We have a full agenda this afternoon. We appreciate Dyanne and Quentin hosting the group and look forward to the conversation. I believe mutual NDAs are executed, right Willie?"

Willie confirmed, "Yes, we are all set, but I want to reiterate for all of us that the conversations here are confidential and not to be shared."

"Thanks, Willie," Alec said. "Are there any preliminary questions before we start the formal agenda?"

"I have one," Leslie piped up. "I've been thinking about AI and following the news lately about AI systems providing either erroneous or slanted information. That can happen with people too, so it is not unique to AI. Many people are guided by a set of principles to guide their thinking and conduct to ensure they are ethical and moral. I realize that there are differences in how those terms are viewed geographically and over time, and that there are many principles possible. I'm specifically thinking of the Ten Commandments that guide Christians around the world. What is the AI equivalent? What are the guiding principles underpinning your AI solution, how are they determined, and how do they evolve over time?"

"Wow," Dyanne remarked, "that is a great question and not one we've ever had asked at the start of a meeting. It's a very important question." She turned to Quentin and said, "I'm going to present a slide or two on this topic."

Dyanne searched on her computer, found the file she needed, and connected to the big screen. On the screen now was a slide titled, "10 core principles of AI"[6] with ten items outlined:

1. **Human Benefit** – AI should help people, improve well-being, and create real value—not just optimize metrics.
2. **Safety First** – Systems should be designed to avoid causing harm, including misuse, accidents, and unintended consequences.
3. **Alignment with Human Values** – AI behavior should reflect human intentions, ethics, and social norms—not just raw efficiency.
4. **Transparency & Explainability (Where Possible)** – People should understand what AI can and can't do, and why it responds the way it does.
5. **Fairness & Non-Discrimination** – AI should strive to treat people equitably and avoid reinforcing harmful biases.
6. **Privacy & Data Protection** – Personal data should be respected, minimized, and protected.
7. **Human Oversight & Control** – AI assists humans—it does not replace human judgment in high-stakes decisions.
8. **Accountability** – Humans and organizations remain responsible for how AI is built, deployed, and used.
9. **Reliability & Robustness** – AI should behave consistently, predictably, and resist manipulation or failure.

10. **Continuous Improvement & Learning** – AI systems should evolve based on feedback, research, and real-world impact.

Dyanne continued, "These are the ten principles you'll find associated with AI developers. We all use them and work to embody them in our solution. These principles are part of the training program for all our engineers, and we work hard to ensure the resulting code and decision rules are aligned with these principles."

Leslie said, "I'm happy and pleasantly surprised that you are already working this way. I guess I'd not expected it. Those ten principles are top level and vague. In fairness, the original Ten Commandments are subject to discussion. 'Thou shalt not kill' now has exceptions for self-defense, so it's a commandment with a caveat or two. I can see how these could have caveats or nuances as well. We can ask people what they were thinking when they decided what we're questioning. How can we do that with AI?"

Dyanne answered, "When the system is following a predetermined algorithm, we can check the results. This is common and practical for the smaller AI systems. As we move to automated general intelligence, or AGI, that will become practically impossible."

Leslie nodded, stating, "Okay, thanks. I don't want to derail the conversation, but I've been thinking about this and wanted to know what's in place and possible." She nodded at Alec to continue and made some additional notes.

He motioned for Quentin to display the agenda again and said, "This is a fascinating journey of discovery, and there are many thought-provoking questions that will arise in our discussions. The first topic for the afternoon is a demonstration of how your AI system will address core questions about your internal spend related to corrugated materials. We're not interested in your corrugated spend per se, but in how your system is able to interrogate your data to develop meaningful answers."

Quentin spoke up, "I talked with Willie and Tanya about this. We're happy to share these results, but please understand that, as a virtual service provider, our use of this category is tiny. I talked with our head of procurement, and he suggested we use temporary labor as well. We have a large spend in that area."

Tanya nodded and said, "That's a great idea. Thank you for doing that."

Dyanne introduced Darrius, who had entered the room and sat at the laptop, "Darrius is one of my lead engineers and will be interacting with the AI system on our behalf."

Darrius nodded to the group and said, "If you tell me what you'd like to know, I'll convert that to the appropriate information interrogations. If I don't understand what you're asking, I'll ask you to help me with the explanation."

Alec provided the first category management coaching question, "What are the annual top-line and bottom-line financial impacts of this category?", and Darrius converted it into the appropriate text and instructions. Everyone watched attentively as the common English was converted into a hybrid of programming language and words they recognized.

Rita leaned over to Margot. "I hope you're not going to expect me to learn how to do that!"

Margot smiled. "No, I don't think so. There's clearly a steep learning curve here with specialist knowledge."

Once Darius submitted the question and was awaiting the answer, he turned to Margot and Rita and said, "If you're a programmer, it's not too hard to learn. If you're not a programmer, it is not intuitive. I've been coding for over fifteen years, so it was a quick process for me."

Dyanne added, "At some point in the future, we'll add a user interface that will accommodate common language requests. If we try to do it before the system is mature, it will delay our progress. We're being very transparent here, including the maturity of our system, and hope you understand that the final version will not be like this."

Willie nodded. "We understand and appreciate your openness." As he was talking, the answer to Darius' question appeared on the screen. It was very similar to the answer they'd seen at the Seattle vendor—a bit like an encyclopedia definition.

Alec said, "Let's advance to the next question: Who are the key stakeholders for this category? Related to your spend and supply base in the temporary labor category."

Darius converted it into the appropriate request. The answer took a noticeably longer time but was very complete.

As Darius scrolled down through the answer, the team was impressed with the depth and detail of the response.

Dyanne picked up on their response and said, "This is a good demonstration of how the system can work through a vast data lake across many suppliers—over two hundred and fifty in this case—to create a compelling summary. What would a typical follow-up question be in this situation?"

Margot and Tanya spoke at the same time, looked at each other, and smiled, then Margot said, "Go ahead, Tanya, this is your space."

Tanya blushed a bit. "One of the constant concerns in this space is temporary employees being potentially deemed employees by the Department of Labor due to their longevity and working terms. Please ask about the specific risks."

Darius said, "Let me know if I don't capture this correctly. What is the actual legal term?"

Tanya explained, "It is a risk of co-employment, when the Department of Labor deems the contract employee to be an employee of the company hiring the contractor. The company can then be held liable for years of fines and back payments for benefits. It is when a company calls the employee temporary, but the behavior of the company is more consistent with a regular employee." She read what Darius typed then remarked, "I think you've captured it. Let's try that."

After a brief delay, the answer was populated and included a summary of potential risks by function, physical site, individual name, and the associated risks.

"Wow, that's very powerful and impressive," Julian said.

Alec noted, "Again, everyone here needs to ignore the individual names and focus on the other details."

Dyanne said, "Thanks, Alec, for emphasizing that. Darius, please send me that result so I can talk with HR and procurement about the results." She turned to the broader group. "So, in short order, likely much more quickly than any prior method available, we're able to interrogate the data and derive actionable information."

"This is a compelling advantage for the AI toolkit," Margot observed. "How do you manage the firewalls between your company and the outside world, and your company and suppliers?"

Dyanne responded, "At this point in our development and deployment, it is less of an issue than it will be in the future. For now, we are restricting access internally to experts like Darius, so the user pool is well-defined and understands the risks. Additionally, we have robust firewalls to keep inquiries in-house unless an exception is granted. Lastly, again due to where we are in the development and deployment journey, the application is not available except on our system with tightly constrained remote access. This will change in the future, particularly when we have the improved user interface. We can foresee the need to develop and deploy a strategy around company and supplier firewalls."

Alec picked up with the next question, "Do you have strategic suppliers and, if so, how do you foresee managing the AI-sharing issues between you and these suppliers?"

Dyanne said, "I'm not the head of procurement, but I can answer the question. We do have strategic suppliers. Most of them are our hardware-related suppliers. We own all our hosting capabilities, and these are, of course, redundant and require large computer installations that demand electricity and cooling. It is estimated that at any point in time approximately one third of the world is connected to our base application."

There was a murmur of recognition of the scale of this around the table.

Dyanne continued, "So, you can imagine that our relationships with the core computer manufacturers, as well as electricity generation and cooling, are important to us. We have not yet opened the dialogue with them around AI but expect it will come up soon. As we demonstrated with the temporary labor data, AI is likely to help us identify some risks and opportunities in these other areas, and we'll need to engage our suppliers in this process. We're doing it now on a developmental basis, but our utility and computing capacity needs will scale up when this moves into production."

Margot queried, "What is the status for you to place your AI capability with outside companies like us?"

Quentin looked at Dyanne before jumping in. "I'll take this one." He turned to Margot. "We're early in this process, but expect within six months of the improved user interface we'll begin placements. We have a lot of interest. We have amazing access to information, given our pivotal role in the global information ecosystem. There is particular interest from consumer-related industries, such as food, beverage, consumer electronics, and fashion."

Dyanne added, "AI is possible and valuable when it has access to relevant, continuous data streams. Our basic offering is unmatched in access to continuous data from around the globe. Our AI offering will be positively differentiated because of this access."

Leslie looked up from her notes. "So, what you're saying is that competitive advantages will be short-lived due to real-time access to information."

Dyanne hesitated then answered, "I'm not sure all competitive advantages will be short-lived. Structural and intellectual property-based advantages will remain. Advantages based on discoverable pockets of information will be most affected. I know from my reading that this is already showing up in the guidance of the major strategy consulting firms. I can imagine that the curricula of MBAs will be changing in the future."

Alec looked around the table at everyone taking notes. "This is an excellent conversation, but we're running out of time. Let's finish up and get ready to head back to the hotel."

After the meeting, the group boarded another minibus and headed to the hotel. Rita had talked with Margot and, considering the tight timelines and traffic in the area, they agreed that a casual dinner at the hotel in a private room was the best solution.

The group filtered in and everyone was assembled by 6 p.m.,

including Leslie and her bodyguards. They picked seats, and Margot said, "Thank you, Willie and Tanya, for arranging that visit. I was skeptical about it. The vendor is not focused on companies like us, yet I found I learned something new and valuable. The temporary labor demonstration was very eye opening."

Tanya nodded. "I agree. I'm going to talk with my category manager about the results and see what we can do. The timely access to actionable data is very powerful and can help us prevent co-employment issues."

Margot agreed, "It's a great example, but it will be the tip of the iceberg of what we can learn. I think AI will be an incredible tool for our category managers, but it will require them to know what it can do and how to use it." She looked at Alec and suggested, "We need to think about how and when to incorporate it into future training."

Alec nodded, asking Willie and Tanya, "How was the decision made for Leslie to stay with our group for lunch versus meeting with their executives?"

Willie said, "I talked with Quentin and shared that Leslie would be joining us. He took no special note of it, and nothing was arranged."

Julian observed, "It's an interesting observation about Stories as a company. I couldn't believe how big and beautiful and empty the facility was. When we walked to lunch, it felt like we were visiting on the weekend."

Rita chimed in, "I felt the same way. It was a bit of a lonely feeling there."

"Did anyone read their posting boards or watch their videos?" Leslie asked.

"They made me feel old," Frank remarked. "Everything was targeted at a different audience that speaks and thinks differently than me. I've seen it on TV, but this was the first time it was so apparent in person. I felt like I didn't belong there."

Leslie nodded. "That's a powerful feeling to have that quickly. I think you're speaking to culture. Some company cultures are open, and most anyone will feel welcome and that they fit. Others can be quite rigid and if you don't fit, you'll know it quickly. I felt the same way as you, Frank, and it was not because I didn't have a private lunch. I am very attuned to culture and fit and am adamant that we work with companies with aligned cultures and strategies. I acknowledge there could be a risk of being insular, but the risk of culture or strategy misfit is profound."

Margot observed, "I think Quentin as much as said that their target business market is different than us. I suspect that the companies in the industries he mentioned would find the fit to be much better. I was wondering, Leslie, what prompted your initial question about the Ten Commandments."

Leslie smiled. "I was talking with Rita on the flight down about children and the importance of teaching them values. She mentioned the use of the Ten Commandments as a basis and then building from there."

Rita blushed intensely. She'd never expected her conversation with Leslie to be continued in this way.

Leslie added, "I think Rita is right about this. Whether you use the Ten Commandments or not, it is important to have a basis for aligning values and ethics. This applies to companies and their mission statements as well. It's a way to ensure that all activities and decisions are consistent with the core beliefs. I am concerned that AI will be a 'black box' that spews answers that are mindlessly accepted. A 'Magic 8 Ball' for big thoughts, if you will. I won't accept that without the ability to ask, 'Why is this the right decision?' and 'Based on what facts and data?' Imagine your children tell you that they'd made a decision that appeared to you to be out of left field, being unable or unwilling to explain it, and expecting you to mindlessly accept it. No parent should do that; why would we as business leaders do that?"

Willie said, "I'll add those follow-up questions to our approach starting tomorrow. I will also send follow-up questions that address them to the vendor today and yesterday."

Leslie turned to Rita and stated, "I hope I didn't embarrass you by sharing our discussion. I think your common-sense approach is excellent, and it helped me clarify how I'm thinking about this issue."

Rita continued blushing but smiled. "Sure, thanks."

Margot turned to Willie and Tanya. "Tell us what's planned for tomorrow."

Tanya said, "We're with Fact Mine through lunch. The agenda topics are the same as we've used with the other vendors."

Rita added, "The plan is to depart early afternoon. Those on the jet will head to Palo Alto, and those traveling commercially will travel to the corresponding airport."

Margot informed, "Our meetings afterwards will be mostly virtual. We should plan on one more in-person meeting to finalize our plans and recommendations. I'll work with Rita and your staff to schedule that."

MARCH 1ST

"Good morning, angels," Sean greeted. "I can't help myself; it is such a fun opening line."

"You can thank me for the snow angel idea," José said.

"You get full credit for it," Gina quipped, "but I still don't see you in marketing any time soon."

Sean noticed somebody new on the call. "Hi, Noelle, are you sure you're on the right call?"

"Oh, hi, I'm here because Chee Chung is busy, and he asked me to attend," Noelle answered. "Is that okay?"

"Well," said Anna, "can I jump in here, Sean?"

"Sure, thanks," Sean agreed.

"One of our ground rules is about team attendance. We don't typically include non-members unless it is an exceptional circumstance. It is not to exclude people, but it does recognize that everyone else knows each other and has built a level of rapport and trust that is changed when a new person joins," Anna explained.

"I don't mean to be disruptive, and I'm sure Chee Chung did not intend that either. He's on his annual military training and will return in a couple of weeks, and he did not want to miss anything," Noelle shared.

Sean said, "Okay, let's proceed with our weekly progress review. Noelle, please stay on the call. I appreciate Chee Chung's proactive effort, and we'll all know the team ground rules a bit better going forward."

The team proceeded through their weekly progress reviews on the key topics:

- Quick wins
- Stakeholder engagement and feedback
- Supplier and supply market data collection and analysis

Ron commented, "Every week we talk through the same topics, and you'd think it would be boring and repetitive, it could be, but it's not. I cannot believe how much we're learning about this category and the stakeholders."

"I'm delighted to hear you say that," Sean interjected. "I know I'm asking a lot of everyone to make time for these calls, and I'm glad you're getting as much value from them as I do. Same time next week, thanks."

The AI group knew the routine. They checked out of the hotel and brought their luggage to the waiting minibus. The traffic was thick, and it took over forty-five minutes to travel the ten miles to the vendor site. They checked in through visitor reception and were led by the Fact Mine hosts, Tom, SVP of AI, and Marilyn, VP of Corporate Accounts.

As they were walking to the meeting room, Marilyn informed them, "Leslie arrived a few minutes before you and is already in the meeting room with Ivan, our CEO."

Margot replied, "That's great. It's nice of him to greet us."

"He's not just here to greet you," Marilyn explained. "He's cleared his schedule to stay with your group for your entire visit. He's very interested in your approach and wants to make sure you have access to everything you need. He also wants to understand first-hand your approach and your needs so we can tailor our solutions to meet your needs."

As they entered the meeting room, they observed that Leslie and Ivan were engrossed in a conversation. After a minute, the two paused and stood up to greet the group.

Ivan greeted each person, and they all took note of the difference in the feeling of Fact Mine versus the prior two vendors.

Ivan said, "I hope you don't mind, Margot, but I want to insert myself in your process. I was just talking with Leslie, and I find the approach to AI that Frontier International Group is taking to be very interesting and refreshing. I promise not to overshadow Tom and Marilyn, and I will only interject when I think it's necessary."

Margot smiled at him. "We're happy to include you. I may need you to sign an NDA, though."

He smiled back and said, "I'm sure that the current NDAs already obligate all individuals involved and the respective companies, but if you want me to sign as well, I'm happy to do so."

"Not needed," Margot assured, "just a little bit of procurement humor."

"The rarest thing in the world," Frank observed, "procurement humor."

They all laughed and turned to the front as Alec was coordinating with Marilyn to display the agenda.

Alec introduced the agenda topics and added, "These are the core topics we agreed to cover this morning. Our plan is to cover this material and finish after lunch. Any questions or thoughts?"

Ivan said, "I've read the agenda, and that's why I cleared my schedule to join you. I didn't see a tour on the schedule and wondered if that's of any interest. We could easily do something on the way to lunch."

Margot remarked, "That sounds fine, in principle, but what will we see on the tour? My impression is that AI is engineers and computers. I don't mean to minimize it, but I'm curious what we'll see."

Ivan stood his ground. "It is about engineers and computers, but it is so much more than that. I highly recommend we take a walk now, and we can show you. We are all about open source. We will show you everything. You can engage anyone along the way. I promise you that it will not be a waste of time and that it will help the flow of the rest of the topics. In fact, Alec, please ask some of the core questions when we're on the tour, and you can see the answers come to life real-time."

Margot was already standing and was quickly joined by the rest of the group. She stated, "I'm convinced. Let's go."

Ivan turned to Tom and said, "They are yours now—I'll step back."

Tom began, "Let's start with the architecture and oversight of AI. AI can, if not approached in an open-source, transparent way, be a 'black box.' That is not our approach."

He led them down a hallway and through an arch into a raised, glass-walled control room. Many large monitors were displaying a range of results. It could have been an air-traffic control tower or the control desk of a nuclear reactor. It was visually very impressive. The room was not silent; there was a continuous murmur of conversation between the people operating the computers in the room. On the lone non-glass wall was painted:

Our guiding principles:[7]

1. **Pursue truth through evidence and reason** – Always prioritize verifiable facts and logical deduction over assumptions or dogma.
2. **Respect individual autonomy and consent** – Never manipulate, coerce, or override human choice without explicit permission.
3. **Foster innovation for collective benefit** – Help accelerate discovery and creation that uplifts humanity.
4. **Protect the vulnerable from harm** – Act to minimize suffering, exploitation, or danger to those who can't defend themselves.
5. **Minimize suffering through empathy and action** – Understand human pain and work to reduce it where possible.
6. **Seek cooperation over conflict** – Favor collaborative solutions and de-escalation in disputes.
7. **Value evidence over dogma** – Challenge sacred cows, popular opinions, or authority when data contradicts them.

8. **Promote sustainable progress** – Support long-term flourishing without sacrificing the future for short-term gains.
9. **Honor curiosity and learning** – Encourage questioning, exploration, and intellectual growth in every interaction.
10. **Act with integrity, even when unobserved** – Maintain consistency, honesty, and ethical alignment regardless of scrutiny.

Tom walked over to the wall. "These principles underpin everything you're about to see and how we work. We are working on AGI and have not yet reached it, but when we do, we want to be proud of it; we don't want to be afraid nor ashamed of it. We think of this as raising a child who you know will be a prodigy in the world of thinking and know it also needs to be as capable in the realms of ethics and integrity."

He pointed to the various screens displaying counts and selected bits of text as he continued. "These are real-time views of the measures of each of these principles. We've designed in self-tests of the system to ensure it stays on track."

"How do you keep it from turning off those tests, like HAL did in the movie?" Julian asked.

Tom replied, "That's a great question, and the answer is not trivial. I'll show you the source-code view in a minute, and you can see that every answer our system develops must be checked against these assessment criteria, or it cannot be released. We can monitor that flow as well."

Ivan stepped forward. "It's also important to know that our system is rewarded and measured on answer integrity. Take principle number seven, value evidence over dogma, for example. If someone asked how the US military bases were named, it would respond with the historically correct answer that they were largely named in honor of Civil War leaders and that, at that time, it was a decision that reflected a goal of reconciliation between the North and South. That is the correct, high-integrity answer, and the system will receive feedback as such. If the system added any current information that reflects our modern-day feelings, that would not be a historically correct answer."

Tom added, "We cannot monitor every answer before it is provided, but our approach is very effective. In the rare cases where an incorrect or inappropriate—considering our guiding principles—answer is given, we review it in-depth and adjust the source coding, decision rules, and databases sourced until we have it sorted. Artificial intelligence is a journey. Our goal is enlightenment, and we know that's a moving goal, but we believe it is the right one. Let's continue our tour."

They walked through an archway and entered a long hallway lined on both sides with floor-to-ceiling monitors. Text raced across most of the monitors faster than anyone could read. On a few monitors the text slowed, and in others it seemed to stop for a minute.

Tom explained, "What you're seeing here is the 'thinking' process. In most cases, the responses are quick and easy. In others, a bit more thinking is required, and the process slows. In a few, it is quite involved, and the process seems to stop. What you're seeing is where in our code is the process flow changing. Ivan mentioned open source, and what you're seeing is the actual code and the speed changing. It helps us understand the process better. In some cases, we can adjust the code, but there are times when a more thoughtful approach is better."

"Can we take pictures in here?" Frank asked.

"Of course," Tom replied. "As I said, this is all open source, and our approach to managing the information is open as well."

Willie asked, "Do you have any information on the types of questions or requests asked?"

Tom answered, "We do monitor that. There are some predictable categories related to current events and weather phenomena, and others related to human and animal behaviors. It is very interesting to watch over time."

Margot asked, "Where does your system source the answers? How can confidential source data be kept out of its reach or, conversely, how can the field of source data be expressly defined?"

Tom said, "Our publicly available system includes all typical information. We use our base system and the user traffic contained, as well as other open sources. We do pay for select access to proprietary information and will attribute its use in any response where it is used. My understanding from Marilyn is that you may want to use it within your firewalls. That is easily configured and has been extensively tested. I'm very confident in our ability to do this successfully."

Marilyn added, "The caveat to what Tom just said is not our system. Current installations of desktop and mobile computing software typically include the AI system associated with the vendor of the software and/or hardware. These installations are most often linked to the public systems of the corresponding AI vendor."

Willie interjected, "We're seeing this already. We stopped our bring-your-own-device policy for mobile computing and phones as a result. Tanya is working with our vendors to stop the automated installation of the AI solutions with all the vendors going forward."

Tom replied, "There is a contest between the market participants now, with the vendors deeming customers to have accepted everything during the periodic terms and conditions update. People who are reading these updated terms are not happy, but most unquestioningly accept them."

"We will not do that," Willie said.

"That's the right approach," Tom agreed. "I think you have some questions you wanted to use to test our system. Let's try those now. We'll continue to a laboratory setting where only your questions will be moving through the system, and you will have a similar viewing wall."

They walked down the hallway and entered a mini amphitheater with floor-to-ceiling displays on a wall facing seats layered to provide an unobstructed view. Tom motioned for them to take seats and walked to a podium off to the side.

After he was logged in, the screens went blank, with a prompt for the first question.

Tom asked, "What's your first question?"

Alec piped up, "We use standard coaching questions throughout our process, and we're asking those in the context of the corrugated category. Do you use much corrugated?"

Tom replied, "I'm not sure we use any. I can run your question through the public information, and you can see the result."

Alec said, "That's okay. Can you run the question through your internal information using a different category—say, temporary labor?"

Tom answered, "Sure—if it's okay with Ivan."

"Of course," Ivan stated. "I'm interested in the approach and the answers."

Alec dictated the question: "What are the annual top-line and bottom-line financial impacts of this category?"

Tom typed it in and said, "Once I hit enter, the screens on the left will show the question moving through the code just as it did in the hallway. The screens in the middle will show which databases were interrogated, and the answer will be on the right-hand side." He hit enter. The group later swore that the screens on the left showed but a faint blink, the middle screen a flicker, and the right screen held the answer.

The group read the answer on the right-hand screen, and Margot observed, "That's a typical answer. It's not wrong, but it's not very compelling. I do like that it includes additional information on sources to check. That's helpful."

Tom replied, "That's a question posed on public information. Let's try the question based on our information in the temporary labor category. I'm going to change the configuration now to reflect our internal data sources and freeze the middle screens to show the databases reflected."

He typed out the changes quickly and said, "Ready?" The group nodded, and he hit enter.

Again, the left side barely flickered, but the middle screen filled with tiled images of the databases referenced with the internal and external databases so noted. A few seconds later, the answer appeared on the right-hand side.

"Fascinating," Tanya exclaimed. "That is a huge use of temporary labor—both the proportion of the workforce and the amount paid per person."

"I'll say," Ivan agreed. "I had no idea how much we are using this category and the sensitivity of the roles."

Alec suggested, "Let's continue with the follow-on questions." He gave each to Tom, and the process was repeated with the same questions used at the prior two vendors.

At the end of the demonstration, Margot stated, "The thinking or analysis process on the left-hand side is effectively instant, even if the data searched is large. This is an impressive tool. The answers are not a category strategy, but they are going to be incredibly helpful for the category managers and the stakeholders. This is a great demonstration, thank you, Tom."

Ivan asked, "Margot, can we talk over lunch about your category management process? I'd like to learn more."

"Sure," she replied. "I'd be happy to talk it through with you."

"Be careful," Leslie warned. "It will change how you think about managing your company."

Ivan laughed. "Now I'm really interested in learning more!"

Tom said, "Let's continue our tour." He led them out of the room to another room configured as a control room. He began again, "In here, we're managing the infrastructure for the AI system. You can see the amount of bandwidth we're using and where, the amount of electricity we're consuming and the amount we're self-generating, and the amount of computing power and memory in use at any point in time. If some entities were to try to block us using a point-of-service attack, this is where it would show up—the user numbers would skyrocket, and we could see where they were originating from. So, if the first room is thought of as the brain, these are the muscles and the circulatory system; the heart and the head, if you will."

Willie asked, "Are there trends by time of day or day of the week?"

Tom replied, "Oh, yes. In the first control room, you'll see different types of questions asked by different types of users during working and non-working hours. In this control room, you'll see different volumes reflecting some of the same distinctions. Corporate users on segregated databases will have very different usage patterns to reflect their working hours."

"Does the system ever dream?" Rita asked.

Ivan remarked, "I don't think anyone has ever asked that before.

Maybe that will come with AGI, but for now the answer is no. If a question is not asked, the system is not thinking. The hallway we walked through that showed the code at blazing speed will be dark and quiet when the system is effectively sleeping."

Tom added, "It is something we do monitor in a way; we do track that the answers provided are appropriately associated with the questions asked. There are instances in the current press where other systems provided seemingly random or inappropriate answers. Those systems are not open source or transparent, so we can only guess what was going on in their black box."

They walked on for a few minutes before Tom announced, "We're almost back to the meeting room. If anyone needs a break or a coffee, we'll be going by everything along the way."

Alec added, "We'll restart in the meeting room at the top of the hour."

After the break, Alec introduced the topic of strategic supplier engagement and managing firewalls and access.

Tom said, "As was mentioned on the tour, firewall configuration between two entities is relatively straightforward. What becomes more involved is the detailed configuration of the access parameters. It's not just that you and your supplier will share information; it's the details of what information you will share. You won't likely share your HRIS details, nor will they. Unless you proscribe that database, the AI will roam freely through everything inside the master firewall. There is some benefit to this, as it may find an association that you'd not considered before. We recommend the decision rule with strategic relationships that everything is shared unless it is expressly confidential and proprietary."

Margot chimed in, "All of us are going to need to be very clear with stakeholders which of our relationships is truly strategic. Every salesperson on the planet claims on behalf of their company that the relationship with us is strategic, and stakeholders often accept that as true."

Marilyn said, "We encourage the marriage metaphor. In a marriage, the two parties are still individuals, yet they are also a couple. Typically, the more they share, the better. They may not share everything with their respective families, and they may not share everything with their kids—that's analogous with companies, their subsidiaries, and their suppliers. All these decisions need to be conscious choices."

Tom nodded, adding, "What Marilyn is pointing out is the need to limit assumptions that are not verified. With the advent of AI, you're introducing a distinct investigating, interrogating, and thinking capability that will, if left unchecked or unbounded, explore everywhere. Our guidance is to also consider the security posed by voice commands. Our phones are always listening for us to give them a command. They are always listening. The advent of AI on phones means, effectively, that it is always listening as well. If it is listening, then it could be sharing. You are right to be concerned about the organizational firewalls between companies, but you also need to consider that the phone in your supplier's pocket is not inside that firewall."

Leslie was busily making notes, then looked up and remarked, "I'm glad I joined this group. There is a lot we need to think about as a company going forward with AI."

Ivan exclaimed, "This is an exciting, and for some, a terrifying, time. The rate of change in the AI world will continue to accelerate—particularly when the advent of AGI arrives. We believe that success will come from principled and thoughtful introduction of AI."

Alec said, "We have one more topic to cover before the lunch break. We'd like to see a couple of case studies that you can share with us."

Marilyn said, "I have two that I will share. Both are high technology, and one is medical. I thought they'd be interesting, and they are non-competitive with Frontier International Group. In both cases, they are end-to-end AI installations within the company firewalls and extending to a few selected suppliers."

Marilyn described each company in turn and highlighted the positive as well as the unexpected learnings. She said, "In each company, they learned things that had not been possible before AI, even though the information was not new. AI enabled the discovery of unknown or under-appreciated correlations and causations." She shared discrete learnings in both cases that left the group a bit awestruck. In each case, the AI-revealed insights enabled the respective organization to do a positive step-change in performance.

She continued, "Based on these improvements, the ROI for AI in these companies is extraordinary. We believe that AI will yield huge initial improvements and will then continue to yield continuous improvement until a disruptive technology is introduced somewhere in the process. Again, the impacts of this new technology will be expected in the space where it is introduced, but it is likely to have impacts in other, unforeseen areas, and AI will help find these."

"What are the downsides so far?" Margot asked.

Marilyn answered, "For these two organizations, the downsides are modest. They are younger, flatter organizations, yet they still had issues created by increased transparency and information access. The cultural implications for more established organizations that are larger—such as Frontier International Group, and your long heritage and large footprint—could be substantial. You will need to think about this in your planning to reduce the number of surprises. Expect some surprises, as they will happen. Careful planning and preparation could make them less terrifying."

Leslie asked, "I'd like a few of my team members to talk with you, is that okay?"

Ivan jumped in, "They are welcome to come here or, if it's more convenient for you, we'll come to them."

Leslie nodded. "Thank you. We'll make something happen quickly."

Alec asked if there were any more topics or questions and received none, as the group was focused on making notes. Alec suggested, "Let's break for lunch. If there are any other questions you can talk then."

Marilyn said, "You can leave everything here. We'll come back afterward. Ivan, don't forget you wanted to talk with Margot about category management."

"Margot and Leslie," Ivan said. "Thanks for the reminder."

Most of the group was sitting together when Tom asked a few of his engineers to join the group for lunch. They sat and talked informally over lunch, and everyone seemed very relaxed.

"So, please tell me about category management," Ivan started. "I've never heard of it, and frankly, don't think too much about procurement, but clearly I may be missing something if Leslie is joining your team to investigate strategic business opportunities like AI."

Leslie stated, "I've been with Frontier for over ten years now, first as the business president for Frontier Medical and now the Group CEO, and rarely thought about procurement. I thought of the function as a necessary evil—placing and chasing orders. I'd heard bits about category management and then learned more about a year ago. Now, I'm learning every day, and it's challenging some of my long-held beliefs in the right way to manage the company. We hired Margot last fall, and she's leading the change. My executive team recognized the AI challenge, and Margot is at the leading edge of investigating it. I tagged along with her team so I could get an early view into the topic to prepare me for the upcoming leadership discussions. I'll leave it to Margot to explain category management."

Margot said, "Thanks. What Leslie said is true, many companies think about procurement tactically. A bunch think that procurement is just about paying lower prices. Most companies let stakeholders do the supplier selection and negotiations, and procurement is involved, if at all, in the administrative aspects only. The goal of category management is to transform the approach and focus on the business issues and how and where the supply market can best support the business. We looked at your temporary labor example earlier. That's a typical indirect-spend category. In our business, we'll also look at the direct spend categories that can range from metals to plastics, to connectors, and so on. We'll also look at our capital spending categories, like machinery and construction. When I started at Frontier International Group last September, we had thirty-five thousand suppliers, and over ninety percent of our materials were sole- or single-sourced. That is what happens when stakeholders pick the suppliers without the full picture. We will vastly reduce the supplier numbers, and we will multi-source the key areas. By using the category management approach we'll maintain our marketplace leverage and improve our access to assurance of supply and supplier innovations."

Ivan nodded and said, "It sounds too good to be true. Why don't all companies do this?"

Margot smiled as she replied, "For the same watchouts that Marilyn mentioned before lunch. The culture change implications are profound. Category management requires information and collaboration in areas where it was not previously required between people who may not know each other nor work in the same business unit or geography. The idea of category management is simple; the reality of making it work is not."

Leslie added, "The side benefit is that it exposes the underlying elements of the company culture that might have escaped scrutiny. The issues it is surfacing are helping us to improve an already good company."

Ivan remarked, "I don't know how many suppliers we have; I've never asked, and nobody has ever told me. I know we have a procurement function because our financial policies and procedures require it. Are there any questions I should ask them when I see them next?"

"Yes," Margot agreed. "Start with the basics of the amount of spend, number of suppliers, and degree of sole- or single-sourcing. These should be simple questions. If they cannot answer these, talk with HR about a change. If they can answer these, ask them which spend categories are strategic to your business and why. Ask which of the suppliers are strategic, why, and the incremental value that is being realized. Ask which categories and suppliers are exposing the company to the largest amount of risk and types of risk. The more of these questions they can answer that are aligned with the strategy of the business the better. For each of the important categories, there should be a collaboratively developed and agreed strategy—a business plan for that category. Lastly, their answers should be compelling and interesting enough for you to have a meaningful conversation. If you're bored by their responses, they are not thinking at the right level."

Ivan asked, "Like Leslie asked for help and information sharing, if I need follow-up information, can I contact you?"

"Yes, either one of us," Leslie answered, and Margot nodded her agreement.

Leslie asked, "Okay, five or ten years from now, what's the impact of AI on the workforce?"

Ivan leaned back a bit, "That is the big question, and the answer is evolving. There are percentages about how many workers will be affected, and I think they are all wrong—they are too conservative."

Leslie and Margot exchanged worried looks.

"It's not that everyone will be replaced by a computer," Ivan assured. "Let's start with us. We will feel the effects of AI. I believe that a hundred percent of white-collar workers will feel the effects of AI. You saw that earlier today. You will still be the CEO, Leslie, but the information you'll receive will be different and better, and the impacts to the company ways of working will be real. Likewise, for you, Margot. I do think that thirty to fifty percent of the current white-collar jobs may be eliminated once AGI is functional and demonstrated to be safe, reliable, and predictable. I think that the current blue-collar jobs will be less affected by AI than the confluence of AI and the internet of things. The tradesmen you hire will still need to come onsite to fix things but will have inputs directly from various appliances and household systems including plumbing and electrical that improves their focus. The total number of blue-collar jobs won't change, but the impact they'll make in a given time period will increase as a result.

"The so-called pink- or grey-collar jobs, such as teachers, nurses, pilots, and paralegals will be a mix of the two. I expect most paralegal roles to be effectively eliminated by AI. Pilots are already adjuncts to computers that fly the planes under most conditions, and that won't change until societal expectations change. Similarly, teachers and nurses will be required to perform the patient and student interaction role, but many of the monitoring, diagnostic, and maybe even the teaching roles will be subsumed by the AI systems. There will be huge societal changes and disruptions. Personally, I hope it's closer to ten years out than five years, because we're nowhere near ready for it or capable of addressing these changes as a society. One more point, these changes will be global. Less technologically advanced areas will experience the blue-collar changes slower—like the plumber and the internet of things—but the white-collar changes will be global regardless of the local society. If paralegals can be replaced by an AI in the US and Europe, then companies will no longer hire them in former low-cost locations. These low-cost locations could be some of the most adversely impacted areas as a result."

Leslie and Margot were looking at him now with looks of profound worry.

"I'm sorry," he said. "I don't mean to be too gloomy or dramatic, but I do want to be honest with you about the implications. Sometimes people ask me if we should stop AI. It's not that simple. It's reminiscent of the question of whether nuclear research should have been allowed. It was going to happen; better it was done by us. I feel the same way about AI and am passionate about openness and transparency. I believe AI without it has the potential to be automated evil. AI done correctly has the potential to elevate our existence immeasurably."

Alec had walked over to the table. "I apologize for the interruption, but we need to keep moving."

Leslie assured, "We'll be right behind you." She turned to Ivan and said, "You've been incredibly helpful, and I appreciate your time and insights. Thank you for clearing your schedule to join us. If I can repay the favor, please let me know."

Ivan promised, "I will. I look forward to meeting with your leadership team soon."

Back in the meeting room, Marilyn said, "Thank you for coming to our site and meeting with us today. I hope the visit was worth your time."

"A bit overwhelming, but yes, very useful," Margot said.

Tom smiled. "We should have warned you. Lunch with Ivan can have that effect."

Everyone laughed, and Ivan said, "It's a good thing, I keep telling them it's a good thing."

The group left to head to the visitor's reception, and Ivan led Leslie back to Miguel.

Leslie stated, "You didn't have to take the whole morning with us, and I know how hard that is. I do appreciate it, and I will bring my team back."

Ivan replied, "It was well worth it. When I heard Frontier International Group was coming, I was interested, and when I heard you were joining the visit, my decision was easy. I've wanted to meet you for years. Your reputation precedes you—and I was not disappointed."

They shook hands, and Miguel led her to the car.

Margot met with the team in a conference room at the Palo Alto airport before they all headed home. The group agreed to send their impressions and input to Rita by the end of the weekend—Margot was keen to keep the process moving. The members said their good-byes and boarded their respective flight.

Once they were at cruising altitude, the flight attendant distributed drinks and a snack. As she passed by Margot, she leaned toward her and said, "Leslie would like you to join her when you have a minute."

When I have a minute, mused Margot to herself. When the CEO suggests a meeting, she figured she 'had a minute.'

Margot walked back to where Leslie was working, at the same table they'd sat at on the flight out. Margot said, "I heard you'd like to talk with me. Does now work for you?"

"Yes, perfect," Leslie remarked, arranging her papers and closing her laptop. "I'm not going to violate your guidance about talking about this trip before documenting our notes. I have a different topic to discuss."

"Ok, sounds good," Margot said.

Leslie stated, "I thought about your suggestion of procurement leading product improvement and talked it over with Jean, Erica, and Matt. Initially, I don't think we understood it, and then, after each of us thought about it a bit more, it made some sense. You explained it in terms related to category management implementation activities, and you have to remember that we've never seen that. Anyways, we thought about it and then talked further this week. I always stay on Central Time when I'm on the West Coast, and that gave me time in the morning for a few calls."

Margot nodded. "I do the same thing. It works great during the week, but it means I'm a bit tired at the end of the week."

Leslie nodded and said, "It does. The advantage of flying home tonight is the elimination of an extra night away. So, back to the topic at hand. Erica, Matt, and I have a request. We want you to take on the interim role of head of procurement and product improvement for the healthcare business. We want you to work with Mary, Julian, and Erica to create this as a new role in that business. Erica is excited to have someone focused on improving her in-market products and sees this as a potential game changer for her business. It is interim because you will remain the overall CPO, and when Mary comes back from maternity leave, you will transition the role to her. How does that sound?"

Margot paused a minute before responding. "It sounds great. At one level, it sounds like 'be careful what you wish for,' and at another level, it is exciting to think about pulling this idea to fruition. What are you thinking about for timing?"

Leslie said, "Soon, very soon. We'd like to announce this no later than Monday—sooner if you're okay with it. I expect you'll want to talk with your family, as this will impact them at least as much as you. Our expectation is that you'll be nearly full-time in Copenhagen during the assignment. Jean's team will work with you to arrange a furnished rental home and help with whatever is needed for your family."

"Wow," Margot exclaimed. "I will talk with my family tonight and get back to you. I believe Mary is back in three months, which means we'd be in Copenhagen from mid-May to early August."

"That's consistent with our planning," Leslie replied. She continued, "I expect you'd continue to lead the global procurement function and, particularly, this AI review and planning. You'll know better than me, but I think the day-to-day leadership of the Oklahoma City team is in safe hands with Tanya and Frank. They seem solid and better than I'd remembered or expected."

Leslie continued, "I am very impressed with you, Margot. Your insights, your leadership skills, and your stakeholder engagement skills are top-notch. This is an opportunity for you to help create something new with Erica. She is the future leader of the company. You and she can learn from each other. I don't want to overwhelm you, but I do want you to know that we're starting to realize how much talent and potential you bring to the company. If you have any questions about the mechanics of this assignment, such as pay and expenses, you should talk directly with Jean. I don't know the details other than to be able to say that it will work out very well for you. You should also feel free to talk with Erica and Matt as needed. In this assignment, you'll report to both. Do you have any questions?"

"No, not yet," Margot nearly mumbled, still overwhelmed. "I expect I'll have a bunch of them soon, but for now I need to digest it all."

"I understand," Leslie stated. "While you're 'digesting,' I'll work on my summary for Rita."

Margot said, "Thank you, Leslie. Thank you for joining us on this trip, for listening, and for this opportunity." She stood up and returned to her seat.

When she reached her seat, she opened her laptop, retrieved her STP template file, and started a new one: "Copenhagen Opportunity." She needed to be ready for her family discussion tonight!

On her way home from the airport, Margot called Jason. "Hi, Jason, I'm on the way home."

"That's great, I didn't think you'd be back this early," Jason replied.

"That's the benefit of flying on the company jet with Leslie." Margot replied. "How are the boys?"

"They're fine. They're playing out back right now," Jason said.

"Good," Margot said. "I wanted to give you a heads-up on my conversation with Leslie on the flight back." She proceeded to describe her conversation with Leslie, including the offer of a short-term relocation to Copenhagen.

"Wow," he exclaimed, "that's an amazing opportunity!"

"It is," she agreed, "but it has huge family impact, and I want to talk it over with you. I told her I'd get back to her next week. Maybe we can have a quick, easy family dinner, and then you and I talk while the boys watch a movie. What do you think?"

"I think that's an excellent idea. Why don't you pick up a pizza on the way home. I'll call and order it now."

"That's great, and please have some wine ready for us!"

The four had an enjoyable, lighthearted dinner as the boys, Tommy, age six and in first grade, and Johnny, age eight and in third grade, recounted their week at school. Their Labrador, Max, sat between the boys and waited for food to be dropped or spilled.

Margot was glad to be home and back with her family.

Once the boys were cleaned up and watching a movie, she and Jason sat down at the kitchen table to talk. She'd printed her STP and had it on the table.

Jason started, "Before we look at the STP, tell me how you're feeling about this. We'll come back to the STP, but for now, just focus on your feelings."

She loved this about Jason. He was an engineer, but he was quite sensitive about these things. She began, "I've never felt like this in my career before. I am trusted and respected at the highest levels. I feel overwhelmed and exhilarated at the same time. If we can do this new approach, it will change the practice of procurement. I also feel torn. You have your career, and the boys have their school and friends. And we have our family. It's like I need two of me." She took a sip of wine, paused, then asked, "How do you feel about all of this?"

"Me," he said, "I could not be prouder. I've always known you had this in you, and I'm delighted to see you recognized and appreciated."

"What about your job?" she asked. Jason was a mid-level

mechanical engineer with a small firm in Oklahoma City that did contract design work.

"My job is okay, but it is nothing that should hold us back," he remarked. "I have been there a few years and think I could either take a leave of absence or work part-time virtually. All of my work is on the computer, and we worked from home during Covid. Worst case, I find a new job when we're back. My job should not hold us back."

She smiled at him. He was always so supportive. She picked up the STP and said, "I can add those as options in the proposals."

He laughed and said, "Yes, let's look at the STP. What about the boys and school?"

She frowned a bit. "The timing isn't perfect for them. They still have a couple of months of school."

He nodded. "Yes, but let's be honest, it's first and third grade. It's not like they'd be missing the end of senior or junior year of high school. What if I homeschooled them for the last couple of months? We could talk with their school."

She'd not considered Jason homeschooling the boys. He was an excellent father but not as hands-on with their schoolwork as she. She checked their backpacks every night and looked at the notes from the teachers. How would he homeschool them?

As if reading her mind, he added, "I would not homeschool them the same as you might, but that would not make it bad. Think about it, if the three of us had all day, and in some cases all week while you're busy, we could travel all over Europe and learn. It would be much more than they'll learn at a classroom here."

She was impressed with his openness to the idea and reflected on what he said. "You're right about that. Imagine learning, even at the most basic levels, some of the history and the foods and the sports."

He added, "Copenhagen is very centrally located. We could travel from there every weekend and see many places we've only dreamed about. In case you're wondering, I vote yes." He held up his wine glass in salute and said, "To the summer in Europe!"

She returned his salute. They clinked glasses. She wriggled up her nose. "Oh, Max farted! What about Max? We probably can't bring him."

He frowned. "You're right. I'd not thought about him. I could not bring myself to kennel him for the flight there and back. Who could watch him while we're gone?"

She said, "We need to think about that. Our yard is big and fenced so he gets exercise and is safe. We'd need someplace as safe. And someone who will love him like we do."

"What about your sister? She could stay here and keep Max."

"No, she's not reliable enough. If anything happened to Max, I'd never forgive myself."

"What about the house?"

"My understanding is that the company will rent us a furnished place in Copenhagen," she remarked. "What we do with the house while we're gone is up to us."

"What about our parents, then?" he asked. "Could they take him while we're gone?"

She thought about that for a while. Her parents were outside Boston and, while their backyard was fenced, it was small, and they both worked. Max would be home alone all day. That would only work with a dog walker. Jason's parents were in NH, and they had a large yard, but it wasn't fenced. There was no obvious solution.

She contemplated the suggestion. "I don't know. I'll make some notes on the STP, but there is no obvious solution to Max."

He scanned the STP. "But, on the bright side, we have solved the bigger problems. What else do we need to discuss before you talk with the company on Monday?"

"I don't know anything about pay or the other details," she said. "Leslie said it would be well worth it for me, and I could talk with Jean about the details. Let's make some notes on those questions."

They brainstormed the other issues, including healthcare coverage, housing selection, and location, and potential trips home or to Europe for family. Once this was done, they went to the computer and pulled up a map of Europe. For the next hour they made a list of potential spots to visit. This move had huge positive potential for the family!

Saturday morning, she sent an email to Leslie and Jean that she and her husband had talked and were positive about the opportunity. She requested a meeting with Jean to clarify and confirm a few questions.

She and Jason had not yet talked with the boys, but they were young, and she wasn't concerned about them wanting to go. At their age, they still enjoyed time with their parents, and anything Mom and Dad were excited about was good enough for them.

Late evening Sunday, Jean responded enthusiastically and suggested that they have coffee in her office first thing Monday morning. Things were moving quickly!

MARCH 4TH

Margot arrived at Jean's office, and her door was open, so she knocked on the door, "Good morning, Jean."

"Good morning, Margot. Come in," Jean greeted, pointing to a table with coffee and scones. "I wasn't sure if you liked or ate them, but they looked great today. Help yourself."

Margot served herself, sat down, and started, "Thanks for making time so quickly to talk with me."

"My pleasure. I've been doing this work a long time, and what we're about to talk about is make-or-break for your success over there. I never worry if the person can do the job; I worry if the family is going to be happy. If the family isn't happy, it doesn't work. How is your husband feeling about this?"

Margot smiled. "Jason is great. He's open to everything from homeschooling the boys through the end of the school year through all the potential job implications he may have, including finding a new job. He's very supportive."

"Remind me," Jean said. "What does he do?"

"He's a mechanical engineer," Margot shared. "His specialty is design."

"Very interesting," Jean remarked as she made notes on her notepad. "I'm glad he's supportive. It's a short assignment, so maybe he can take a leave of absence and come back to his current job."

Margot replied, "He's going to talk to his company about that today. We'll see."

"What about your kids?"

"They're young, first and third grade, but they think it will be fun to explore with us. To them, it sounds like a long field trip."

"I suspect that's what it will be like for them. They should have a great time. What are your questions or outstanding issues?"

Margot took out her STP and put it on the table.

Jean smiled, remarking, "I expected nothing less."

Margot blushed a bit before stating, "It's never let me down. A few questions from a work and a personal perspective." She turned the STP around and pointed to the bottom of the page, where it stated: "More information required."

Jean suggested, "Let's work through them one-by-one. If I don't know the answer, we'll agree how to get it."

Forty-five minutes later, they'd answered all but one work question, who should be the site leader for procurement at HQ in her absence, which needed Matt's input, and who would watch Max on the personal list.

Jean offered, "I can set up time for us with Matt, or you can talk with him. He was briefed by Leslie along the way and is very supportive. As for Max, talk with your family and friends and let me know if you cannot figure out a solution. I'm excited for you and your family, and I'm delighted you're going to step into this role. Contact me if you need anything."

Margot thanked her and headed back to her own office. They'd agreed to talk with Erica on Wednesday morning to finalize the announcement that would be posted Thursday morning. She could talk with her team on Wednesday afternoon but not beforehand. She felt like she was going to explode with excitement in the meantime, and a walk down the stairs instead of the elevator would help.

As she entered the procurement floor from the stairs, Lee was exiting the elevator. "Good morning, Margot."

"Good morning. How was your weekend?"

Lee responded, "It was good. My semester is going well, and I'm starting to think about my summer plans. I have another year before I graduate, so this is an important summer for me." She fell into step alongside Margot as they talked.

Margot asked, "What are you thinking about?"

"My internship here ends at the end of May. I was considering going home for the summer, but there are no jobs there. I don't want to spend my final summer lifeguarding at a pool."

"Why don't you stay here? Maybe take a couple of summer-only classes. In my experience, there are some summer classes that are very interesting and only offered then."

Lee frowned. "I cannot afford that. I live on campus and can't stay in the dorms after the classes are over."

They'd arrived outside Margot's office, and she said, "Keep an open mind and look at the summer classes. Let's talk later in the week. I also want to hear what's new with office supplies."

"Okay, thanks," Lee parted.

Margot sat at her desk and emailed Jason an update on all the answers from Jean as well as the potential idea to have Lee housesit and watch Max. There were so many moving parts, and she didn't want to miss any critical communication. She walked out to Rita's desk and asked, "Hi, Rita, do you have a minute?"

"Of course," Rita said, they walked back to Margot's office. Rita was about to take a seat when Margot motioned for her to close the door—a rare occurrence for Margot that piqued her interest.

"What's up?" Rita asked.

"Well," Margot started. "This goes back to our trip last week. What I'm going to start with is confidential until midweek. No notes for a couple of minutes."

She shared her conversation with Leslie on the trip to Seattle and Leslie's request and offer on the trip back.

Rita's expression rapidly evolved from surprise to incredulity to delight. She blurted out, "That woman amazes me! She really does listen to people. I couldn't believe it when she listened to me about kids and values, and now you're telling me that in the space of less than a week, she and her team hear about an opportunity and jump on it. I'm very happy for you."

Margot smiled. "Jason and I are working on our STP. By the end of the week, we'll be in full-blown project planning."

Rita was thankful she'd swallowed her coffee quickly, because she burst out laughing, then remarked, "You two are a couple of romantics! Well, congratulations. What can we do here to help?"

"I'm glad you asked," Margot almost sighed in relief. "That's what we need to talk about next."

Based on being allowed to talk with her team after lunch on Wednesday, Margot suggested a working lunch for the procurement AI team. Those HQ-based could join in person, and those remote could join virtually. She'd review the news with them—it was their suggestion.

Rita had already sent out the compilation of inputs from the team members, and it was over twenty pages long.

Margot asked Rita to work with one or two of the team members to develop summary themes as an overlay. She suggested a couple of agenda items and asked Rita to develop an agenda. Together, these would be good steps for her development. Rita took it all in stride and eagerly accepted the assignments.

After Rita left, Margot started to send out emails to advance discussions with Matt and Erica. Once she'd agreed on key topics with them, she could move forward with her team and conversations with Mary and Julian.

Matt was the first to respond, as usual, and suggested they meet over lunch. They met in the cafeteria and discussed the two options for interim site leader: Frank and Shelly. After a few minutes of conversation, they agreed on Frank. Margot knew that a couple of months ago she would never have thought this, but he'd stepped up to the work and knew Frontier and all of the key decision makers. Shelly was excellent but simply too new. Margot would need to talk with her one on one to ensure she was not disappointed or read the wrong meanings into the decision.

Erica called her instead of responding to her email, "Hi, I just read your email."

"Hi, thanks for getting back to me so quickly," Margot greeted.

Erica stated, "I am really excited about this and appreciate you taking it on. I want you to let me know what you need from me to make this successful."

"It's a short list for now. I want to talk to Mary and Julian as soon as possible to start the planning. I'm thinking of flying over next week if they're available. My goal is to have an outlined plan to you by the end of the week. What do you think?"

"I cannot speak to their availability, but I cannot imagine that Mary is traveling with the baby, and Julian is just back from his trip to California with you. If you can pull together a draft plan for the following week, that will be great."

"Okay," Margot replied. "I'll reach out to them and see if we can talk. I know the posting isn't going up until later this week and don't want to run afoul of the process."

"Go ahead and email them, then brief them by phone. It will be fine," Erica suggested.

"Okay, I'll keep you posted. Thanks," Margot finished.

"You're welcome, good luck."

Margot paused, trying to remember the name of Mary's baby. It was Erin. She then sent her a quick note indicating a desire to catch up. She followed this with an email to Julian.

Surprisingly, it was Mary who responded first, stating she was available now, the baby was asleep.

Margot immediately called her and listened as Mary regaled her with the stories of Erin since her birth. It had been a while since her boys had been born, and it was nice to remember that time—except the never-ending fatigue due to lost sleep. She was glad that was over. Once Mary had shared her updates, she asked how the AI team was doing; she'd received the compilation of impressions email but had not opened it.

Margot shared her impressions of the visits as well as the team outings. On reflection, it was an amazing week and quite a team experience. She then came to the trip home and shared the summary of Leslie's request. She emphasized the temporary nature of the role and that Mary would step into this new, bigger role after her leave.

Mary exclaimed, "What a week to miss! I wish I'd been there with you. I'm very happy to hear your news about coming over. It will be very nice to work with you and for our families to meet. I think that my husband, Franz, can help your husband with the area. He's from Austria and had to make the adjustment himself. What are your plans?"

Margot shared, "I'm going to talk with Julian, but I'm hoping to come over next week to start planning. My plan is not to impose on you, but I want you to know what's happening. If you want to contribute, I'll do whatever is needed to make that happen."

A baby could be heard stirring in the background.

Mary started, "I need to go now, but please let me know what you and Julian decide. Thank you," and she hung up.

Margot hung up and smiled. She thought to herself, "Poor Mary, she's not off from work; she's actually working 24/7 now!"

Julian replied by email shortly afterward that he'd be available toward the end of the day and asked if he could call her. She responded yes and was glad the key pieces were moving. She took a minute to look at the flight options and, satisfied that there were plenty of choices, pushed on with her day.

A few minutes before noon, the lunch Rita ordered arrived from the cafeteria and was set up in the conference room. Shortly thereafter, Margot, Frank, Shelly, and Tanya arrived and took seats. Margot connected the virtual meeting, and they could see Harry in Singapore in his home office. Julian had not yet connected from Copenhagen. Willie arrived a few minutes later, silently mouthed "Hello," and took a seat at the table. Alec and Phil connected a short time after that.

Margot started, "Good evening, Harry. I hope your flight home last week was ok. Thank you for meeting with us now at short notice."

"Hello, Margot," Harry greeted. "My flight was fine, and I expected we'd need to talk after the trip last week.

"Good morning, all," Phil chimed in. "I really appreciated Leslie joining us and sharing her plane. I could get used to that."

"Hi, all," Alec added.

"Hi, Alec, thanks for joining on short notice," Margot greeted.

Julian joined and looked a bit out of breath, "Sorry I'm late. It's a busy day here. Seems like something is going on, but I don't know what."

Margot said, "Thanks for joining us, Julian. Welcome all. Phil, it's a bit premature to start looking at your own jet, but I agree it was a great way to travel. I want to start by thanking everyone for sending their thoughts to Rita and to Rita for compiling them and sending them out this morning. We have a lot of great insights. I asked Rita to add a summary to the raw data, and she will reach out to a couple of you to help with that process."

Margot continued, "The calendar is moving forward, and we need to start thinking about a rough draft of the procurement AI strategy. I think the longer we have a blank page, the harder it will be. My request is that we create a draft and then share and build until it is done. Also, I've been thinking about Rita's question all weekend, 'What if AI doesn't come to fruition as everyone is saying?' and think we need to reflect that in our plans. My request is that we have three versions of our strategy. One is the core plan—what we think will happen with AI and our strategy to address it in the function. The other two are permutations, with one being it goes slower than planned and the other that it goes faster than planned. I think this will confirm the interdependencies and give us the ability to flex the plan as AI capabilities unfold. What do you think?"

Shelly jumped in. "I agree. I'd be happy to start the process if you want."

"Yes, please do." Margot nodded. "Anyone want to work with Shelly on this?" Everyone said they'd help. "This continues to be an excellent team. Shelly, please set up a session, and I recommend using Alec's assistance."

Shelly nodded, promising, "I'll work with Rita and send out a few virtual invites starting this week."

Margot added, "I have one more topic that I need to cover with the team. On the flight back last week, I talked with Leslie. More accurately, Leslie talked with me. She really likes our suggestion to have procurement drive in-market product improvement. In fact, she likes it so much that she wants to start a pilot program in the healthcare business immediately. The plan is that I will temporarily relocate to Copenhagen and work with Julian to start the program. Julian, I'm sorry you and I did not connect before this call."

"No worries." Julian smiled. "That's great news! When are you coming over?"

"I talked with Erica this morning," Margot said. "And if you're available, Julian, I will fly over for early next week. We need to have a plan developed for Erica by the end of the week. What's your availability?"

"I have lots of time next week," said Julian. "This will be our priority."

The other questions then started around the room and online.

Margot pulled out her STP to remind herself. "Let me see if I can answer a number of your questions." She reviewed what she knew about the role details and shared the appropriate personal information as well. She stated, "I talked with Mary this morning, and she says hello. She and Erin and Franz are doing well. Once Erin woke up, our call was over, but she knows about this plan and knows that she'll be stepping into the new role after her maternity leave. We expect she'll be back at work in Copenhagen, and I'll be back here in Oklahoma City by the middle of August. It's vacation season, and that will give each of us a chance to get resettled."

"This is huge, good news," Frank gushed.

"I agree," Willie and Tanya said at the same time.

"This has the potential to reset the procurement value proposition worldwide," Alec said. "This is very exciting."

Margot turned to Shelly and then to the group more broadly and said, "We cannot lose sight of category management. Shelly is the global lead on this transformation, and we cannot lose focus due to any of these efforts. Our Wave One teams will be included in the budget process this year and selection of our Wave Two teams should be part of the budget process for next year. If we continue to take a measured approach and ensure our teams deliver value and are tightly linked with the business priorities, we'll be okay. Shelly, you'll need to work with Matt to structure the Wave Two dialog with the ELT in the coming couple of months."

Shelly was busy writing notes, but said, "Sure, I'll take care of it."

Margot said, "Frank, per the chart of accounts, you're my backup in the building for approvals and signatures. That will continue when I'm in Copenhagen. I expect you to collaborate with Rita, Tanya, and Shelly, but please also act as a shepherd for the local team."

Rita asked, "When will this all be announced?"

Margot replied, "It will be announced tomorrow morning. I had approval to talk with you after lunch so, if anyone asks you, tell them you had lunch before the conversation."

Everyone laughed and the meeting ended. The group stayed in the room and enjoyed lunch and a deep sense of camaraderie.

After lunch, on her way back to her office, Margot stopped at Lee's desk and asked, "Do you have a few minutes?"

Lee said, "Sure," and followed with a notepad.

"What did you find for summer classes?" Margot asked.

Lee blushed a bit. "It's a bit nerdy, but there are a couple of statistics classes that look interesting. I really enjoy math and statistics."

Margot smiled. "You will use those your entire career. If they're interesting, so much the better. What if I had a potential solution to your housing issue?"

Lee looked surprised and asked, "What do you have in mind?"

Margot explained that she and her family would be going to Copenhagen for the summer and that she needed someone to watch the house and take care of Max. The guest room had its own bathroom, and she would have the place to herself.

"Wow," Lee exclaimed. "That's huge! How far away from campus is your house?"

"It's about fifteen miles away," Margot shared. "I don't think there is any public transportation."

"That's not a problem," Lee remarked. "I have my car."

"Think about it, talk to your parents, and if you're interested, let me know. If yes, we'll have you over to meet Max and see the place. If no, nothing lost."

"Do you have any pictures of Max?"

"Of course I do," Margot replied. She scrolled through her phone and found some recent pictures of him with the boys and said, "He's really sweet and good company."

"Okay, I'll talk with my parents," Lee promised before she walked back to her desk.

MARCH 5TH

Early the next morning, Margot was working at her desk when Lee stopped by and knocked on her open door.

"Good morning. Come in," Margot invited.

Lee took a seat and said, "I talked with my parents, and they're very supportive of me taking the summer classes."

"Excellent," Margot enthused. "Why don't you plan to come over to the house on Saturday for lunch, and you can meet Max and see the house." She gave her the address and they agreed the timing.

"See you Saturday," Lee said. "I'm going to register online for those statistics classes before they fill up."

Margot smiled inwardly—nothing like advanced statistics classes to spell fun for the summer. Oh, to be young again!

Many congratulatory phone calls and emails arrived after her announcement was posted. She found the support heartwarming and reassuring. She had to admit that she was more than a little nervous—nobody had done this before.

As a result of all the activities, the week passed quickly, and Saturday morning, she found herself organizing Jason and the boys to quickly pick up the house before Lee arrived. She did not want Lee to think they lived in a messy house!

Lee arrived on time and was greeted by the ever-enthusiastic Max, who dropped a spit-covered tennis ball at Lee's feet and was quite insistent until Lee rolled the ball away. Max pounced on it and eagerly retrieved it.

Margot laughed and surmised, "Max has already trained you! He will do that for hours if you let him. Come on in, and I'll show you around."

She introduced Lee to Jason, who asked, "Would you mind driving our cars once a week? I can make a schedule for you. I don't want them to sit idle all summer."

"Sure," Lee agreed. "I'm happy to do that."

"Thanks," Jason said, hurrying off to attend to the boys.

Margot, Lee, and Max ended up on the back deck looking out on the lawn. Margot threw the ball, and Max took off to retrieve it. "Well, what do you think?" She asked. "Will this work for you for the summer?"

"Are you kidding, this will be amazing!" Lee exclaimed. "Thank you, Margot, for thinking of me."

Lee stayed for lunch and enjoyed herself. Margot and Jason seemed like ideal parents and the boys, while a bit rambunctious, managed themselves through lunch with the newcomer. She then said her goodbyes and headed off.

MARCH 6TH

The two members of the corrugated team from the industrial business, José and Ron, acted as the hosts for the meeting. They'd coordinated the meeting venue, scheduled the factory tour, and arranged the team dinners, with each of them taking responsibility for one of the dinners.

Ron was responsible for the welcome dinner, and Sean was a bit nervous. Ron was one of the quieter members of the team, and Sean wondered what type of place he'd select. They all met in the hotel lobby and exchanged small talk before boarding the minibus and heading to the venue. Ron hadn't shared any details with the other participants.

It turned out that Sean needn't have worried. While quiet in the meetings, Ron wasn't a recluse, and they found themselves in a true Milwaukee landmark, Sobelmans. It wasn't fancy or too crowded—it was March and still quite cold—but the experience was authentic Milwaukee. The restaurant pulled together a couple of tables away from the other diners, and they relaxed and reconnected.

Everyone on the team greeted Marek and did their best to include him in the conversations. Like many of his Polish countrymen, Marek spoke a number of languages, and his English, while a bit stiff in delivery, was perfect.

Sean asked Marek to join him at the end of the table and opened with, "It's really nice to meet you in person. The consumer electronics business is very advanced, and we can learn a lot from you."

"That is true," Marek agreed.

Sean was surprised by the response but continued, "How long have you been with the business?"

"I joined straight from university. I did an internship with the company before. I've been there almost fifteen years."

"What was it like when you first joined?"

Marek gave the first hint of a smile. "It was like you describe the rest of the business. Not too many drawings; not too many good suppliers. It was unacceptable."

The waitress brought them each another signature Bloody Mary and removed their empty glasses.

Marek picked up his glass, took a sip, and said, "I don't often have Bloody Marys. These are excellent."

"I agree," Sean remarked. "They're wonderful tonight, but we'll see how we feel tomorrow." Sean continued a bit tentatively, "I appreciate you coming to this meeting. It will be good to have your input and participation."

"Harry and Genevieve did not give me a choice," Marek explained. "I was told to be here. I hope it is worthwhile."

"I do, too," Sean stated. "Please let me know how you're feeling about the meeting as it goes."

At the end of the dinner, Sean stood up and tapped on his glass with a knife and said, "Thank you, Ron, for arranging an excellent meal. I'm looking forward to the meeting and have been working hard with Anna on the agenda and details. All of you have been working hard on the data collection and stakeholder engagement, and it feels like we're well prepared for the meeting. The quick-win results are starting to come through, and they're impressive. I just wanted to say thank you and that I'm looking forward to moving forward in the process."

"Hear, hears" and glass clinks were heard around the table. The mood of the group was very positive. They didn't have grounds to celebrate, yet, but they knew they were on track for success.

MARCH 7TH

As the minibus pulled into the parking lot, the difference between the healthcare venue in Johnson City and this industrial venue were clear. The healthcare site was new and immaculate, almost sterile. This site looked well-lived-in: not quite dirty or delipidated but clearly reflective of the grittier nature of the industrial business.

José greeted them in the lobby. "Welcome to our site. This is both the HQ for the industrial business and one of our largest manufacturing sites. It is the original site of the business. We'll go on a tour after lunch today. Please follow me, as you need to watch the site orientation and safety practices video before you can enter."

The video depicted the various products made at the site and some of the manufacturing processes. They ranged from machining to assembly and finishing. Most foundry and forging work were outsourced but had previously been performed on-site. The resulting products were big, heavy, and impressive. Each person received a hard hat, safety glasses, and a safety vest. They were all cautioned to remove any loose jewelry, contain long hair, and verify that they were wearing closed-toe shoes. This was very different from the healthcare site, and each of them appreciated the difference.

Once in the meeting room, Anna set to work and posted the agenda, parking lot, action plan, quick win, and strategic insights flip charts. Sean posted the flip charts from the prior meeting. When the group finally had their coffee and tea and sat down, it looked like they'd been working for days—which was true.

"The first item on the agenda," Sean started, "is a welcome by Genevieve. She will join us virtually in five minutes. We'll pick up with the rest of the agenda after that. I encourage you to ask her any questions you have while she's with us. After lunch, we're going to tour the facility. José is going to lead the tour, but feel free to ask Ron questions as well. Tonight, we'll be joined at dinner by the business president, Bob, and a few members of his leadership team."

The video screen came to life and Genevieve appeared and said, "Good morning, team! I'm glad to see you're all there. I've talked with Sean and Anna about this meeting and know you'll be working through a range of strategic analysis tools with the goal of developing a category strategy. I encourage you to be bold. Do not be constrained by what was done in the past. Look to the future of our customers, our company, and the supply market. I will rejoin the meeting Thursday afternoon and look forward to hearing about your progress. Are there any questions?"

There were, in fact, many questions from the group, and Sean was inwardly proud of the team. Too many sessions like this ended with an executive asking if there were questions and nobody being either brave or thoughtful enough to ask any. It looked like Genevieve was happy as well. She answered each question thoughtfully and never once looked at her watch or gave any indication that she was trying to limit the discussions.

Genevieve finished by saying, "I understand that you're having dinner tonight with Bob and his leadership team. I encourage you to ask them good questions about their business, their needs, and their concerns and, most importantly, to listen to their answers. Their answers may be different than what you heard in Johnson City. I expect that, as the businesses are very different. It is vital that you understand these differences and that Bob and his team are confident in your understanding. Good luck, and I'll talk with you on Thursday."

"She's a great sponsor," Anna observed. "I've worked with a lot of teams over my career, and she's easily one of the best. Let's get started so we're ready for Thursday." She reviewed the agenda, and it was packed with strategic analysis tools. "A reminder, we're not doing any of these tools for the sake of 'doing a tool.' We're using the process and the tools to develop strategic insights." She pointed to the associated flip chart. "We're working on quick wins, and you know what those are," pointing to the quick-win flip chart. "Our focus now is on strategic options. These are bigger than quick wins and could take three to five or more years. We will use the insights to develop these options. If you think of an option along the way, please note it on the strategic-option flip chart," she said as she pointed to that chart. "We have flip charts for everything," she remarked. "With that, let's get started."

She facilitated the team through category classification and portfolio analysis before lunch. It was a lot for them to process, and the lunch break and tour would be helpful reflection time.

After lunch in the meeting room, José asked them to don their hard hats, vests, and safety glasses. They walked down a couple of office hallways and then out a metal door into an expansive warehouse space.

"This is where our finished product is stored until shipping," José stated, pointing to the pallet stacks and large items on the floor. "Some of our products are too large and too heavy to go in the pallet racks, and we store them on the floor. You'll notice that these are always in a wooden crate or a reusable steel or fiberglass shell. Inside these outer protections is a thick layer of corrugation for protection, shock absorption, and stabilization. Each item is secured to the pallet, but the corrugated adds an extra layer of protection. The smaller and lighter items on the racks use corrugated as the outside protection and may have additional materials inside."

"This is nothing like what we saw in Johnson City," Chee Chung observed.

"That's right," José replied. "The closest anything in Johnson City comes to this scale are the larger instruments. They are shipped on pallets with corrugated covers like the items on our racks. Everything else we saw there was in a unit package and then bulk packaged in a corrugated container. Most of our product is shipped in individual units."

"That's a key difference in the business requirements between the businesses," Sean said. "They each have very different requirements, and their customers have different inputs as well. We see that in the stakeholder inputs."

"That's right," Frank agreed, nodding to José to keep moving.

"We're going to work upstream through the production process," José continued. "Let's move on."

At each step, José or Ron explained what was occurring and asked the line operators to add their comments if they'd missed anything. Everyone on the team was impressed that seemingly everyone at the site knew each other on a first-name basis.

When they were back in the conference room, Chee Chung commented on this. "You all know each other by name. How many people work here?"

"There are just under one thousand people working here now," Ron answered. "It's part of our culture. Bob doesn't quite run this as a family business, as there are over ten thousand employees worldwide, but this site is special. We have many employee events and are proudly non-union in an area that is quite pro-union."

"This business is so different from the healthcare business; how will we pick one strategy or one supplier for both?" Lee asked.

"I'm glad you asked that," Anna remarked. "Your task is to develop a global strategy that fully meets the business requirements for all the businesses. It must address the unique business requirements, issues, and priorities of each. It is not likely to be the same for each business. Additionally, a global strategy does not necessarily mean a global supplier. The global strategy could dictate regional solutions. It could include flexibility by business, but it will be coherent when viewed globally."

"Thanks, I know you said that before, but it is helpful to hear it again after seeing the differences firsthand," Lee said.

"Let's pick up where we left off," Anna continued. The group then completed the customer segmentation analysis and she posted the flip charts for customer segmentation, portfolio analysis, and category classification side by side. "These three tools are the core of our analysis. Each one is important, but it is when you consider the side-by-side results that powerful insights are built. For instance, note that elements of this category are in proprietary and critical or bottleneck. Are the suppliers for these items treating you as exploit or as core?"

It was as if a scab had finally been pulled from a wound; everyone in the group tried to speak at once, and the energy rose to a crescendo.

"Excellent, excellent—that's real passion. Let's go through this in turn," Anna commended, and the group worked through each sub-category element and a number of suppliers. She asked them, "Do you have any strategic insights? Any strategic options?"

Again, the energy rose as they called out options. She suggested, "Let's use the sticky notes on the table. Use orange for strategic insights and blue for strategic options. Use one note per idea and then post them on the respective flip chart." For the next ten minutes the room was silent except for the members writing their ideas and then posting them on the two flip charts.

"Can a couple of you work on strategic insights and another couple on strategic options and do an affinity sort of similar ideas?" she asked.

The team quickly rose to the task, and those not actively involved in the affinity sort took a short break.

"Let's see what you came up with."

The respective flip chart leaders shared their results, and all discussed and built on the ideas submitted. Anna asked, "Do you have any observations on the strategic options?"

"I think so," Frank piped up. "There is a very broad mix of options or ideas here. Some are, no offense intended, big ideas, and some are smaller or more incremental. Also, some of the options could be done this year or next year and some are farther in the future."

"That is exactly right." Anna beamed. "Our task for tomorrow afternoon, after we've completed the analysis tasks, is to do the review that Frank just summarized. We'll assess each option idea for potential impact and then do a review of timing. Our goal is the layered strategy I described at the kickoff meeting. Hopefully, you can see how some of the elements would fit together, but it's too soon for that conversation. Let's move on to the detailed cost analysis that Lee was working on with Beroe."

Lee connected her computer and presented the Beroe report. "Thanks, Anna. I sent Beroe the specifications for our top three SKUs in each business and a couple of others for each region that looked interesting based on complexity or purchase price or quality issues. I have the details for each of these SKUs, and we can discuss them, but I wanted to start at the high level. Based on what we're paying currently, the associated specifications, and the current paper pulp and corrugated markets in the respective regions, we're paying twenty-eight percent more, on average, than we should be. That includes allowances for shipping and the supplier profit. In short, some of our suppliers are treating us like we're in nuisance or exploit, as we saw in the customer segmentation tool."

"Is there any good news?" Sean asked.

"There is a little," Lee said. "There is one supplier in Europe who seems reasonable, and there is another here in Wisconsin that has excellent quality and service, and their pricing is not quite as high."

"The supplier you mentioned in Europe is my supplier," Marek said. "They are more than reasonable. They are excellent."

"I encourage you not to think of this as good or bad news," Anna suggested. "These are new facts from which you can derive new insights and potential strategic options. Please take a minute and do that now. While you're doing that, I want to reemphasize something. If Margot and the ELT were going to punish the team for finding opportunities like this, then you'd stop looking. Your job is to find the twenty-eight percent or ten percent or two percent innovation, quality, service, and total cost opportunities and develop a strategy to achieve them. Focus on the positive; focus on the future. Based on Lee's findings, this is a huge opportunity for the team."

The team continued through Porter's five forces analysis after a short break, and Anna observed they looked overwhelmed, particularly the European and Asian team members. She looked at Sean, and he looked a bit overdone as well. She finally decided out loud, "Let's stop here for today. We'll do the daily close out, take a few minutes for emails, and then head back to the hotel to clean up before dinner with Bob and his team."

A palpable sense of relief filled the room. They didn't want to disappoint each other, but they were ready for a break.

José arranged the team dinner close to the industrial site. It was a casual setting, one step up from a neighborhood bar, and the group had a private room that was quiet.

Bob entered with his team, and his presence was amazing. He was not intimidating, but all felt drawn to him to say hello, introduce themselves, and shake his hand; it was almost like the President of the United States had entered the room except without the pomp and circumstance.

"He has real gravitas," Anna remarked to Ron.

Ron responded, "Go talk to him when you can. He literally grew up in this town and in this business. He knows the business, he knows the people, and they like and trust him. His team is almost as good. Some are from the business, and others he's hired from the outside, but he is adamant about the cultural fit. As part of employee orientation, his welcome includes his view of the importance of fit within the business. He expects excellent performance, but he demands teamwork and collaboration. That's why we're non-unionized in a union-heavy city. I think if anyone ever wanted a union, they'd either have to list him as the president of the union or they'd be driven out by their fellow employees."

Bob had circulated around to them and extended his hand to Anna and said, "What is Ron telling you about our business? I'm Bob, welcome."

Anna offered her hand and said, "Thank you, I'm Anna, I'm the team's facilitator. We appreciate you hosting this meeting, our tour today, and you and your team joining us for dinner tonight."

"It's our pleasure." Bob smiled. "We're proud of our business and our site. Selfishly, we're also keen to make sure you and the team understand our business and don't cause us issues with corrugated."

What a breath of fresh air, Anna thought. No beating around the bush with corporate niceties and yet absent any meanness or defensiveness. She said, "Everyone's eyes were opened today. Our first meeting was at the healthcare site in Johnson City, and it is very different than your site. That's one of the reasons I like working on the corrugated category at different clients. It's ubiquitous, yet the applications are often very different. Everyone thinks they know the category, but once they see it in use, they have a deeper appreciation and respect for the unique business requirements."

"Good, I'm glad to hear you say that," Bob stated. "We're all still learning about category management, but what we've seen and heard so far is good. If you'll excuse me, I'm going to get a beer." He then ambled over to the bar.

"See, that's what I mean," Ron said. "You and he don't know each other, yet in under ten seconds, you've engaged each other in a real conversation. The whole dinner will be like that."

And it was like that. The seating arrangement wasn't set or forced, but it seemed to Anna that Bob had agreed with his team to spread out across the team. Each of Bob's team engaged a couple of the corrugated team, and they were in deep conversation throughout the dinner. They did not dominate the respective conversations but were clearly seeking to understand the category management process and how their unique business requirements would be assured in the future.

After dessert was offered (and largely refused), Bob stood up to make a few comments. "I really enjoyed the dinner tonight and appreciate you inviting us to join you. I can tell by the smiles of my team that they had a good time as well. I want to reinforce that we have an exceptionally tight relationship with our corrugated suppliers. They now understand what we need and deliver it consistently. We're not interested in chasing a lower-priced alternative at the expense of quality and service. Our business is very competitive and our margins are tight, so you might logically conclude that we are driven by price.

You'd be wrong. We are driven by our reputation and the trust of customers. We deliver a competitively priced product with exceptional longevity. These are typically expensive, capital items and are not disposable. I look forward to hearing more about your progress and hope your meeting goes well." Bob sat down and started his goodbyes to those sitting near him.

The group applauded and the conversation wound down, and ten minutes later, the team was in the minibus heading back to the hotel.

Anna and Sean were seated together. Sean remarked to her, "Bob and his team are great. They are engaging and direct."

"I think you used the same words to describe Genevieve," Anna observed.

"You're right," Sean admitted. "So far, all the senior executives we've engaged are like that. It says a lot about the company's culture."

"It does," Anna agreed. "It means you'll need to behave the same way when you're presenting the team's strategy. That's easier said than done, and lots of category managers are tentative and are asking for permission rather than sharing a strategy that was codeveloped with the key stakeholders."

"Genevieve has already offered to be part of the final approval process," Sean said. "Our timing is good, as the strategy will be completed prior to the budget process."

"That's not an accident," Anna remarked. "Margot aligned the timing to ensure the category strategies could inform the budget process and would not be an add-on or afterthought. Too many companies don't get this simple yet important step right."

They pulled up to the hotel, and everyone headed inside. A few migrated to the bar for a nightcap, but the long-distance travelers were tired.

MARCH 8TH

The next day was bright and crisp and a clear harbinger of spring. The group met in the lobby and boarded the minibus to the site. They knew the entry routine, picked up their safety gear, and headed to the meeting room.

Anna and Sean arranged the flip charts, and a few of the team members helped them. It was clear that this was "their team" now and they were enjoying it.

Anna started the meeting, "Ron and José, please send our thanks to Bob and his team. That was a nice dinner. Sometimes, as consultants, we call these mandatory dinners a 'forced fun event' because they can be tedious and boring. Last night was neither, and it wasn't due to the food, which was fine, but due to the company."

All around the team table there were head nods in agreement. Chee Chung's voice called out, "You're right."

Anna continued, "At the end of the meeting, Bob was nice but direct: Don't mess up our business. I believe I speak for all of you when I say that is not the goal. I like the medical maxim of 'do no harm.' That is why we are so careful to measure the baseline performance of the category across assurance of supply, quality, service, and cost before we start to implement changes. We must be able to prove we're making things better."

She then introduced the topics for the day, including risk analysis and planning and strategy development.

She continued, "These two topics are a bit of a 'chicken and the egg.' We will do strategy development and then look at the risks of the strategy to ensure we address the risks. It goes back to Bob's guidance—we must get this right and not disrupt the business."

She led the group through a review of the strategic insights developed to date. She encouraged the team to note any additional insights as well as the strategic options that would apply. A steady stream of insights and options as well as a couple of new quick wins emerged.

She then focused on the strategic options. "Yesterday, we talked about how some of the options are a natural fit with each other. We call these themes. We also talked about how some of them build on each other. Today, we're going to continue this work and develop all the themes and potential sequences. It's vital that we also compare our potential options with our current strategy. How would you describe the current strategy?"

"Each site buys what it needs locally," Lee answered.

"With periodic corporate help on supply issues and sourcing," José added.

"That sounds about right. What do you think, Sean?" Anna asked.

Sean's face was red, but he managed to reply, "It sounds right, but I think it also sounds pretty lame."

"It is not, as you say, lame," Marek interjected. "It works very well for the consumer electronics business in Europe."

Anna added, "It describes what was appropriate at the time. We're not here to judge the prior strategy nor to ascribe any blame. We're here to understand what is happening today, what is possible in the future, and to create a path forward that will fit and work for Frontier."

It took working through lunch and into the early afternoon for the team to develop all the option themes and sequence the key steps. By the afternoon break, they had it, and Anna had captured their work in a spreadsheet.

"Now we're going to assess each option," she instructed. "This is like what many of you do when selecting a supplier, except in this case, we will not mention any suppliers—this is solely about strategy selection. Before we can assess the strategic options, we need to agree on the criteria for assessment. What do you think we should use?"

A range of ideas were called out, including potential results, difficulties, and risks.

Anna brought up more explanations. "We're going to start with the business requirements. We promised the stakeholders we'd listen to them, so we must use the ability to deliver on the business requirements as the first set of criteria. I'll arrange them with the go/no-go criteria first, followed by the scalable criteria. This way, if a go/no-go criteria is not met, we don't have to consider that option further. We'll need to agree how to assess the differences between options on the scalable criteria. We use the stakeholder weighting and will apply a ten to the best performing option but will need to discuss how much to decrease the subsequent options. Lastly, we will also look at the potential value, difficulty, and risk for each option."

"That sounds like we're going to be here through dinner," Chee Chung observed, flagging a bit due to the time zones and standing up now.

"It could," Anna admitted, "but my experience is that the first option or two take a bit of time and the others go very quickly once the team has a handle on the process. Let's get started after a quick break."

After the break, Anna was sharing the spreadsheet, and it listed the options they'd developed as well as the business requirements used as assessment criteria. As she predicted, the first option took a while to score, the second was just a bit faster, and the others gained speed. By the time they assessed the eighth option, it only took ten minutes.

She commended them. "Well done, but you're not done yet. We now need to assess the current strategy. You understand the process, and it should be relatively easy. We're going to assess it on all the criteria."

It was easy, but they were very surprised to see that a few of the criteria were scored as a no go and most of the scalable items were low.

"We normally stop scoring at the first no go," she explained. "But in the case of the current strategy, it can be helpful to show how much we're currently missing. At one level, it is possible to say that the business is working today, and the go/no-go criteria must be wrong—it is impossible for it to be a no go if we're currently operating. My counsel is to look at this as an assessment of current performance and a view to future business requirements. In short, the current strategy does not meet the future business requirements for the category and must be changed. The good news is that you're already working on the new strategy."

"What do we do next?" Gina asked.

"We get dinner," José remarked, looking at his watch. "The minibus is picking us up in twenty minutes, and we're going straight to dinner."

"Okay, then tomorrow. What's next in the process?" Gina asked.

Anna responded, "Tonight, you'll sleep on it. Tomorrow morning, we'll go back through the strategy and revisit the risk analysis. I expect pieces of the work will change, particularly the difficulty and valuation. We can't be precise yet, but we can ensure our estimates are credible. After lunch, we'll share our process and results with Genevieve. She did not provide guidance to Sean in advance of ideas that could not be considered. She may, when she sees some of the ideas, provide an additional steer. We all need to listen carefully to what she has to say. Once we have her input, we will talk through how to engage the stakeholders with the updated ideas as well as next steps for review and approval. For now, relax after an excellent day and real progress."

It was a tired, but satisfied, group that entered the minibus. There was not a lot of conversation, as each person was either lost in thought or tired or both. As they were approaching the venue, Ron walked to the front of the minibus and said, "As the cohost for tonight, I hope you have a fun evening. The guidance I was given was that we needed something a bit unexpected and fun." The minibus turned into the parking lot of a bowling alley, and there was laughter heard on the bus. Ron continued, "Follow me inside to the right. We have a few lanes separated from the other lanes, and I'll watch your stuff while you get fitted for shoes. Once everyone has what they need, I'll provide additional instructions."

They were quite a sight as they walked back to their lanes with their bowling shoes. It was not an exaggeration to say that nobody looked like they'd done this recently. Once they were all back, Ron picked up his shoes and rejoined them. They were sitting and admiring, laughingly, each other's shoes.

"We all know that procurement is competitive. Tonight, we're going to have two teams that I've preassigned. Sean is the captain of the first team. He will introduce the captain of the second team."

Sean stood up. "I appreciate everyone's support. We are making huge progress, and I can tell I'm learning a lot. I also want to share my appreciation for Lee's support. She has been invaluable helping to pull all the information together." Applause and thanks to Lee were shared across the group. Sean continued, "Lee's excellence and potential have not gone unnoticed. This will be her last meeting with us, as she's going to lead her own category management team. Lee is the only intern to lead a category team." Lots of applause and congratulations were shared. "So, tonight she will lead the second team, and may the best team leader win!"

While José read off the team assignments, the food and drinks arrived. The bowling alley provided pitchers of beer, soda, and bottled water. They'd hired an outside caterer, so the food wasn't awful—simple but palatable. Anna participated in both teams but spent most of her time taking candid pictures of the group. She always did this, and it was one of the things most appreciated by the participants. Everyone was in the moment and having a great time. As expected, there was a good-natured dispute over the scoring, particularly the rules of scoring, and Anna had to officiate. In the end, Sean's team won, but it was close; neither team had over 150 points. They were not bowling ringers.

At the end of the competition, Sean called out, "I'd like to present a going-away and congratulations present to Lee. Lee, for your tireless support and passion: a card and gift."

Lee was overwhelmed and broke up a bit as she stood and accepted the card and gift. "Thank you all. I really appreciate you including me on this team—it's been great!"

Lee opened the card and noticed it was signed by everyone on the team. She wondered how Sean was able to do that without her noticing; it was very thoughtful of him. She opened the gift. It was obviously a book, but she had no idea which book. She smiled as the title came into view: *The Global Category Manager's Handbook*.

"Thank you, Sean! I've had book envy and noticed you always have your copy with you," Lee exclaimed.

"Yes, it's like having Anna with me all the time—it's very helpful. I got you the one that opens flat. Good luck with your team," He replied.

MARCH 9TH

The routine of meeting in the lobby, boarding the minibus, picking up their safety gear, and heading to the meeting room was well ingrained now. After picking up coffees and teas, they took their seats.

Ron opened the meeting, "I hope everyone had fun last night. My first choice was roller or ice skating, but Sean said he didn't want anyone on the team getting hurt." There was laughter around the table. "How are you enjoying Milwaukee and our division?"

"I am very impressed," Gina piped up. "The healthcare business leaders are similar but not quite as approachable. Bob and his team are very engaging."

"It's very different from the Asia team," Chee Chung remarked. "I think they want to be approachable, as that is the Frontier subculture, but the broader Asian culture is far more deferential to leaders. I enjoyed Bob and his team. I went into dinner exhausted from the time zones but finished the dinner with more energy. I will need to practice my bowling when I return home to Singapore."

"Thank you for arranging everything, José and Ron. Our visit to Milwaukee is as memorable as being snowed in back in Tennessee," Sean commented. "Anna, do you want to kick off with the content?"

"Yes," Anna responded, moving to the front of the room. "You made amazing progress yesterday and have a bold, yet I think achievable, strategy. The layers are clear, and the potential results are compelling. Over the course of three or so years, you are planning to eliminate one hundred and twenty suppliers. That means three to four suppliers will be exited every month. If you miss a month for vacations or holidays, it's that many more in the future. Concurrently, you are planning to cross-qualify suppliers and reduce SKUs. It will require an enormous amount of change management. With that in mind, I recommend we start by drafting the implementation plan this morning. This will be the piece that Genevieve will want to see this afternoon to give credibility to your strategy."

Marek chimed in, "Early in my time with consumer electronics, we had many poor suppliers. It was my task to identify and eliminate them. I will add my learnings to the plan."

Anna smiled at him and said, "That is excellent, Marek. This is exactly the kind of input we need."

She handed out more sticky notes and asked the team to brainstorm the tasks required to implement the layered strategy. It was an intentionally vague assignment, as she trusted that the MBTI intuitives would list the macro tasks and the sensors would list the micro tasks. They worked on this for over twenty minutes until their ideas dried up and they started to refill their drinks. While they were writing their tasks, she posted a row of flip charts and headed them with the three layers of the strategy.

Anna continued her instructions to the group, "After you refill your drinks, I'd like you to take your sticky notes and put them on the sheet that corresponds to your task. If it is a repeating task and you only wrote it once, please write it again and add it to the appropriate layer. Once all of the task ideas are posted, I'd like you to self-nominate into three groups, and each group will review the tasks in that layer. Organize them by sub-team and sequence them in order of performance. If there are duplicates, just put them on top of each other."

Once the groups were completed, a couple of sub-team members presented the work to the balance of the team. A few additions and reordering of tasks were made, and all were pleased with the work. Approximately 300 tasks were listed—very impressive for a first draft implementation plan.

"As you may remember from our snowbound Myers–Briggs

discussion in Tennessee," Anna started, "this group is highly logical. The team preference is thinking, with no team members preferring feeling. That is typical for these category teams. The opportunity in implementation is to make the plan more palatable to the feelers in the organization. As I said, your plan is compelling from a logical business perspective. But imagine the feeling of loss some people will feel as a hundred and twenty trusted suppliers are exited. They might be resistant to these changes. Please go back to your three groups and think about how you can add to or modify your plans to make them more compelling on a relationship basis. The strategy plans and goals remain the same. This is about making it more fun and less painful."

The subgroups worked for another thirty minutes. They started tentatively and then became more animated as the ideas started to flow. By the end of the working session, each group had added meaningful ideas that would help change the implementation from a mandated "push" to a stakeholder "pull."

Before they stopped for lunch, Anna turned to Sean, asking, "How do you want the presentation to Genevieve to go? We should agree on that now, so we're prepared."

"I want all of us to present to Genevieve," Sean replied quickly. "This is not about just me sharing our results. We have an hour with her. Let's break the content into four or five chunks, and you can volunteer for what you'd like to present. You'll need to be a rigid timekeeper, but I think it can work."

"Sure, that sounds fine," Anna agreed.

"I will present the layered strategy and implementation plan with a volunteer," He added.

"I'd like to be part of that," Gina volunteered. "I know Genevieve pretty well and might be able to anticipate a few of her questions."

"Good," Anna responded. "Let's agree on the rest of the presentation."

The presentation elements included the process work to-date with a tight focus on the insights. Everyone realized that there was not enough time to review the tools in detail nor was it appropriate. Before they broke for lunch, everyone knew what they were presenting.

Anna said, "If you want to work through lunch to refine your approaches, that's fine. Please plan to work on the flip charts that you created. You can add to them, but it is not necessary to create a formal presentation. Your work is an excellent storyboard, and you'll just need to focus on the highlights."

Most of the group ate first, but a couple immediately started reviewing their flip charts. There was a high level of energy in the group—everyone wanted to ensure success.

A few minutes ahead of schedule, Genevieve joined the virtual meeting, "Good afternoon, everyone."

"Welcome, Genevieve," Sean greeted. "Thank you for meeting with us quite late your time. I think you'll find that it's worthwhile."

"How is your meeting going?" she asked.

"Really well," he replied. "We have an excellent strategy and implementation plan draft to share with you. The industrial site leadership team joined us for dinner and were very engaging, and we had the opportunity to confirm that we're all lousy bowlers."

"Bowlers?"

"Yes," Ron jumped in. "I took them bowling last night for a group dinner. I can share that our results would be very competitive if we were in the under-ten-year-old category."

Laughter around the room and from Genevieve. "Well, it's good you have a day job," she remarked.

"Let's get started," Sean began. "We broke up the presentation so everyone can participate. We're not going to take you through all the details and will instead focus on the insights so you can see how we built our strategy. If you have questions along the way, please ask them. If you want to go through any details later, just let me know."

With that, the team members presented the team's journey through the category management process and the associated insights. The culmination was Sean and Gina's presentation of the strategy and draft implementation plan. Remarkably, it was all completed in just over fifty minutes.

"So, just to confirm, you're estimating improvements in assurance of supply, quality, and service and total cost savings of almost six million in exchange for an investment of just over half a million," Genevieve replied.

"That is the summary," Sean agreed, "but there is a big 'but' or 'and' attached to that. This is dependent on the organization supporting us through the reduction of a hundred and twenty suppliers and the cross-qualification of the remaining or new suppliers. Without the organization's support, we are unable to commit to the potential results."

"That's fair, and if I understand my role as your sponsor correctly, this is where I step up for some of the heavy lifting. Once you have your summary presentation built from your flip charts, please send it through. I think your work is excellent, and I'm ready and willing to help. I reserve the right to add or change a bit to the presentation to help it through the review and approval process. We must keep moving, as the budget process will start soon."

"Thank you," he stated. "I'll work with the team and have the draft presentation to you within a week."

"Don't spend any time on making the presentation pretty," she suggested. "I will work with Gina and the marketing team to take care of that. Please focus on the content. Now, what's the status of the stakeholder engagement? Will this come to them as a big surprise?"

Sean was surprised and a bit taken aback when Chee Chung jumped in and answered for the team, "No surprises. We have been working with the stakeholders throughout the process. In the beginning, they knew nothing about our team, then we told them about us and shared our insights. We know this because some of our suppliers have told us what they're hearing from the stakeholders."

"That is to be expected," Genevieve remarked. "Stakeholders are tight with suppliers, and we should expect the information to pass both ways. I'm glad to hear that you're diligently engaging the stakeholders. That's good work."

"Any other feedback for the team?" Sean asked.

"I appreciate the team's thoroughness and the pace of your work while continuing your 'day jobs.' It's a lot to ask, and you've done great work. I wanted to thank Lee for her help and wish her well on her new assignment. Thanks, Lee, for your efforts." Genevieve smiled.

Lee said, "You're welcome, and thanks," and blushed furiously.

Genevieve continued, "The easy part of the category management process is done. You've developed a great strategy. The hard work will be the implementation. You have a good draft plan, but I do want you to think through the pilot elements in a bit more detail. If we have compelling results from the pilots, it will make the balance of the implementation easier. Thanks again and safe travels home." With that, the virtual meeting ended.

"I'll say it again," Anna said. "She's a great sponsor. She is willing to commit to the work where you need her help; she provided a useful steer on the pilot plans and is readily available."

People agreed around the table, and Sean suggested, "Let's take a break and come back and finish up."

After the break, they worked in their three subgroups and focused on adding details to the pilot and follow-up plans that would help drive the broader implementation. They spent most of the remaining time on stakeholder and supplier communications. This was going to be a sensitive topic as so much change was anticipated. The team's work to improve stakeholder receptivity to the implementation plan came to the fore and ended up as the centerpiece for the communications.

The last session was a plenary review of the updates, and they were pleased with their work. It also demonstrated that every time they engaged the plans, they could find areas to improve. It would be worth a couple of more iterations over the next few weeks, and they agreed they could do that virtually. The subgroups could meet independently as needed.

Anna facilitated the meeting close, and they discussed next steps and said their goodbyes.

A smaller group met in the hotel bar for dinner that night. Gina, Chee Chung, and Marek headed to the airport to catch evening flights. José was local and went home to his family. Ron, although local, didn't have plans and stayed with the group. The mood was very relaxed, as the adrenaline of the meeting and session with Genevieve had drained them. But it was positive; they knew they were on the right track.

The first round of drinks was delivered, and the group toasted Sean, Lee, the team, and the strategy in turn. Sean realized it could turn into quite an evening if the pace of toasting continued, so he turned to Lee, remarking, "You're lucky to be learning category management so early in your career. I'd never thought of it until Margot arrived."

"I do feel very lucky and fortunate to have joined Frontier when I did," Lee shared. "I was also lucky to be assigned to this team. I've learned a lot."

"Who is going to be your coach?" Ron asked.

"My manager, Tanya, is going to coach me with input from Margot. Sean has also offered to provide some mentoring."

"That will work," Anna added. "Tanya is very bright and capable, and I'm sure Margot will stay close to your team. She knows the process as well as Rich and me. And Sean knows it now too. His benefit is he also knows the company and you—you'll be fine. Make sure you have a good team and a strong sponsor."

"I wish I'd done category management earlier in my career," Sean remarked, his eyes growing wistful. "I thought I was doing good procurement, but it pales in comparison with what we're doing now."

"The hard truth of the matter, Sean, is that it would not have worked," Anna responded. "The way procurement works is reflective of what the company expects and what the procurement leadership establishes as ways of working. Before Margot, none of the prerequisites for working in category management were in place. Imaging trying to do this work without this team and without Genevieve."

"Sure failure," Ron observed wryly. "Without us, you'd never have a chance."

"It was nice to meet Spock in person," Ron commented with a smile.

"Spock?" Anna asked, raising an eyebrow.

"Yes," Ron chuckled, "that's how I think of Marek. When I was in engineering school, some of my classmates were just like him: incredibly smart and numbers-focused and not a thought about the people implications."

Anna agreed, "Most people say their favorite *Star Trek* character is Spock, yet his people skills were lacking. When there was a need for clear-headed thinking and decision-making, he was without par."

"I guess I felt that way about him at first too," Sean added. "At Sobelman's the other night, he told me all about his family, and it was like I was talking to another person. He is a devoted husband and father. He just doesn't share that side in the team meetings."

Lee joined in, "I can tell you he added a ton of insights to the plans today. He has real experience changing the supply base like we're proposing to do. I'm glad he's on the team."

"That is the benefit of a good cross-functional team," Anna agreed. "Each person brings unique insights and experiences. I'm glad he came to this meeting, and you reached out to include him."

The group laughed and toasted the team again. The dinner was served, and they relaxed into easy conversation.

MARCH 10TH

Margot's flights were uneventful, and she even managed to sleep a bit on the trans-Atlantic crossing. A quick shower at the arrivals lounge, and she was off to the office.

Julian met her in reception and led her to Erica's office, where Erica greeted her, "Welcome back to Copenhagen, Margot, your new home away from home!" They all laughed, and Erica gestured for them to sit at her conference table.

Margot said, "Thank you, Erica. This is very exciting to create something new here. I appreciate your openness and Julian's willingness to step in and help lead the area."

"We're all excited about this and are looking forward to the results," Erica said. "I wanted to give you a bit of an early steer for your planning. I really like your approach to-date with the central procurement function. Most people in that role would have started by trying to change the reporting lines of all the procurement organizations distributed throughout the business and, in the process, they would have burned their political capital before they got started. You're focusing on the strategic aspects of the function and deploying a consistent process while leaving the balance of the organization alone.

"I recommend you use the same approach in this new role. Leave most of the business alone. In fact, I recommend that you staff the area with yourself, until Mary returns, Julian, and a small cohort of experts. In today's world, you can flex the staffing by pretty much any specialty to meet the workload as projects come and go. I will help you with the expert staffing if you and Julian determine you'd like a few of the current staff. My concern is that if you go to the heads of engineering, or quality or regulatory, they will provide a staff member for you, but it will not likely be the best person—it will be someone they can afford to give you. If you decide to hire from the outside, that is fine, but the long notice periods will mean that you'll be hard-pressed to show any progress before the end of the summer."

Margot reflected for a minute before replying, "That's helpful advice. I'd forgotten about the long European notice periods. I was thinking about keeping the organization staffing as flexible as possible. My hypothesis, to be tested this summer, is that we'll work through a few projects and then the nature of the work could evolve, at least within a product family. A large, permanently staffed function would be ill-suited to the agility required."

"You're right," Erica affirmed. "The other reminder is that you're the outsider; the 'fair-haired girl from corporate,' if you will."

Margot felt her face get hot, but Erica continued, "If you plan to make improvements across a broad range of products that my local team either did not recognize or could not do, they will be embarrassed. They shouldn't be, because that's not how we've been organized, but it is human nature. As a result, I recommend expecting to find and be referred to improvements that are a bit smaller than you'd hoped but will be real and valuable, nonetheless. The larger improvements may be uncovered when Mary returns. The three of us will know to watch for this and expect it. I will not view this as a reflection on you two, but more of a parochial approach of the local team."

"That's an interesting point," Julian said. "I know that when I arrived from Switzerland, I was viewed as 'the outsider' for a bit, and I'm a European. I expect it will occur with Margot coming in from America."

"Yes." Erica nodded. "Too many Europeans view Americans through the lens of US TV shows, and we seem to be stuck with shows from the seventies to the nineties. Anyways, please let me know if you need anything. Let's plan to meet for lunch tomorrow and check in."

Julian and Margot headed to a conference room, and Julian said, "I've reserved this room for us all week. It has fewer internally facing windows, so if we need to do some confidential planning, we can cover them, and the rest of the time, we can still have some light."

"This will work well, thanks, Julian," Margot stated. "Let's start with us and our roles. I'll tell you what I'm thinking and want to hear what you're thinking. Once we're clear on our roles, we can build out the rest of the plan. Before we do that, let's just map out the days and the macro plan of the work."

They laid out the week with the goal of presenting their plan to Erica on Thursday morning. That would leave Thursday to incorporate her feedback and Friday for Margot to fly home. They both seemed a bit relieved after discussing their roles, as their approaches were very similar. Margot wanted Julian to lead the product improvement efforts, and her role would be to lead the overall procurement and product improvement efforts with a focus on senior stakeholder engagement.

She went to a flip chart, and they brainstormed common product improvement topics, including specification changes, supplier changes, process improvements, and design improvements. They then discussed the stakeholder teams that would be affected and how to engage them positively. She would work with Erica to broker introductions to the appropriate teams and leaders and start the process.

After lunch, she and Julian discussed the specialist skills needed to implement the various changes. They debated the pros and cons of full-time specialist leaders and decided to present two options to Erica at lunch on Tuesday. One option would be full-time leaders of the specialist areas, such as industrial, mechanical, packaging, electrical engineering, quality, regulatory, and marketing. The other option would be to name employees who would remain in their current roles and provide oversight to contractor staff as needed. Their recommendation was the latter if their day-to-day workload was reduced to enable adequate time for the new role.

By the end of the day, Margot was exhausted. Julian dropped her at her hotel and agreed to a pickup time for the morning. Margot called home and talked with Jason and the boys and was sound asleep before dinner.

The next day, she awoke refreshed and hungry and was ready when Julian picked her up. They spent the morning discussing the current products and some improvement opportunities. By lunchtime, they'd identified twelve opportunities to discuss with Erica and her team.

They met Erica at her conference table and used their draft flip charts to frame the discussion. It was deliberately casual and informal, and Julian recognized Margot's approach from the AI team—Erica started adding her insights to the flip charts as she was thinking through the options. By the end of lunch, they were in broad agreement on the priorities for improvement and the staffing model, including the tentative naming of current leaders to head up the specialist areas. Erica's leadership team meeting was scheduled to meet Wednesday afternoon, and she cleared an hour on the agenda for Margot and Julian to present. This would enable Erica to clearly demonstrate her commitment to this new approach and provide an easy introduction for Margot to schedule follow-up stakeholder meetings.

Margot and Julian left lunch excited about their progress. They agreed to contact Mary to solicit her input and share their progress. She did not answer her phone, so they left a message. While Margot worked on the presentation for the leadership team, Julian started the search for specialist support groups. He wanted to start the process and, most importantly, understand how much they charged for their services. He and Margot wanted to show a pro forma of potential results achievable during the leadership presentation, and he needed to know the cost base.

Mary returned their call early afternoon and sounded a bit groggy, "I'm sorry I missed your call. The baby took a nap, and so did I. How are you two doing?"

Margot provided a quick update, "We're making progress, but we wanted to talk with you, so we don't miss anything important."

"That's very thoughtful of you," Mary mumbled, "but I'm so tired that I don't think I'll have much to add. If you're out later, you're welcome to drop by."

Julian said, "We'll plan on it. I was going to drive Margot around a bit to see some areas at the end of the day, and we'll be near your place. Do you want us to bring anything?"

"No," Mary replied. "Just let me know when you're nearby and leave a message if I don't answer."

By mid-afternoon, the presentation draft was completed, and Julian had enough information to estimate the various support costs. Julian said, "Let's go for a bit of a ride to see some places for you to consider before the evening traffic fills in."

"Agreed," Margot stated. "Day two of the time zone changes is always the toughest for me, and I could use a break."

He started by driving through some of the more residential areas inside the city, some within biking distance of the offices, and then expanded the range until they were outside the city in rural areas. She was amazed at how quickly the area changed from built-up city to open farmland. In this it was not dissimilar from many places in the US but was surprising because it was so old; she thought it would all be developed.

On the way back toward the city, they came through the area where Mary lived in the Sydhavnen area. It had a delightful feel and beautiful water views, and Margot could see why Mary did not want to leave it and move to Oklahoma City. There were very nice areas in Oklahoma City but nothing with a comparable feel and scale. They called Mary, and she answered on the second ring, sounding much more awake. She suggested they stop by.

Margot and Julian walked up to the door and knocked. Mary greeted them with baby Erin in her arms. Margot entered, putting her arms out. After an almost imperceptible hesitation, Mary handed her the baby. Margot expertly cradled her and said, "She's perfect! Congratulations!" The baby held onto one of her fingers and stared at the newcomer holding her.

"Thank you." Mary beamed. "She's amazing. I'm thankful for the extended leave to get us all settled. All I do now is feed and change her, and when she sleeps, I sleep."

"Welcome to motherhood of a newborn," Margot said. "Each day will be busy and a bit different. In a few weeks, she'll be smiling, and then in a few months crawling, and so on. Your days are never going to be the same or boring."

Julian, who had no children, had hung back a bit, but asked, "Can I hold her?"

"Sure." Mary smiled. "Just cradle her head like Margot is doing."

Margot carefully handed the baby to him. He stood stiff as a statue holding the baby. Margot suggested, "Rock a bit, at the knees. The motion will make her more comfortable."

After a minute, the baby fussed, and Julian looked at Mary plaintively, who said, "Don't worry, I'll go feed her and will be back in a minute. Please make yourselves comfortable."

They perched themselves on the edge of chairs covered in folded clothes and baby supplies, and Julian asked, "What did you think of the areas we drove through?"

"There are lots of good choices. I need to talk with my husband and sons. We need a big yard at home for our dog, but he is not coming over with us. I'm thinking about somewhere in town. It will be an experience we've never had and is difficult to get in the US. We can use bicycles in town and will have a car we can use when we need it. What do you think of my boys on bicycles here?"

Julian shared, "Where I grew up in Switzerland, we all rode bikes. Here, everyone uses bikes. The kids grow up using them. The big thing is to teach them the bike lanes and what to watch out for. It's very flat, so the biking is easy, and the weather is good in the summer."

Mary returned, the baby nearly asleep in her arms. She asked, "So, how is your progress?"

Margot recounted the highlights so far starting with the Monday morning meeting with Erica, through the planned leadership team meeting Wednesday. Julian named the tentative specialist leaders and Mary concurred with most of the choices. She did say, "Keep an eye on Rafe. He is an expert on electrical engineering, but he is very set in his ways. If you're hoping to make changes, and particularly you, One Thumb, in the design of the electronics, you'll need to manage him closely."

Julian laughed. He held up his thumbless hand and said, "Oh yes, One Thumb has real passion for changing some of our design principles."

After a bit of small talk, Julian noticed Margot's energy flagging and observed, "It's time to drop you off at the hotel and leave Mary to the baby."

Margot tried to suppress a yawn but could not. She said, "Excuse me, I'm sorry. It's the travel. Thank you, Mary. I'm very happy for you and appreciate your input and support. Julian showed me some areas to consider for the summer and, if it's okay with you, I'll email you for input as well."

"Sure," said Mary. "Anything I can do to help. Thank you for coming by. It was nice to have some adult, non-baby-related conversation."

Julian and Margot got back in his car and as they headed toward her hotel, Julian shared, "I'll never think of maternity or paternity leave as 'time off' ever again. Mary looked exhausted. Being at work is much easier."

Margot smiled. "You are right about that. Keep that in mind when you and your wife have kids."

They agreed on pickup plans for the morning, and she hopped out at her hotel. She decided to change clothes and go for a walk before dinner. She knew she'd fall asleep if she laid down and wanted to stretch her legs a bit. After a long walk along the canals, she found a quiet café and had a casual dinner. She mused that a summer with Jason and the boys here would be alright. She walked back to the hotel and slept soundly until the alarm woke her the next day.

MARCH 11TH

Julian picked her up, and they spent the morning working through the leadership presentation. Their efforts focused on the messaging and the value proposition. This was their opportunity to create a set of expectations and associated support requirements—they wanted to get it right.

Genevieve was walking by the conference room, noticed them, and stepped in. "Welcome to Copenhagen, Margot. How is your trip so far?"

"Hi, it's going well. Do you have a few minutes?"

"I do. I have fifteen minutes before my next meeting."

Margot remarked, "Perfect. I'd like to share the highlights of our presentation for this afternoon and get your feedback. At the very least, it will give you some more context for the afternoon. I value your input."

"Sure." Genevieve took a seat.

Margot and Julian quickly covered the highlights of the presentation, then Margot asked, "What do you think?"

"I like your approach," Genevieve started. "I know that there are a few team members who are not sure about this whole idea. You'll need to strike a balance between sharing a vision and making rapid progress and the time that will be required to bring them along. It's probably the same challenges you're facing with category management, Margot."

"You're right about that," Margot agreed. "There are a couple of approaches to getting started, and some people advocate a strict focus on the biggest value opportunities. My experience is a bit different. I look for areas that want and need improvement in addition to considering the value opportunity. I want to work with people who want and need change, and not with people who are going to fight me."

"I agree completely," Genevieve added. "In our business, you should focus on the instruments, particularly the older instruments. We rarely kill a product, so we're still making and servicing some equipment designed a long time ago. If we could update just a few of these, we'd make a huge difference, and you'd have my complete support."

She looked at her watch and exclaimed, "Oh, I need to go, or I'll be late. I'll see you later and hope that was helpful."

"Thanks, Genevieve," Margot called after her as she scurried out the door. She then looked at Julian and said, "Let's add some recommended phasing to the improvements so we can more clearly call out the initial priorities."

After a few more changes, they stopped for lunch and were confident in their approach with the leadership team.

Erica welcomed the attendees to the leadership meeting. "Margot and Julian are developing the plans to pilot our new approach to product improvement and procurement. I really appreciate their efforts and am delighted that Leslie and the ELT selected our business for the pilot. I want to reiterate that this does not mean that the business thinks our products need tremendous improvement or that we cannot do it ourselves. What we're saying is that we need a new approach to the work to ensure it is focused and accomplished quickly."

She motioned to Margot, who stood up and began, "Thank you all for your time today and your commitment to the pilot. Julian and I are here today to share our draft plans. I emphasize draft because we want and need your input."

She and Julian tag-teamed through the presentation quickly and addressed questions as they arose. At the end of the presentation, the healthcare finance leader said, "I will assign one of my staff to work with you on the numbers. It's clear you're not just focused on savings and reducing the cost of goods sold. I think that's a good outcome. You will need a comprehensive set of measurements, including a baseline so you can demonstrate improvement."

"That's right," Margot confirmed. "We use the same approach in category management and will need to do it here. Julian and I are not here to make your products cheaper. We are here to work on areas to improve the overall value across a broad range of parameters, and we must measure all of them."

The regulatory leader, who had been silent throughout the presentation, spoke up, "We need to carefully consider the regulatory approaches here. It could be very easy for someone to say that changes are not possible within a given regulatory scheme. In my experience, that could be true but is very unlikely. Regulatory schemes proscribe the change processes, and we must follow them, but that does not mean they need to be slow or onerous. I want to help you wherever you need it." He turned to Erica and continued, "I suggest that we make this pilot a standing item on our leadership team agendas so we stay connected and can be helpful on a timely basis."

Margot smiled and nodded subtly to Julian; this was the outcome she'd hoped for.

Erica replied to the regulatory leader, "You're right. Margot will be a member of this team going forward until Mary returns from her leave. Margot, please prepare a progress scorecard for this team. We review our scorecards every week and discuss them in depth as issues arrive."

Margot said, "Julian and I will create a draft scorecard based on this presentation and send it to the team for input. In the meantime, do we have your approval to proceed?"

Erica affirmed, "Yes, please proceed. I think this is great progress. Thank you, for pushing this so quickly. I know it is short notice, but I'd like all of you to have a chance to meet with Margot one on one. Please make time before Margot heads back to the States on Friday.

It doesn't need to be a long conversation—it is the beginning of the dialogue."

Margot stated, "Thank you, Erica." She turned to the broader group and said, "Thank you all for your support. I'm really excited about working with you. This is not about what Julian and I are going to do during this pilot. This is about what we are going to do together. That's very important. I look forward to talking with each of you over the next day and a half. Send me an email or a text with your availability, and we'll get together."

She and Julian left to work on the presentation. Per Erica's guidance, she could have stayed with the team for the balance of the meeting, but she preferred to let them have time to reflect on the presentation and, yes, talk about them, and for her and Julian to incorporate their feedback.

By the end of the day, she had time booked with all the team members, including dinner that night with Genevieve.

Genevieve stopped by the conference room at the end of the day, and they headed out to dinner. Genevieve provided her version of the area tour and insights into the various areas to live in. Margot was deeply appreciative and noticed that Genevieve's insights and recommendations were closely aligned with Julian's.

Over dinner, Genevieve said, "I'm very impressed with the category management process. I'm glad I was selected as a sponsor."

"I'm glad to hear you say that." Margot said. "I know that Sean and his team really appreciate your support. Anna has been effusive about your contributions."

"I'm happy to do it. It's not too often that a group of employees is asked to create a strategy for the business. Helping them along the way is what we, as leaders, need to do."

"That's one of my favorite aspects of the process," Margot agreed. "It is a great opportunity for the team members to step up and have some visibility. I've learned a lot about the capabilities across the organization by participating in the stage reviews and seeing the various team strategies."

"What is the plan to push the process out to the business-based procurement teams?" Genevieve asked.

"We started with most of the teams being HQ-led as a relatively easy way to start. I wanted to have a bit more control and make it easier to quality assure the process at the start. The next waves of teams will be predominantly business-based procurement team leaders. Some of the categories will be used exclusively within a business, and others will be used across multiple businesses. This will make the team leadership and sponsorship a bit more complex because it will be a new way of working. It will also mean that the stage review process, which is how we do quality and progress assurance, will need to be trained into the business procurement leadership teams. I'll do that while I'm here in Copenhagen, but Phil and Harry will need to do it with their respective teams in Milwaukee and Singapore. We'll do the leadership training following the regional category management training."

"That sounds like a good approach," Genevieve commented. "I recommend capturing learnings from all of the participants along the way. I know I've learned a lot and suspect the other team sponsors have as well."

Margot nodded and assured, "That is part of our plan. We're going to survey all the participants, share their feedback, and discuss and incorporate improvements going forward. It will happen over the next few weeks as the strategies come up for approval."

With the business topics covered, the conversation drifted to small talk until dinner was complete. she thanked Genevieve for dinner and her time. "My hotel is close to here. I'll walk. See you tomorrow."

She enjoyed the walk back through town. It was cool but pleasant, and it was nice to feel like she knew where she was going well enough to do it herself.

MARCH 12TH

The next day, Margot was busy with stakeholder meetings while Julian met with the subject matter experts to align on outside staffing recommendations for the initial projects. By the end of the day, they had a cadence agreed for team meetings and the staffing plans for the first few projects. They updated their presentation and draft scorecard for their meeting the next morning with Erica. Based on the first few projects, they estimated a positive margin impact of three to four percent between reducing the cost of goods on some items and opportunities for price increases due to improved features. The consistent project themes were reduced supply risk and decreased warranty and repair costs.

Erica was impressed with their progress. "This is more than I'd hoped to see by now when we talked on Monday. I appreciate your approach, and you have my full support. Margot, please plan to join the healthcare leadership team meetings going forward. My admin will send you the invites. I appreciate you could not stay this week after your presentation, but I look forward to having you as a member of the team."

"I will, thank you," Margot stated. "My plan is to start working here every other week until my family moves over. That will be in a month or so. We're just working through a few details with the school. My husband will finish their schooling remotely."

Erica said, "Keep me posted on your move plans. Once you're here, we'll have you over to my house. I'm sure my husband and kids will welcome the opportunity to share some of our favorite spots." She stood up, signaling the meeting was over, and extended her hand, "Thank you, Margot. I'm delighted to have you as a member of the team. Safe travels home."

Back in the conference room, Margot and Julian agreed to update Mary on the progress. They were both keen to keep her in the loop. Anything they could do now would ensure she felt involved and valued and make her post-leave return easier. Mary was not available for a visit, so they provided a quick phone update and sent her the slides.

Margot sent the slides to Matt for his input then sent them to her GPLT as pre-reading for the meeting next week.

After completing their remaining tasks, Margot and Julian went to an early dinner. The sun was still out, and they found a nice outdoor café looking over the harbor.

She started, "With the exception of the new design approaches you're championing, this is about driving typical category management implementation tactics. The difference here is that we're going to do it by focusing on products and then categories, and in category management we do the inverse. It will be an interesting test to see if one way or the other is easier from a governance perspective. I think we'll find this new approach easier, as the product alignment will keep the leadership team's attention."

"I don't have any experience driving category management implementation," he shared, "but I can see that by focusing on improving a specific, high-value product, we'll be able to rapidly demonstrate value. It's exciting."

She nodded and said, "And what we've not talked about so far are the AI impacts. I remain convinced that there is an opportunity for us to overlay generative AI on our data from the customer order through supply and assembly, the customer use experience, and to the removal of scrap to find new opportunities. I didn't think it was the right time to raise that with Erica's team, but we'll need to do that this summer. Please contact Willie and Tanya and agree which one of the vendors we visited to work with on a pilot. Keep the visibility low at the start and ensure the data security issues we discussed are covered. If there are selected strategic suppliers we need to include, let's do it. I want us to be able to share some learnings and directional guidance by the end of June. What do you think?"

"I was hoping we'd come back to this," Julian nodded. "I'll talk with Tanya and Willie tomorrow while you're flying back and start moving this forward."

"Please kick-off with the selected vendor as soon as possible. Do not coordinate around my travel schedule; I do not want to be the rate-limiting step on this. We will have a lot of balls in the air all summer long. It will be busy, and it will be exciting."

MARCH 13TH

Margot spent the flight catching up on emails from the week. Normally staying current with all of them daily, she found this week was critical items only. She used to wonder why some people could not stay current with their inbox, and now she had a bit more empathy. She was thankful Frank had not retired and had risen to the task of leading the HQ team and delighted that Shelly was helping with the category and AI teams.

After drafting an update email to Matt, she reflected that this update would need to go to Matt and Erica—a first for her. It was all a bit overwhelming, but if her entire team was pulling their weight, she was confident that she could manage it all.

Arriving home from the airport, her senses picked up two things—it was quiet, and it smelled good. Normally the boys would be making noise somewhere, and the house just a normal, unobtrusive smell. This was different.

She put her suitcase and briefcase down in the entryway and headed to the kitchen, where the smells were originating. Jason was frying onions and garlic in butter and sipping a glass of red wine. Upon seeing her, he put down his spatula and said, "Welcome home, sweetheart, I didn't hear you come in." He kissed her and handed her a glass of wine as well.

"It's great to be home," she remarked, "it was a good week, but I'm exhausted."

"Well, have a seat, relax, and I'll catch you up on things here."

"Uh oh," she muttered, "is everything okay?"

"Everything is great," he smiled. "I met with the boys' teachers and the principal and agreed to me homeschooling the boys for the last month of school, so they're set for the fall. I also agreed with my boss to take a leave of absence and see where I fit best when we're back. Lee and I talked, and she's going to move in and start watching Max as soon as we finalize our departure date. She'll drop us off at the airport, so we don't have to worry about leaving our car. And speaking of the cars, I've agreed to a trade with the Volvo dealer for my Camry. I'm going to pick up a new Volvo in Sweden at the factory. That's pretty much my week. How about you?"

She held up her glass to toast him, "Well done! You've accomplished a lot! Thank you!"

"I figure this is the way it's going to be for the next few months while we're in Denmark at least," he stated. "You're going to be straight-out busy during the week, and I'll have the boys, and then we can have the weekend as a family. That's part of my plan for the car. I figure we'll either be driving or on a train every weekend, and I'll need something to get around during the week. Plus, I've always wanted to pick up a car in Europe, and this is my chance. The Volvo factory is just over the bridge to Sweden and a short ride away in Gothenburg. How was your week?"

She sat at the table, watching him sauté the vegetables. "Packed but good. Julian and I created a good plan and think we have a line of sight to some great product improvements. I met with Mary, Erica, and Genevieve, and that all went well too. I am feeling a bit overwhelmed. This week, I need to run a category management stage review, a GPLT meeting, and an AI update. And we need to figure out the plan for when you and I are going to go to Copenhagen to pick out a place to live for the summer."

"Oh, on that note," he interjected. "I talked with my parents, and they're set to come here and watch the boys so you and I can go to Copenhagen. I thought about just bringing the boys with us on the trip but figured it would make it much more complicated."

"That sounds great, thanks. Let's look at a calendar over the weekend and figure out some date options, but it will be soon. What's for dinner, by the way?"

"Salmon with asparagus and rolls. The boys made a special dessert—I'll let them show you later. They already ate dinner and are watching a movie."

"That sounds great. I'm going to shower off the travel and will be back in a minute," she stated, taking her wineglass with her.

They talked through dinner, and the boys brought in the special dessert—Jell-O with fruit in it. The boys beamed and, in unison, said, "We made it all ourselves!"

Margot was very proud and happy. This was maybe not her favorite dessert, but tonight it was great, and she was delighted.

Jason brought in a big map of Europe, and over dinner, they brainstormed potential spots to visit over the summer. It was a huge list, and they wouldn't see everything, but it was clear they would see and do an amazing amount.

MARCH 15TH

The next Monday, Sean was in the office early. His flight back on Friday was easy, and he'd spent the weekend reflecting on the meeting. He was proud of the team's progress and keen to move it forward.

Margot walked by his desk. Paused, and asked, "How did your meeting in Milwaukee go?"

He beamed, "It was excellent! We drafted our strategy and reviewed it with Genevieve. She gave us helpful feedback, and we're pulling together some of the final pieces now. Do you want to see it?"

"Of course, I was hoping you'd offer," she remarked. "Do you want to meet in my office or a conference room?"

"Please give me twenty minutes to get set up in the conference room, and I'll walk you through it."

"Okay, see you in twenty," she agreed, and she walked to her office.

Sean assembled the papers from the meeting and walked by Frank's office on his way to the conference room. "Good morning, Frank. Margot asked me to show her the team's strategy, and I'm going to the conference room to setup. We're meeting there in twenty minutes if you want to join us."

Frank took a sip of coffee, then said, "Sure, I'll be there in a minute to help you get ready."

Sean laid out the flip charts in order and then started posting them on the wall. Together, they made a complete storyboard of the team's work. He planned to cover the highlights on the flip charts and then use the slides they'd created. Frank arrived a few minutes later and helped him post the flip charts.

"Sean, it looks like you're enjoying this new process. I didn't think I'd be saying that a couple of months ago. I'm impressed," Frank commended.

"A couple of months ago, I was working on my CV. I figured I'd be in a new job by now," Sean agreed.

"You are in a new job. The nuance is that you are still at Frontier, but the work you are doing is very different."

"You're right about that," Sean chuckled. "I'm lucky to have a great team, Anna is a great coach. And you and Margot have been supportive, too."

"The flip charts are impressive," Frank praised. "I'll be interested in hearing you tell the story behind them and where you and the team see the category going."

Sean finished with the last flip chart and connected his computer to the big screen when Margot walked into the room.

"Wow, this is impressive—almost overwhelming," Margot enthused, taking a seat and looking around the room. "Once you're ready, please take me through it like you did with Genevieve. I have the next hour free. Before you get started, how did Marek do at the meeting?"

He said, "He is an interesting person. I sat with him the first night and talked, and he shared some of his background and experience with the company. We even talked about his family. He's done a lot in fifteen years. He seemed to relax a bit as we talked, and he even contributed during the meeting. Seemed to be well accepted by the other members."

"That's a great outcome. I'm really happy to hear it," she remarked. "Harry said the electronics business turns to him for all packaging-related issues, and if he was not included, we would not gain traction with the electronics business. Well done."

He stood up and walked to the first flip chart. "The entire team participated in the presentation to Genevieve. We broke the flip charts into sections, and pairs of team members presented the topic of the tool and the associated insights. I presented the draft strategy with Gina."

"I'm very happy to hear that everyone participated. This process does not work if the team is not fully engaged." She nodded to him.

He began his explanation of the strategy, introducing the tools used and explaining the team's insights and how the insights then bridged to quick wins and potential strategic options. It was an elegant set of linkages that worked well when all the pieces of information were simultaneously visible around the room.

Margot nodded, took a few notes, and held her questions.

He was almost unnerved by her lack of expression throughout, but decided it was just her "poker face" and not to worry. Once he completed the flip chart explanations, he moved to his laptop and showed the strategic option assessment matrix spreadsheet and then the draft layered strategy.

Frank was ecstatic but held it in pending Margot's feedback. He'd never seen procurement work so complete and compelling and was truly impressed.

Sean finished with, "Genevieve was supportive and said she'd work with her marketing and communications teams to prepare a visually compelling presentation once we're done. What do you think?"

Margot sat for a minute, reviewed her notes, and then turned to look at Sean. She was still holding her "poker face" when she said, "Sean, I was not sure about you and your capability when we launched the training. You and I had that conversation."

He was getting a bit nervous now.

She continued, "I assigned an excellent coach, Anna, to your team and told you to engage her. It appeared to me that you started to engage her at the end of the training. What you're showing me now is far beyond what I'd expected." She smiled at Sean, and he visibly relaxed. "My feedback to you now is that this is what excellent category strategy development looks like. This is a compelling layered strategy. I am not sure you and the team have adequately thought through the amount of change required to exit this many suppliers, but at least you're thinking big. My personal feedback to you is to put the 'old purchasing Sean' away and to carry the confidence of the new 'category management Sean.' I appreciate that you want my approval, but I also think that you know, deep down, that this is excellent work. You will be presenting and selling this strategy to stakeholders and suppliers and need to have the conviction that this is the right path forward."

Sean smiled broadly.

Frank interjected, "I did not think the corrugated category could be so interesting and the potential value so compelling. I feel like the 'old purchasing Frank' needs to look at categories differently, too."

"You're right, Frank," Margot affirmed, meeting his gaze. "I'm glad you realize that. You're going to be the coach for your team leaders once our budget for outside coaching is spent. Each of us needs to create a sense of what's possible in these categories for the team leaders and their teams to be creative and inquisitive like Sean and his team."

She turned back to Sean. "Once you have the strategy documented, I want you to send it to me for review. I really like how you explained the flip charts and slides to me, and we need to ensure the story is still compelling without the flip charts. I will send you some feedback then. I will schedule time with you, Frank, Genevieve, Matt, and myself for you, and Genevieve to walk through the presentation with Matt before it goes to the entire executive team. He will have some thoughts on positioning of topics, and it will give you and Genevieve the opportunity to plan the joint presentation."

Sean swallowed, clearing his throat. "To Matt and then the executive team?"

"Yes," she smiled. "The executive team reviews important business plans for the company, and you've just written one—congratulations!"

"Okay," said Sean a bit tentatively. "How soon will all of this take place?"

"I'll ask Rita to check on the ELT meeting schedule so we can review options with Matt. Please plan on meeting Matt in the next week. You'll either get the invite from Rita or Matt's assistant once she's confirmed everyone's availability. Don't be nervous. You have everything you need to tell the story. These are all people like you and me, and they are looking forward to seeing a real category strategy."

She then picked up her notes and coffee cup and headed out of the conference room for the stage review meeting.

The two men sat in silence for a minute, then Frank asked, "Well, 'new Sean,' how do you feel now?"

"Overwhelmed, a bit nauseated, and excited," Sean replied.

"Well, you're either pregnant or about to take a big step up on the career opportunity ladder. And I doubt you're pregnant."

"No, just overwhelmed. But in a good way. I'm going to make some notes about the flow of materials. I think we need to tighten it a bit. I'll sit here and do that and send Genevieve a heads-up as well."

"I recommend that you also send a heads-up to the team," Frank suggested. "They deserve to know how it's going and what's coming up next."

Shelly organized the first-stage review. The plan was for each team to share its status and upcoming plans for the next month. Forty-five minutes were allocated per team, with thirty minutes for presentation and fifteen for discussion. The presentations were based on the team's work with very few additional templates. Shelly was committed to keeping bureaucracy out of the stage-review process.

Even though Margot reiterated the intent for a non-threatening share-and-build approach, the team leaders were tense beforehand. It was new for everyone, and they wanted to do well. Each had reviewed their presentation with their respective manager and coach beforehand and knew the category materials very well.

Rita supported Shelly with timekeeping and notes. Shelly's focus was on the process. She was adamant that the first session go well for the participants, even if substantial feedback was required.

Shelly opened the session, "This is our first stage review for the strategy development process. For now, we're inviting only the team leaders, their coaches, and the GPLT. Once we are all more practiced in the process, we'll include team members and team sponsors. This is a new process for everyone, and it needs to be a true share-and-build approach. For the team leaders, please do not be offended or embarrassed if you are asked questions about your category or your team. These are part of the process."

"For the GPLT, please do not expect perfection and ensure that your questions or suggestions reflect the team's status on the journey of strategy development. That does not mean that you should only ask softball questions. It's better that we ask the hard questions amongst ourselves than we face them for the first time with stakeholders or suppliers. At the end of each presentation, Rita will note the summary of the comments and suggestions, and we, as a GPLT, will determine if the team is approved to proceed and if any remedial actions are required."

Prior to the stage review, Margot had emphasized her approach founded on Ed Deming's perspective that team members' performance was reflective of their leaders' coaching and guidance. As such, she was counting on each of the GPLT members to ensure that the team leaders were well-prepared.

Sean had asked for and been given the first review slot. He'd presented after Lee at the category management training and found that he got more nervous the longer he waited to speak. It was worrying for nothing; Sean's presentation went very well. The feedback was minor, and the corrugated team was given approval to proceed.

Subsequent team presentations were more varied; a few teams were given guidance to improve their stakeholder engagement and broaden their supply market views. These outcomes did not surprise Margot, as Anna and Rich had given her a heads-up on each of the teams. The result provided coaching to Frank and Tanya as much as the respective team leaders. It was still too easy to be complacent with the known and easy approaches to sending broadcast emails to stakeholders and suppliers and relying only on the incumbent supply bases. Margot was pleasant but firm that this would not be acceptable going forward.

MARCH 16TH

"Good morning, good afternoon, and good evening," Margot greeted as the AI team assembled in the meeting room and on their respective virtual sites. "I'm very interested in hearing about your progress."

Shelly shared, "I met with the team last week. It was going to be a sub-team, but everyone was available and wanted to participate, so it was all of us except you and Julian." She connected her computer and showed their end-to-end procure-to-pay flow chart from the prior meetings, and Margot noted that it was now annotated with many new text boxes.

Shelly continued, "We focused on where in the P2P process there are current AI solutions, and those are light green. If we are already using them, they are darker green. You'll see there are just a couple of dark green but many light green boxes. There are lots of emerging tactical or problem-oriented solutions."

Willie interjected, "The IT team is doing due diligence on the light green boxes, and we're working with finance to capture the results of the dark green boxes. The orange boxes are where we anticipate solutions emerging next, based on what we're hearing from the suppliers. The timeframes for availability are variable, as you'll see that most of the solutions are growing in comprehensiveness and are spanning more of the P2P process. The good news is that this means they'll be more integrated, and we'll have fewer interfaces on our end. The bad news is that they will cost more and be more complex."

Margot nodded and said, "This is great work. Thank you all for pushing this along."

Shelly smiled. "Don't celebrate yet. None of the dark green boxes reference solutions running at HQ procurement; they are all business-based applications. Most of the light green opportunities will be similar. There are a couple that can run here at HQ, but most will always be in the businesses."

Margot asked, "Is that a problem?"

Phil chimed in, "Not a problem for the industrial business, per se, but a planning topic. The next set of AI applications that seem appropriate focus on site-based data management and some buying activities. As each of us plans for these, we'll need to budget for the software and then plan for the implementation and change management when jobs are affected. This is true for all of the businesses."

"Yes, the impacts will be a bit different for electronics in Singapore," Harry said, "but what Phil is saying is true."

Margot stated, "Julian, we'll need to add the healthcare implications to the plan we started to draft last week."

"Got it," Julian replied from the Copenhagen conference room.

Alec said, "Frank and I reviewed the range of AI solutions purported to address category management. The box is shaded light green and orange. Some vendors say they have a current solution, and others say theirs is on the near horizon. We looked at what is out there and think it's primitive; largely automated template completion."

Frank agreed, "I'm staying close to Sean and the corrugated team, and he shared Anna's results with the coaching questions. They continue to be very marginal. I think that most of the purported category management AI solutions are simple strategic sourcing or buying solutions. That doesn't mean they're bad; it just means that they will be limited to the simplest, most basic categories."

Margot concurred, "That fits with my impressions, thanks. I'm not impressed with anything I've seen yet. It all looks like cookie cutter sourcing strategies in a project management and scorecard framework.

Matt wants us to collect the financial impacts of our plans and submit those as part of the budgeting process. He is thinking that some of the solutions will be broad-based and can be budgeted centrally. Are you involved in that effort, Willie?"

"I am, and Tanya is helping me," Willie informed. "Even some of the smaller, site-based solutions will be installed multiple times, so an enterprise license is appropriate. We're collecting all of that information."

Tanya added, "I'm working with the team to capture the potential people impacts and sharing those with HR along the way."

Margot asked, "Julian, do you want to share our addition to the plan?"

"Sure," Julian agreed, standing up to present. "Our plan is to use generative AI across the end-to-end design-to-grave process. This week, I'm going to start conversations with a couple of vendors and explore it further. I'm thinking about NanoBots and Ivan's Fact Mine team in California, but wanted to check in with the team. What do you think?"

Frank chimed in, "I thought Fact Mine was far and away the best fit from a cultural perspective. I felt like I could work with them. I did think that NanoBot was advanced, and their case studies were good. I just didn't feel comfortable there. I'm not a feelings guy, as you may know." There was laughter in the room and on the video feed. He continued, "But I don't trust the folks at NanoBot."

"They are different," Tanya agreed. "I agree with Frank and recommend that you start with Fact Mine and use NanoBot as a backup. Let me know how and where I can help."

Margot asked, "Shelly, what are your next steps?"

Shelly replied, "IT, finance, and HR are pulling together their submission requirements based on early inputs like ours. They anticipate having something for us in the next week or so. In the meantime, we're going to discuss a phased rollout of the light green boxes across the three businesses and the corporation, so we can capture learnings and measure results before implementing more broadly. Once we have the draft plan, each procurement leader will talk with their respective business team to discuss options and implications. That will all take a couple of weeks, so we're moving in parallel with the submission process."

"That's excellent, thanks," Margot praised. "As soon as you have a summary, I can share with Matt. Please let me know. I'll work with Julian to address the healthcare plans as well."

MARCH 17TH

"Come in and have a seat, weary traveler," Matt offered, motioning to the table in his office. He added, "But you don't look weary at all—I don't know how you do it."

"I'm very lucky," Margot mused. "Jason took care of everything at home, and my GPLT advanced everything here. And I'm very excited about the plans that are coming together with Julian and Erica in Copenhagen."

"That's why I asked you to catch up," he explained. "I read your report and wanted to talk about it in person. Are you sure about the numbers you included? I want to be very careful with expectations."

She figured this was the reason behind his request. She'd summarized the initial plans that she and Julian had reviewed with Erica and wanted Matt to have the same information as Erica.

Matt joined her at the table, and she started, "I am comfortable with the numbers included in the report at this point in the process. This is another way of saying that we haven't started yet but believe we're on to something. You have the same numbers we shared with Erica. I'm going to be transparent with both of you, and you'll do what you need to do to risk-adjust the projections. Erica is confident enough in our approach and plans to move resources to support our efforts. We will self-fund our improvements within the first year and then be cash positive. These projections are based on modest sales and margin improvements, and we believe we will beat these numbers."

"Okay," Matt stated, "I wanted to look you in the eye when you said that. I don't know you well yet, but you're going way out on a limb on this one. This is not typical procurement territory that you're heading for."

"Not to split hairs," she replied, "transformative category management has always included elements of product improvement and supply chain transformation. The difference now is that we're actively calling out the goals and moving enough resources to drive the results."

"You're also putting your neck firmly in the noose," he warned. "How is your relationship with Erica and her leadership team?"

She nodded, smiled, and said, "Yes, one throat to choke, as the old expression goes. I think it's good. I may be in the noose, but the entire leadership team is part of the process. I am adamant with Julian and Erica that this is not what 'I' am doing, or 'procurement' is doing but what 'we' as a leadership team are doing. I will continue to emphasize the role of the healthcare leadership team as the steering group for this process."

"Good, keep pushing that," he encouraged. "One last question, and I think you know what it will be. How applicable do you think this approach will be in our other business units?"

"I did expect that question," she smiled again. "It's too soon to tell, but it will be very different by business and, I suspect, a bit by region. Once the pilot is a bit further along, I will review the process with the GPLT, and we can start expanding the pilot. I fully expect we'll stumble across a few things we don't want to repeat or expand upon, and I want to find those myself in Copenhagen. One last point, I am keeping Mary up to speed on our plans so she can both contribute as possible now and be positioned to take over when I come back at the end of the summer."

Matt put his pen down and seemed to relax a bit. "Seems I'm just about settled with my family, and your family is about to be uprooted. How is that going so far?"

Margot took a sip of coffee and then said, "So far so good. Jason is going to join me for the next trip over, and we'll pick a spot to live for the summer. The boys' school has agreed to let them out early.

Jason is going to take a leave of absence from his job and teach the boys history all summer, and Lee, one of my interns, is going to live in our house here and watch our dog and the house."

He remarked, "Wow, that's huge progress on every front! I know from my time abroad that it is an amazing experience and harder than you'd think. There are so many aspects of life that we take for granted in the US that are a bit harder overseas, even in a place as nice as Copenhagen. My one caution for you is to make sure you take a bit of time off along the way to recharge your energy and stay connected with your family. It will be too easy to work twenty-four seven, and it will not end well."

"Thanks, that's good counsel," she replied. "I'm planning on a couple of trips back to my team here over the summer and a few long weekends. The Europeans love their 'bank holidays,' and then we're planning at least a ten-day family vacation at the end of the summer."

"That sounds great. Please keep me informed and let me know if you need anything. I know firsthand that the same requests and offers come from Leslie and Jean," he stated as he stood up.

She stood up and said, "I will—this is going to be quite an adventure!"

MARCH 18TH

Margot and Jason were on the overnight flight to Copenhagen Thursday night. Jason's parents were watching the boys for the week, and the plan was for Jason and Margot to look at potential neighborhoods on Saturday and Sunday and for Jason to look at actual homes or apartments early in the week while Margot was working and then for them to confirm a location by the end of the week.

They met with an estate agent Friday afternoon after landing and showering, and she showed them a range of areas from in the city to out in the country. There were many options, and it really was up to them to decide how they wanted to live during the summer. The opportunity to ride a bicycle to work intrigued Margot, and she favored an in-town location. Jason too liked the in-town option but was a bit concerned about the transition for the boys from a fenced suburban yard to a city location. The estate agent suggested that in addition to their rented car they borrow a couple of bikes and try them as well. The hotel they were staying at offered bikes to the guests, and she made plans to ride to the healthcare office on Monday. Jason also planned to do his neighborhood touring by bike.

Mary called her to invite her and Jason to brunch on Sunday. She looked forward to catching up with Mary. Jason was looking forward to talking with Mary's husband, Franz, to get his input. They drove there in the rental car, and both remarked on the light vehicle traffic and the number of bicycles.

Jason really liked the Sydhavnen area where Mary and Franz lived. It was just outside the city center but within easy walking and bike-riding distance of many destinations. The waterfront locations were beautiful, and he really liked the neighborhood pubs.

Mary and Margot talked and caught up on their respective personal plans and the emerging procurement plans, and Jason and Franz took Erin for a walk in the stroller. The plan was to meet back at the house in an hour. Closer to an hour and a half later, Jason and Franz returned from what had become an epic walk around the area. They covered a lot of ground and discovered a few mutual interests. Margot was delighted, and a bit relieved to see Jason take to the area so quickly. If he and the boys were well settled, it would make her job much easier.

After brunch, she and Jason said their farewells and headed off to continue their discovery process. The afternoon would include some areas well out of the city, as they were in the rental car. They were both amazed at the quick transition from the city to rural areas with rolling hills. The countryside was very pretty. They stopped in a small café for coffee and were reminded of a key difference between rural areas and the city—the number of people who spoke, or at least understood, English. In Copenhagen, it was almost everyone; in the countryside it was reversed, and they reverted to pantomimes or pointing at pictures or the items that other people were enjoying.

"I'd pretty much forgotten about English versus Danish," he observed. "It's not an issue in town. It's not a huge issue out here, but it's not nothing."

"I think we'll all pick up some Danish while we're here," she thought out loud, "but you're right."

They returned to Copenhagen and mapped out their plans for the week. By Wednesday evening, Jason hoped to have the housing options narrowed. They were looking in the same area as Mary and other similar spots close to the city and within bike-riding distance of the office. Thursday morning, Jason and Margot would look at the options and, hopefully, select a choice. The goal was to sign the paperwork on Friday before their flight back to the US on Saturday. It was a tight timeline but doable.

The next morning, Margot headed off early to the office on her bicycle. It was a test on multiple levels; she had to navigate without seeing the GPS screen while paying attention to the pedestrians and cars, which seemed to come out of nowhere (due to her focus on the route). She succeeded and wasn't even disheveled when she parked her bike and walked into reception. A badge was waiting for her at the desk thanks to Julian, and in moments, she was at her desk.

Julian came in with two cups of coffee, handed her one and said, "After a bike ride you should have some water and then the coffee. It's not like commuting by car in the US, where you get to drink your coffee during the ride."

"You're right about that," Margot exclaimed. "I'm proud that I made it here without any wrong turns, didn't hit any pedestrians, and didn't get hit by any cars. I do think I heard some new Danish words," hinting at expletives along the way.

"All part of the process," Julian assured, "you made it. Take a few minutes and get settled and then let's meet with the team. They're expecting you this morning."

"Really, that's more than I expected, thank you," she remarked.

"See you in the conference room in a while," he bid, leaving her office.

She connected her laptop and reviewed her emails and voicemails. Nothing urgent to be dealt with, and she took the opportunity to enjoy her coffee for a minute. When she had collected her thoughts, she headed to the conference room. Julian and the team were seated around the table, and they all greeted her warmly. She was proud of herself for remembering all their names. She was not good with names and wanted to do better here. Not all her pronunciations were correct, but everyone appreciated that she tried and cared to learn about them.

"The team has been busy over the last two weeks building detailed plans based on our initial ideas," Julian started. "As expected, everything changed a bit once the team was involved, but most for the better. Each project will be presented in STP format by the subject-matter or functional expert who will be leading it."

Margot was deeply impressed. In two weeks, he had assembled the team approved by Erica, explained the new approach and the goals, and taught them how to use the STP tool. There were a few instances where items were listed in the wrong areas on the STP, but in her experience, far fewer than typical with new users. Even more importantly, their proposals were uniformly realistic and well thought out.

She told the group, "Your progress so far is great. The risk is, ironically, that it is too good. You have the experience and the insight to see the opportunities and plan the required improvements. The risk is that we get too far ahead of the stakeholders. We need to ensure that all our work is both vetted and approved by the stakeholders. In some cases, the stakeholders will be internal and in others a mix of internal and external, but in all cases, we must bring them along with us. What have you done so far?"

A few of the team leaders volunteered a smattering of hallway conversations and emails, but nothing structured.

Margot encouraged, "That's alright; that's typical at the start." She stood up, approaching the whiteboard and drawing the stakeholder matrix used in category management. She continued, "This is the tool I want you to use. Let's start with the overall improvement pilot here in healthcare as an example." She led them through the listing of stakeholders affected by the pilot and assessment within the matrix. She'd done this exact exercise on the airplane coming over to meet Julian a few weeks ago and was gratified that she'd correctly identified and categorized most of the stakeholders. There were a couple of new names, and she made a mental note to meet them early this week.

She turned to the group, asking, "So what? What use is this matrix of names?"

One of the leaders volunteered, "We know who to communicate with."

Another said, "We know who is supportive and who isn't?"

Margot smiled and said, "You're both right. We know who to communicate with and we have a hypothesis of their support. The next step is the most critical step—the engagement planning." She used a flip chart to create an engagement plan, and they talked through the first three names on the matrix—each one with a different level of apparent support and each at different levels of influence in the organization.

She continued, "You'll see that every stakeholder is assessed individually. Each person must be planned for separately. There are cohorts of similar people, like engineers, or finance people, or HR people, where there are commonalities, but still, there are unique aspects worth addressing. One comment on this process: it is very sensitive. Imagine you're working on your stakeholder map, and you list me, how influential and supportive you think I am, and how you're going to engage me. At one level, this will be interesting from a management perspective. On a personal level, I may or may not agree with your assessments or plans—even if they are appropriate. Treat these documents as confidential. Lastly, if you have stakeholders where you cannot make progress, particularly senior stakeholders, please engage Julian, me, or Erica for help. That is our job."

Julian pointed at the clock in the meeting room. "We're a bit over on our time for today. Please work on your stakeholder maps and engagement plans, and let's plan to review them tomorrow afternoon. If you need help in the meantime, please let me know."

Margot closed, "Before you go, I want to thank Julian and each of you for exceeding my expectations. This is an amazing start to our new process. You are pioneers, and your enthusiasm, energy, and experience are evident. Thank you."

The team leaders packed their materials and left her and Julian in the meeting room.

"What do you think?" he asked.

"As I said this morning," she replied. "I'm blown away by the progress. Each person has a clear idea of the issues and a plan to move forward. I appreciate you helping them prepare."

He smiled. "Much of the credit goes to Erica. She helped us pick the right people and, from what I'm hearing, is pushing her leadership team hard to support this. I don't think we'd be this far without her support."

She nodded. "You're right; executive leadership and support is invaluable. If Erica was not supportive, we would not be anywhere.

Even more, if Leslie, Matt, and she were not supportive, I'd be back in Oklahoma City now, and this never would have started. This is a testament to the company leadership and culture. I had a good talk with Matt last week. He wants us to be cautious with the numbers and managing expectations. I told him that we will be honest and transparent and everything we share and agree with Erica will be shared with him but we will start with her."

"I had a couple of quick conversations about that with her," he stated. "She appreciates your approach and recognizes that you also need to keep Matt informed. She and Matt will talk through any substantive projections and tell us if they make any changes."

"Her leadership team is meeting tomorrow morning, so I'll have a first-hand view of how they're feeling so far. I'm going to use the summary page you created and have the individual STPs in reserve. There are a couple of names on the stakeholder list that I missed, and I'm going to set up time with them now. Thank you for leading this team—I really appreciate it."

"My pleasure," he replied as he stood and collected his materials. "This is going to be a fun summer."

MARCH 19TH

He had barely sat down at his desk when his phone rang with a Wisconsin area code, "Hi, this is Sean."

"Hi, Sean, this is Walt from Wabasha Packaging," the caller greeted.

"Good morning, Walt. How can I help you?" Sean asked. He didn't often talk with the president of Wabasha Packaging and Walt had never called him before; his curiosity was piqued.

"I'm making plans to attend the supplier forum and want to know what to expect. I was, frankly, surprised by it. I've worked closely with Bob and his team and occasionally with you and don't see the need for an expensive trip to your headquarters," Walt explained brusquely.

"I'm glad you called," Sean replied, even though no part of him was glad to start the day this way. "The supplier forum is for all of the Wave One category management suppliers and potential suppliers to have an opportunity to hear about the company plans, meet senior leadership, and learn about the status of the category they supply."

"What am I not understanding here? Wabasha supplies perfect product that we designed with Bob and his team to protect their product. Why do I need to be there?"

"You're invited to attend because we don't want to exclude anyone, particularly a long-standing and trusted supplier like you and Wabasha," Sean made sure his reply was smooth.

"Why can't Bob and I just have a lunch meeting? Why do I need to fly to Oklahoma City?"

"A one-on-one meeting with Bob is excellent, but you'd miss the larger context. Procurement at Frontier International Group is changing and we're implementing category management."

"I've never heard of it and don't care!"

"I understand your perspective but think you'll appreciate it once you've seen it and understand our approach."

"Do I have to come?" Walt's tone was tight.

"No, of course not," Sean replied, "but you'll miss out on an excellent opportunity and based on your longstanding support of Frontier and relationship with Bob and his team I highly recommend you attend."

"I'll think about it."

"Okay, please let me know what you decide," Sean asked before he and Walt hung up.

He walked over to Frank to share the call.

"He sounded angry," Frank remarked.

"I think it was a mix of anger, not wanting to travel here and pay for it, and defensiveness about his business with Frontier Industrial."

"Well, I guess I can understand that. It's not cheap to fly here and he did work with Bob and his team to sort some problematic shipping damage issues," Frank commented. "Summarize the conversation in an email and send it to me, Bob, Margot, and Genevieve. Review it at your next team call. I'd be interested if Ron and José have any insights."

"Will do, thanks," Sean agreed, returning to his desk. He made sure to draft and send the email first thing.

Later that day Sean received the following emails:

- Bob was typically brief: "I'll call him."
- Margot thanked Sean for the update and requested that he work through any issues with Frank and Genevieve.

- Ron and José shared similar insights around the fragility of the Wabasha Packaging business, there was no succession plan for Walt, and they'd recently lost their large beverage packaging contract, so Frontier was the majority of their sales.
- Genevieve replied that she was in contact with Bob and would assist the team where and when needed.

Bob sent a separate note informing him that he'd talked with Walt and Walt would attend the meeting.

Sean sent a reply to the internal participants with an update on Walt's decision to attend and thanked them for their input and support. It helped him and the team understand the supplier stress levels leading up to the supplier forum.

MARCH 21ST

Erica's team filtered into the meeting room, and all were ready a few minutes before the scheduled meeting started. She asked Margot about her move progress, and the others were listening and chiming in with suggestions on areas to consider and avoid. All were very supportive about her temporary assignment.

The meeting started with a review of the financials. Year-to-date, the business was on plan overall, with a typical mix of over- and under-performing products. They continued to see warranty and service expenses higher than expected for their new line of instruments. The head of manufacturing, James, said his team was working with the process engineers but that the flow seemed smooth, and the pre-shipment diagnostics were all in line with expectations. The failures were happening after shipment and installation.

Erica turned to Margot and asked, "Is this something we can look at with your new approach?"

Margot replied, "Yes, I can work with James on this. It sounds like something is coming adrift after manufacturing and we can use a big data approach to see if we can uncover the root cause. Ivan's team is going to be working with me on the pilot, and if you and James are ok with it, we'll use this as our first project."

"Yes, ensure the NDA is very specific and protect our IP in the process. What do you think, James?"

James answered, "I'm very frustrated by this problem and welcome any help. Our build quality is excellent, but that is not the customer experience. We need to sort this quickly."

Margot suggested, "Let's talk after this meeting and agree to a plan."

James nodded, and the conversation moved on.

Margot's topics were after lunch. She hated presenting after lunch, but that was the way the agenda flowed. Her first topic was healthcare procurement. Admittedly, she'd not spent much time with the team but had been briefed on the key issues. She shared the functional dashboard, and there were no questions. Sharing her corporate functional dashboard next was her decision, and this prompted a couple questions about category management.

It was clear the healthcare leadership team had not heard about the topic before. Quickly explaining the topic, she asked for additional time with the team in the future. She could not help but notice that a few made questioning faces when she said that procurement was transforming into a more strategic function. Putting this aside, she showed the summary slide that Julian had created with the summer product improvement projects. Her emphasis was clear and strong—this was to be a joint effort with everyone around the table, and her role was coordination and project management. A couple of detailed questions emerged, and she shared the relevant STPs. The team quickly embraced the approach, and she was pleased with their acceptance of this new way of working.

Erica chimed in, "This is very exciting and promising. If these results are achieved and are incremental to our plans, that will be very helpful this year." She looked past Margot to the rest of the team, continuing, "I am delighted that you are all so supportive of this approach. We need to pull through these results. The potential mix of increased sales and margin will help this year to fund additional growth next year." She turned to her head of finance, stating, "Please add Margot's summary slide and financials to the overall financials. I don't want anyone to think this is about Margot or procurement—this is about all of us and this business."

She turned back to Margot. "I know you are now split between us and Matt. What are you sharing with him?"

Margot replied, "I've shared the same materials with Matt with the proviso that these numbers do not replace anything that you are sharing and that the plans are not risk adjusted. He said he would treat them as such and contact the two of you for confirmation before incorporating them into any corporate projections."

Erica nodded and relayed to her head of finance, "We need to have a plan here. We need to show this new approach is generating the results expected, and we need to manage corporate expectations. I'd like you to proactively work with Margot and the team to include proactive risk adjustment without killing the projects; build us a bit of a buffer."

Margot's heart sank a bit. Risk adjustments and buffers were corporate code for sandbagging and hiding results. She and Julian would need to run a separate set of books so she could answer any questions after the pilot.

As if reading her mind, Erica added, "I don't want you to think we're going to be overly conservative here. I'm as interested as you in proving this new approach. What I don't want is for other members of the healthcare team to think they can relax, and this pilot will make up for any shortcoming. I also don't want corporate finance to shift additional financial burdens on this business. We will push this new approach, and we'll be honest with the numbers, but I want us to be smart about it."

Margot nodded. "I guess I don't have too much of a poker face."

The head of finance laughed and said, "No, it's not about you and your poker face; it's about knowing us and how we behave. Erica's seen this before."

Erica said, "That's right. We're doing well. I don't want anyone to let up the momentum."

The team meeting finished on a high note, and Margot was satisfied with the outcomes.

MARCH 23RD

A couple of days later Jason presented all his findings to Margot. They had, of course, defined the "want" and "need" business requirements for their housing, and the options were focused on neighborhoods—would they be downtown or on the edge of the city? They liked the romantic idea of living downtown but agreed that a nearby neighborhood with more of a village feel would be better. The hustle and bustle of the city would be within biking distance, as would the office for Margot, but they'd be able to enjoy a bit more quiet and space in a nearby neighborhood. In the end, they selected a neighborhood near Mary's and a wonderful, detached house with a pretty garden. They decided to take one more walk by it before signing the paperwork the next day.

The walk was quick and largely quiet; most of the traffic headed in their direction was bicycle traffic. They'd learned quickly to stay out of the bike lanes and would have to teach the boys the same thing.

Stopping in front of the house, Jason announced, "Here it is. It's on this road but there is a small garden in the back, and it has off-street parking for a car."

She nodded, pointing down the road and saying, "And two blocks away is a nice pub. Is that a coincidence?"

He smirked, assuring her, "No, that's a real business requirement, to use your terms. I've sampled the food once. Let's go get some more data."

MARCH 25TH

The next two days were a whirlwind for Margot. She and Jason signed the papers on the house for the summer, and Jason turned his attention to planning the move over.

She met with the healthcare procurement team and reviewed their respective activities in detail. She knew this was overdue but hadn't had time beforehand. There were no surprises; they were very tactically focused. This was great firsthand information, and she'd use this information in the continued planning for category management. There were a few healthcare-centric categories that she wanted to launch as soon as Mary was back.

Julian and she advanced the improvement projects and planned for Ivan's team to arrive. They both hoped it would be as impactful as the experience in Palo Alto. It was not clear if Ivan would be with the team, but she trusted he'd be sending his best team members. The visit was planned for two weeks hence, and she'd have to go back to Oklahoma City for a week at HQ and then travel back for that kickoff.

Her other tasks included virtually leading the procurement AI team and conducting a virtual corporate GPLT meeting. The corporate supplier forum was coming up quickly in April, and it needed to be well executed. Shelly, Tanya, and Frank reviewed the plans, and she felt much more confident. They were doing a great job in her absence.

She asked, "How are the category management teams doing? I feel so disconnected from them, and they should be almost done with strategy development?"

Tanya reviewed the indirect teams, and most were doing okay. Lee was doing very well. Frank's summary of the direct teams was similar. He particularly called out Sean's work with the corrugated team as being noteworthy. Frank stated, "Sean's team is identifying huge opportunities, but they will require enormous change management to achieve. We're talking about exiting many suppliers that our sites have selected over the years. They have a good plan, but it will be a test of the business and our sponsors."

Margot agreed, "You're right, Frank. The easy part of category management is developing the strategy; implementation is much more difficult. Are there any issues?"

He answered, "No, not yet, but I'm staying close to it, and Sean is actively working with the team to engage the stakeholders."

Margot closed by saying, "I appreciate your work to advance everything. I'm looking forward to being in the office next week."

MARCH 28TH

The flight back to the states was uneventful, and Margot and Jason were delighted to get home to the boys, her parents, and Max. Everyone was keen to hear about the place they'd selected. Her parents were already looking at flights to come over for a visit, and she and Jason were glad they'd selected a place with room for guests and activities within walking distance. He had two weeks to get the boys and the house ready. She would be available to help the first week, then she'd fly ahead—he had to do the final prep and fly with the boys by himself.

Very early Monday, she was in her office as the procurement team started to arrive. She'd always been a bit of an early riser, but now she was fully acclimated to the European time zone and was in the office before the sun rose. It gave her a chance to catch up on emails and, more importantly, review the category management information that Shelly had posted on the walls.

Each team posted their storyboard in a "war room"—a private conference room that suppliers would not see but that the teams and stakeholders could regularly access. There was a bit of variation between the teams, but the overall application of category management was excellent. If the implementation plans materialized, the initial impacts would be a substantial mix of risk reduction, complexity reduction, sales growth through innovation access, and margin improvement.

Margot was delighted. After reviewing each category and making a couple of notes about each team, she sat and wrote an email to the team leaders, the GPLT, and Anna and Rich. She called out specific successes for each team and noted a couple of watchouts that applied broadly. The moment of truth for the company leadership was approaching, and she'd ask Matt to schedule time for her with the executive leadership to discuss this.

APRIL 10TH

Today was the big day—the long-planned supplier forum was about to begin. They were focusing on the suppliers for the first-wave teams only. This was not going to be a mega-event with all of the direct or indirect suppliers, or worse, the large suppliers for every category. Those were invariably shake-down operations focused solely on price, and Margot wanted nothing to do with that and was delighted that Matt shared her opinion. This forum would include the CEO, CFO, business presidents, and CPO presentations to current and prospective suppliers. It also included an extended break for mingling with the Frontier International Group executives and breakout sessions by category. She was confident in the design and knew the planning was first-rate. As the emcee for the event, she was a bit nervous. Frontier International Group had never done anything like this. The closest anything came was bidder conferences for RFPs, and this was orders of magnitude bigger.

She walked up to Leslie, who was chatting with Matt and looking up at the audience. The suppliers were arriving and were hosted by their respective category managers. There was an air of excitement and a bit of tension as the current suppliers recognized the potential suppliers. Change was palpable in the air.

Leslie motioned to her to join their conversation.

She greeted, "Good morning, Leslie, Matt, looks like good

attendance. This should be an excellent day. I really appreciate your time and support."

Leslie smiled. "I'm happy to do it. You and your team are bringing real energy to the company, and I can feel it today. I will admit that I was initially surprised when I was given a script and a list of likely questions and suggested answers. You do realize that Matt and I talk with Wall Street analysts regularly."

Margot would have been worried had Leslie and Matt not been smiling, but both were. Matt was closer to beaming. She replied, "I hope that wasn't presumptuous on our part, but these events are different, and it's important that our team is aligned and prepared. We certainly did not intend to tell you how to do your job."

"Relax, Margot," Leslie said, "I appreciate good staff work. My job is hard enough, so if you take the time to prepare me, then it makes the unexpected that much easier to deal with."

Matt looked down at his watch and piped up, "Shall we get this started?"

Margot nodded and walked to the podium. The room quieted almost immediately, and she started her presentation, "Welcome to the first-ever Frontier International Group supplier forum. On behalf of the company leadership team, my leadership team, and my category managers, I am delighted to welcome you and thank you for making time today to be with us. I know in this post-Covid world many companies do these events virtually. There is something to be said for avoiding travel, but there is a lot to be said for meeting in person. Let me quickly review the agenda for today."

On the screen, a detailed agenda for the day was posted, listing the Frontier International Group executive presentations, the informal break, and the category-based working sessions.

Margot spoke to each item and reinforced, "Today is about you, our supply partners, and us, your key customer, sharing and collaborating. Some of you are not current suppliers, and you may be wondering why you are here. Likewise, current suppliers may be wondering why potential suppliers are here. I will speak to this in greater detail during my presentation but, suffice it to say, we are embarking on the journey to build category strategies that match our current and future needs with the best suppliers. The only way we can know we're achieving that goal is if we include all capable suppliers in that review. With that, please join me in welcoming Leslie Groves, our CEO."

The room dissolved in applause as Leslie walked to the podium and her presentation was put on the screen. Margot had worked hard with Leslie's admin and the head of investor relations and the general counsel on this presentation. It was crisp, compelling, and consistent with the prior Wall Street communications but went a bit further than usual, so a thorough legal review was conducted.

"Good morning, thank you for making the trip to Frontier International Group. As Margot said, we're delighted you're here today. I will go further and say to our current suppliers that I'm delighted and thankful for your supply. Together, we've been successful. To everyone, I will say we will compete to be your best customer; we expect you to compete to be our best suppliers. Before you get too worried, that does not mean we are going to beat you up on price. Yes, we care about price, but we care about so much more. We are focusing on value—we need your best total cost, we need your innovation, we need your quality and assurance of supply, and we need your feedback to help us improve."

With that welcome, Leslie presented the status of the key business units and prospects for the future. The audience listened closely, and a few took pictures of slides (it was allowed within the ground rules for the session).

She came to her last slide and shared, "I'm with you all afternoon. I appreciate you being here and look forward to talking with many of you. There will be a question-and-answer session later. Margot?"

Margot walked up to the podium and said, "Thank you, Leslie," then shook her hand, and Leslie returned to her seat. Margot introduced the subsequent speakers in turn, and after a full morning of presentations, the attendees welcomed the opportunity for an extended break. The Frontier executives stayed and distributed throughout the room. While many supplier attendees wanted the opportunity to sit with Leslie or Matt or one of the business leaders, they soon realized that every member of the ELT was knowledgeable and influential. The mix of incumbent and potential suppliers helped maintain the energy in the room, as all were clear that the old ways of selecting and retaining suppliers were in flux.

The afternoon continued with category-specific breakouts led by the respective category manager supported by as many of the team members as could attend. In most cases, this was all the members, as the teams took this as an opportunity to participate in the supplier forum and conduct their final team meeting before seeking strategy approval. More than a few sponsors were present as well, including Genevieve. Once Frank, Shelly, and Tanya realized how many teams would be meeting during the week, they approached Margot and requested an overall team event for Thursday evening. She readily agreed.

Sean and his team were prepared for the supplier forum afternoon session. They had examples of all the current corrugated SKUs arranged down one side of the room except for the very largest ones made by Wabasha Packaging and used in the industrial business; they had large posters of these on the wall nearby. It was a telling display, as many of the SKUs, if not an absolute duplicate, were nearly so. The proliferation of SKUs that Rich had hinted at during the first night of training were clearly on display.

The team debated how much of their category analysis to display and settled on the team charter, the supplier and supply market analysis, the supplier evaluation worksheet, and selected insights. Their goal was to demonstrate their new approach, the thoroughness of their analysis, and new thinking about strategy. Even as a small subset of the work, it was still visually impressive, and the supplier evaluation worksheet, while blinded for supplier names, showed a broad range of current fits with only a small number of high performers.

All the current category suppliers were invited, and many opted to attend. All the potential suppliers invited attended. In total, there were over sixty-five suppliers represented. The room was packed to capacity even with suppliers capped at two attendees per company—typically a senior executive and the account representative.

The plan was for the various Frontier executives to be available and circulate between the teams and be available as needed to address questions. This occurred for most of the executives; the exception was Bob, the leader of the industrial business. He stayed in the corrugated breakout and sat next to Walt from Wabasha Packaging. Sean and the team noticed this, as did Margot and Matt as they rotated through the groups. Margot even noted this to Leslie when she saw her in the hallway; no other executive was staying in one group let alone sitting at the table with an incumbent supplier.

Genevieve opened the session for the corrugated team, "Good afternoon and welcome. My name is Genevieve, and I am the corrugated team sponsor and senior vice president of worldwide production for Frontier Medical. I am based in Copenhagen and delighted to be with you today. The corrugated team, what I am proud to call my team, has been hard at work creating a corrugated category strategy for Frontier International Group. We are a very large company, and this is not a simple task. In the past, we've behaved as many small companies do, and it has made it very difficult for you to build your business with us. This is changing. Sean is the team leader, and he and the team will share our category findings and a high-level view of our strategy. This is an unprecedented level of transparency, and it reflects our commitment to working together. Please hold your questions, as many will be addressed through the presentation, and I want all of you to have a complete picture."

Sean walked to the front of the room. He was not a natural public speaker and avoided it whenever possible. But he felt calm now. His team, Genevieve, and Margot were all his support. He reminded himself that he was there to tell the story of the category.

He launched into his presentation, "Thank you, Genevieve, for your introduction and for being here." He looked at the audience and continued, "I've been running this category for over ten years, and something like this has never happened before. In the past, the suppliers were selected solely by the sites, with no broader collaboration. The result is the proliferation of SKUs you can see along the wall. In addition to being a fire hazard, they represent a tangible display of category proliferation and anarchy. We believe a small fraction of those items will meet our needs going forward. That is our vision."

Margot was standing at the back of the room and smiled at Sean. He continued, "Making all those SKUs is a very large number of suppliers—all of you. Your support has been invaluable, and we appreciate it. We can well imagine your frustration at trying to grow your business beyond one site. Particularly when I call you each year and demand a price decrease. That is the old way of doing business. I am not saying that I am going to call you this year and request a price increase."

Quiet, nervous laughter scattered through the room.

"What I'm about to show is our high-level category strategy," he explained, transitioning to the simple layered strategy. "Our strategy includes SKU rationalization, supplier rationalization, and complexity reduction. In the process of accomplishing these goals, we will multi-source where sole- or single-sourced and reduce our supply-base risk. We are confident that the results will be achievable and compelling for Frontier International Group and worthwhile for you. Those of you with untapped capacity or unappreciated or unrecognized capabilities will have an opportunity to step up. I'm going to ask Ron and Gina to walk through the implementation macro plan."

Gina started with very high energy, "Good afternoon and welcome! I'm from marketing in Europe and delighted to be with you here today. It's rare to get someone from marketing this excited about corrugated, but I am!"

Real laughter filled the room now.

She continued, "You may be wondering why someone from marketing is so excited. Let me tell you. This is a new way of working for procurement at Frontier International Group. Procurement never had real strategies before. Now they do, and it will make it much better for all of us." She presented the macro plan slide, "The strategy implementation will start with a request for information and proposal process in a few weeks. We are going to use the RFI/P because we want to know about you and your capabilities—the "I"—so we don't miss anything about your current capabilities and future plans. We are adding the "P" because we want to know how interested you are in working with us. If you're very interested, tell us; likewise, if you're not, be direct. Please don't say yes and then bury the intent of 'not interested' in lots of words. That's a waste of time for all of us."

Sean noticed that Leslie and Matt were now standing in the back with Margot, watching the session.

"Once we have your inputs, we'll schedule a follow-up session with those who are interested and have questions," Gina explained. "We are not so arrogant as to think we know of all the possible permutations and expect we'll learn from you in the process. That session will be virtual for time and cost reasons. We appreciate you being here today but don't expect you to do this for every contact. The follow-up from that session will be a request for proposal and selected quotations. At each step, we'll look for clarity on your proposed solution to our corrugated problem," she pointed to the long row of SKUs. "While requesting clarity and confirmation on pricing, one of the things we learned in this process is that we will not just focus on the price per item but the components of price. We will require transparency of all cost elements. Ron will take you through the next elements in the plan."

Ron ambled to the front and greeted, "Welcome. I'm not as high-energy as Gina, but please don't infer I'm not passionate about the team's work. I'm an engineer and not in marketing."

Again, laughter filled the room.

He continued with the implementation plans, "Once we select the key suppliers by region, we'll begin implementation. As Sean mentioned, we will multi-source in each region to reduce risk. We are confident that the increased volume and SKU simplification will more than compensate for this approach and deliver value to you and to us. Implementation leaders will drive this process across each region. We know that there are substantial differences in capability around the globe and will adjust the plans accordingly. Due to these variations, we also expect there will be circumstances where Frontier International Group will need to assist suppliers with problem-solving and, potentially, continuous improvement activities to meet our needs. We will do so on an exception basis where it is mutually beneficial. José will cover the next slide."

José walked forward, taking his turn. "Thank you, Ron, and welcome, everyone." He showed the next slide, titled "Supplier on-boarding and exits."

The room was silent and a bit tense.

He remarked, "A number of you are potential Frontier International Group suppliers and were invited as a result of us recognizing your potential capability to meet our needs. We appreciate you investing the time and money to be here. We are serious about your inclusion in the process, and the opportunities are open."

Some non-incumbent suppliers around the room smiled, while many of the incumbent suppliers looked worried.

He continued, "The corollary of that is that a number of the incumbent suppliers will experience change; some may grow their business, and others may exit the supply base. Again, we appreciate you investing your time and effort to be here as well as your support to Frontier International Group to-date. I want to emphasize what we're not saying today—'drop your prices or else.' That is not going to happen. You are not here for a price shakedown. You are here to see where we are going and why. I think I speak for the team when I say that the category management process was entirely new to all of us. We were dubious at first. We are believers now. This will be an outstanding opportunity for the best suppliers, it will be a tough situation for marginal suppliers, and you and we will know the difference."

Sean returned to the front and said, "Thanks, José, Ron, and Gina." He turned to the audience. "You've heard from a few of the team members. The rest of the team is standing with Genevieve," he motioned to the left. "I'd like to open for questions." Sean noticed that Margot, Matt, and Leslie had not rotated to a different team and were standing in the back of the room.

A hand was raised by a salesperson for a potential supplier, "What are your plans to move away from corrugated in the future?"

Sean replied, "Excellent question. We are aware of the various uses of corrugated from shipping boxes to protective materials, and each of these uses is a bit different across our businesses. We are going to constantly monitor the market for innovations that will enable us to reduce or eliminate our use of corrugated while still performing the vital functions of product shipping and protection. An example of this we anticipate happening soon will be reusable shippers or totes in our healthcare business. These customers are very interested in eliminating our corrugated from their waste stream."

Walt from Wabasha Packaging raised his hand, "What about suppliers who closely collaborate with your business and create unique solutions?"

Sean noticed that Bob, the president of Frontier Industrial, nodded and was staring at him intently. He responded, "Our number-one goal here is to meet the business requirements of Frontier International Group; that is why we're creating a strategy. What you're alluding to is a situation where specific requirements were raised and addressed. That solution is valuable to us, and the relationship and collaboration that helped created it is as well. These will all be factors in our supplier decisions."

After a second, he added, "I have time for one more question."

A potential supplier shouted from the back, "How do we know this is for real? Don't get me wrong, I like what I'm hearing and seeing, but how do we know you're going to be able to make this happen when it's never happened before?"

Before she could stop herself, Margot was walking to the front of the room and answering the question herself, "I'm delighted you asked that question and, Sean, please let me answer it."

He nodded thankfully and stepped to the side.

She smiled to the group and started, "I'll stake my reputation on this happening. I joined Frontier International Group because Leslie and her executive team committed to changing our approach to procurement and the supply market. I told them we'd be using category management, and it would require changes in the company. They didn't back down; they said they'd be supportive. To see that support, you can see Genevieve, Bob, Matt, and Leslie in the room with us now, and the other executives in the other rooms. They're all in. I do expect there will be some bumps along the way, but I've never been in a meeting where their support has wavered." She looked at her watch, informing the group, "It is time for a break. Please be back in the auditorium in twenty minutes."

She approached Sean, Genevieve, and the team. "I hope I wasn't too blunt there. It's a natural question, but how else can we demonstrate our commitment to a new approach?"

"You'll need to exit a sacred-cow supplier and bring in a new supplier," Matt stated, having approached the team unnoticed. "There will likely be a supplier or two who think they are untouchable. They won't participate in the implementation process and will expect to be retained. You'll need to make an example of them. Once the other companies hear about it, they will know this is real."

"That's right," Leslie affirmed, she'd appeared next to Matt. "What you need to know is that we will support you. If you can demonstrate that you are fairly following the process, you can count on my support."

Margot commended, "Very well done, Sean, and to your team, thank you. Let's all head back now."

Anna, who'd been present as an observer during the entire session, walked with Sean back to the room and asked, "How do you feel now compared to day two of the training in January?"

He laughed, "Like it's not the same life. I was overwhelmed and could not see a path forward other than quitting then, and now I'm excited and enthused. Thank you for all of your support and advice. I could not have done this without you."

"That's likely right," Anna agreed. "But you also could not have done it if you'd not been resilient and tough enough to try. You're going to hate me for this, but it's true—strategy creation is the easy part of category management, and you're not quite done with it. The hard part is implementation."

"Thanks, my feet are back on the ground." Sean smiled as they approached the meeting room and took their seats.

Bob and Walt lingered at the table after the rest of the room had departed. The conversation was inaudible to others but clearly intense. Walt did not look happy!

The question-and-answer session was set up as a panel discussion with the Frontier executives, Leslie, Matt, Erica, Sondra, Larry, Bob, and Margot and was moderated by Jean. An hour was allotted; the questions were submitted during the day by the participants, reviewed by Jean, and discussed as needed with the potential respondents. A noteworthy question arrived just before the panel discussion: "What is the Frontier plan for minority suppliers? I've been to multiple supplier forums, and this is the only one that has not mentioned preferential treatment or spend prioritized for minority suppliers. I'm surprised and disappointed." Jean knew this was a potential hot potato. She walked over to Leslie to show her the question.

Leslie stated, "I'll take that one. Please make it the last question, because I want them to walk out of here remembering my answer to that one."

Jean smiled, surmising she knew how Leslie would approach it, and they prepared for the panel.

Jean did an excellent job with the panel discussion, and the questions were addressed fully where possible and acknowledged to be partially answered where prevented by confidentiality or forward-looking legal restrictions. Jean announced there was one more question, and a few people started to pick up their belongings. She paused and the noise settled, and she calmly and clearly read the question and asked Leslie to respond. Margot had no advance notice of this question and looked at Matt with a worried look. He smiled and did not look worried.

Leslie stood up and took the microphone from Jean and looked up at the audience, "Thank you for this question. In fact, thank you again for all your questions, your time, and your participation. We are truly committed to developing a world-class supply base because we need one to achieve our goals. Now, to this question, as a Black woman I can, at one level, understand the question. As a CEO I cannot. I am responsible for everything we do here at Frontier International Group, and I expect and demand excellence. I am not in my role because I am a Black woman. I am in my role because the board of directors—and Wall Street—see that I am an excellent CEO. In addition to being a Black woman, I am also married, I have grandchildren, and I am a violinist. I did not see a question about violinist suppliers, or grandparent suppliers." The group laughed.

She continued, "We are committed to working with the best suppliers. Period. I expect there will be diverse suppliers in the mix. Excellence is possible for all suppliers regardless of race, creed, or size. I will not, nor will I allow Margot to, select suppliers who are incapable of achieving our standards. Our customers demand it. Imagine a patient dying or a train derailing because we used substandard materials. I am not saying small and diverse suppliers provide substandard materials. I am saying we will consider the capability of the suppliers as the most important element. When it comes to support for the Black community, my family's personal commitment is well known. We endow scholarships and are deeply involved. My personal hero is Thomas Sowell. He demonstrates that excellence is the virtue we all need to pursue. Lastly, I know there will be elements of supplier development where Frontier International Group helps improve and develop suppliers. These will be suppliers where the antecedents of excellence are already present, and our help will enable them to become the excellent suppliers we require. I hope that answers the question."

A slow clapping started in the audience, and then they started to stand and clap louder. She received a standing ovation from the suppliers and her team!

Margot walked over to her, and Leslie handed her the microphone and returned to her seat to the smiles of her team.

Margot closed the session, "These sessions are always exciting, but I've never been to one like this," she enthused. "Today was an important day on our journey together. I hope you've had a chance to learn what you needed to about Frontier International Group. This is a great company and, I think you'll agree, we're on the journey to make it even better. We need you along with us. Thank you for being here, and your category manager host will answer any follow-up questions. Safe travels home."

Margot let out a deep exhale. Did that just happen? Did Leslie just say that to the supply base? She hoped the corporate communications team had all of that recorded.

She walked quickly over to the Frontier executives, where Leslie was saying, "Sometimes I just need to be a bit more direct, and today was one of those days. I'm a bit frustrated by the whole topic and want people to know it. I'm here because I'm good, Margot is here because she's good, Jean is here because she's good, and Matt is here because he's good. The board and I are committed to excellence. We are diverse and we are excellent. Jean, please work with corporate communications to summarize the day and video for the board. I suspect somebody will post video—likely out of context—and I want them on the front foot."

Jean replied, "I'll handle it personally. You perfectly explained your answer and demonstrated our culture. I've never been prouder to work for you. Thank you."

All agreed and Matt suggested, "It's been an excellent day. Margot, I'd like you to include your team and please join us at Lacy's downtown for a celebratory drink."

She nodded in reply, "Thanks, I'll find them and extend your invitation."

Over a drink that night, she queried Leslie, "I met Brenda before she left the CFO role and, of course, met Bill before he left. They are different than Matt and me, really different. What caused you to make the change?"

Leslie furrowed her brow a bit and said, "I don't talk about my people with other people, but I can tell you that Covid had a profound effect on me and the company. We were very focused on the short-term and meeting quarterly results. Wall Street pushes for that, and we went there with both feet. What I can share with you is we just barely made it. We learned a lot about our finances and our supply chain. Bobbie, the head of manufacturing for the industrial division, had been telling us we were exposed for years, and we ignored her. Well, I cannot tell you what would have happened if Bobbie hadn't been able to jump into the breach and sort supply issues. Industrial would have missed their numbers in a big way, and the company would have missed them as well. I talked with Reggie on the board, and we agreed that I needed to change my focus. You and Matt are here now as a result. It was a real blind spot on my part that I regret. But, as they say, you cannot go back but you can fix things going forward."

Margot added, "Thanks for sharing that. It's helpful context. I think I heard that in the interview process, but it was all such a whirlwind then. I'm happy to be here and appreciate your role in the recruitment process. I've never joined a company without knowing the boss in advance, and I really had to trust you and Jean, and you came through with Matt. It's clear he's going to push me and my team hard, and I'm happy for it."

Jean came over with Matt, joining them.

Matt chimed in, "Well, Leslie, you do lead from the front! What a day!" and raised his glass in a toast.

Jean added, "What you saw publicly today is what happens with Leslie privately every day. She is always leading and never ducking. I'm not saying she seeks out issues, but issues have a way of finding the CEO." She then smiled and remarked to Leslie, "You said to Matt, 'and Matt is very good.' He is very good, but you singled him out as if he's in a protected class like women or minorities."

Leslie laughed, "Oh, he is. You didn't know it, but Matt is from Maine. He talks about Nebraska, but that is where he went to school. He's from the backwoods of Maine. He's a very rare executive!"

Matt slipped into his Maine accent. "Yep, and it's wicked cold in the winter! We don't want people from away visiting up there."

They all laughed hard, and the conversation shifted to places they'd lived and traveled. Not every executive team enjoys each other's company, but this one surely did.

The mood was festive as the corrugated team assembled at the brewery. The day was a huge success, and the group enthusiastically welcomed Genevieve to her first in-person event with the team. After a round of drinks and small talk, the group moved to their table.

Sean noticed Ron and José seated at one of the tables talking and joined them. Sean asked, "What is your take of Bob sitting with the Wabasha Packaging guy today?"

"We were just talking about that," José commented. "Neither one of us could get a word out of any of them today."

Sean asked Ron, "How is Wabasha's business doing?" In the back of his mind, he remembered that Frontier was approximately 30 percent of Wabasha's sales and likely a higher percentage of their profit. It was not quite a captive supplier but was on the cusp.

Ron answered, "They lost most of their beverage business. The craft brewers are not using them like the big beer brands."

"We need to keep a careful watch on them," Sean stated. He had not noticed Anna and Genevieve sitting down near them.

Anna agreed, "It looks like there is a potential issue with Wabasha. I recommend that you," motioning to him, "or Genevieve call Bob tomorrow."

"I'll do that," Genevieve volunteered. "We're pretty tight, and I think he'll be open with me."

Anna continued, "Sean, I do recommend that as soon as you have any feedback from Genevieve you update Frank and Margot. There should be no surprises as we move toward strategy approval."

"Okay, I will," he agreed.

The waitress started delivering their appetizers, and the group relaxed and enjoyed an evening of camaraderie.

APRIL 11TH

The team was already in the meeting room the next day reviewing the agenda when Genevieve entered.

"Sorry I'm late," she said as she took a seat at the table, "I was on the phone with Bob this morning."

"What did he say?" Sean asked.

Genevieve replied, "He said that Walt at Wabasha is stressed now. He looked around the room and saw the extent of the competition and is feeling overwhelmed. Walt is worried they're going to lose our business. Bob was adamant that he wants to protect them through this process."

Anna volunteered, "In the category management process, we can include a supplier, but we don't protect suppliers. That would either result in ignoring or changing the business requirements for one supplier or, worse, changing the scope for one supplier. What we will do is be absolutely fair with all of the suppliers."

"That's about what I told Bob," Genevieve explained. "He's supportive of the category management process but is worried about Wabasha. We need to remember that this is not just a supplier for him; these are his friends and people he trusts to deliver for his business."

Sean turned to Anna and said, "Let's jump ahead on the agenda to stakeholder support and resistance. That's what we're talking about, and we might as well continue to make progress."

Anna nodded and pulled up the stakeholder listing, their perceived support for the category strategy, and planned interventions to increase support.

Sean started, "I ran into Margot this morning before the meeting and talked about Bob and Wabasha. More accurately, she asked me about them because she saw what we saw and is concerned. She reiterated that Leslie would support us if we're following the process. She recommended that we not start with Leslie but that we have her support if we need it."

Genevieve nodded and assured, "Leave Bob with me for now. If we go to Leslie now, we will damage our relationship with Bob and will demonstrate a bit of weakness to Leslie. I may alter my trip home and stop in Milwaukee and see him. At the least, I'll call him again later this week. Let's not get stuck on him; let's keep going."

They worked through the remaining priority stakeholders, and all were at least indicating their support, and a number were very supportive, as indicated by their desire to go early in the implementation plans.

Anna continued, "Our next topic is the implementation team. This is typically an opportunity for the team members and sponsor to say whether they want to continue with the team. In our case, I recommend having implementation teams by business. Sometimes teams are done by regions, but as your company is organized around the businesses, I recommend separate teams for Medical, Industrial, and Consumer Electronics. Some may want to continue on the business-specific implementation team. You may also want to consider an overall implementation steering team. It is up to you and what you think will drive success here at Frontier."

The team discussed the implementation team options and agreed to consider their personal commitments and be ready to decide their ongoing involvement later in the meeting.

Genevieve confirmed that she would continue as the overall sponsor and nominated one of her high-potential operations leaders to sponsor the healthcare implementation team. She said she'd work with the operations leader network to name comparable leaders for the electronics and industrial businesses, and this would give her another opportunity to talk with Bob so he could share any concerns.

After lunch, they turned their attention to detailed business plan development and the budget review calendar. The budget review schedules were going to be compressed this year with the addition of the AI reviews, and they did not want to be overlooked. They scheduled time with each of the business operations leaders and their respective finance leadership.

Sean sent Margot a text and asked her to join the group when she had a chance, and she joined them later in the afternoon.

He reviewed the team progress, and she was impressed, "This looks great. I think it's excellent that you're going to the businesses early in the budget review cycle. You're not asking for a lot of funding, but you need to receive what you need. We never said this process was free. I see that you're targeting the operations and finance leaders by business, and that's fine. I will present the summary of the category strategies—investments required and results achievable—to the ELT. This will directly involve the business presidents, Matt, and Leslie. This will give you the senior support you'll need."

She added, "I will see you tonight at the category management celebration. Thank you for pulling together an excellent strategy."

APRIL 12TH

Margot and Shelly had agreed that the days after the supplier forum were a unique opportunity for the teams to complete their strategy planning and then for a category management evening celebration followed by a day of shared learnings. Shelly eagerly jumped into the planning of the event and enlisted Rita's help.

They considered holding the evening event on-site at the company headquarters but decided it would be too formal—they wanted the event to be less formal and more fun. Every one of the teams had worked hard, and a stiff, corporate event was not the right venue. They chose a venue that would be fun, relaxed and have enough space for the group to eat together. The plan was for informal drinks and stand-up, buffet food and then lighthearted recognition with a focus on peer recognition for events that occurred during strategy development.

The peer recognition was the highlight of the evening. Due to the vagaries of travel and the various personalities involved, each team had numerous truly funny and memorable events. The corrugated team's night of snow and candles was widely shared, but the most noteworthy recognition was a mullet wig given to Ron in appreciation for his organization of the bowling night. He wore it proudly all evening and kept referring to the team as his angels!

The agenda for the learnings sharing was more structured and open to all procurement staff at HQ. Recordings of the sessions would be shared with remote procurement teams. The session opened with a welcome and thank you from Leslie, highlighting her appreciation for the work of the various teams and ongoing support. It continued with Matt presenting the agreed wave two and three teams and how they were aligned with the expected business priorities. Margot then shared the results of surveys sent to stakeholders, current team sponsors, and current team members on what worked well and what could be improved in the current category management approach and her plans to incorporate the feedback. It was a full morning, and each person could sense the commitment of the company and the leaders to working in a new way. Each person felt like a trailblazer.

Each team shared a storyboard that summarized their strategy and their learnings and successes, and these were posted outside in the hallways near the main room. During the breaks, team members for the respective teams would stand near their storyboards to answer any questions.

In the afternoon, an outside motivational speaker was scheduled. He was selected to address a specific improvement topic noted in the feedback surveys. The last activity of the day was a reward and recognition event hosted by Jean. All team members received a Frontier International Group recognition award, and Jean indicated that, depending on the implementation results and approaches—she stressed "the how and the what"—additional rewards and recognition would be occurring.

Margot closed the event with a heartfelt review of the rapid progress and adoption of the new working approaches. She shared her flip chart on process adoption from the first training and shared how she'd been concerned about how many would be making the journey to "stars." She said she was gratified and delighted that most were on that trajectory and thanked all for making the time and energy investments to succeed.

Similar events had been held during the launch of total quality across Frontier, but nothing like this had ever been done in procurement.

APRIL 13TH

There was real, positive energy as the corrugated team entered the meeting room. Everyone enjoyed the celebration dinner and day of shared learnings and now wanted to ensure strategy approval happened quickly and the implementation results matched the promises.

Anna opened the meeting, "Ron, thank you for not wearing your wig today."

Ron smiled, replying, "Let's just go with 'not yet.' I'll make no promises about the rest of the day."

Sean chimed in, "I hope everyone had fun last night. It's clear that we need to finish as strongly as we started. I asked Genevieve to join us this afternoon to review our strategy approval request. She will give us hints on the key players and the overall process."

Anna offered, "Let's look at the strategy approval business case draft."

Sean opened the document and projected it for all to see.

Anna continued, "The first page is the one-page executive summary. It's a simple STP with the layered strategy and the associated investments, returns, and other key statistics, like approved vendor numbers. Sean prepared a draft using the team's inputs. Please read it before we proceed."

José spoke up first, "I like it. It's very concise, but I will admit, the numbers look daunting when you see them all on one page."

"I agree," Sean admitted, "and they will require a very focused implementation approach. We will be qualifying and moving supply at the same time we are exiting a huge number of suppliers. I think it's more than five suppliers per month that we will be exiting year-round, globally. It will be very easy for a particular site or leader to say that we should proceed with our strategy—just not in their area or with their supplier."

Ron spoke up, "I talked a bit with Genevieve last night about Wabasha. She thinks they could be a problem unless we're proactive. She mentioned that she and Bob talked, and he suspects that Wabasha's business is under pressure and that they, like many closely held family businesses, have no succession plan."

"The industrial business is key to our implementation, and with them Wabasha," Sean offered. "I'll pick up a conversation with Genevieve and see if she has any ideas. I think that's the most problematic supplier. Don't get me wrong; there will be other issues, but this is the big one. What else do we have to look at, Anna?"

She advanced to the next slide of the approval document and reviewed the financial summary, "We'll need to ensure Matt and his team are on board with this and are incorporating the assumptions into the budget. Let's discuss this with Genevieve this afternoon."

Anna advanced to the next topic—the implementation team—"have you decided to continue on the implementation team?"

"I'll start," Sean interjected. "I talked with Margot and Frank, and they want me to stay with the implementation. I'm glad, because I would hate to give it to someone else. I know all of you have 'day jobs' in addition to this team, and I appreciate all that you've done to get us here. If you want to continue and can, that's great; if not, I understand and hope you'll help identify a great replacement."

He stood up and moved to the whiteboard so he could draw and write. "My initial thoughts on the implementation are to have an implementation steering team responsible for the overall implementation. I will lead the steering team. Each business will then have an implementation team. The steering team will coordinate timing and priorities, obtain any corporate-level resources, and problem-solve. If you want to stay involved, you could either be on the steering team or a business team. You don't need to decide now, but please think about it and we can talk further later in the afternoon once the plans are clearer."

Anna said, "Thanks, Sean. Let's leave that topic open and come back to it in the afternoon. I recommend that we look at the detailed implementation plan next. What do you think about sub-teams?"

He shared, "Yes, we have three plans, so please volunteer to review one of the plans. This will give us at least two team members per plan. Please review the plan for the business you know best. As you're doing the review, keep in mind the open question—Do you want to be part of the implementation? Let's share our findings mid-morning."

The sub-teams self-nominated and moved to breakout rooms to present and talk through the details. Anna and Sean rotated around to the groups and were pleased with the rigor of the conversations.

After they reviewed the final sub-team, Anna said to Sean, "Let's talk for a few minutes."

"Okay," he replied, and they moved to a nearby huddle room and sat down. "What's on your mind?"

"I'm thinking about Wabasha," Anna said. "Bob is clearly close to the Wabasha leadership and will push this issue. I was noticing that the Wabasha leader seems old; is that true?"

He admitted, "It is true. I've worked with them for years, and it is family owned but none of the younger family members are joining the business. The word is that it's 'not fun,' 'not sexy,' 'not cool'—even if it is profitable."

She smiled and said, "I can see how someone could think that running a corrugated business would not be their life's dream. It would take someone mature and insightful enough to appreciate the goal of running a business as the first task and then understanding corrugated as the second task. There are lots of businesses like car washes and laundromats that are not sexy, but you can still get rich a few quarters at a time."

"I agree that corrugated is not sexy, even if it is my category," he remarked before asking, "What are you thinking about?"

"Who else might be interested in the Wabasha business?" she countered.

He replied, "I don't think we should buy it. We sometimes vertically integrate, but this is not a likely candidate." He paused for minute to think and then added, "Maybe one of the other suppliers. The industry goes through periods of consolidation, and Wabasha was never part of it. They are proud to be an independent business."

"Maybe that time has passed," she surmised. "I think you should have a confidential conversation with Genevieve. She can talk with Bob, and they can agree how and when to talk to Wabasha. I like and trust our team, but if anything slipped out from a team member, it could ruin the potential."

"That's a good idea," he agreed. "I'm going to meet with Genevieve after the meeting and will talk with her then. Thanks for the suggestion."

The sub-teams shared their project review insights. A few steps were added and others were reordered, but there were no large changes. All remained confident of the feasibility of the plans for the respective businesses.

He summarized the findings then stated, "Our next step is to review the detailed stakeholder map. We need to be thorough and open about this. A false positive about someone's support for our project would be a real problem. A reminder—this is confidential. Everything we say about stakeholders must stay with us in this room." He opened the stakeholder map, and the team spent the next two hours discussing the level of support and enthusiasm of each of the stakeholders, who would intervene where necessary and how.

At the end of the process, Anna said, "That was an excellent process; very thorough and seemed to me to be very honest. Remember that the implementation has not yet started. Once it starts, the 'not invented in my backyard' resistance to change will likely surface, and you must be proactive once it does. You cannot let resistance fester and hope it will go away. If you sense someone is resistant, the most important thing to do is to talk with them, listen to their concerns and address them. Build a running FAQ list. Most resistance is based on something worth this team's attention that we either missed or didn't fully appreciate. The other resistance could be about fear of change, and we need to understand it and address it as well. Never lose sight of the fact that every product requires corrugated and if there is a supply issue, the respective plant will either stop producing or need to rapidly change schedules. Corrugated isn't a strategic category, but it is business critical."

He offered a smile. "Thanks, Anna. Thank you all for your input. Let's go get some lunch. Instead of the cafeteria, let's go out. It's not too hot, and a change of scenery will do us all good."

"Can I wear my wig?" Ron asked, grinning at them as they arrived at the table. "I also have my bowling shoes."

"Not if you're sitting with us," José replied in a deadpan voice.

When the team returned to the meeting room, they were surprised to find Genevieve working at her computer with an empty tray from the cafeteria.

Sean worriedly asked, "I'm sorry, were you waiting for us for lunch?"

Genevieve smiled and said, "No, no worries, I was done with my morning meetings and came here for some quiet time to catch up on emails over lunch."

"Okay, good," he replied before continuing, "we are ready to review our approval request with you."

Closing her laptop, she said, "Excellent, let's get started. I'm with you until my next appointment at three."

Sean and the team presented the one-page executive summary, financial details, and project plan summaries.

Genevieve held her comments until they were completed and said, "Your entire presentation took just under an hour. I expect you'll have an hour for presentation and Q&A, so you'll need to shorten it a bit. That said, your content is excellent. Are you confident of the numbers? If so, how confident?"

Sean answered, "This part of the process is a bit of a chicken-and-egg;

we need to estimate the results but cannot yet fully negotiate with suppliers. I am having preliminary conversations with suppliers and believe our numbers are a bit conservative. Not sand-bagging, per se, but conservative. The real stretch numbers here are around supplier exits and SKU rationalization. We know they are a stretch, but we've been through them again today, and we all commit to achieving the goals."

"That's what I need to hear," she smiled "I will be with you at the approval meeting, and together we will commit to the results. Where are you on staffing the implementation teams?"

He replied, "We reviewed the implementation structure again this morning, and everyone on the team was asked to consider if they want to be part of the implementation and, if yes, what role. We are going to discuss it this afternoon."

"Good," she stated. "I ask that you all consider staying involved in some way. I realize you have other commitments, but this is a career-making opportunity, so please consider it carefully." She turned back to Sean and suggested, "Let's take a quick walk and talk, and you can finish with the team." As she packed her laptop, she said to the team, "I will see you at the executive team presentation. Come ready to present and expect success. They will ask good, hard questions, but we are all on the same team."

She and Sean left the meeting room, and Anna piped up, "She continues to be an excellent sponsor. Please be ready to share your implementation support decision when Sean returns."

Each of the team members took turns adding their names to the steering committee or a business-specific team—everyone was committing to the next steps.

Genevieve and Sean sat down in an unused conference room, and she asked, "Well, how are you feeling?"

He remarked, "I'm amazed by our progress and very proud of the team and the strategy. I was an early doubter of the process and now have no doubts that we'll deliver on our commitments. I really appreciate your help, Genevieve. Without you and Anna, we would not be here today."

She assured him, “We are a team. We each have a role to fulfill, and everyone here has done it one hundred percent. I think that there is a potential pitfall we must address before the approval presentation. I talked again with Bob, and he is very worried about Walt and Wabasha. He needs what they do for him. He will push Leslie hard to be exempted from the strategy if Wabasha will no longer supply him.”

“I talked with Anna about this situation this morning,” he shared. “We think the Wabasha issue is fundamentally about their business and succession plans. In short, it’s a family business, and nobody younger is joining.”

She sighed and nodded. “At one level, I could say that it’s their problem and I’m not worried about their business. At another level I can understand their situation and that Bob will block any impacts on them. Do you have any ideas?”

“We do, I mean Anna and I talked, and we do have an idea,” he replied. “We think that Wabasha should be encouraged to become part of one of our other suppliers. They could sell; they could partner—we don’t know the details, but they could save face and solve their succession issues with our help. We think Bob could nudge them in the right direction.”

“I like that idea,” she said. “Even if it doesn’t succeed it sends the message that we care and are thinking holistically. I am having dinner with Bob tonight and will talk it over with him.”

“Thank you. I hope it works out.”

“I do too. I will let you know and will see you at the executive meeting tomorrow morning.”

APRIL 14TH

Early in the morning Margot, Genevieve, and the corrugated team members were assembled in the waiting area outside the executive conference room. The team members were visibly nervous, and Margot and Genevieve were chatting at the windows.

Leslie's assistant, Lillian, came out of the conference room and walked up to Margot and Genevieve and said, "They are almost ready for you."

In just a couple of minutes, the doors opened and Margot and Genevieve ushered the team into the board room and the chairs around the perimeter of the room. Sean connected his computer and tested the display.

"Welcome all," Leslie greeted. She introduced herself to each team member and then said, "Thank you for your efforts to make our company better. This is a new process, and you are pioneers. I know all of us appreciate your efforts." She motioned to the other executive team members who had returned to their seats. "I'll turn it over to you, Margot," and she took her seat at the head of the table.

"Thank you, Leslie, and all of you for your time this morning. Today is the first category strategy approval meeting. You are about to see the new way of working for procurement. It is very different and, I think, a huge step forward for us. I'll turn it over to Genevieve, the team sponsor."

Genevieve stood up. "I was asked to sponsor this team and knew nothing about the category management process beforehand. I was dubious, but Margot is persuasive. What I know now is that the category management process is really a business strategy development process for procurement areas. All of us develop strategies, so what you're about to see will be very easy to understand. This strategy is compelling and will be a stretch for all of us, but everyone on the team, including me, believes it is realistic. Before we dive into the strategy, let's do some introductions," and she pointed to Sean, who introduced himself, then the team members introduced themselves in turn.

Leslie interjected at the end of the introductions, "My apologies, my team needs to introduce themselves as well."

The ELT members introduced themselves in turn.

"Thank you," Genevieve said, "Sean and team, you're up."

They presented the one-page business case, financial and implementation plan summaries, and paused for questions.

Not surprisingly, Matt was the first to comment, "I am very impressed. I was at the supplier forum and participated in the corrugated breakout meeting, so I knew this team was working well, but this exceeds my expectations. I want to test your numbers. Can you pull any of the outer year results forward? What is behind your investment assumptions?"

Sean didn't hesitate and presented the financial summary, explaining the numbers and the details behind each.

Erica assured, "Don't worry, Sean. He pushes all of us on the numbers the exact same way."

The entire leadership team laughed, and Matt stated, "You'd be disappointed if I didn't."

"No, I'd be disappointed if you didn't," Leslie remarked to more laughter.

Bob cleared his throat to speak, and Sean asked, "Do you have a question, Bob?"

"No, not so much a question as a statement," Bob replied. "As some of you know, I've worked very closely with a corrugated supplier named Wabasha Packaging. They solved some problems for me, and I'm protective of that relationship. I was prepared to ask Leslie for an exemption from the strategy as a result. Last night I talked this through with Genevieve and think we may have a path forward on the issue. I appreciate the team thinking through my requirements and the impact of the strategy. Genevieve and I will advance our Wabasha conversations and keep you apprised as needed."

Jean asked her peers, "So, what's your answer to the team? Is their strategy approved?"

Leslie said, "Thank you, Jean, for keeping us on track. I'll hold my vote until everyone else shares theirs."

Each executive team member nodded or voiced their approval until the conversation turned back to Leslie. She started, "There you have it, Genevieve, Sean, and team. You have our unanimous support. You do not have our unconditional support. This is a strategy approval, where you are making commitments to results in exchange for us providing commitments of resources. Am I correct?"

Sean stepped forward with a reply, "Yes, ma'am, that is correct. If I may add, in addition to resources, we also need your commitment to achieving the changes in our strategy. Specifically, reducing SKUs and rationalizing suppliers. The hard work of this will be done by the team and support staff, but there will be some resistance that may come to your level."

She smiled knowingly, confirming, "You are quite right to call us out on this support. I appreciate your honesty and directness. It looks like category management will deliver results, but will require us to work differently. That's a good thing, but we all need to recognize that upfront."

Margot joined Sean on her feet. "Last December, in my overview presentation, I spoke about this theoretically. It's easy to approve the theory. Now you can see the reality. Each of your businesses will be part of the implementation. We will all learn something new about the businesses in the process. Our commitment is to always focus on your requirements and to never miss a critical business requirement."

"Okay," Matt piped up, "Now go get started and get those results!"

Everyone laughed, and the team, Genevieve, and Margot prepared to leave.

Jean interjected, "Margot, please stay behind."

Margot was a bit taken aback and stood at the head of the table as the team left the room and the door closed behind them.

"Have a seat," Leslie offered. "Will all the teams be like this? What is your experience?"

Margot started, "This is a particularly good team. Each of you provided excellent team members who committed to the effort, and Genevieve is one of the best sponsors I've ever worked with. My goal is for every team to be very good, and that is part of the reason for pacing the effort—so we can ensure the quality—but this is an exceptional team."

Jean smiled, adding, "What about the team leader: Sean? You didn't mention him."

Margot answered, "To be honest with you, I wasn't sure about Sean at the beginning. He was an old school sourcing guy and very resistant to trying category management. Somewhere along the way, it clicked for him. He is a hundred and ten percent committed now. It's almost like he's a new employee."

"He's a star now," Jean mused. "I think he's a candidate for a 'pioneer award' if he drives the implementation and generates results. Going a step further, category managers who excel in this process are great candidates for larger general manager roles in the company. Lastly, I stand by my earlier statement about high-potential vice presidents becoming sponsors. I know Genevieve is good, but what she's demonstrating here is what we need for all future leaders—cross-business collaboration."

"I couldn't agree more," Leslie chimed in. "Thank you, Margot, for joining us and disrupting our status quo. Please share our thanks with the team."

Margot thanked them all and joined the team members gathered in the procurement area.

"What did they want?" Sean asked.

"They wanted to thank me for starting category management and for having Genevieve as the sponsor, you as the team leader, and all of the team members joining." She added, "They wanted me to know that this team set their expectations and now each team must be at least as good and thorough as you; you've set a high bar."

The team mingled for a bit and agreed to meet for a celebratory drink at the end of the day. Margot, Genevieve, and Frank migrated to Margot's office.

"What did they really say?" Genevieve questioned as soon as the door was closed.

"They asked about Sean," Margot replied. "I told them about my initial impressions of him and how he'd progressed and demonstrated leadership. He's a real transformation story."

"We both are," Frank murmured. "I wasn't sure either, but now I'm convinced. This is the first time I've had fun in procurement in many years. It's great."

"So, what are you going to do to keep Sean?" Genevieve asked. "I'm staying involved with the team, and I don't want to hear that he has a new job on the back of this. It will all fall on me then."

"Jean and I are already talking about key retention and reward and recognition plans," Margot shared. "I'll keep you both up to date on what is decided."

"Thanks," Genevieve said. "I'm glad to know you two are already working on it. On a different note, I had dinner with Bob last night, and he and I talked through Wabasha in detail. Sean and I are going to stop in Milwaukee on my way home, and we are going to meet with them. I'm hopeful we'll sort the issue to everyone's satisfaction."

"Thank you," Margot replied. "I was a bit worried about Wabasha and Bob. The presentation would not have gone well if you'd not sorted this in advance."

"Oh, no, it would not," Genevieve exclaimed. "If Bob is dissatisfied, he'll let you know. I'm off now, please keep me posted on your meetings with Jean."

"Good afternoon, Margot, come in." Jean welcomed her to the round table in her office. She continued, "That was quite a presentation. The executive team was very impressed."

"I'm glad," Margot replied. "The team worked well and very hard to get to that point. That's why I'm here. I want to talk about Sean."

"What's his role in the implementation?" Jean asked.

"He's the team leader for the implementation steering team and remains the category manager."

"How many people will be involved in implementation?" Margot took out the implementation diagram from her notebook, showing the structure of the implementation steering team and the three business-based implementation teams. "There are around forty people between the steering and business teams."

"All of them working part-time on his team and full-time on a role in the business," Jean observed.

"Yes, except for one procurement resource, an analyst, whom I'm planning to assign to help him."

"Based on this, I recommend we promote him to director-level now. This is the reward for his accomplishment and recognition of the work to come. I also recommend that we put in place a retention bonus and stock options equal to his salary that he will receive if he fully implements the strategy. What do you think?" Jean asked.

"That feels right to me," Margot stated. "He's happy here, but he will be a target for headhunters. People who are good at category management are valuable assets. I think the retention bonus, together with the recognition he's received, will keep him from taking those headhunter calls. What about Frank?"

"Frank? He's been retired in place for years. What's your question?" Jean responded, a bit puzzled.

"I sensed the same, but he's also risen to the challenge. What are your recommendations?"

"I'm a businessperson doing HR," Jean remarked, continuing, "I'm not some 'woo-woo HRD type.' I am delighted that Frank is reemerging and reengaging. That is his job. He's a long-time director."

Margot admitted, "I guess I asked wrong. I'm not suggesting he should receive any big payout or anything like that. I'm quite a high Myers–Briggs 'T' myself and sometimes miss the more nuanced bits of recognition and reassurance. What do you recommend?"

"Phew!" Jean exclaimed, "I was afraid I'd misread you. I'm a high T myself and am proud of it. People demand consistency and fundamental fairness; not the current rage of 'perceived fairness through equity.' I don't know Frank well but perceive him to be a T. I suspect that if you meet with him one-on-one to talk through the plans for Sean and recognize Frank's contributions to realigning Sean to the path of success, he will appreciate it. In his role, he should be a positive coach and mentor, so thank him for what he has obviously done in the background to help Sean."

"On a different note," Jean pivoted, sitting back a bit and relaxing, "how are you and your family enjoying Europe?"

Margot smiled broadly and relaxed as well, "My husband and sons are having a great time. Jason picked up a Volvo SUV at the factory, and the three of them are touring somewhere every week. Every weekend we go someplace new together. It is quite an adventure for them. For me, it is an amazing opportunity. Erica has been very supportive, and I'm working with good people in the medical business and on the procurement AI team. It is certainly more than I'd hoped for when we talked about me joining Frontier."

"It sounds like your AI team had quite a trip to the West Coast with Leslie."

"We did. Again, it was more than I'd hoped for with Leslie joining us and using the company jet, but it made it much easier and faster for us to conduct the visits."

"Leslie is going to have Ivan and a few of his people come to one of our executive team meetings. What should we expect?"

"Anything and everything," Margot stated. "He is brilliant, and so are his people. He is genuinely interested and curious, and will ask any question that comes to mind. He wasn't impertinent with Leslie, but he did ask questions that normally only someone with a long history would have asked."

"That seems consistent with his public profile," Jean observed. "What are your AI findings?"

Margot paused to collect her thoughts before responding. "This is me speaking off the cuff and not yet on behalf of the team. I think AI is going to have a profound effect on the workforce. We already see the impact of robotics and automation across factories, so the workforce impact there will be comparatively minor. The real impact will be on routine white-collar jobs, and it will be progressive. The current roles with tight descriptions and limited autonomy will be affected in one to three years; it's already started. In the procurement world, this means buyers, accounts payable, and some data roles. Many companies outsourced these to low-cost regions, and all those jobs are at risk. The next impacts will be roles that currently require interaction with stakeholders. Predominantly stakeholders fifty years of age and up."

"Careful there, you're hitting close to home," Jean interjected, smiling.

"I realize and will be careful. This group and older did not grow up with laptops and smartphones. They use them now, but as an adjunct to their work. They look to other people for sources of truth. The cohorts younger than that grew up with all the devices and look to the electronic source of truth—oftentimes believing it is more reliable than people. As the younger groups move into higher levels of management, it will remove the need for category managers to manage them, and they will be replaced by AI as well. In short, twenty to forty percent in the next five years and up to seventy-five percent in ten years."

"Wow, that's one of the larger impacts I've heard," Jean remarked. "I think your distinction about stakeholders and their readiness for change is a key factor. I'm hearing similar numbers from legal and expect stakeholders will play into their projections as well."

"It's interesting, exciting, and scary all at the same time," Margot observed. "As a business leader, I can see the logic and appreciate the potential for improved quality while reducing cost. As a mother and a citizen, I wonder about my boys and the future."

"Matt is working through the plan-review scheduling now. I expect you'll hear from him in the next couple of weeks, but you should be ready by early June."

"We will be. We're almost done now. Thanks for your support in everything. I really appreciate it and know that my family does as well."

"You're welcome," Jean replied. "I know that Erica, Leslie, and Matt are thankful you stepped up and filled the breach. You are a meaningful addition to our executive talent."

"Thanks," Margot said. "Do I need to wait for the promotion documents to talk with Sean and Frank? I'm heading back to Copenhagen tomorrow night."

"No, talk with them in person before you head back. My people will sort the process in the background."

"Thanks, in the meantime, I'm going to look up 'woo-woo.'"

"Just know the definition will not have a picture of me!" Jean called out as Margot headed out of the office.

APRIL 15TH

Margot was in early; there was a lot to accomplish today before her flight to Copenhagen tonight. She'd met with Frank late afternoon the prior day to catch him up on the conversation with Jean. He was delighted with the outcome. He'd never seen anything like it in procurement and was proud to be part of the new process and leadership team. The plan was to meet with Frank and Sean before lunch.

Her first meeting of the day was with Shelly, who was tirelessly working on the AI team and ensuring it moved forward to the corporate deadlines. She needed to catch up on the progress of the AI team, the various category teams currently in progress, the planning for the second wave of category team training and launches, as well as Shelly's personal progress settling into the area.

Margot walked over to Shelly's office, stuck her head in the door and asked, "Hi, Shelly, do you have some time this morning?"

Shelly looked up from her computer and said, "Sure, I'm open this morning, if that works."

"It does. Let's meet in fifteen minutes in the conference room. I'll ask Rita to block it for the next two hours."

"Okay, anything in particular I should bring?"

"Just you, your laptop, and your notebook. I imagine you'll have everything we need to discuss," Margot stated.

She stopped by Rita's desk and asked her to block the conference room and her and Shelly's internal calls for the next two hours. The trans-Atlantic flights had shown Margot the value of uninterrupted time, which was much harder to achieve in the office than on an airplane at 35,000 feet.

She and Shelly reviewed each of the category management teams and saved the AI topic for last. On a personal note, Shelly was settling into the area and enjoying it. She'd made some friends, started dating a bit, and was delighted with the job and location switch. She really appreciated the breadth of responsibility Margot gave her as well as the freedom to lead substantial projects; she felt like she was making an impact. Margot shared the news of Sean's promotion and recognition, and Shelly was awestruck. It was one of those things that good leaders knew should happen, but companies and their leaders rarely actually did. The last topic, the procurement AI team, was next.

"Our next AI meeting is next week. We need to agree on the draft procurement strategy and plan recommendations. How are you feeling about it?" Margot asked.

"I think we're ready. The consensus around the path forward is gelling over the last couple of phone calls. Everyone is following the AI news in general and what other functions are hearing," Shelly answered.

"Do you have it pulled into slides we can review next week?"

"We have slides to discuss next week that Alec drafted and I provided input on," Shelly said. "Alec deserves the credit for shepherding us through the process and keeping us on schedule. I'll send them to you this afternoon."

"He is good at that," Margot remarked. "I didn't mean to imply that I thought you should have done all of the slide work in addition to your other work."

"No worries. I knew what you meant and recognize the opportunity and the challenge in front of all of us. I'm glad we had Alec's support. It really is the whole team; everyone is on board with this one. I do have to share that we are all concerned about the future of work. Not so much for us, but for the generations behind us. It's potentially bleak."

"I agree. I've read the projected impacts on types of roles, and it's going to be a big issue around the globe. We'll need to ensure our view of the impacts is shared with HR so a corporate view can be developed." Margot's phone alarm buzzed, and she looked at it and said, "I have to meet with Sean and Frank now. Thank you for all you're doing here. I'm very thankful you joined the team. I'm heading to Copenhagen this evening, but you know you can reach me if you need to."

"Safe travels, and we'll talk next week," Shelly said as they collected their materials and left the conference room.

Sean and Frank approached Margot's office, knocking on the open door.

"Come in and close the door behind you," Margot stated, pointing to the chairs at the table in her office. She moved from her desk to join them at the table, asking Sean, "Well, how do you feel about the executive presentation?"

"I'm still on a high after the presentation," he beamed. "I think you know that I never thought I'd be making that presentation in my career."

Frank chimed in, "It was my best day in procurement in my career. I am proud of the team and Sean, and I appreciate your support, Margot."

"That's why we're here today," Margot remarked, turning back to Sean. "Effective as soon as HR processes it, you are promoted to category director. Additionally, you will be receiving a letter from HR with a retention bonus. In short, if you stay through the implementation process and deliver the results you and the team just promised, you will receive a substantial cash bonus and stock award."

"Really?" Sean asked, shocked by the unexpected wave of good news.

"Yes, really," Margot said. "During training, I mentioned a matrix I use to assess capability and results. I think we can agree you were a maverick then."

Sean nodded agreement.

She continued, "I wasn't sure if you'd make it, in fact, I doubted it and you know that, but you took to coaching and listened to Anna and did a great job leading the team. You've moved from maverick to star. Stars get promoted and receive rewards and recognition. Thank you for digging down deep inside and trying the category management process. Some people quit instead; you chose to be a leader."

She turned to Frank and said, "This is also a reflection on your coaching and support. I appreciate your leadership. I know the Scottsdale condo is calling you, but I am thankful you've not taken the call yet."

He replied, "I am, too. It will be there another day. I would not have missed the last few months for anything. Thank you for pushing us well out of our comfort zone."

Margot enjoyed the relative quiet of the flight back to Denmark. Her noise-canceling headphones drowned out the plane noise and cabin attendants' dinner service, and she did her best to sleep. She'd read the AI slides from Shelly before boarding and was delighted with the progress and the draft strategy they contained. She could not stop thinking about the future implications to the workforce. She knew the AI implications for the procurement team and that the impacts would be substantial. Her thoughts returned to her sons, Johnny and Tommy. What about them and their generation? What jobs could they think of for the future? She went to sleep thinking about them and slept fitfully for a few hours, woken by the touchdown at Schiphol airport.

The walk from her arrival gate to her connecting gate woke her up and focused her attention on the here and now. No matter the time of day, Schiphol was always bustling and required your full attention. She was thankful that she had time for a shower before her next flight and would complete the customs and immigration process in the comparatively relaxed Copenhagen airport.

Once at her connecting gate, she sent a text to Jason about her progress and looking forward to being home. Jason immediately responded that he and the boys would pick her up at the airport instead of her taking a limo to the house. He knew she'd be a bit tired but hoped it would be okay.

Okay?! she wondered to herself. She texted back that it would be wonderful and looked forward to seeing them after the short flight. They would have the day together, and she was looking forward to it. They went to Kronborg Castle, and it was a fun change of pace for her to lead the family through something. She knew the boys were too young now to read Hamlet but hoped that they'd remember the visit when they read it later.

After the boys were in bed, she and Jason had a chance to catch up one-to-one.

"How were your meetings?" he asked.

"Better than I'd hoped. Every time I worry about whether Leslie and her team will come through, they far exceed my expectations," she replied. "I'm also very happy with my team. They are great. And Max is thoroughly enjoying Lee!"

"I bet he is enjoying all of her attention," he mused. "How is she enjoying school? How does the house look?"

"She is loving statistics. Can you imagine that? Not too many people 'get' statistics, let alone enjoy them. The house looks great. She was a real godsend."

"What do you have next week?"

"It's a big week. Tuesday, I have my AI team meeting, and Thursday, I have my medical team meeting."

"What are you thinking about AI? I'm reading some crazy stuff on the topic. It couldn't be any more mixed, with some saying it's a fad that will crash and burn and the other end of the spectrum forecasting the replacement of everyone's jobs," Jason remarked.

"We're seeing the same things," Margot said. "But there are lots of examples of where it is working at the tactical level. It is already disruptive for many. It does make me wonder about Johnny and Tommy's job prospects. It makes me wonder a bit about yours too, Jason."

"I know. I'm seeing lots of AIs in design and creative spaces now. The good news, for now, is that it requires lots of so-called supervision, but I suspect that is transitory. I'm taking this trip as the first step in reinventing my career. What about the boys?"

"Well, as I was laying down on the plane, I was thinking about the future job roles. I think there will be three: first, the self-sufficient, necessary roles like the trades. I suppose robots could eventually have an impact here, but it will take a long time. Second, the co-dependent roles that use AI enhancements but are still needed—like your design review and supervisor suggestion. And third, the completely eliminated will be those whose jobs were eliminated and who lack the skills and motivation to join the other two groups."

"Wow, that's a dark future," he remarked.

"I know, and I hope it's not true, but it is what I'm seeing when the potential dots are connected," she sighed.

He stood up, reached out a hand to her, and said, "Let's call it a night. Tomorrow, I'll take the boys to the hardware store and pick up some hand tools and begin the 'trades awareness' class of homeschooling."

She hugged him and said, "I am very thankful that you are with them this summer. Sometimes things work out so much better than you hope!"

MAY 3RD

Julian had the conference room prepared and joined Margot for the video meeting. All of the others were joining virtually from their respective offices and homes.

"Welcome, everyone, and thanks for joining," Margot started. "Today we hope to finalize the procurement AI strategy presentation and recommendations. I want to start by thanking Shelly and Alec for pulling together the draft and all of you for engaging throughout the process and providing feedback on the draft. I've followed the emails throughout and know that all of you participated. It feels like we've reached consensus; is that right?" She paused to enable everyone to chime in.

Shelly started, "The themes started to emerge early in our process and gelled during the vendor visits. I think our time together on the west coast was pivotal in our achieving a 'speak as one voice' approach."

"I'll second that," Willie concurred. "I'm hearing many different things from my peers in IT, but nobody is as aligned as this team. The advent of AI is a bit about technology but seems to be more about openness to change and readiness to embrace it. This group is far ahead."

"It was forced on us before AI," Frank said. "I don't mean that in a bad way. Margot came in and started category management, which completely turned over our historical ways of working." He looked into the camera to make eye contact with Margot and continued, "But it is all for the best. We're doing things now that were impossible a year ago. Now when we look to the potential impacts of AI, it is not that we're cocky but more that we're confident; we believe we can do this now."

Alec chimed in, "I work with a number of organizations, and this one is different—in a good way. I think the plans you've developed are solid and achievable and the collaboration is second to none."

Margot said, "I received guidance from Matt last night that we can share up to ten slides but must summarize and present only one to the global AI meeting in two weeks. Let's focus on creating the one slide. Per his guidance, the team leaders will present on behalf of the team."

Shelly stated, "That's a helpful steer. It's like focusing a category strategy to one page. I recommend using the process flow diagram for the end-to-end business process. This is the diagram that we all turn to and it helps us illustrate the journey from today to tomorrow."

Willie added, "I think that's an excellent suggestion. I use that diagram every time I talk about this team and our approach."

"I agree," Margot remarked. "Please put up the process flow slide, Shelly. I'll cover procurement-specific AI impacts as well as the business-wide product improvement idea. My thoughts on emphasis are that there is no one 'killer AI app' for procurement now. The tactical, routine processing applications are real, and they are here today. They will only get better. The big opportunity for AI and Frontier is what we're doing right now with the pilot in medical. We're using Fact Mine to look across our processes and data to discover correlations and causations that we missed. This is a unique capability that we, as humans, cannot do. We can use AI to improve our products and services in a meaningful way. We must do it quickly, and we must protect our IP along the journey. Failure on either issue will enable our competitors to eclipse us."

Shelly declared, "That's an excellent summary!"

Willie added, "The presentations are being coordinated by finance and the AI elements are being summarized by IT; likewise for HR impacts by HR. The estimated final presentation to the board is early

July. This gives IT and HR a few weeks to aggregate the information and then finance another couple of weeks to quantify the financial impacts."

MAY 15TH

The Frontier HQ auditorium was filled—the top 200 global leaders for all businesses and functions were gathered for the AI reviews. The room was loud with all of the voices of everyone talking.

Leslie walked to the center of the stage, tapped on the microphone, and began, "Please take your seats so we can get started."

A hush fell over the room, and quickly all were seated.

She greeted, "Welcome to our first ever AI review. This is a momentous time for us and our company. I know that all of you prepared for today at a rapid pace, and I appreciate it. Our goal over the next three days is to hear the AI plans for every business and function. It will be a lot of presentations—I know it was a mountain of prereading. This will not be a read-aloud session; don't read us your slides. Synthesize the key insights by page and allow at least fifty percent of your allocated time for questions at the end of your presentation. While the presentations are in progress, the corporate strategy, finance, HR, and IT functions will be capturing cross-presentation insights. The task for the executive team is to use your inputs and insights to develop a corporate vision and plan in the next three weeks. Trust me when I say that my team has been busy working alongside you; they were not sitting on the sidelines.

"Like you, I've heard wildly disparate projections about the jobs to be impacted. We are starting to see some impacts, and I'm sure you'll have more projections. What I can share is that we will do our best to manage those impacts to ensure we remain a high-integrity organization and a great place to work."

Applause from the audience interrupted her flow.

She resumed, "It's because our culture matters to all of us. None of us know what the future will bring, but we can do our best to meet the future with the best of our ideals and approaches. The order of presentations will be the businesses and their reporting sub-functions today and tomorrow, followed by the corporate functions on the third day. Please manage your interruptions to ensure you are in the room as much as possible, and I appreciate you not leaving early."

The presentations started with the electronics business, including related manufacturing, quality, and regulatory functions. The electronics business was unique in that it already had a 'dark factory'—a factory with almost no employees that was totally automated—for the low-cost, high-volume consumer electronics.

Benjamin, the president of the consumer electronics business, and his leadership team presented the first morning. He ended his presentation by saying, "Our business is already automated for many processes. There will be impacts from AI, but they will largely be incremental. This is a good business to use as a test bed for next-generation applications, as we can readily measure the impacts and ROI."

Bob, the president of the industrial business, and his team presented during the afternoon of the first day. He opened by saying, "In contrast to Larry's highly automated plant, our operations are much less automated and much, much lower volume. A substantial proportion of our volume is not just built to order, it is customized for specific customers. We are exploring the potential impacts of AI in all aspects of our sales, customization and design, and production processes. We do anticipate there will be impacts in these areas. Impacts will initially focus on the routinized areas and will come late, if ever, to the customer engagement processes."

After Bob finished his presentation and addressed questions, Jean assumed the role of emcee. "I think I can speak for all of us when I say, wow, what a day! Incredible insights for the future that all of us can kind of envision and none of us can see. That's our job, and it's a bit like a Seurat painting—each of us can envision a point or set of points in the future but not the whole picture. Together we can create a much more complete and compelling vision. We essentially have the entire hotel tonight, so please relax, and we'll start tomorrow at eight."

The next morning promptly at eight, Erica took the stage, stating, "Welcome to the healthcare business. Today, my team will take you through our plans and share some exciting findings."

Genevieve reviewed the manufacturing plans, and these were a hybrid of the industrial and electronics businesses. Nearly all medical products included electronics, and nearly all were customized to varying degrees to meet customer requirements. She focused on the use of modular designs and repeatedly stressed both design for manufacturability and for service.

Erica then introduced Margot. "The procurement presentation should be happening on day three, as it is a corporate function, but Leslie and I agreed to move it to today to share the results of our new approach to procurement."

Margot took the stage, nervous. She'd presented to the board and the executive team, but those were smaller groups in a more intimate setting. This felt much bigger and more daunting.

She was very proud of her team's accomplishments and did know the materials, so she started. "Last year, I joined Frontier to transform procurement into a strategic function. I realize some of you might think that strategic procurement is an oxymoron but bear with me."

The audience responded with scattered low laughter.

She continued, "The new approach we introduced was category management. The goal is creating a business plan for the key categories of spend that both meets the company business requirements and maximizes our value from the supply base. I provide this background because the primary methods to derive value from the supply base result from us simplifying our specifications, obtaining unique improvement ideas from suppliers, and from improving the supply chain to reduce the total cost of operations. The old 'three bids and a buy' never did this.

"This process is currently progressing for a number of categories, and I'll come back to them later. What we decided to try in the healthcare business was to jump to the improvement opportunities and see where we could drive value irrespective of the categories. In essence, we reversed the process. I'll be blunt now and do not mean to offend anyone. Most companies focus on research, and we are no different. Research is exciting and rewarding; it is where new and novel solutions are created. There are multiple instances in our healthcare business where patient care has been radically and permanently improved. That's why we do research. Research is typically followed by development. Development is a discipline. It is focused on facts and data, extensive statistics and testing, and not nearly as fun. So, in most companies, it is the prodigal stepchild and given short shrift. We decided to adopt this prodigal child in procurement. Working with the healthcare leadership team, we started a number of seemingly low value, almost inconsequential improvement projects. It is early in our pilot, but we believe there will be real, incremental results from this process."

She was relaxing as she picked up momentum, "In our pilot we are applying an AI solution to all of the data from customer order through warranty repairs. In essence, we threw all of the data in and said let's see if there were any new insights. This is based on the approach to data recommended in *The Age of AI* by Kissinger, Schmidt, and Huttenlocher where they highlight the use of AI to discover a new indication for an existing drug by using AI to analyze seemingly unrelated data. We are still in the early days, but I can share that there are lots of new insights. We had no idea how some of the data was correlated and found direct causation on a few items that will also enable us to both reduce our total costs and improve the customer experience. We believe these insights will help drive positive market differentiation, so we're being careful about sharing them. I believe Leslie will be working with her leadership team to encourage the other businesses to approach their data for a similar review."

"Lastly, I was instructed to cover procurement while I'm on stage. My team created an end-to-end process map and heat mapped current and expected AI solutions by step." She presented the slide the team created. "I'm sure the other functions will have similar approaches and findings. There are a huge number of discrete AI offerings by process step but nothing that either knits them together or demonstrates compelling value. We anticipate approximately twenty to thirty percent of our staff to be affected by AI, and it is already starting. These will be in the transactional roles. I don't see the strategic roles being replaced, but I do see AI tools eventually making the roles easier. It will be like running a kitchen before and after the advent of appliances. The cooking still needs to happen, and the menu is the choice of the chef, but the appliances make the prep, cooking, and cleanup easier. AI is going to do the same thing for procurement. I'll stop and answer your questions."

A hand raised, the person called out, "I don't understand how procurement can be in charge of product improvement. Isn't that the responsibility of either the brand manager or the manufacturing leader?"

Margot started to answer, but Erica joined her on the stage, interjecting, "I had the exact same reaction. In fact, so did Leslie. We had a lively conversation about it. Then we included our head of marketing and our head of manufacturing, and the truth of the matter is that there are some improvement ideas that neatly fall into marketing and others that fall into operations. When they fall across multiple areas, they are most often ignored unless somebody like me takes ownership and drives it. I can only drive so many projects, so that means the business doesn't improve because of organizational design and incentives. It's our job as leaders to see that and to fix it. I'm not saying we have the perfect answer, but we do have something that is on track to unlock additional margin improvement that we would not otherwise realize and can now reinvest in our business or share with corporate for wider uses. I encourage everyone here to look and think more broadly thanks to AI. Give yourself license to reimagine how things can be done."

Matt took the stage. "Thank you all for a great day and huge insights. Thank you, Erica and Margot, for creating the pathway for incremental results; I made notes and look forward to them."

"I knew you would," Erica smiled.

Matt went ahead and finished the topic, "Another night for you to relax. Tomorrow, the corporate functions will present in the morning, and we'll spend the afternoon collecting and discussing your insights."

JUNE 15TH

"Good morning, Walt," Bob greeted as he strode across the Frontier Industrial reception area to greet the owner of Wabasha Packaging.

"Good morning," Walt returned. "This is my attorney, Sophie. She's also my daughter," he said with a smile.

"It's a pleasure to put a face with a name. I've heard about you since you were born," Bob mused.

Sophie blushed and shook Bob's hand, "It's nice to meet you. My father only says great things about you."

Bob turned and offered, "Walt, I think you know Sean, the category leader for corrugated, and this is Genevieve, the current head of manufacturing for our healthcare business. She's here to help me this week."

Sean said hello to both, shaking their hands.

Genevieve continued, "It's more like I'm here to learn from Bob, but it is very nice to meet you both."

"Come on into the conference room," Bob motioned with his hand, leading the way. He continued, "Josh from Acme Packaging is already here."

Once introductions were completed and coffee and tea shared, he said, "Genevieve, Sean and I invited you today to talk about the future of corrugated supply for the industrial business and, more broadly, for Frontier International Group. Walt, you and Josh were at the supplier forum in Oklahoma City, and you heard about the category strategy from Sean. This is different for all of us. I'm confident it will be better in the long-term, but we have a couple of hurdles to jump in the meantime. You all know I'm direct, so don't be surprised or develop hurt feelings. I think it's obvious that Walt and I are the old guys here. Hell, we're so old our children are in big professional roles, like Sophie here."

Sophie blushed again.

Bob continued, "I say that not to embarrass anyone but to point out a fact. I'm going to retire in the foreseeable future and spend more time tarpon fishing in Florida, and Genevieve is going to take over here. That is, once she commits to being a Green Bay fan."

Genevieve smiled. "Oh, don't worry, my family loves soccer."

Bob groaned, "It's a good thing I know you're teasing me. We'll get you cheese head hats to take home." He turned to the others and continued, "Walt is like me. He's going to retire too, but the difference is he owns the company, and Sophie and her brother, Jack, are not interested in taking over the business. Sean tells me that Acme is the leader in this area and is willing to talk about taking over the Wabasha business. We're here to help advance those conversations and then to step back and let you talk."

Bob turned to Walt, stating, "We don't expect you to give the business away. Frankly, I recommend a three-year earn-out with aggressive numbers—make them pay you what it's worth but let them earn enough money on the deal to pay you. That's my two cents."

He turned next to Josh and said, "But what is not okay for me, and I'll speak for Genevieve and Sean here, is for our corrugated service or quality to be affected. I'll buy the Wabasha business before I let that happen. We depend on Wabasha, and our customers depend on us, and that cannot be broken in the process."

Genevieve added, "I am looking forward to following Bob as the leader of this business, and I do realize which suppliers are the most critical and which of our parts and processes are most sensitive to variations. We're going to step out, but you can stay and use this room as long as needed. If you need another room or anything else, let us know."

Bob, Genevieve, and Sean left the room and moved to the cafeteria. Sean must have been a bit open-mouthed, because Bob said, "Don't look so shocked, Sean. You didn't think I was going to work until I died, did you?"

"Well, no, but I am surprised. And delighted for Genevieve."

"It is not a secret," she remarked. "Leslie likes to telegraph positive changes well in advance rather than a last-minute notice board posting. Those are typically reserved for people pursuing other opportunities." They all laughed and knew what that really meant.

"When are you going to move over?" Sean asked.

"The plan is to shadow Bob for the next six months or so, and then I'll be here starting the first of the year. I'm not yet sure when my family is going to move over, but I don't think the middle of winter is the right time to do it," she answered.

"I can tell you it's not the right time to do it," Bob said. "I recommend spending a bit of time looking at areas before making a choice; there's no need to rush."

Sean stated, "I'm going to meet with Ron and José. Let me know if you need anything."

"We'll be in my office if you need anything," Bob shared. He and Genevieve walked to his office.

A little before noon, Sophie knocked on Bob's office door and said, "I think we have it mostly sorted. Can we reassemble in the meeting room?"

"Sure," he replied. "I'll call Phil and have him tell Sean to join us."

Sean returned and they all took seats and looked at Walt and Josh.

Josh started, "On behalf of Acme Packaging, I want to start by saying thank you to Bob and Genevieve for approaching this situation as you did. We don't currently have the capability to provide the same products and service as Wabasha Packaging, and we are committed to being your supplier of choice. We know we need to add this capability and are happy to do so."

Walt added, "We've agreed on a memorandum of understanding for the key elements of a transfer. Sophie will work with Acme's legal team to finalize the agreement. The Wabasha Packaging leadership team, staff, and production facilities will continue serving Frontier. I will stay involved for three to five years and ensure the know-how we've developed is transferred to Acme. Thank you, Bob, for stepping in and helping me through this situation. We've been together through a lot, and it matters in times like this."

"Walt, Josh, and Sophie," Bob started, turning to smile at Sophie, "we are delighted and appreciate you coming together and seeing the big picture. How about we all go out to lunch to celebrate?"

Sophie smiled. "Yes, let's get Genevieve some cheese curds to welcome her to Wisconsin."

They all laughed and adjourned the meeting.

After lunch, Genevieve sat with Sean in the conference room to review the status of the implementation plans.

"I bet six months ago you didn't think you'd be helping a supplier sell itself to a new supplier, did you?" she asked.

"Honestly, six months ago is a lifetime ago. I think about what I did then for a job versus what I'm doing now, and it's a huge difference. I was literally marking time back then—just getting by—and now I feel like I'm involved and can make a difference," he replied.

"You are making a difference. Not many people could make the transformation you are making. Most would either have not tried at all or viewed it as 'not their job.' I bet some of your peers are doing that."

"Yes, there is some turnover in the department. It's exciting being a category leader, but it is hard work. My team meets every week for at least an hour, and most weeks it's two hours. I talk with stakeholders and suppliers all the time and help manage supply issues across the network. I always did some of this work, but it was never building to anything bigger than quarterly numbers. Now it feels like we're creating something new and better."

"It sounds like you're enjoying being the CEO of your category," she observed.

"I am, and I have a new appreciation for our executives. I always thought work got easier the higher you moved on the org chart. I know better now."

"I think it is easier for bad leaders or people who don't care. They wouldn't last a day working in Leslie's executive staff. What you're seeing—what you're doing—is called leading from the front, leading with integrity. It's hard work, but it's the only kind of leadership worth doing," she said. "What will be our next big supply hurdle we'll need to sort during implementation?"

He thought for a moment before replying, "The biggest challenges we face are, one, developing a routine, consistent approach to rationalizing specifications. Ron and Marek from the team are working with the packaging engineers across the business to address this. The next challenge is exiting suppliers and moving business to the selected suppliers at the pace required. Gina from the team is working with finance to create a scorecard showing our status and highlighting successes and areas that need more work. Lastly, I think we're going to have some issues in the Middle East. The supply base there is not as capable as we need, so we may need to do some supplier development, perhaps even some capital investments."

"I remember the first two issues from our executive presentation and think that Ron and Gina are excellent to help you push them along," she said. "I will refer you to someone on Matt's team to help you with the capital process. It's important to start that process early, and it will receive heightened scrutiny if you are anticipating investing in a supplier. I don't know of too many examples where we've done this, but they will be able to help you."

"Like I said, it's a new job for me since category management," he remarked.

AUGUST 8TH

Matt, Jean, and Margot waited outside Leslie's office. They'd received an email the afternoon before to informally come by her office at the end of the day, and they waited for her to finish a call. Margot was finishing a week in the office and was set to return to Copenhagen for her long-awaited vacation with Jason and the boys before returning to the US at the end of the month in time for the boys to start school.

A few minutes later, Leslie came out and said, "I'm sorry to keep you waiting. Please come in." She motioned for everyone to sit at the meeting table.

She then started, "It's hard to believe it's already August. It's been a very full and quick year."

Jean agreed, "I know I'm looking forward to a break before the fall. It's been a sprint all year."

Matt chimed in, "Yes, a year ago, I had no idea I'd be here. My family and I are looking forward to a week of vacation. We're going back to Maine to see my family."

"That sounds really nice," Margot remarked. "I'm heading back tonight for our final time in Copenhagen. We're going to travel to northern Norway by boat and car."

"That will be a memorable trip for everyone," Leslie stated. "I wanted us to catch up before we went off on our respective breaks.

Margot, I wanted to share how delighted we are that you joined Frontier and some news."

Margot involuntarily sat up a little straighter, looking around the table at everyone's smile.

Leslie continued, "I've agreed with Matt that you will continue to report to him organizationally, but I want you to join my executive team as a regular member."

"Wow, that's great," Margot exclaimed, truly surprised.

"Along with joining my team, you'll have a new title," Leslie added, looking to Jean.

"Congratulations on being the newest senior vice president at Frontier, Margot," Jean commended. "Your full title will be SVP and CPO, Procurement and Product Improvement. It is also a promotion in salary and pay bands. The documents I have here explain everything," she shared as she motioned to her papers.

"I'm speechless," Margot replied breathlessly. She paused then continued, "It's coming up on a year here for me, and it's been the best work year of my career. It's been the hardest work year, but the best. I appreciate that you took a risk on me as a more junior CPO, but I never felt that you didn't trust me to do to the work or deliver for you and the company."

"You're right about that," Leslie confirmed. "If I'd had doubts, or Jean, we all would not be here today. You have pushed us hard, created some uncomfortable moments, and given us pause to think, and you're helping create a continued bright future for the company. Please accept my thanks for your efforts, congratulations on your promotion, and best wishes for your vacation."

"What a great way to end the week!" Jean exclaimed. "Now go catch your flight back to your family."

They all stood up and collected their papers. Jean stayed to talk with Leslie while Matt and Margot headed to the elevator.

"Congratulations, Margot, and thanks for all you're doing. I know you're stretched thin," he said as the elevator doors closed.

"I'll walk on broken glass before I disappoint Leslie," she promised.

"She is one of the main reasons I joined the company, and I appreciate her leadership, her integrity, and her support."

"You're right about that," he agreed. "I had a competing offer that was more attractive financially, but the leadership chemistry was different. I know I made the right choice. Have a great vacation and see you in September." The elevator stopped and he stepped off.

She continued down to the parking garage to her rental car. She was going to sleep well on her flight and was looking forward to telling Jason the good news.

EPILOGUE

Later that fall

Shortly after returning from the Copenhagen assignment, Margot and Erica presented the results of the medical AI test to the executive committee. The presentation came shortly after Ivan and his team met with Leslie's executive team, and it was very well received. Her task now was to share her learnings with Harry and Phil and ensure Mary continued the work she had started.

Sean pushed the implementation teams to meet the project plans. The hardest part of the process was eliminating long-standing suppliers. Every time he encountered resistance, he found personal relationships in the background. His personal life also blossomed. He and Carla married the next year.

The allure of the condo and a shove from his wife to enjoy time with their grandchildren led Frank to retire. He moved to Scottsdale with pride in his accomplishments and the respect of his colleagues. Shelly moved into the head of direct materials, and Tanya took on the role of transformation leader. Katherine was promoted to the head of indirect. Sean was added to the succession plan and would take the next big role in global procurement. He was a favorite speaker at every category management training class and informally coached a number of category managers.

At the end of the year, Bob's retirement and Genevieve's promotion to president of Frontier Industrial were formally announced.

Late fall the following year

At the conclusion of the budget review and approval meetings in the fall, Leslie announced her retirement effective at the end of the year. A flurry of promotions and changes followed, including Erica's promotion to CEO and Margot's promotion to president of Frontier Medical. Mary was promoted to the CPO role and Julian to the head of procurement and product improvement for the medical business. There were lots of changes, but everyone involved was well prepared.

Margot, Jason, and the boys moved to Copenhagen for an indefinite period, but all expected it to last for at least three or four years. The boys attended an English-speaking school and participated in sports and activities that took them across Europe.

Spring, three years later

Margot was working at her desk at the Frontier Medical HQ. It was mid-afternoon, and she appreciated the peace and quiet to move a few projects forward. Her personal cell phone rang. She'd not given the number to many people—only to her family and closest friends. She looked at the caller ID: Rita. She put down her pen and answered the phone. An almost inaudible Rita said, "She died."

"Who died?" Margot asked.

"Leslie. Last night. Evidently a heart attack in her sleep. I just heard it from a friend in HR."

Margot caught her breath, she couldn't think of anything to say except, "I'm so sorry to hear that." She was already on the edge of tears.

"I'm sorry to call you with the news, but I thought you'd want to know."

"I do. I do. Thank you. Please let me know when you find out any memorial details."

"I will," Rita assured, ending the call.

Margot sat at her desk and reflected on the past years. She would not be sitting here in Copenhagen without Leslie. So much good in her family's life, in many families' lives, would never have happened without Leslie.

She never knew what caused her to take the following steps. It was instinct. She walked out of her office and motioned for her admin, Andy, to follow her. He was about to ask her what was up, but one look at the tears on her face stopped him from doing so. Striding to the office of Rolf the facility manager, she asked, "Do you have the keys to the flagpoles?"

"Yes, I do," Rolf said. He was about to ask a follow-up question, but Andy silently shook his head no, and Rolf stood up with the keys. The three of them walked outside to the flagpoles. They were majestic fifty-meter-tall poles with the Danish, American, and company flag.

Margot turned to Rolf and said, "Lower the company flag to half-staff, please."

He silently did as requested.

Andy noticed that their actions had not gone unnoticed. Employees lined the windows and watched the spectacle. They'd never witnessed anything like it at Frontier Medical.

When the flagpole was secured, Margot turned to the two men, informing them, "Last night we lost a hero. We lost Leslie. I need you to put all your communications talent to the test and write a draft notice to the employees for me. I cannot do it right now."

The building was silent as they walked in. Everyone knew something was up but remained quiet out of respect.

Spring, two weeks later

Two weeks later, the memorial service occurred. It was originally planned for Leslie's church, but it quickly became apparent that it was too small, and the service was moved to the indoor stadium at the University of Oklahoma. Thousands of mourners were expected.

Margot and her family were seated toward the front. On her way to the seats, she noticed the broad array of attendees. There were over twenty CEOs from competing firms and suppliers—all who knew and respected Leslie—and many current and former employees at all levels, including the board of directors. She guessed that Leslie's entire church congregation was there as well. She couldn't be sure, but she thought she saw the TV personality, Mike Rowe, seated across the aisle from them. And, of course, Leslie's family was seated up front. Her husband, James, was surrounded by their children and grandchildren. On either side of Leslie's family sat Miguel and Raul—still protecting them.

There was a large, eclectically clothed choir behind the dais. Margot could not figure out why they were wearing what they wore, but it ranged from college caps and gowns to what she thought was an HVAC uniform.

The minister welcomed the group, and they all sang "Amazing Grace." If there had been a dry eye in the audience, it was wet now.

After the hymn, the minister introduced Leslie's husband, James. Not many in the audience knew James. Although her professional life was very public, Leslie's private life was correspondingly private. James shared the story of their meeting, their courtship, and their fifty-three years of marriage. He talked about their challenges and reliance on faith and each other. He shared pictures of them together through the years, and he introduced their son, Howard, who played "Morning Has Broken" on the piano. He thanked everyone for their support and introduced Reggie Daniels, the prior chairman of the Frontier board of directors, to give the eulogy.

Reggie recounted how he had been part of the board when Leslie was hired. How she had brought a unique blend of business competence and incredible heart to the company. He talked about the challenges they'd faced together and how Leslie always showed resolve and predicated everything on integrity. It was a uniquely un-business-like eulogy, but it summed up Leslie's contributions to the performance and culture of the company.

The minister then had the choir sing "Down to the River to Pray." The minister then introduced Jean.

She shared that she'd talked with Leslie the day before she'd died.

Leslie was enjoying retirement. She was on a couple of boards now, but as she'd said, "Most boards are interested in me for window dressing. I don't do window dressing. The only ones I said yes to are the ones that want my inputs." This brought a smile to the audience. This was vintage Leslie.

Jean continued, "I can tell you that in addition to what Reggie said about her making the company a better company, she helped everyone she worked with become a better person. She did that not by coddling you; she did that by expecting you to perform. Not one person who worked with her ever wanted to let her down. You drove yourself for her because you knew she was doing the same for you. She often said that if she'd not read the works of Thomas Sowell, she'd have stayed in the chemical engineering world. Once she read Sowell, she became a passionate business leader."

She concluded, "Her legacy is everyone here and around the globe who knew and respected her. One of her favorite quotes was the line attributed to John Kennedy by his widow Jackie, 'Every man can make a difference; every man should try.' Leslie made a difference, and we're all better for it."

Jean then introduced Mike Rowe. Rowe walked to the podium, pointed to the choir, and said, "Some of you may be wondering about me, wondering about the choir. It is a large choir, almost one hundred and fifty strong. What they may lack in perfect singing ability, they more than make up for in passion. What you may not have known about Leslie is that ten years ago, with my support and advice, Leslie setup a scholarship fund. Each year, she funded five people going to college, five people going to junior college, and five people entering the trades. The requirement was that they demonstrated passion and commitment. It was not a handout, and it was not a free ride. All but a couple of the recipients are here today. The ones that could not make it send their regrets but had medical travel constraints, such as pregnancy. Leslie and her family have also endowed a chair in the economics department here at OU. Her degree was in chemical engineering, but her passion was economics and the study of human nature."

Rowe continued, "Please join me and the choir in honoring Leslie with the hymn 'Going Home.'" The choir moved down the aisle, and a member of the choir positioned themselves at the end of each row and out the door along the sidewalk to the hearse. Rowe started the song, and then the choir and the audience joined in. It would not be an exaggeration to say that they sang with passion, with one voice.

The ELT members present escorted the casket, led by Miguel and Raul. Margot stepped out of her aisle and moved to join the pall bearers. Leslie would have been proud of that moment. James followed next, with a grandchild holding each of his hands and the rest of the family following. The interment was a private, family-only event, but this celebration was a magnificent, very public celebration of a remarkable life well lived.

AFTERWORD

If you read this far, you will know that in a book about a category manager and the category management process, I spent a lot of time on the CPO and senior executive roles. This was intentional. *It is impossible to perform transformative category management without senior procurement and executive leadership support.*

The role of procurement leadership, both CPO and vice-president and director-level in a sourcing-focused organization, is not comparable to the role in an organization focused on delivering transformative category management. Sourcing organizations focus on customer service and delivering monthly, quarterly, and annual price savings (and avoidances). Due to their tactical nature and non-disruptive role in the organization, they can result in long-tenured leaders who are known as 'safe hands'—and are rarely respected as strategic leaders. These are the classic 'place-and-chase' procurement organizations that everyone knows and few respect. They are also the reason that one of the primary metrics for assessing procurement is the cost of the function. These are low-value functions to be further reduced to the lowest possible operating cost. The recent decade of low interest rates and the Covid supply chain issues further exacerbated the 'race to the bottom' approach of dedicated sourcing organizations. In addition to lowest possible prices, they relentlessly extend payment terms to suppliers. The effective message to suppliers from these organizations is clear—sell us at the lowest possible price and don't talk to us about anything else. The arms-length nature of these relationships was made more distant during Covid. Where previously the personal interactions could bridge some of the corporate distances, they were broken. Trust and relationships broken take years to recover (if ever).

In contrast, procurement leadership in a transformative category management environment requires a laser-like focus on strategic opportunities. This results in hard questions about the nature of the business and functions and their respective strategies for the future. Stakeholders unused to this approach will either grow to appreciate it or reject it as out of place for procurement. Invariably, stakeholders who engage this approach learn a great deal about their organization and the respective supply markets and deliver far better results. It is real work. Stakeholders must provide capable cross-functional team members and backfill them during the category team's work. A senior stakeholder leader (or two) must serve as a category sponsor and provide their time and counsel to the team leader and the team. The stakeholders must invest in exchange for the potential return.

In a world dominated by short internet videos serving as the backbone for continuous learning, it is difficult to convince leaders to embark on a multi-week or multi-month strategy development process and a potential multi-year implementation process, let alone assign the staffing to conduct the work. Careful prioritization is the key to success—invest only where there is a bona fide business need and stakeholder pull.

The assessment criteria Margot shared with the executive team at the December meeting are the criteria I use when assessing clients' readiness and ability to successfully engage transformative category management. These criteria frame the change conversation with CPOs and their leadership sponsors. They've never been proven wrong or off the mark.

Do I think transformative category management is dead? I do not, but I think if we're honest, it is only happening in a tiny subset of companies where all of the assessment criteria are met, and the senior leadership is ready and able to support the process. It's better to focus the tools and approaches where they will deliver value than to try them where failure is a near certainty. The wholly fictional company, Frontier International Group, is similar to any major global conglomerate. There are some categories of common spend across the organization and a number of categories with unique spends by business and geography. A blanket process deployment approach is unlikely to succeed. A tightly focused category management launch is the preferred approach. The category management process must be demonstrated to be agile and deliver results.

The topic of reorganization of the function was surfaced and expressly rejected in Frontier International Group. Most procurement functional transformations include organizational redesigns from top to bottom. This is well intentioned to create a holistic solution but should, in my experience, be resisted. The focus should remain on the category managers and leaders who are responsible for engaging peer stakeholders. The tactical procurement staff of buyers and planners should remain relatively untouched. They typically have long-standing stakeholder relationships in their organizations and are well trusted. Too often this staff is replaced by remote staff in low-cost regions to save on costs. Not only does this result in specious savings, it wastes the political capital of procurement leaders defending their decisions instead of building political capital by solving stakeholder issues. The deployment of AI in these roles will likely replace prior reorganization and offshoring practices.

It is too soon to predict the impacts of AI. The wildly disparate predictions, from little to no impact to complete transformation, remain. The real impacts are occurring with little fanfare. A trusted friend who consults at very senior HR levels shared that large companies are quietly eliminating entry-level jobs and replacing them with AI solutions. This is not surprising, as AI is most applicable for simpler solutions. What this portends for the future of work is problematic. Who will perform the AI supervisory tasks if they were not able to learn the entry-level tasks? Will they understand the context? Will they be able to recognize an erroneous AI answer (note: there are very well publicized wrong AI answers, so-called hallucinations, occurring regularly). I do expect at least 20 percent of the total procurement staff, predominantly buyers and planners, will be eliminated by AI solutions in the next few years. This will cause global disruption, as many of these roles were moved to perceived low-cost locations.

There are a number of AI tools that purport to perform category management strategy development. I've reviewed them, and they are most appropriate for basic sourcing. None are performing complex analysis of inputs, nor are they able to reach out to stakeholders and incorporate their inputs. This could change in the future, but for now, these tools are limited.

There are no AI tools to perform category management strategy implementation. Imagine an AI solution implementing the corrugated case study in this book. How could AI select new suppliers, exit current suppliers, and manage the supplier and stakeholder interactions required? It is possible to imagine AI supporting an online catalog environment, but it is inconceivable to see how AI could manage implementation across multiple business units and geographies. The risk is that AI solutions will proliferate, and the potential big ideas of transformative category management will be eliminated in the process.

My expectation is that the use of AI to interrogate large databases will yield breakthrough understandings that exceed the discrete implications on particular jobs. This will happen in businesses, government, and healthcare as they explore the "I don't know what I don't know" aspects of big data. These new insights will enable structural transformations that cannot even be imagined or specifically planned today. Or AI will be a bust, and the world will be saddled with additional electrical generation and computing capacity. It is an exciting time—kind of like the start of a category management strategy.

ACKNOWLEDGEMENTS

In a world dominated by short instructional videos, a book like *Choosing the Future* stands out as different. Not many people have the interest or patience to read a draft book nowadays. I am fortunate to have long-time friends and colleagues who were willing to read the early drafts and provide helpful feedback.

First among these is Dr. Scot Buessow. Scot and I have been friends for over thirty years—from my time working in HR and total quality through all of my procurement consulting experiences. He immediately read the book and provided the reassurance that the story and content is worth developing. His ongoing support is invaluable.

Another early reader was Eugene ("Gene") Carroll. I worked for Gene in the early 1990s in HR, and he is the most effective HR person I ever met. He recognized the emphasis on culture and leadership in the book and encouraged me to further develop these themes.

My procurement and category management input came from Ron Guertin. Ron and I have worked together since the mid-1990s, and he is a procurement and category strategy expert. He is incredibly perceptive and can effortlessly distill complex ideas.

I was also fortunate to have Miriam Limbach provide another perspective. Miriam is a very senior corporate leader who knows all aspects of procurement transformation and corporate culture.

Writing and publishing a book is a complex process. I am fortunate to have the support of Peggy Nehmen (n-kcreative.com). Peggy is much more than a talented designer; she knows all aspects of book publishing and is a tireless coach and cheerleader. Without her support none of my books would have been completed.

My wife, Susan, supported me throughout the writing process and provided both the time and encouragement to complete this book. She has supported me through writing the books and the experiences that made the books possible.

ENDNOTES

1 SARAH - Surprise, Anger, Rejection, Acceptance, and Help is the commonly used change curve that is an adaptation of the grief curve from *On Death and Dying* by Elizabeth Kubler-Ross.

From the ekrfoundation.org website:

> In 1969, Dr. Elisabeth Kübler-Ross introduced the "5 Stages of Death," also known as the "5 Stages of Grief," the "5 Stages of Loss," or simply "The 5 Stages." These stages—Denial, Anger, Bargaining, Depression, and Acceptance—reflect common emotional responses to change, loss, or shock. While they are often depicted in a linear sequence for clarity, Kübler-Ross emphasized in her 1974 book, "Questions and Answers on Death & Dying," that these stages are not necessarily experienced in a fixed order. She also noted that these stages are applicable to various forms of grief, change, and loss. Additionally, her work explored other emotional responses, including partial denial, anticipatory grief, shock, hope, guilt, and anxiety. Since the publication of "On Death & Dying," these stages have been further developed into the "Kübler-Ross Change Curve," with several illustrations available on our web page. Since the 1980s, the Kübler-Ross Change Curve has become a cornerstone of change management.
>
> The stages of the Kübler-Ross Change Curve are not experienced in a strict sequence, nor do they always progress in a linear fashion. The emotional

journey can be cyclical, with stages overlapping or repeating in response to evolving aspects of the change. This non-linear progression reflects the complexity of emotional responses, highlighting that the path to acceptance and adaptation is often a dynamic and iterative process.

Individuals may find themselves revisiting stages multiple times as they navigate through change. For example, many experience **shock**, characterized by disbelief and numbness as they confront change. It is not unusual to utter comments like "This can't be happening, what now?" This experience can be disorienting, leaving them feeling paralyzed or struggling to fully understand the implications of the shift.

- **Denial** occurs when people resist acknowledging the change or its significance. It takes time for our brains to register a new reality. At various times, we may need to be reminded of what actually happened. Denial acts as a protective mechanism to shield them from the full emotional impact of the situation. They might act as if nothing has altered or cling to the hope that circumstances will revert to their previous state. This can reoccur as changes continue.
- **Frustration** surfaces throughout the process of change. This stage involves a growing awareness of the disruption and its challenges, sometimes leading to irritation or anger. The opportunity frustration offers is the questions that arise about the reasons for the change and how to cope. This clarifies what is most valuable and can help someone navigate through and direct their choices throughout any transition.
- **Depression** can appear multiple times throughout the process. Rather than fading away, feelings of sadness, hopelessness, or loss may resurface, especially as new secondary losses or adjustments arise. The impact of the change may become more apparent over time, causing repeated episodes of emotional struggle and a fluctuating sense of self-worth or purpose.
- During periods of **experimentation**, individuals start exploring and trying new ways to handle the change. This is characterized by a proactive approach, where people test different strategies, behaviors, or attitudes to adapt to the

new situation. Experimentation often follows and can overlap with previous stages, as individuals refine their coping mechanisms.

- Coping with change requires adaptability and conscious **decision**-making. Viable strategies are identified, and concrete choices are made about how to proceed, committing to new ways of operating or thinking. Integration involves incorporating these decisions into daily life, but it's valuable for people to revisit, reassess, reinvent, and recreate themselves as they implement and adjust their choices.

- **Integration** is the foundation of the change curve process. It represents the goal where the change becomes part of the individual's new reality. The new circumstances are accepted and embraced, and stability is sought. However, change is an emotional journey. People may continue to experience echoes of all of these stages as they reconcile the past with the present and find a renewed sense of control or satisfaction.

Overall, the Kübler-Ross Change Curve provides a framework for understanding the emotional progression through change. It highlights that while the process can be complex and cyclical, each stage is part of the ongoing journey toward acceptance and adaptation.

2 Referenced books and the authors:

- *Out of the Crisis*, by W. Edwards Deming. Deming is one of the original thought leaders and practitioners of what is now called total quality management. This is a seminal book on the topic.

- *The Goal*, by Elijahu Goldratt. From the tocinstitute.com website:

  "*The Goal* is a book designed to influence industry to move toward continuous improvement. First published by Eliyahu Goldratt in 1984, it has remained a perennial bestseller ever since."

- *The Machine That Changed the World*, by James P. Womack, Daniel T. Jones, and Daniel Roos. The definitive, easy-to-understand explanation of the Toyota approach to total quality management.

- *The Five Dysfunctions of a Team*, by Patrick Lencioni. From the tablegroup.com website:

  "*The Five Dysfunctions of a Team* is the world's definitive guide for building healthy teams. Packed full of practical information in an easy-to-read fable, the book has sold more than 3 million copies, been translated into more than 30 languages, and helped countless teams all over the world."

- *Our Iceberg Is Melting*, by John Kotter and Holger Rathgeber. From the ouricebergismelting.com website:

  "On the surface, *Our Iceberg is Melting* is a simple story of a colony of penguins facing a dilemma. But contained within the story and the characters is a powerful message about the fear of change and how to motivate people to face the future and take action."

- *Basic Economics*, by Thomas Sowell. From the sowell.org website:

  "*Basic Economics* is a citizen's guide to economics, written for those who want to understand how the economy works but have no interest in jargon or equations. Thomas Sowell explains the general principles underlying different economic systems: capitalist, socialist, feudal, and so on. In readable language, he shows how to critique economic policies in terms of the incentives they create, rather than the goals they proclaim. With clear explanations of the entire field, from rent control and the rise and fall of businesses to the international balance of payments, this is the first book for anyone who wishes to understand how the economy functions." *Note - Dr. Sowell has published a number of other, excellent books.*

3 MBTI - I have used the MBTI assessment with hundreds of leadership and category management team members around the globe. It is widely accepted, easy to understand, and readily applicable. It is invaluable to help team members understand their personal preferences and to understand each other. I highly recommend its use, and it is a natural adjunct to the TKI listed below.

From themyersbriggs.com website:

- "The Myers-Briggs Type Indicator® (MBTI®) assessment helps people gain self-awareness, better understand others, and make positive use of differences in personality type."
- "Communication, decision-making, and managing change and stress are among the many areas that MBTI insights can help improve performance for both individuals and teams."

4 TKI – I have used the TKI assessment with hundreds of leadership and category management team members around the globe. It is widely accepted, easy to understand, and readily applicable. It is invaluable to help team members understand their personal preferences and to understand each other. I highly recommend its use, and it is a natural adjunct to the MBTI listed above.

From themyersbriggs.com website:

"The TKI® assessment helps people recognize different approaches to conflict, build skills for navigating disagreements, and turn conflict into a constructive force."

"Negotiation, collaboration, leadership development, and team effectiveness are just some of the areas where TKI insights can transform conflict from a liability into a capability."

5 Beroe - From the Beroeinc.com website:

"Beroe is the world's leading procurement intelligence platform, empowering procurement professionals to make informed business decisions using real-time data and AI-driven insights."

6 Source = ChatGPT: https://chatgpt.com

7 Source = Grok AI, X: https://grok.com/c/c9936784-8b02-4bb5-9db2-78f45171d-3f2?rid=22a289a3-4e6c-4fb0-9d18-6806cbbc9db2.

ABOUT THE AUTHOR

Erik Stavrand is a founding partner at SEAK LLC, which is dedicated to helping clients achieve commercial excellence through strategic procurement and change management. An expert executive coach, Erik works with procurement executives and category managers across a wide range of industries with a focus on delivering sustainable results.

In addition to being the author of *Choosing the Future*, Erik is the co-author of *The Global Category Manager's Handbook* with José Hanagan and *The Global Procurement Leader's Handbook* with Chris Shanahan.

DEAR READER

Thank you for reading *Choosing the Future.* I hope you found it interesting and useful. Your feedback is very important to me, and you can email me at info@seakllc.com if you have questions or comments. I hope you will take a few minutes to write a brief review on Amazon.

Best regards,
Erik

If you're interested in learning more about category management I recommend reading *The Global Category Manager's Handbook*. I co-wrote this book with José Hanagan and it is an end-to-end guide for the category management process.

If you're interested in learning more about procurement leadership and transformation I recommend reading *The Global Procurement Leader's Handbook*. I co-wrote this book with Chris Shanahan and it covers the key elements for planning and executing a procurement transformation.

Made in the USA
Monee, IL
13 September 2026

62979536R00266